School of American Research
Advanced Seminar Series

DOUGLAS W. SCHWARTZ, GENERAL EDITOR

SCHOOL OF AMERICAN RESEARCH
ADVANCED SEMINAR SERIES

Explorations in Ethnoarchaeology

Advanced Seminars are made possible
by a gift in recognition of
Philip L. Shultz
for his efforts on behalf of
the School of American Research

EXPLORATIONS
IN
ETHNOARCHAEOLOGY

EDITED BY
RICHARD A. GOULD

A SCHOOL OF AMERICAN RESEARCH BOOK

UNIVERSITY OF NEW MEXICO PRESS • Albuquerque

Library of Congress Cataloging in Publication Data

Main entry under title:

Explorations in ethnoarchaeology.

(Advanced seminar series—School of American Research)
"A School of American Research book."
Papers prepared for a School of American Research
advanced seminar held in Santa Fe, Nov. 17–21, 1975.
Includes bibliographical references and index.
1. Ethnology—Methodology—Congresses. 2. Archaeol-
ogy—Methodology—Congresses. 3. Man—Influence of
environment—Congresses. 4. Industries, Primitive—
Congresses. I. Gould, Richard A. II. Santa Fe,
N.M. School of American Research. III. Series: Santa
Fe, N.M. School of American Research. Advanced seminar
series.
GN345.E96   301.2   77-89438
ISBN 0-8263-0454-0
ISBN 0-8263-0462-1 pbk.

Foreword

The ethnoarchaeologist is an anthropologist conducting ethnographic research for an archaeological purpose, linking material remains to the human behavior from which they resulted. From the
inception of archaeology, its practitioners have drawn conclusions
about prehistoric material by making comparisons or analogies to
ethnographically derived observations of living people. This seminar
volume clearly demonstrates how that practice recently has raised the
study of human residues and material behavior to a new level of
systematic sophistication.

The archaeologist is so used to seeing ancient lifeways through
the filter of decay and the passage of great spans of time that much
of their human character is completely missing. Yet when this same
archaeologist interacts with living people whose lives are similar to
those seen in archaeological contexts, the complexity of the
humanist's real world is brought home in the strongest possible way;
and this kind of field experience will never again permit a simple
interpretation of archaeologically observed material. Then, in the
course first of fieldwork and later of laboratory analysis, regularities
and patterns emerge from the ethnoarchaeological observations,
allowing the ethnoarchaeologist to develop a fresh scientific
orientation toward hypothesis testing. The interrelated papers of

this volume provide an insight into this critical dual avenue to knowledge—the humanistic and the scientific.

Each chapter presents the reader with a substantive example of a stimulating and productive interaction between archaeology and ethnology. Jones's case study of the change in occurrence of fish bones in 7,000 years of Tasmanian deposits provides a view of an extreme case of cultural isolation and its consequences. Rathje's analysis of contemporary Tucson garbage relates directly to the reliability of interview data and the effects of human behavior upon patterns of discard. Gifford, through controlled observation of site decay sequences, examines the nature of cultural and natural factors influencing patterns of human discard with special reference to the refuse of pastoralists in northern Kenya. Kirch uses an ethnographic analysis of agricultural adaptation to generate several major hypotheses on western Polynesian prehistory. Hole, who entered into the culturally rich but personally trying world of pastoral nomads in southern Iran to determine how they cope on a day-to-day basis with the problems of caring for their animals, uses these data to reflect on the origins of pastoralism. Tringham explains how experimental research on materials can play an integral part in hypothesis testing and the formulation of probability statements in archaeological research. Stanislawski's work on the pottery of the Hopi in northern Arizona shows how ethnoarchaeology can allow for the stronger development of inference and analogy for use in reconstructing behavior in prehistoric societies. Schiffer reviews past ethnoarchaeological studies, discusses their weaknesses, and suggests remedies encouraging the investigation of cultural laws. Finally, Gould's work on lithic selectivity among the Desert Aborigines of Western Australia demonstrates the value of interpreting archaeological correlates in a behavioristic context.

Presented in these chapters is a range of topics, with ecologically varied settings, in situations of substantially different levels of cultural complexity, interwoven with a heuristic series of concepts and methodological considerations. They dramatically illustrate the breakthrough ethnoarchaeology is making in the general growth of contemporary anthropological method and theory.

Douglas W. Schwartz

School of American Research

Preface

This volume is the product of a School of American Research Advanced Seminar held in Santa Fe, November 17-21, 1975. Nine scholars participated: Diane P. Gifford (University of California, Santa Cruz), Richard A. Gould (University of Hawaii), Frank Hole (Rice University), Rhys Jones (Australian National University), Patrick V. Kirch (Bernice P. Bishop Museum, Honolulu), William L. Rathje (University of Arizona), Michael B. Schiffer (University of Arizona), Michael B. Stanislawski (Museum of New Mexico), and Ruth Tringham (Harvard University). All of the papers were prepared and circulated to each of the seminar participants in advance of the meeting. Afterward they were revised for presentation in this volume.

Anthropologists have been doing ethnoarchaeology for a lot longer than they have been aware of what they were doing. This seminar met with the aim of developing a clearer and more self-conscious view of ethnoarchaeology and what it can accomplish. For some of us it was a question of looking at the past history of ideas and events that have influenced the development of ethnoarchaeology, while for others it was an invitation to look forward to ways of studying behavior in contemporary human societies. In other words, some aspects of ethnoarchaeology clearly have to do with traditional interests of long standing in anthropology, while other aspects are novel and will require new ideas to guide them.

One of the "traditional" interests of ethnoarchaeology is the concern with limitations of archaeological evidence. It is a truism among archaeologists that we must constantly be aware of the limitations of our evidence. Not only do we face the obvious problems of poor or differential preservation of material remains, but the sample of human behavior represented by those remains that survive is likewise limited. Furthermore, there is what I shall term the "no rerun problem." One cannot go back and redo an archaeological excavation in the same way that a chemist can repeat a laboratory experiment. These considerations and others like them are all familiar to archaeologists and are stressed, rightly, by the profession in textbooks and critical papers. Yet archaeology would never have amounted to much if these limitations had been accepted as final. Indeed, the whole history of archaeology is a record of scientific opportunism showing how scholars have found ways to overcome these limitations, and one can only admire the ingenuity and resourcefulness of archaeologists in devising solutions to problems of this kind.

Ethnoarchaeology, too, has presented and at times been exposed to criticism concerning such problems as the weaknesses of analogy, ambiguities of interpretation in distinguishing natural and cultural variables that might affect a given archaeological occurrence, and the like. Indeed, there is a whole literature today of "cautionary tales" based upon ethnographic observations (Heider 1967; R. Lee 1966; Deetz 1968b; Bonnichsen 1973; White and Modjeska 1974) that reveal the ambiguities and errors that can occur in archaeological interpretation. These cautionary tales are valid and present problems that cannot be ignored by ethnoarchaeologists, yet we cannot allow such problems to inhibit efforts to carry out useful research. These problems, like all other archaeological limitations, must be overcome, and the eventual acceptance of ethnoarchaeology as an approach rests largely on success in overcoming these limitations.

In planning this seminar, it was understood from the beginning that we did not wish ethnoarchaeologists to seem like "spoilers," out to carp and moan about the defects of work already done. Instead, we tried to arrange for papers that would offer steps toward resolving defects and clarifying ambiguities. To this end, we sought papers that would be varied in approach. Rather than asking the question "What is ethnoarchaeology?" we tried to find out what ethnoarchaeologists do. Some ethnoarchaeologists have an abiding interest in theory and the formulation and testing of laws and lawlike propositions, while others are concerned more with elegant demonstrations based on particular fieldwork. So we sought participants and papers that would represent the widest possible sample along this continuum of interest. With respect to fieldwork, there has been a tendency in the past for ethnoarchaeologists to stress data gathered in the context of hunting-and-gathering societies, leading to the impression in some quarters that this is the only kind of society that can usefully be studied in this way. So we sought scholars whose work demonstrates the effectiveness of ethnoarchaeological approaches in a wide variety of ethnographic contexts that includes complex as well as hunter-gatherer societies. Thus not only do we find the Australian and Tasmanian Aborigines represented, but also such diverse adaptive systems as those of southwestern Pueblo villages, pastoral nomads of Iran, Polynesian island settlements, and modern, urban Tucson. Finally, we realized that ethnoarchaeology cannot expect to operate effectively in isolation from other special disciplines, so particular expertise was sought in matters like experimental archaeology and taphonomy.

In short, from a series of negatively stated propositions we hoped to evolve a positive approach which, for convenience, we are calling ethnoarchaeology. The diversity of this gathering was so great that at times there were misgivings as to whether or not we would have enough mutuality of interests to establish common grounds for action. What happened, however, was that our diverse interests remained intact while, at the same time, we increased our recognition of and appreciation for a set of related goals and ideas that represent an important first step toward understanding perhaps not only what ethnoarchaeology is but, more important, what it can accomplish in the study of human behavior. Having said what ethnoarchaeology is not, let us now see if we can discover what it is.

Acknowledgments

There is something quite special about the Advanced Seminars of the School of American Research. For one thing, there is Dr. Douglas Schwartz, Director of the School and General Editor of the series of which this volume is a part. Thanks to his efforts, the Advanced Seminars are undoubtedly the liveliest and best-run scholarly gatherings of their kind in the field of anthropology. For another thing, there is Mrs. Ella Schroeder, whose hospitality and attention to the details of the day-to-day running of the seminar helped make it such a success. On behalf of all the participants in the ethnoarchaeology seminar, I wish to thank both these individuals for doing so much to make this gathering so thoroughly pleasant and intellectually rewarding.

I wish especially to thank Dr. Schwartz for his editorial assistance and advice during the period when the contributed papers were being revised and assembled for the final manuscript. As a volume editor I am in a unique position to appreciate the careful organization and good sense that are required to edit a series of this kind. It is no mean feat to be able to maintain high standards of excellence over a wide variety of topics, as Dr. Schwartz has done since this series began. Again, speaking on behalf of the other contributors to this volume, let me say that we are all pleased and proud to be associated with the School of American Research Advanced Seminar Series.

Finally, I wish to thank each of the contributors for writing such outstanding papers and for the keen interest they showed in all of the discussions. These discussions will, no doubt, be continued in many quarters and will ultimately advance the development of ethnoarchaeology beyond its present frontiers. But I think all of us will remember this seminar as a landmark in the course of our endeavors, and I wanted to take this opportunity to record my gratitude to all of those who made it possible.

Contents

1
From Tasmania to Tucson: New Directions in Ethnoarchaeology

RICHARD A. GOULD

University of Hawaii

In attempting to draw together and relate the ideas proposed in a book like this, one always runs the risk of overorganizing. Where does agreement really lie in a gathering of minds as diverse as those represented here? Too much apparent consensus can easily stifle and inhibit creative research. Yet, as the discussions in this seminar revealed, there is more agreement on basic principles among the participants than is readily apparent from the individual papers. Much of the excitement in the seminar arose from our shared discovery that we do have many things in common in the various ways we look at human behavior. It would be a disservice to readers of this volume to gloss over the progress we made in isolating some of the essential elements of an ethnoarchaeological approach. In the preface I proposed some ideas about what ethnoarchaeology is not; now I should like to present the seminar's views about what ethnoarchaeology is. As long as our readers understand that we do not wish to seem doctrinaire in making concrete suggestions about the basic nature of ethnoarchaeology, all is well.

THE ANTHROPOLOGY OF RESIDUES

Although ancient Tasmanians and modern Tucsonians differed greatly in their behavior, one thing they both produced was refuse. Most of the information presented by Jones (Chap. 2, below) about the ancient Tasmanians has been derived from studying their midden deposits, and Rathje (Chap. 3) has demonstrated how much we can learn about the inhabitants of modern Tucson from examining their garbage. Perhaps we are on the verge of discovering a Great Truth in scientific archaeology, which is that all our ideas about past and present-day human behavior are founded on rubbish. The garbage heap is where archaeology and ethnology meet, in spirit, if not physically. What brings us together there is a common interest in studying human residues.

Residues, for the purposes of this presentation, are defined in the broadest possible sense to mean any physical remains that result, either directly or indirectly, from human activities. Thus, the concept of residue includes not only such obvious items as discarded tools, food refuse, workshop debris, and architectural and camp remains, but also such less obvious things as spatial relationships between material remains, as well as soils, biotic elements, and other natural features that have been altered in some way by human activities.

This interest in residues possesses both a cultural and a natural dimension. The laws or "lawlike propositions" advocated by Schiffer (Chap. 9, below) depend ultimately upon the physical and spatial relationships of materials left behind in their final context of discard. Thus the proposition, offered by Yellen (1974) and echoed by Schiffer, ". . . the longer the stay [of a group of people at one place], the more likely it is that a greater variety of maintenance activities will be carried out and corresponding refuse discarded" could be established only by observing the behavior of living groups of people in relation to their refuse. Schiffer's chapter presents us with many such lawlike propositions pertaining to human residues. Rathje's observations of modern Tucson operate in the same way, to such an extent that they lead inevitably to the conclusion that observed "waste behavior" is a more reliable indicator of human patterns of consumption and use of food and other resources than any number of direct interviews or questionnaires that ask people about their behavior in such matters. Recent studies of refuse behavior at modern campgrounds, cited by Schiffer, further reinforce this conclusion. While Schiffer's and

Rathje's arguments stress the effects of human behavior upon patterns of discard, this same line of reasoning has been applied by Gifford (Chap. 4) to the study of natural factors that influence the patterning of discards—in this case, of animal carcasses. Controlled studies of the kind being pioneered by Gifford are essential if archaeologists are ever going to be able to distinguish between natural and cultural factors leading to the actual patterns of deposition and disposal in their sites.

The ethnoarchaeologist starts with patterns of disposal of material remains as they rest in their context of ultimate discard. The archaeologist's task is to record and document the context of discard as accurately as present techniques will permit, noting all significant associations and correlations derived from them. The ethnoarchaeologist then tries to establish the behavioral patterns that will account most economically for these correlations. Whether he is concerned with fish bones in a Tasmanian midden or lamb chops in a Tucson garbage can, the research approach used by the ethnoarchaeologist is basically the same in its primary concern for the anthropology of discard.

THE MATERIALIST BIAS OF ETHNOARCHAEOLOGY

Efforts of outspoken critics like Marvin Harris (1968b) notwithstanding, the dominant approaches in anthropology today are concerned with human symbols, values, beliefs, and social organization. That is, they are nonmaterialist in nature. Interest in material culture has been disparagingly regarded by some anthropologists as a kind of intellectual stamp collecting. It is hard to imagine an approach like ethnoarchaeology evolving out of orthodox anthropology without a significant impetus from archaeology, and, indeed, one might go so far as to suggest that only archaeology could have led us in this direction. Although there are some useful ethnographic studies of tool making and tool use, domestic architecture, food gathering and food production, and the like, there exist virtually no reliable ethnographic accounts of behavior associated with discard. As Stanislawski (1969b) and Heider (1967) have pointed out elsewhere, most ethnographic studies of material culture tend to emphasize aspects of manufacture and use or else look to elements of symbolism in design and artistic representation. Those ethnographic studies of material culture that do exist also tend to lack the detail necessary for discovering those aspects of be-

3

havior most crucial in explaining the pattern of discard involved. So ethnoarchaeologists invariably turn out to be trained archaeologists who have turned their attention to the study of present-day human material behavior.

Ethnoarchaeology is thus a peculiar kind of ethnography, one with an unabashed materialist bias. The ethnoarchaeologist looks *first* at the ways in which material items are made, used, and discarded (or collected, processed, and disposed of), and he tries to make these observations as empirical as possible. Although ethnoarchaeologists have, at various times, examined emic categories pertaining to material remains (White and Thomas 1972; White and Modjeska 1974; Gould 1974), the results for archaeological interpretation have been essentially negative and have led to a general acceptance of the idea proposed by Clarke (1968:59-62) and echoed by Kirch (Chap. 5, below) that emic categories and cognitive codes exist as a "black box" for the archaeologist. We can observe inputs and outputs in a human society without specifying the content of the cognitive "black box." Kirch's studies of tropical agriculture on Uvea and Futuna stress the physical, ecological, and locational aspects of food production, as does Hole's discussion of nomadic pastoralism among the Baharvand people of western Iran (Chap. 6). Although both these modes of adaptation are rich in symbolism and ideational content, the main concern has been to analyze them as adaptive systems, relating specific behavior to particular resources and environmental factors. Not only do these case studies demonstrate the materialist bias of ethnoarchaeology, they further show the importance of the concept of the ecosystem, and of processes of adaptation within an ecosystem, in this materialist view. Ethnoarchaeology does not study *things* so much as it looks for processes of *behavior* that will explain the way material remains come to occur where they finally do. Kirch has proposed that these processes of behavior can be viewed in an adaptive framework, and that idea was further elaborated by Jones during discussions about networks of trade and other social contacts needed by hunter-gatherer societies to maintain themselves under different ecological conditions. Jones noted that with the worldwide rise in sea levels at the close of the Pleistocene, about 11,000 years ago, Tasmania was cut off from the Australian mainland and became an island. He suggested that many of the unique characteristics of Tasmanian Aborigine life as known at the time of historic discovery may have resulted after this geographic

4

separation occurred, following a severing of social networks that formerly extended to groups on the Australian mainland. He proposed that this same adaptive argument could account for the occurrence of backed blades and other implements made of "exotic" lithic materials at Puntutjarpa Rockshelter in the Western Desert of Australia. That is, the long-distance trade and transport of these materials reflect the existence of a network of social relationships needed to maintain a secure life for the Aborigines under conditions of unreliable rainfall and basic resources. Further, Jones proposes that changes in the percentage of exotic lithic material at any time in the cultural sequence at Puntutjarpa may reflect changes in rainfall and resources. This adaptational argument adds an important dimension to the interpretation of both the Tasmanian and Western Desert archaeological data and further demonstrates the value of an ecological frame of reference in the materialist approach in ethnoarchaeology.

The concept of *adaptation* in ecological anthropology generally carries two levels of meaning. It refers to *adaptive strategies*, or "patterns formed by the many separate adjustments that people devise in order to obtain and use resources and solve the immediate problems confronting them" (Bennett 1969:14), as well as *adaptive processes*, that is, "changes introduced over relatively long periods of time by the repeated use of such strategies or the making of many adjustments" (Bennett 1969:14). While the ethnoarchaeologist's direct observations afford a view of a group's adaptive strategies, or coping behavior, on a day-to-day basis, his archaeological orientation leads him to consider the directions that result cumulatively from such day-to-day adaptive strategies over the long run. Adaptive models proposed by the ethnoarchaeologist must account not only for short-run, synchronic phenomena but must also help to explain variability in long chronological sequences. In dealing with nomadic pastoralism as an adaptive system, not only has Hole sought to understand how Baharvand pastoralists cope on a day-to-day basis with the problems of caring for their animals, but he has also inquired into the origins of pastoral nomadic behavior in relation to other, contemporaneous modes of adaptation in the Deh Luran region. Some of the most useful discussions during the seminar occurred when other participants proposed adaptive models along similar lines that dealt with both levels of adaptation in relation to cultural sequences in particular regions of the world, most notably Australia, New Guinea, and Polynesia.

At the risk of sounding like a "filthy mentalist," I should note that the materialist approach in ethnoarchaeology is not a materialist philosophy. As Stanislawski pointed out, one may observe the manner in which Hopi potsherds are discarded and conclude from these observations that many sherds are recycled in a variety of ways that preclude their occurrence in a trash heap. One way in which Hopi potsherds are recycled is as "templates" from which designs are copied onto new pots, thus helping to maintain the continuity of certain "schools" of ceramic art. Hence the empirical study of patterns of discard, with its emphasis on materialist assumptions, is useful in any study of the style and symbolism of ceramic designs in the Southwest. As anthropologists we are interested in questions of symbolism and expression, but as ethnoarchaeologists we look at such questions from a materialist point of view. While the materialist approach may not, in and of itself, furnish explanations for various kinds of symbolic behavior, it provides a means for discovering basic patterns of behavior that any student of symbolic behavior cannot afford to ignore.

In other words, because ethnoarchaeology is based upon a materialist approach to human behavior, it must confront the *totality* of behaviors that may account for the observed patterns of material remains. Human beings do manipulate symbols, and their symbolic behavior can affect the total pattern of material residues in any society. By empirically observing the pattern of lithic artifacts discarded by Australian Desert Aborigines, it is possible not only to see how practical considerations of edge-holding properties and relative ease of procurement affect the choice of particular kinds of stone but to discover as well how religious beliefs also operate as a determining factor in such choices. That those religious beliefs (in this case totemism and its importance in maintaining long-distance social networks and wide geographical knowledge) can also be seen as adaptive at the level of the desert ecosystem adds to rather than diminishes our view of the importance of such symbolic systems in understanding the totality of behavior related to discard. Symbolic systems play a vital role in human adaptation. They can be approached from the same materialist point of view by the ethnoarchaeologist as such items of "behavioral hardware" as technology and subsistence.

It is no accident that the contributors to this volume have avoided the use of the term *culture*. Most concepts of culture used today by anthropologists are based on normative principles; that is, they assume the existence of shared patterns of belief, values, and social organization, and they extend this assumption into the study of material culture. This is where ethnoarchaeology diverges most sharply from orthodox anthropology, since the study of human residues does not permit such assumptions. Rather, patterns that may reflect shared norms within a human society must be discovered by the ethnoarchaeologist through empirical examination of processes of human residue formation. The empirical skepticism engendered by archaeological training is especially evident here, since archaeologists are constantly discovering patterns in their excavations and regional surveys that require explanation. The first task an archaeologist faces in providing such explanations is to distinguish between cultural and natural processes that may account for the patterns, a responsibility which, quite naturally, leads him to take very little for granted. Gifford has stressed the need for improved research to provide better control for natural processes as they relate to residue formation, since without such basic studies we will always run the risk of confounding natural and cultural patterns when they occur in or on the ground. So from the point of view of orthodox anthropology, the ethnoarchaeologist might be viewed as a congenital misanthrope, forever investigating people's garbage and throwaway behavior without ever inquiring directly into their normative attitudes.

Do ethnoarchaeologists ever discover norms? Certainly they discover patterns that reflect consistencies in human behavior, and these patterns may be highly predictable under sets of known conditions. For example, one can, without too much difficulty, observe and record the patterning of campsite remains for a hunter-gatherer society until it is possible to note specific associations with geographic and biotic features of the local habitat. Moreover, one can also observe certain kinds of behavior that occur in such contexts and give rise to these patterns of association. What one has in such cases is a kind of "rule" akin to rules of grammar in speech (Rowe 1959). That is, the rule is operationally defined, without particular concern for its cognitive dimension. Native speakers are usually unaware of the phonological and grammatical rules in their language, but this lack of awareness does not inhibit their ability to communicate effectively; the same can be said for people's awareness of their behavior toward their material residues. Stanislawski refers to patterns of this kind as "deep structures" in behavior, and he points out the effectiveness of ethnoarchaeology in discovering them. Stanislawski's use of this expression does not presuppose any sort of universal human "deep structures," though, indeed, certain patterned relationships of this kind may, upon testing, prove to be common to man as a species.

Thus the empirical attitude of the ethnoarchaeologist in studying anthropological processes leading to human residues enables him to move from his discovery of "rules" of behavior as they occur in particular human societies to the possibility of discovering in residue formation "laws" of behavior that are universal to mankind. It is thus evident that any living human society may be studied effectively by ethnoarchaeology, since residue behavior, like language, is universal to man. In the past, ethnoarchaeologists tended to study traditional hunter-gatherer societies; indeed, there was an urgent need to do so because of the rapid encroachment of Western technology and the world market. But with a research philosophy evolving now in the direction of generalizing principles of human behavior, the range of subjects for ethnoarchaeological study has correspondingly widened to include any human societies where processes of residue formation can be observed.

EXPERIMENT IN ETHNOARCHAEOLOGY

One reflection of the materialist bias in ethnoarchaeology is the increasingly important role of experimental approaches. As one scholar recently stated concerning experimental archaeology,

> By definition the words suggest a trial, a test, a means of judging a theory or an idea, and this is exactly so; experimental archaeology provides a way, one way, of examining archaeological thoughts about human behavior in the past. (Coles 1973:13)

In Chapter 7, Tringham offers a useful distinction between "laboratory" and "ethnographic" experiments and then goes on to alert us to the dangers of leapfrogging from inadequately controlled low-level demonstrations to high-level propositions about human behavior in the case of both kinds of experiments. In the case of ethnography we may further need to distinguish between studies that are set up in the field in a controlled, scientific manner but are carried out by native operators (White and Thomas 1972) and controlled,

8

nondirective field observations of traditional behavior relating to material remains (Gould, Koster, and Sontz 1971). In either case, the ethnoarchaeologist is studying primarily the *by-products* of manufacture and use, rather than manufacture and use activities as such.

The concept of by-product experimentation advocated by Tringham is probably the most useful experimental approach for ethnoarchaeology. Being concerned with behavioral processes leading to human residues, ethnoarchaeologists tend to look to this kind of experiment more than to behavioral experiments that test the relationship of human operators to materials. Just as Gifford sought controlled observation of natural processes that affect the deposition and deterioration of animal bones, so Tringham advocates controlled observation of natural phenomena (stone, clay, earth, and the like) in terms of how they are affected by human actions. Low-level, by-product experiments can be used along with ethnoarchaeological observations to form propositions (that is, rules or lawlike propositions) to test against archaeological data.

By-product experiments of this kind were vital in establishing that lithic raw materials of "exotic" origin were less mechanically efficient for scraping hardwoods than some locally available stone materials at Puntutjarpa Rockshelter in the Western Desert of Australia (see Chapter 10, below). These experiments were combined with observational data to propose that long-distance transport of lithic raw materials was as much a result of nontechnological aspects of tool procurement (ritually reinforced social networks) as of such technical factors as edge-holding properties and natural availability. This case provides positive confirmation of Tringham's argument and demonstrates how effective such experimental finds are when combined with observational data from ethnoarchaeology.

Thus the question is not, Should experimental approaches be included within the ethnoarchaeological approach?, but, How do experiments work best when combined with ethnoarchaeology? Tringham and Gifford have shown that experimental studies of naturally and culturally altered by-products are entirely consistent with the residue-oriented approach of ethnoarchaeology. Analytic results like those cited from Puntutjarpa indicate that controlled by-product experiments should be considered whenever ethnoarchaeological work is being attempted.

9

RICHARD A. GOULD

NEW DIRECTIONS IN ETHNOARCHAEOLOGY

Ethnoarchaeology is a new kind of ethnology. It is an approach that is based upon an inescapable irony, namely, that the materialist examination of patterns of human residue behavior may be one of the best ways to identify the idealist determinants of human behavior. As Schiffer has suggested, anthropologists may have had a tendency to rush into accepting idealist propositions before they have adequately· tested materialist arguments that could explain the behavior in question more economically. Perhaps there is a kind of scientific leapfrogging taking place in anthropology that bears some resemblance on a larger scale to the tendencies described and criticized by Tringham in connection with the experimental approach. That is, materialist propositions must be developed and tested to their limits before one can accept an idealist explanation for particular behavioral responses. The irony, alluded to earlier, is that by doing this the ethnoarchaeologist is in a stronger position to discover just when and under what conditions idealist propositions really do explain human behavior. Ethnoarchaeology is not a negation of symbolic or ideational variables in human behavior. Rather, it is an empirical approach designed to discover the totality of variables that determine human behavior in particular situations and to posit general principles that will show how these variables consistently interact.

2
Why Did the Tasmanians Stop Eating Fish?

RHYS JONES

Australian National University

SAVAGE MEN AND FOSSIL MEN

The practice of making inferences from ethnoarchaeological evidence hardly had an auspicious start in Tasmania. In 1642, a landing party from Tasman's ship came ashore in Frederick Henry Bay and noticed large trees which

> bore notches made with flint implements, the bark having been removed for the purpose; these notches, forming a kind of steps to enable persons to get up the trees and rob the birds' nests in their tips, were fully five feet apart, so that our men concluded that the natives here must be of very tall stature, or must be in possession of some sort of artifice for getting up on said trees. (Tasman's journal, in Plomley 1969:125)

With the sound of voices approaching in the woods, and seeing great plumes of smoke rising from the dense bush, the Dutchmen decided not to test their alternative hypotheses by further experiment or observation. Having hastily planted a flag on the beach, they left the

11

place for the relative safety of their ships and sailed away to the unknown seas in the east. It is strange to think that at this time—when Newton was wrestling with the laws that moved the universe, and Descartes and Leibniz were exploring the bizarre intellectualisms of calculus and of integral functions—European man's concepts of himself and his place in nature and in time were colored more by the paranoia of Salem, the fantasies of a Mandeville, or the fundamentalism of an Ussher than by either sweet reason or cold observation. The paradigm was a parody, such that sixty years later, in 1726, Swift could place his Houyhnhnmland in the ocean to the west of Tasmania, and his Lilliput in what is now the Nullarbor Plain.

The first man ever officially to be called an anthropologist was François Péron, serving in that capacity in the scientific expedition led by Nicolas Baudin, which did its most important work in Tasmania in 1802. The intellectual aims of the anthropological work were minutely set out in a memorandum from Baudin to the Société des Observateurs de L'Homme, the world's first anthropological research group, operating between 1799 and 1803, whose rationale had been outlined by Degérando in 1800 (F.G.T. Moore 1969). A museum was proposed to house "a collection uniquely devoted to the progress of the study of the science of man" (L. F. Jauffret c. 1800, in Cornell 1974:594), which was to be organized in the field under various headings. Section 6 of the memorandum dealt with

> man considered in the use of his means of nutrition and in relation to the basis for subsistence which he has discovered, created, conquered or modified. (Cornell 1974:596)

Under this heading collections would be made of "specimens of food-producing plants, their seeds and fruits," while in other sections would be obtained "various implements for hunting and fishing," huts, clothes, and so on. Finally, if they proved willing, some of the people themselves might be invited "to put an immense distance between their cradle and their grave," and—unlike Omai returned to his homeland with his suit of armor or Ishi janitoring the collection of his dead society—"their remains, later cherished and preserved through the genius of science and the requirements of a gentle sensibility, would find a place in our museum amongst the articles of their homeland, of which they would then complete the picture" (Cornell 1974:595).[1]

12

Why Did the Tasmanians Stop Eating Fish?

The humanity of the Tasmanians had been ascertained thirty years before this time and their putative gigantic stature refuted by the unassailable proof of measurement. In 1772 Marion Du Fresne's expedition brought face to face representatives of the two most separated peoples in recorded history. The one, whose ancestors had been separated from mainland Australia for twelve thousand years, had been within Greater Australia itself in at least partial isolation from Asia for a further twenty thousand years (Jones 1973); the other had come from the western seaboard of the European continent. Yet despite this vast geographic and historical gulf, each side recognized the other as human; in this recognition was enacted on the windswept shores of southeastern Tasmania the final proof of the unity of man. The Tasmanians threw stones at the landing Frenchmen, and one of the former was shot dead in retaliation. His corpse on the sand measured five feet three inches in the old French measure, or 1.7 m (Crozet 1783; Roth 1899:9; Plomley 1969:28).

The scientific study of the Tasmanians, though fleeting in duration and uneven in quality, was to play an important role in the development of Paleolithic archaeology. Scholars as long ago as Edward Lhuyd in 1699 had referred to ethnographic accounts from the Americas to give some meaning to prehistoric stone implements, saying of tools from Scotland that "they are just the same chip'd flints the natives of New England head their arrows with at this day" (Gunther 1945:425; Piggott 1976:19). Even such a confirmed skeptic as Samuel Johnson, on his tour of the Hebrides in 1773, felt that proof of long human occupation of the Isle of Raasay

> is afforded by the stone heads of arrows which are very frequently picked up. The people call them *Elf-bolts*, and believe that the fairies shoot them at the cattle. They nearly resemble those which Mr Banks has lately brought from the savage countries in the Pacifick Ocean, and must have been made by a nation to which the use of metals was unknown. (1775:56)

Yet John Frere's paper describing hand axes as "evidently weapons of war, fabricated and used by a people who had not the use of metals" (1800:204) was ignored for over half a century because of the implications that such a contemporaneity of human artifacts and extinct animals would have had on the then established view of man's short antiquity.

13

Only two years later, on the other side of the globe, we get a foretaste of the kind of direct ethnographic observations which were shortly to play their part in the overthrow of this view. Baudin was shown by some Tasmanians how they sharpened their spear points. "Firstly they use a stone, as we would a piece of glass, and then, for polishing them, they employ an oyster shell that they have sharpened on one side" (26 February 1802, in Cornell 1974:350). A little later, we become vicariously the witnesses of the very interface between the Age of Stone and that of Iron, when the expedition's gardener gave one of the Aborigines his pruning knife and showed him how to use it. The latter "used it for the same purpose as his stone and then gave it back when he was ready to perfect his work with his oyster shell" (Cornell 1974:350). We have come a long way since the "thunderbolts or 'Elfin' arrows" of folklore (Lubbock 1869:416).

A year after the first publication of Edouard Lartet and Henry Christy's excavations in the Perigord, Tylor (1865), in a chapter entitled "The Stone Age—Past and Present," searched the ethnographic literature to find examples of the uses of various kinds of stone tools. Tasmanian gastropod-shell middens were described as having associated with them small spherical stones used by the Aborigines to break open the shells, whereas in the case of middens of "oysters, mussels, cockles, and other bivalves, there flint-knives, used to open them with, are generally found" (Tylor 1865:192, using data from Milligan 1863:128). So deeply were ethnographic analogies embedded into pioneering archaeologists' conceptions of the ancient societies responsible for the remains they were excavating that Boyd Dawkins in his *Cave Hunting* felt that the very aim of archaeological research might at first sight

> seem a hopeless quest to recover what has been buried in oblivion so long, and is successful merely through the careful comparison of the human skeletons in the caves and tombs of Britain, France and Spain, with those of existing races, and of the implements and weapons with those which are now used among savage tribes. (1874:8)

Lubbock was also quite explicit about the intellectual processes involved; see his celebrated statement that

> if we wish clearly to understand the antiquities of Europe, we must compare them with the rude implements and weapons still,

or until lately, used by the savage races in other parts of the world. In fact, the Van Diemaner[2] and South American are to the antiquary what the opossum and the sloth are to the geologist. (1869:416)

This great alliance between the methods of geology and of ethnography, epitomized perhaps in the very title of de Quatrefages' book *Hommes fossiles et hommes sauvages* (1884), served for the first time to give some order to the historical relationships among contemporary peoples and also to allow an investigation of man's deep past.

BUT WE NEVER SAW ANY FISH BONES

Between 1772 and 1802, nine major scientific exploratory expeditions and at least five mercantile ones visited the coast of Tasmania (see Roth 1899; B. Hiatt 1967-68; Plomley 1969; Jones 1974:319-23). Detailed descriptions were made of the diet, camps, and technology of the Aborigines, and from these the conclusion emerges that the Tasmanians did not eat fish. In assessing this literature, we must remember that in common English, as in French, the term *fish* is also loosely used for molluscs ("shellfish"), crustacea ("crayfish"), and even for sea mammals ("whale fisheries of the Greenland shore"), so that a few ambiguities do occur. In most cases, however, these are resolved by context or by further description. Thus Péron (1807-16:198), having supposed that a group of Aborigines "were on their return from fishing," gives as his reasons that "they all had some crabs, a kind of lobster and some other sorts of shell fish which they carried in their bags of rush." G. A. Robinson (21 June 1832, in Plomley 1966:619) described "women fishing and caught crawfish and mutton fish," the prey being colloquial words for a cray (*Jasus* sp.) and an abalone (*Notohaliotis* sp.) respectively. Whenever I use the word *fish* in this paper, I refer exclusively to animals, both bony fish (Teleostomi) and cartilaginous (Elasmobranchii).

We may consider the evidence in two ways. First, despite detailed descriptions of a wide range of foods seen eaten or whose remains were left on the campsites, there is not a single unambiguous reference to fish or to any technology associated with fishing. While negative evidence is always dangerous, I consider this silence to be highly significant, especially when we contrast it with the voluminous descriptions of fishing methods by both men and women written by the same authors in other places, such as along the shores of mainland Australia.

The only possible doubtful reference is that of Labillardière in 1793. when he and the expedition's gardener went on a walk through the bush, they "perceived through the trees a number of natives most of whom appeared to be fishing on the borders of the lake. The men and youths were ranging in front nearly in a semi circle; the women, children and girls were a few paces behind" (1800:295). Whether they were in fact getting fish is not known, since the prey is not described. Whereas such group actions might have been appropriate in herding shoal fish into lakeside narrows, they might also have worked for crabs or even for some waterfowl. Later Labillardière states that "from the manner in which we had seen them procure fish, we had reason to presume that they had no fish hooks" (14 February 1793, in 1800:312). If these two statements can be taken as sufficient evidence that some shoal, brackish, or freshwater fish were indeed part of the diet of these southeastern Tasmanians, then they are the only such direct observational references in the entire literature. It is important to note that Rossel, the writer of the official report of the expedition, said that on the campsite midden heaps "we perceived moreover no debris of fishes" (1808:1:56; see also Roth 1899:88).

The second class of evidence comprises direct statements as to the absence of fish from the diet. Perhaps the most widely quoted is the episode described by W. Anderson (1776-77) on Cook's third voyage, when Tasmanian Aborigines from Adventure Bay, Bruny Island, "refus'd some Elephant fish[3] which were offer'd them with a sort of horror as if they never did or were afraid to eat them" (28 January 1777; Beaglehole 1967:2:786). This was despite the fact that they

> seem'd fond of birds and easily made us understand they ate them, and seem'd delighted with the sight of two small pigs which had been brought on shore to be left in the Bay. (Anderson: 28 January 1977)

David Samwell, on the same expedition, also remarked that the food of the Tasmanians

> consists chiefly of shell fish, it did not appear that they were

16

acquainted with the means of catching any other, nor to have any
Notion of a fish hook when it was shewn to them and its use
explained. (28 January 1777; Beaglehole 1967:2:994)

Cook's own men in the same bay had put out a seine net and "caught
more fish than was sufficient to serve the ships' company," the net
breaking with the weight (Anderson: 27 January 1977; Beaglehole
1967:2:784). Fishing with hook and line in a nearby swampy lagoon,
Samwell and friends "catched a great Number of very fine flat fish" (27
January; Beaglehole 1967:2:991). Altogether, during their brief stay at
Adventure Bay, twelve species were caught, including mullet, sole,
bream, elephant fish, and flathead (Anderson: 30 January 1777;
Beaglehole 1967:2:793). The absence of fish from the diet of a coastal
people staggered Cook, who could scarcely believe the evidence. As he
said,

> we cannot suppose but that people who inhabit a Sea Coast must
> have ways and means to catch fish altho we did not see it. . . .
> Either fish is plenty with them, or they did not eat it, for they
> absolutely rejected all we offered them; but I think the first the
> most probable. (Cook 1776-79: 29 January 1777; Beaglehole
> 1967:1:54)

On Baudin's expedition some quarter-century later, the same
responses were solicited from Aborigines at several places along the
southern coast, both in structured situations where Aborigines were
specifically offered fish, cooked and uncooked, but refused it, and
during casual long-term meetings in the bush, where again the
Aborigines refused to share the Europeans' fish diet (Baudin, in
Cornell 1974:318, 345, 347).

On one occasion, Baudin described his own men drawing a net in
the presence of a group of Tasmanians:

> There were no bounds to the delight of the children and even the
> grown men when they saw the fish caught in the net. Their capers
> and exclamations showed plainly how pleased they were. We
> offered to share our catch with them, but they would accept
> nothing, making signs that they did not eat fish, but only shell-fish
> or crustacea. (1 February 1802, in Cornell 1974:323)

This was not merely politeness, for later that day, when the
Frenchmen were cooking their fish and "invited the natives to share in
it," not only was the offer refused, but the Aborigines were even "quite

amazed to see people eating fish" (Cornell 1974:324). It was as if fish was not classified as food for humans.

Finally, from the maritime explorers we have two interesting episodes where inferences about the behavior and diet of the Aborigines were made from detailed observations of recently abandoned campsites. William Bligh (1792, in I. Lee 1920:25) described huts having "large heaps of mussel shells and some oysters and crayfish in them but we never saw any fish bones." George Bass, in what he called "a most scrupulous examination" of middens and fireplaces on the north coast, "discovered nothing except a few bones of the opossum, a squirrel [sic], and here and there those of a small kangaroo. No remains of fish were ever seen" (Bass, in Collins 1789-1802: 2:169).

Decisive support for this conclusion comes from the field journals of G. A. Robinson, who between 1829 and 1834 carried out five major expeditions in the Tasmanian bush in order to persuade the last of the Tasmanians to come into a government settlement. He was accompanied by friendly Aborigines and lived unarmed in the remote bush and along the coastlines of the island, hunting and gathering his food and having long-term contact with most of the various tribal remnants still roaming their land at that time. His extraordinary journal of almost half a million words, lost for over a century, has recently been edited by N. J. B. Plomley (1966), and, together with the impact of modern archaeological work, has revolutionized our knowledge of the Tasmanian Aborigines. Despite hundreds of descriptions of hunting and gathering episodes, documenting scores of different vegetable and animal foods (see B. Hiatt 1967-68), there is not a single description of fish being eaten in the bush. There is no chance that Robinson might have missed fish by inadequate sampling, as he spent well over three-quarters of those five years camping with and talking to various Tasmanian groups, and he was meticulous in his inquiries.

At the very beginning of his work in 1829 at Bruny Island, he described cooking some perch and rock cod for breakfast and "with great difficulty persuaded the natives to partake of some" (30 April 1829, in Plomley 1966:58). These Aborigines had been living for several years in a government settlement and had had long-term contact with the whites at Hobart and with whaling crews along the shores of the Derwent Estuary. In a confrontation scene three years later on the banks of the Arthur River on the west coast, Robinson had persuaded some women to leave their kinfolk and join his Aborigines. In a rage an old man taunted the delinquent women that when they had been taken to the European settlement at Flinders Island, Robinson "should feed them on fish and [he] mimicked the pulling up of the fish with a line" (4 September 1832, in Plomley 1966:653). Finally, in a somewhat bizarre episode, the women in Robinson's group, camped by the Wanderer River about eight kilometers inland from the west coast, "made fishing lines of thread and bent a pin for a hook: baited with worms which they found in the sand and caught a great many fish—trout. This was fine amusement for them. Although they do not eat this sort of fish, it afforded me and my sons a tolerable repast" (12 May 1833, in Plomley 1966:719). That evening the Aborigines themselves ate lobster and wombat instead.

Once, while walking along a sandy ocean beach, an Aborigine in Robinson's party speared what was probably an eel, but no mention was made that it was eaten (19 July 1833, in Plomley 1966:759). In a fireside discussion about star mythology, Aborigines referred to the dark patch in the Milky Way in two of their languages as a stingray, and said that "the blackfellows are spearing it" (13 March 1834, in Plomley 1966:861). Clearly, Tasmanian Aborigines both knew about and were capable of spearing eels and rays, but again there is no mention that these formed part of their diet.

One of the pitfalls of Tasmanian ethnography, common indeed in the use of all historical documents, has been the failure by some authors to distinguish carefully between direct observations made by people in a position to understand what they were seeing, and those reports which depended on hearsay, often without reference to sources and without any specific regard to accuracy. From about 1816 on there were many accounts of the second type, some—such as the works of Bonwick—very influential. Assessments of this literature have already been made by Roth (1899:88, 101-2), Howitt (1940:15), B. Hiatt (1967-68), and Plomley (1969:vi-vii, 14-15) and will not be repeated here, except to stress that most of these accounts perjured their authenticity by confusing the Tasmanians with Aborigines from the neighboring continent.

In a vivid account of a mass stingray hunt in a shallow bay, Lloyd (1862:50-52; Roth 1899:102) has his "serried cordon" of "skilful young savages" wielding a "keen-edged tomahawk" and "barbed spears." Neither tool formed part of the Tasmanian technology, but both were prominent items of those of New South Wales or Victorian Aborigines. Lloyd, writing thirty years after the events he was describing, had confused or embellished his memory. If there was a kernel of truth in this account, which purports to have been observed directly by him in a specifically named location on the east coast of Tasmania, it is of interest that the hunt was done "not with the object of obtaining food, but merely as a matter of sport." The Aborigines

> having satisfied their warrior propensities by destroying numbers of these dangerous creatures. . . . would retire to their camp fires and regale themselves upon the usual coast fare, oysters and steaming opossum. (Lloyd 1862; Roth 1899:102)

A SUMMARY OF THE TASMANIAN DIET

We are thus faced with an extraordinary fact: ethnographically observed Tasmanian Aborigines did not include fish as part of their diet. Furthermore, they showed positive abhorrence at the thought of fish being human food. This is even more strange when we note that about 70 percent of all the bands into which the 4,000 Aborigines were divided had their home estates along the seashore (Fig. 2.3), and that there was not a single band which did not at some time of the year visit the seashore and partake of its resources (Jones 1974). This coastal diet was focused on shellfish, crayfish, seabirds and their eggs, seals, stranded whales, and kelp (see B. Hiatt 1967-68; Jones 1974). Along the rocky coastline, shell species eaten were mostly abalones (Haliotidae) and other gastropods such as turbos (*Subninella* sp.) and whelks (*Dicathais* sp.). These were collected by women, who dived below water, prying the shells off the rocks with a wooden wedge and putting them into small rush baskets suspended from their throats. There are several good descriptions of these collecting occasions, observers stating that the women were excellent swimmers and that they stayed underwater for a long time, diving repeatedly until their baskets were full (see Labillardière and others in B. Hiatt 1967-68:127-28, 209). Crayfish were also obtained in this way, being grabbed from under their rocks in up to three or four meters of rough water and thrown up on shore. To get down to such depths, the women would sometimes use long, thick fronds of kelp as an underwater ladder. Women also swam up to two or three kilometers across open sea straits with dangerous cross rips in order to get to the offshore islands where there were seals and mutton birds (*Puffinus* sp.). Along the western, southern, and southeastern coasts, watercraft consisting of rolls of bark were used by both men and women to cross rivers and to get to islands up to eight kilometers offshore (see Jones 1976). I mention these facts to underscore the point that the Tasmanian economy focused on the seashore and its products, and that members of most local groups were highly adept both in and on the water.

The land component of the diet came mostly from wallabies, wombats, possums and other marsupials, birds and their eggs, and several species of vegetables, among which only bracken-fern rhizomes, orchid roots, the pith of tree ferns, and tree fungi played any significant role. Altogether some sixty species of animals and seventy species of vegetables were eaten (Jones 1975:23). The absence of all fish, either teleosts or elasmobranches, seems even more strange in such a catholic inventory.

AN EXPLANATION AND A DOUBT

The first kind of explanation that was offered is well paraphrased by Sollas (1911:76), who said that the Tasmanians did not eat fish "simply because they were ignorant of the art of fishing, nets and fish-hooks being unknown to them." This somewhat tautologous explanation ignores the high level of skill required to catch many of the staple Tasmanian foods, such as possums from fifty-meter-high trees or cormorants and other birds from exposed offshore rocks, but it was one that came easily from the pens of scholars steeped in a rigidly evolutionist ordering of societies. Somehow it seemed only right that the Tasmanians, technologically the simplest society ever recorded in the literature—and thus perhaps representatives of the oldest surviving cultural stratum of mankind—should be ignorant of the means of catching one of the basic foods of man. Somehow this absence did not even need further explanation.

The first seeds of doubt of this monolithic point of view were planted one afternoon in 1929, on an excursion after the Association of Advancement of Science meeting in Hobart (Pulleine 1929), where, amidst much excitement and speculation, a single premaxilla of a parrot fish (*Pseudolabrus* sp.) was found on the surface of the midden

in the mouth of what later became known as the south cave at Rocky
Cape (Fig. 2.1). A few more fish bones of the same genus were found
in the same deposit from a series of rather rough but extensive
excavations carried out there between about 1930 and 1937 by A. L.
Meston (1956); confirmation for substantial numbers of such fish
bones came from a later small excavation in the same deposit (Gill and
Banks 1956:38).

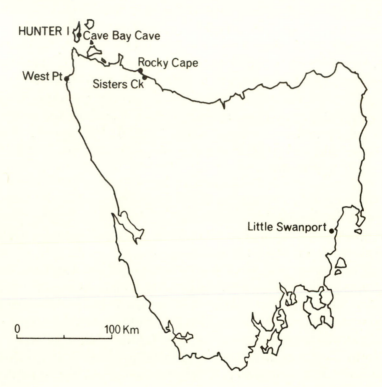

FIGURE 2.1. Map of Tasmania showing locations of archaeological sites discussed in
the text.

Clearly, if such finds were substantiated on a larger scale, they
indicated that at least some of the Tasmanians did eat fish, and it was
the resulting explanation, namely one of tribal or regional tabu, that
most commentators favored (e.g., Gill and Banks 1956:38; Kemp 1963).
Plomley (1966:36 n. 22), for example, stated that "there is evidence that
some of the northwestern tribes may have eaten fish."

My own Tasmanian archaeological work started in 1963 with an

22

excavation at Blackman's Cave, Sisters' Creek, where I found hundreds of bones of parrot fish. If I thought about the question at all, it was to decide that my finds had filled a gap, an example "where archaeology can correct or supplement ethnology" (Jones 1965:200). It was only in my second season in the field, having excavated at West Point, and more particularly in the two caves at Rocky Cape, that I slowly realized, on seriating the various elements from my excavations, that I was faced with a chronological sequence: those units containing fish bone were at the base, and those without were at the top (Jones 1966). It appeared that what was the case in Tasmania in 1800 may not necessarily have been so at all periods in the past. The craft of archaeology was beginning its own inexorable pressure.

THE SEQUENCE AT ROCKY CAPE

The two caves at Rocky Cape (Fig. 2.1) contain midden deposits with a combined depth of over six meters, giving a continuous sequence from just before the ethnographic present back to 8,000 years ago, when the sea in its postglacial rise once more reached the foot of the plunging cliffs that form the cape. General descriptions of my excavations have appeared in Jones 1966, 1968, and in press, with a detailed report in my Ph.D. thesis (1971).

On stratigraphic and other grounds, I divided the middens from both caves, which are about three hundred meters apart, into seven analytical units, which were dated by C^{14} as shown in Figure 2.2 (dates are presented in rounded form without standard errors). It can be seen that a continuous sequence existed and that Unit 4, the basal one of the North Cave, was contemporary with parts of Units 6 and 7 of the South Cave. For convenience in presenting some of the data, I will exclude Unit 4, and proceed straight from 5 up to 3 in my master sequence.

Briefly, the stone tools indicate a continuous technological tradition operating throughout the sequence, with long-term changes such as diminution in size and increasing use of better raw materials brought from specialized quarries as time went on. The result is a complex interrelationship among typology, raw material, and ratio of manufactured pieces to waste. The tradition of steep-edge scrapers, core tools, and the like stemmed from a late Pleistocene pancontinental one that extended back in time to at least 30,000 years ago (Jones 1973; Gould

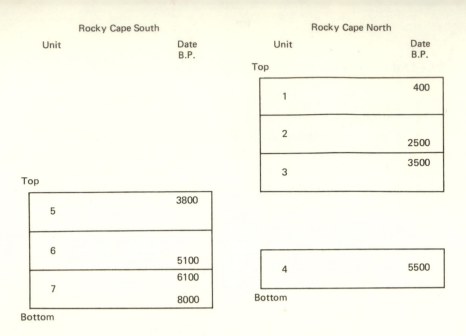

FIGURE 2.2. Midden unit dates, Rocky Cape caves, northwest Tasmania.

1973; Bowdler 1974b; Mulvaney 1975:128-97). The postglacial sea-level rise isolated this tradition within Tasmania, where it was unaffected by the many technological innovations seen in the mainland archaeological record especially from about 5,000-6,000 years ago on (see Gould 1973; Mulvaney 1975:210-37). Given a fundamental background of cultural continuity, I have explained the details of the Rocky Cape sequence in terms of the reassertion of a regional coordinated economic system, by people who had, because of the postglacial sea-level rise, been successively forced back into new and previously unused country. I might remind the reader that along most of western Tasmania occupation of the landscape by the ethnographically observed Aborigines extended only the width of one band's estate back from the coast (Fig. 2.3), the interior being clothed in a dense vegetation complex of rain forest and sclerophyllous trees which itself during the past 10,000 years had been proceeding through a succession responding to late and postglacial climatic changes and to a heavy, humanly maintained fire pressure.

Within all levels of the Rocky Cape middens, about 60-80 percent of the matrix by weight consisted of shells, the dominant species being the rocky coast gastropods, *Subninella undulata*, *Dicathais textilosa*,

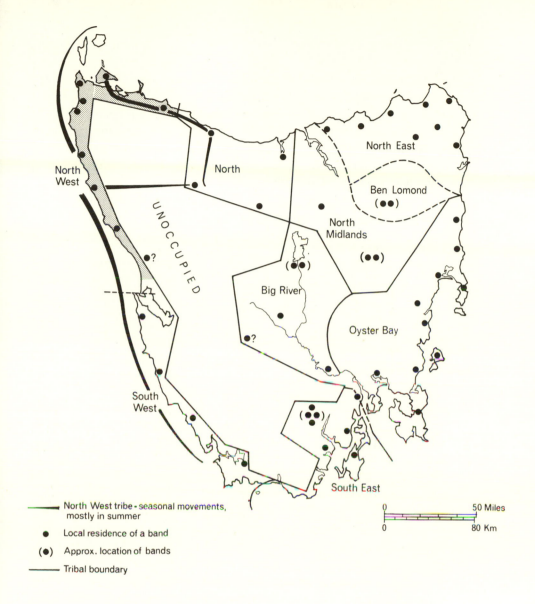

North East

North

North West

UNOCCUPIED

Ben Lomond
(●●)

North Midlands
(●●)

(●●)

Big River

Oyster Bay

South West

South East

0   50 Miles
0   80 Km

FIGURE 2.3. Tasmanian Aboriginal tribe and band territories during the ethnographic present. The territory of the North West tribe is shaded; arrows indicate the major seasonal movements of constituent bands, which took place mostly in the summer months. During the lean winter months, bands tended to return to their own estates.

Notohaliotis ruber, and *Cellana solida*. Although they only constituted some 2-3 percent by weight of the midden, there were numerous bones of seals, marsupials, other land mammals, birds, and—in the lower half of the sequence—fish. The distributions of these bones per unit, in terms of numbers, weights, and the minimum numbers of individual animals, are shown in Tables 2.1, 2.2, 2.3, and 2.4, and visually in Figures 2.4 and 2.5.

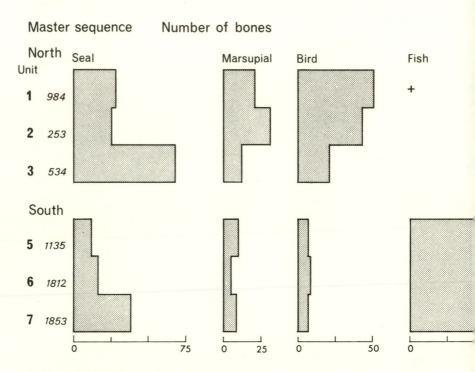

FIGURE 2.4. Relative numbers of bones of various categories of animals excavated at Rocky Cape caves, northwest Tasmania, within the seven units of the sequence.

Fish Bones

Out of a total of 3,196 fish bones, all except one came from the lower four units, dated to between 3,800 and 8,000 years ago. Fish bones in these units constituted 60 percent of all bones. In the top three units, dated from 3,500 years ago to the subethnographic period, out of 1,771 bones, only one was from a fish. This latter, a small vertebra, could easily

26

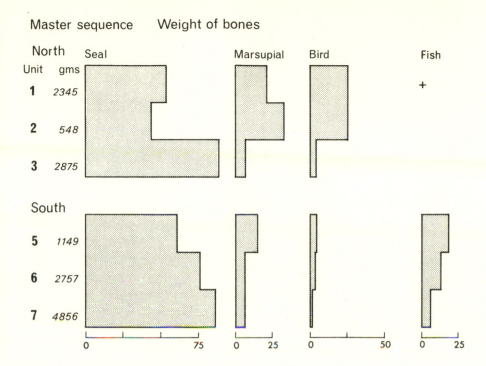

Master sequence   Weight of bones

FIGURE 2.5. Relative weights of bones of various categories of animals excavated at Rocky Cape caves, northwest Tasmania, within the seven units of the sequence.

have been brought into the site in the guts of a seal or a cormorant and will not be discussed further. Translating these figures into minimum numbers of individuals based on counts of various bone elements (Table 2.4), we see that the minimum of 500 fish represented no less than 90 percent of all vertebrates brought into the site during the lower phase, this proportion being maintained steadily in all spits; yet apart from that one vertebra, fish are not represented at all during the excavated sample of the succeeding 3,500 years. Despite the relatively small numbers involved, the odds that this result was due purely to chance, assuming that Units 1-3 and 5-7 represented roughly equal cultural "quanta," was a figure fifty digits long to one against.

All except four bones come from Labridae *Pseudolabrus* sp., known in English as "wrasses" (or, incorrectly, as "parrot fish"). The other four are from three unidentified species. Identical species of wrasses are common around the rocks and reefs of Rocky Cape nowadays. They are somewhat sluggish and can be caught either with a line and

TABLE 2.1
NUMBER OF BONES, ROCKY CAPE MIDDENS

Unit	Total	Seal		Marsupial		Bird		Fish	
		No.	%	No.	%	No.	%	No.	%
North Cave									
1	984	273	28	204	21	506	51	1	0
2	253	63	25	81	32	109	43	0	0
3	534	361	67.5	63	12	110	20.5	0	0
4	540	191	35.5	68	12.5	53	10	228	42
Total (1-4)	2,311	888		416		778		229	
South Cave									
5	1,135	140	12	112	10	78	7	805	71
6	1,812	285	15.5	92	5	144	8	1,291	71.5
7	1,853	699	37.5	163	9	120	6.5	871	47
Total (5-7)	4,800	1,124		367		342		2,967	
Grand Total	7,111	2,012		783		1,120		3,196	

TABLE 2.2
WEIGHT OF BONES IN GRAMS, ROCKY CAPE MIDDENS

Unit	Total	Seal		Marsupial		Bird		Fish	
		No.	%	No.	%	No.	%	No.	%
North Cave									
1	2,345	1,268	54	485	20.5	592	25.4		
2	548	237	43	173	32	138	25		
3	2,875	2,553	89	184	6.5	128	4.5		
4	1,610	1,395	86.5	107	6.5	44	3	64	4
Total (1-4)	7,378	5,463		949		902		64	
South Cave									
5	1,149	700	61	177	15	56	5	215	19
6	2,757	2,107	76.5	161	6	111	4	378	13.5
7	4,856	4,194	86.5	306	6.5	80	1.5	276	5.5
Total (5-7)	8,762	7,001		644		247		869.5	
Grand Total	16,140	12,464		1,593		1,149		933.5	

TABLE 2.3
MINIMUM NUMBERS OF INDIVIDUAL ANIMALS, ROCKY CAPE MIDDENS

Unit	Wallaby		Other land mammals		Seal		Bird		Reptile		Fish		Total
	No.	%	No.	%	No.	%	No.	%	No.	%	No.	%	
Rocky Cape North													
1	5	20	9	31	4	14	8	29	1	3	1	3	28
2	2		2		1		2				0		7
3	4	31	2	15	4	31	3	23			0		13
4	2	9	0	0	5	23	1	4			14	64	22
Rocky Cape South													
5	1	1	7	5	1	1	2	2			119	91	130
6	2	1	6	3	5	2	3	1			199	93	215
7	4	2	9	5	5	3	1	—			170	90	189
													604

TABLE 2.4
MINIMUM NUMBERS OF INDIVIDUAL ANIMALS, ROCKY CAPE MIDDENS

Units Rocky Cape sequence	Approximate dates B.P.	Wallaby		Other land mammals		Seal		Bird		Reptile		Fish		Total
		No.	%	No.	%	No.	%	No.	%	No.	%	No.	%	
1, 2, 3	400 -3,500	11	23	13	27	9	19	13	27	1	2	1	2	48
4, 5, 6, 7	3,800 -8,000	2	2	22	4	16	3	7	1	0	0	502	90	556

hook or by spearing off the rocks (Roughley 1953:87; Bowdler 1970:86; and personal experience). Indeed Roughley (Gill and Banks 1956:38) thinks that they might even be caught by hand in some circumstances, and it is worth remembering that people diving for abalone and crayfish would have been foraging within an environment favored by wrasses. They are widely distributed throughout Australian and New Zealand temperate and subtropical rocky coast and coral reef waters, and they are available in all seasons.

As might be expected from their relative robustness, the most common bone elements present were the upper and lower pharyngeal plates of the dental mill, and the premaxillae and dentaries of the jaws. Nevertheless, no less than 56 percent of all bones were vertebrae, ribs, and bones from around the gill area, suggesting that whole fish were brought up to the site and eaten there. Comparisons of the dimensions of the prehistoric jaws and dental-mill bones with those of modern fish from Rocky Cape showed that the prehistoric fish had a median weight of about 0.5 kilo and a range of between 0.2 and 1.0 kilo.

Other Bones

Two other features of the faunal sequence need to be discussed. First, in terms of the weights of bones, there was a steady diminution in the contribution of seal, from about 86 percent in the lowest level to about 54 percent in the top. This could also be seen in terms of the numbers of bones of seal compared to those of all land mammals and birds when fish bones were excluded from the calculations. This trend seems to be belied when assessed according to the minimum-numbers method, but here the numbers involved may be too small for a detailed analysis. I must state it simply as a feeling that a larger sample would confirm such an erosion in the relative importance of seal.

Second, in the top two units, deposited within the past 2,500 years, there was a small increase in the importance of wallabies (*Macropus rufrogriseus*), and perhaps a more significant increase in birds, mostly cormorants. Among the other land mammals, there was a tendency toward a diminution in the range of species as time went on, from a suite of wet scrub forms in the basal spits to a preponderance of the bandicoot (*Isoodon obesulus*) in the upper ones. The difference in composition of the land mammals in lower and upper units was just significant at the 5 percent level, hinting at a subtle change in the land predation pattern, which might have reflected local vegetational readjustment to the postglacial coastal conditions. It must be noted, however, that the increase of wallaby and bird occurred only in the top two units, a good thousand years after the disappearance of fish. The latter event resulted in impoverishment of the Rocky Cape diet and not a replacement, at least not immediately.

I have gone into the minutiae of this sequence only to indicate that it is only in these terms that any change can be documented in the nonfish faunal component of the prehistoric Rocky Cape diet. They are subtle changes, and a larger sample may well be needed to substantiate them. Against this gentle trend, the sudden and irrevocable absence of fish, after having been a major component within the diet for some four thousand years, stands out as the one bleak and significant fact of the Rocky Cape faunal sequence.

The Contribution of Fish to the pre-3,800 B.P. Rocky Cape Diet

The contribution of fish to the pre-3,800-year diet can be assessed in two ways: (1) in terms of the total flesh intake as expressed finally in calories, proteins, minerals, and vitamins; and (2) in terms of the number of individual units of game, reflecting the number of different hunting actions.

The total amount of food energy represented in both middens, being present at a rate of the order of half a million kilocalories per cubic meter, probably adds up to some 330 million kilocalories. Against this large figure must be balanced the eight millennia during which the energy was consumed, and so even if we take into account several significant stratigraphic breaks indicating occasional periods of nonoccupation of the site, and even of partial midden clearance to make more headroom, this energy would only have been sufficient for a party of a few families to have camped there for a short period, say 5 to 10 days every year (calculation done in consultation with B. Meehan). Excluding vegetable food for the moment, shellfish contributed about half the total flesh weight, the rest coming from the vertebrates discussed above. I have translated their minimum numbers into relative meat weights as shown in Table 2.5. Assessing the weight of seal meat was difficult, since many of the bone elements, such as

TABLE 2.5
WEIGHT OF MEAT

Units Rocky Cape sequence	Approximate dates B.P.	Wallaby %	Other land mammals %	Seal %	Bird %	Reptile %	Fish %	Total Weight (kgs)*
1, 2, 3	400 - 3,500	18	5	73	3	—	—	600
4, 5, 6, 7	3,800 - 800	7	5	67	—	—	21	1,200

* Assuming the weight of meat eaten at the site per seal = 50 kgs.

vertebrae, ribs, and pelvic and pectoral bones, were missing or were greatly underrepresented, implying that the animals had been butchered elsewhere and the meat brought in as cuts. Robinson described Aborigines at Coxes Bight killing a seal which was then "cut up in flitches. Their appearance was very ludicrous, some having long strips dangling over their shoulders, others with it fastened behind their backs and some dragging it along the ground" (10 February 1830, in Plomley 1966:118). Species represented at Rocky Cape were both the fur seals (*Arctocephalus* sp.) and southern elephant seals (*Mirounga leonina*), the individuals being relatively young, probably providing about a hundred kilograms of meat each. I have done my calculations assuming a contribution of 50 kg per individual, assuming that only a portion of the animal was consumed on the midden camp.

It can be seen that the main contributor to the vertebrate meat diet was indeed seal, with some 70 to 80 percent of meat coming from this source in both the upper and the lower halves of the sequence. Note, however, that in the lower half of the sequence the second most important element was fish, giving about 21 percent weight of meat, about three times as much as the next element (wallaby) and almost twice as much as all land mammals combined. Translating these meat weights into their calorific values increases the relative importance of vertebrates against molluscs, and reduces somewhat the role of fish compared to mammals—especially seals, with their high calorific fat content. We need also to consider the somewhat imponderable role of vegetable food. Fecal and dry plant material from a sealed inner chamber dated to about 6,700 years ago indicate that at least bracken fern (*Pteridium esculentum*), grass tree (*Xanthorrhoeia australis*), and a Liliacea formed part of the diet. These plants are still to be found on the flanks of the cape, together with orchids and other plants known to have been eaten. In Tasmania, however, there are no great vegetable staples such as yams, cycads, millets, or macrozamias, which feature so prominently in some mainland diets, and I doubt very much that plant foods could have contributed more than, say, a third of total calorific intake; even this may, in fact, be an overestimation. In the relatively high latitude of Tasmania, it was meat, and especially coastal meat, that was the staff of life.

Given all these imponderables, I would estimate that throughout the lower half of the Rocky Cape sequence, fish contributed about 10 percent of the total calorific intake, the genus *Pseudolabrus* ranking

ranking third behind seal and shellfish in terms of contribution from all available animals.

Despite the fact that the Rocky Cape middens may well contain the remains of a thousand seals, this only meant an average of one seal every eight years, or, put more realistically, seal meat might only have been eaten on one of every four or five visits to the cave. A single seal can provide enough food for 100 man-days, but without storage techniques the span of time when it is edible may only be counted in terms of a few days, even for people with a higher tolerance for decaying meat than ourselves. A successful hunting strategy needs to provide not only an adequate total intake of food, but also a steady intake (Meehan in press), and it is here that shellfish and fish probably played their most important role.

Clearly shellfish were the most commonly collected animals, the work presumably being done by women. Among the vertebrates, we can see from Table 2.4 that during the fish-eating phase, for every bird that was caught, there were 2 wallabies, 3 seals, 4 other land mammals, and no less than 90 fish. Fishing might indeed have been the second most common hunting activity, and, if caught by being trapped or speared by men, fish might have constituted the most frequent contribution to the diet. We can see the structure of this hunting strategy as an interweaving of opportunistic attacks on seals and wallabies which provided sporadic glut periods, complemented by a steady input of shellfish, fish, and vegetable food.

There is a strong seasonal rhythm in the Tasmanian environment, with the greatest amount of food being available in the summer months. I have shown elsewhere (Jones 1974, 1975:31) that for the Tasmanians, winter was the stress period, when they fanned out into small groups along the west coastline and lived on those resources which were still available if less rich in absolute terms than during the summer. Shellfish was a major food during this period. Robinson states explicitly for Aborigines on the southwest coast that during mid June "The wild natives had no spears with them, they not having occasion for them during winter, at least but seldom, remaining chiefly in their huts on the sea coast living on [shell] fish" (14 June 1833, in Plomley 1966:736).[4] To have been able to bring fish into play as a complement to molluscs and crustacea during such stress periods would have been a great advantage, and, conversely, removal of fish from the strategy outlined above must surely have caused significant deprivation.

THE DISAPPEARANCE OF FISH
AS A PAN-TASMANIAN PHENOMENON

The Rocky Cape sequence is confirmed on a regional basis by several other excavations and field surveys in northwest Tasmania. At Blackman's Cave, Sisters' Creek, on the quartzite cliff coast some eight kilometers east of Rocky Cape (Fig. 2.1), a dense shell-midden deposit some 1.75 m deep with a basal date of 6,000 B.P. contained numerous fish bones of Labridae, together with other artifactual and stone raw materials which seriated well with the upper units of Rocky Cape South (Jones 1966:5-6, 1971). Here were also crab claws, and many more small animals, such as bandicoots, possums, rat kangaroos, and rats, than at Rocky Cape; seal remains, in contrast, were few, consisting mostly of teeth and other small fragments. These differences reflect the microenvironmental and perhaps human-use contrasts between the two sites. It is significant, despite these, that fish was as common here as at Rocky Cape.

Moving to the later, nonfish phase, we can look at the massive shell midden of West Point (Fig. 2.1), situated adjacent to what must have been an elephant seal breeding ground, on the west coast, some sixty kilometers west of Rocky Cape. From its size, and from circular depressions believed to be hut sites on its surface and revealed within the excavations, I believe that this midden served as the base camp for an entire band of, say, forty people, who lived there for at least three months every year, carrying out a wide range of industrial and other activities, from manufacturing and using stone tools to cremating their dead. Here some four million kilocalories obtained from flesh were consumed per year for about 500 years between 1,800 B.P. and 1,300 B.P. Twenty-five percent of the energy came from shellfish, especially abalones (Coleman 1966), 65 percent from elephant seal, and the remainder from a wide range of sea and land birds, and from most of the land mammals from the surrounding scrubs and swamps. Out of more than 20,000 bones from my excavations, which measured some 70 cubic meters, only two or three fish vertebrae were found—all of which could have reached the site in the talons of sea eagles, or in the guts of seals. The reefs in front of the midden contain many different kinds of fish which can easily be speared from the rocks or caught by stone walls placed across natural traps exposed by the large tidal range. Since the faunal collection from this site can be treated almost as a total vertebrate and molluscan sample of the coastal scrub and littoral environments, the absence of an entire class of animals, namely fish, is quite eerie.

Recently, further confirmation has come from the work of Bowdler on Hunter Island, five kilometers off northwest Tasmania (Fig. 2.1). At Cave Bay Cave on the east coast of the island, a faunal sequence extends back to a basal level of 22,000 years B.P. (Bowdler 1974a, 1974b, 1975). These Pleistocene layers contain a few stone and bone artifacts left by people exploiting a continental fauna on what was then "Hunter Hill," some distance inland from the sea, the cave itself overlooking the exposed Bassian Plain. In its rise the sea reached the base of the cliffs at about the same time as it did at Rocky Cape, and people with a coastal economy also followed it here, leaving a shell midden dated to between 7,000 and 4,000 years ago. Within this were bones of Labridae, together with those of sea birds and land mammals. A contemporary thin midden in a small rock shelter on the west of the island also contains some fish bones. Then, according to Bowdler's analysis, the sea in its final rise severed the island from the main, and it became abandoned for some two thousand years, to be reclaimed by man about 2,500 years ago, in what may in fact have been part of a more widely coordinated regional economic system discussed above. The reusers of what was now Hunter Island did not eat fish, despite the fact that they exploited a wide range of shellfish, sea birds, seals, and the surviving elements of what was now an impoverished island land fauna (Bowdler 1974a, 1975).

The span of sites in northwest Tasmania, ranging from major home bases to small meal-type middens and encompassing all of the main locations within the annual cycle of the ethnographic "northwest Tribe" (Fig. 2.3) (Jones 1974), ensures that we have an adequate sampling of the various seasonally distributed activities within that region. The discontinuity in eating fish was a regional phenomenon that overrode the internal nuances of the seasonal deployment of diet or of activities.

The possibility that it was a phenomenon restricted to the northwestern region was dispelled by Lourandos's excavations (1970) in a large shell midden at Little Swanport (Fig. 2.1), a sheltered tidal estuary on the central east coast of the island. The midden, consisting of oysters and mussels collected from the muddy banks of the estuary, was some two meters thick, its top truncated by recent agricultural and/or shell-mining activities. Some crayfish remains (*Jasus* sp) were found throughout the midden. Bone was scarce, but a minimum number of about 24 individuals of identifiable land mammal species were found, of which 11 were the large macropods, kangaroos and wallabies, and the others bandicoots and rats, all typical of the open, dry, sclerophyll savannah woodland surrounding the site today. A minimum number of 13 fish of the Aluteridae or leatherjacket family were also found, 12 of which came from the lowest zone, III (dates to between 4450-4750 B.P. and 3550-3850 B.P.), and one only from Zone II. These numbers of individuals were, of course, calculated from many more actual fish bones. There were, however, no fish bones in the top zone, I, which had a top date of 1550-1850 B.P. Comparing Zone III with the other two by chi square in terms of the minimum numbers of all land mammals and birds against those of fish showed the differences to be significant at better than the 0.1 percent level. Leatherjackets are small, fast-moving fish (Pollard 1969:327) and are found today in the Little Swanport estuary (Lourandos 1970:42). Lourandos interpreted this and several other similar sites around the shores of the estuary as having been primarily shell dumps; the home camps where stone-tool manufacture and other maintenance activities were carried out were distributed on the woodland edge away from the shore. Limited though it is, the evidence at Little Swanport for the cessation of fishing corresponds remarkably well to that from Rocky Cape and Hunter Island, though ecologically the two areas display a contrast as great as any in Tasmania.

Before proceeding to an explanation for this cessation, I should like briefly to look at the role of fishing in some mainland Australian economies.

A YEAR WITH THE ANBARA

It was in order to gain quantitative data about the economy of a coastal hunting and gathering society that Betty Meehan and I spent a year (1972-73) living among members of the Anbara community of the Gidjingali (or Burerra) tribe at the mouth of the Blyth River, Arnhem Land, northern Australia. The Gidjingali lived a totally traditional life until 1957, when the government created a settlement for them at Maningrida, on the land of another language group, almost fifty kilometers from their own country. Most Gidjingali then moved to this settlement, where their social structure was analyzed by L. R. Hiatt (1965). During the past five years the Aborigines of north and central

Australia have made a major and sustained move, or have shown a desire to move, away from European settlements and back to their own lands to live largely traditional lives. Partly because of their confidence in dealing with strange societies (they were hosts for visiting Macassan trepang fishermen for hundreds of years), partly because of their intact linguistic religious and demographic structure, due to recency of contact and medical care, and partly because of the richness of their own environment, the Gidjingali have been among the most successful Aboriginal groups in such reestablishment. Since late 1971, about a hundred persons have been living in communities on their estates, hunting and gathering their own food and living in camps that coalesce and move with the flux of the seasonal cycle.

During 1972-73, we made observations on about 330 days of the year, concentrating our attentions on the diet of about 35 persons, who constituted the core of the Anbara camp during that time. Meehan worked with the women and I with the men. In terms of gross weight, about three-quarters of the carbohydrate food was bought from the settlement store and brought into the community each two or three weeks by truck, or, for most of the year, by boat, and paid for by pensions, craftwork moneys, and so forth. The remaining carbohydrates were gathered from the land, as were all the fruits. All of the flesh food was hunted from the sea, the shore, or the land itself.

Altogether, the Anbara hunted and gathered some 250 species of vegetables, fruits, shellfish, crustacea, fish, reptiles, birds, and land mammals during the year. Their consumption of these was organized according to a seasonal pattern, since some elements, such as fruits, were highly seasonal in their availability. Their hunting strategy had two important features (Meehan in press and personal communication). First, while they maintained as broad a spectrum as possible of potential food, within each class as well as between classes, there was a marked concentration on a few favored species. In other words, they had a narrow target in actuality, while keeping all of their options open in case of need. Second, they organized their food gathering so that major intakes, such as a large game animal or a good day's fishing, had steady support from less spectacular, though dependable, foods. In general, the men obtained the major items and the women provided the backup, usually in the form of shellfish and vegetable foods (Meehan in press).

Why Did the Tasmanians Stop Eating Fish?

Some 60 to 70 species of fish, including stingrays, were caught, usually by the men, from a variety of habitats and by many different methods. These included the use of multipronged fish spears from the shore, while wading, or from canoes; fishhooks and lines; traditional and European nets, the latter used in a traditional way with spearmen to usher and stampede the fish into it; and several kinds of fish traps including wickerwork ones placed in gaps in dams or fences. Some fish were caught by hand in small inland pools. Inland groups used vegetable poisons to stun fish. In many of these technologies, European materials were employed, but usually as direct replacements for traditional ones, which were also sometimes used. Even fishhooks made from wire, obtained from the Macassans and later brought in from white Australian camps and properties, were used before 1957, and there were Gidjingali terms for their various elements, including the sinkers.

As an activity, fishing occurred almost every day, with great variation in the number of men actually taking part. Sometimes fishing would be the main foraging activity, with most men participating. On other days it was the work of a few—an adjunct to the expected haul from some other hunt or an insurance against its failure. In this sense fish and shellfish played similar roles in the total strategy, the one caught by men, the other by women.

To gain some idea of the net contribution of fish to the total diet, one may look at Meehan's analysis of the month of April 1973, when the average daily consumption of energy was some twenty-four hundred calories per head. Of this about 50 percent was provided by bought carbohydrates; fish, the second highest item, contributed 21 percent. During that month, the 35 people in the group ate a total gross weight of 500 kilograms of fish, which was 22 percent of the total gross weight of all foods (including bought food). In terms of weight of edible meat, fish contributed 62 percent of the total, the next highest being shellfish with 22 percent, followed by reptiles with 9 percent, crustacea with 4 percent, and mammals and birds combined with only 2 percent. Such a preponderance of fish, followed in importance by molluscs, was maintained throughout the year, with the relatively minor foods such as reptiles, wallabies, and birds making their various contributions according to the season.

The Anbara shared Captain Cook's amazement on being told of a coastal people who did not eat fish; as Gurmanamana said on one occasion, "Silly bugger, eh?"

Bass Point, N.S.W.

To put this rich mainland coastal economy through an archaeological sieve, I will briefly turn to Bowdler's excellent analysis of a coastal midden at Bass Point, New South Wales (1970).

This midden, deposited over the past 3,000 years, overlooked an ocean-washed rock platform and consisted mostly of mussels in the top levels and gastropods in the lower ones. Among vertebrate bones, those of fish predominated to such an extent that Bowdler stated, "Fish was undoubtedly the main vertebrate eaten at this site, while birds and land mammals provided a subsidiary but constant source of meat; and seal afforded an intermittent but substantial supply" (1970:80). Altogether in her excavations, a minimum number of some 252 individual fish were recovered, comprising 244 bony fish and 8 cartilaginous ones—divided altogether into at least 16 families or 17 species. The most numerous fish was the snapper (*Chrysophrys* sp.), followed by *Labridae*; leatherjackets were also important. Bowdler demonstrated a change in the relative frequencies of fish species through time, which she interpreted as being due to the introduction of shell fishhooks, and a consequent shift from men's spearing predation to one based on women fishing with hooks, presumably from the shore or from bark canoes, as described in the ethnographic literature. Despite the preponderance of fish as a vertebrate target, the half-dozen odd seals in the excavations would still have provided substantial portions of meat at spasmodic intervals. Indeed, if we ignore for a moment the sheer diversity of fish species at Bass Point, we are struck with the similarity between the structure of its fauna and that of the lower half of the Rocky Cape sequence.

Taking into account the lack of shell fishhooks or hafted multipronged fish leisters within the technology of the ancient Tasmanians, and giving full regard to the higher latitude of the Tasmanian coast than the mainland examples alluded to above, what strikes one is how much the older half of the Rocky Cape midden seems to be the debris of a typical Aboriginal coastal economy. It is the upper half of the midden—the last 3,500 years of Tasmanian exploitation of their coastline—that is so bizarre.

ICHTHYOPHOBIA: TOWARD AN EXPLANATION

In searching for an explanation for the Tasmanians' strange abnegation of fish, an important element in their diet and in their

42

strategy for survival, I hope that I have already disposed of some of the more obvious contenders.

Physical survival of the evidence is no issue, since the fish bones appear at the base of the sequence and not at the top. Indeed, when first excavated, the fish bones from the lower levels of Rocky Cape constituted the oldest direct evidence in the whole of Australia for Aboriginal use of fish, and—apart from the calcreted golden perch and Murray cod bones from Mungo (Bowler et al. 1970)—they are still in that position. It has proved difficult to draw upon mainland Australian archaeological evidence to help elucidate the Tasmanian problem, simply because nowhere on the mainland Australian continent do we have direct physical evidence of coastal diets before about 4,000 years ago. Indeed, the northwest Tasmanian sites rank with any in the world as witnesses to man's adaptation to the postglacial sea-level rise and consolidation.

I also feel that the question of sampling has been met—in the sites themselves and in terms of the sites as samples of local economies, and of local economies integrated into long-term cultural systems (Fig. 2.3).

Ecological arguments based upon some changes in seashore environments do not carry much weight since there is no evidence that the waters themselves are sensitive to such changes, that the fish genera concerned are narrow in their ecological tolerances, or that diseases and the like are rife in such cold waters. Nor indeed do we find any evidence for such changes in the archaeological record in the cognate littoral fauna of shellfish and seals. I have to stress that the same wrasses swim around the rocks of Rocky Cape, and the same leatherjackets around the shallows of Little Swanport, as was obviously the case 8,000 and 5,000 years ago, respectively. The ecological differences between the littoral environments of western and eastern Tasmania far outweigh any possible putative changes in either region during the past ten millennia. Yet fishing as a human activity was abandoned in both areas at the same time by people caught up in a single cultural net.

Technological arguments do not convince either. At Mungo, 20,000 to 30,000 years ago, people caught large quantities of perch and cod (Bowler et al. 1970; H. Allen 1972), some of which weighed 15 kilos or more, from the deep lakes and rivers of Pleistocene western New South Wales. Fishing was part of the cultural hegemony of Pleistocene Australians; it was brought to the cliffs of northern Tasmania as the sea isolated one tiny splinter of humanity to play out its destiny apart from the rest of mankind for the next 500 generations.

Bone tools are found in the basal layers of several of the sites mentioned above—Cave Bay Cave at 18,000 years ago, Rocky Cape from 8,000 to about 3,000, Sisters' Creek and Little Swanport at their bases. No bone tools were recorded among the tools of the ethnographic Tasmanians. Seductive as it might seem at first sight, we cannot look to these bone tools as an explanation for the cessation of fishing, although both are discontinuous elements in Tasmanian prehistory, and both may indeed be reflections of a higher cultural process. The bone tools consist mostly of stout points and spatulae often made from wallaby and kangaroo fibulae. Their shape, use polish, and analogy from identical ethnographic examples on the adjacent mainland strongly suggest a function as awls and reamers for skin working. The big possum-skin rugs of the nineteenth-century Victorian Aborigines contrast markedly with the rough kangaroo skins slung over the shoulders of the Tasmanians.

In the Rocky Cape sequence, bone tools show a pattern of disuse different from that of fish. They are most typologically diverse in the basal Unit 7, where three bone tools were made for every retouched stone one, but show a steady contraction in form and a decline in relative industrial popularity in the succeeding two units. The last bone tools occur in small quantities in Unit 3, some hundreds of years after the cessation of fishing. Examination of Tables 2.1-2.3 will show that the practice of fishing, though steadily a major hunting activity for four thousand years as represented in all spits in Units 7 to 5, was suddenly discontinued between 3,800 and 3,500 years ago.

Having disposed of all the plausible ecological explanations that I can think of, I am forced back to a cultural one. I feel that the only possible explanation is that the Tasmanians made an intellectual decision which had the result of constricting their ecological universe.

Within Tasmanian ethnography there were several instances of potentially useful arts not being practiced and food not being eaten by certain tribes. Watercraft were made and used by the coastal peoples all along the west, southern, and east coasts as far north as Freycinet Peninsula (Jones 1976). The people of northeastern Tasmania did not use them, nor apparently did they know (or want to know) how to make them (Robinson: 25 July 1831, in Plomley 1966:399). Such craft would have been useful in crossing coastal rivers and bays. The northeasterners had regular contact with people from the southeast. I see this absence of watercraft as a deliberate cultural choice. The Aborigines of eastern Tasmania did not eat penguins despite seeing a Bruny Island man eating them (Robinson: 4 November 1830, in Plomley 1966:267). Some Aborigines would not eat a buck kangaroo, or at least one that had been caught by a woman (Robinson: 28 April 1832, in Plomley 1966:601). One woman did not eat wombat, even though everybody else in the party partook of some (Robinson: 11 July 1834, in Plomley 1966:899). Grease floating on European-prepared soup, presumably from mutton or beef, induced nausea, and Aborigines refused even to touch bread which had been cut with a buttery knife (Backhouse 1843:166). It is in this area of prohibition and of sanction that we may have to look for an explanation as to why the Tasmanians stopped eating fish. The general question of why certain foods become defined as inedible needs psychological or structural anthropological analysis. One can but wonder with Voltaire

> Why must we ask our bishop's permission to eat eggs? If a king commanded his people never to eat eggs, would he not be regarded as the most ridiculous of tyrants? What strange aversion do bishops have against omelettes? (1764: "Lent, Questions on Lent")

Archaeologically, the more profitable question is to consider the evolutionary implications of such a decision; to isolate the initial social or ecological conditions where it was spawned; and to show how it could continue to be observed despite selective pressures against it. In this paper, I have tried to show that fish, having been a significant element of Tasmanian food for at least four thousand years, was suddenly dropped from the diet throughout the island, a situation which persisted for over three thousand years until the ethnographic present. This constituted a net loss of food, and was not a case of one food being replaced by another, or of one less efficient hunting strategy being replaced by a more effective one. To proscribe for thousands of years the use of this abundant food was an economic maladaptation. Food and other proscriptions in ethnographically observed Tasmanian society functioned, like that of different cicatrix and hair style patterns, to distinguish one band or tribe from its neighbor (Jones 1974). These socially defining devices may have been thrown up randomly, but there is an equal possibility that such ideas could also have been used to categorize one set of animals against another—edible against inedible. Whereas one can conceive of a random-number model, throwing up strange and sometimes maladaptive combinations including one whereby all Tasmanians eschewed all species of fish, the important question then to be asked is, How could such practices have persisted?

To answer this, we may need to look not only at the ideology of Tasmanian society but also at its total size. In an open or continental-sized social system, a grossly maladaptive strategy would be corrected by the operation of selective forces. Either the example of neighbors or the flow of other ideas would correct a bizarre aberration, or, ultimately, the participants in an inefficient economy would be replaced by those practicing a more effective one. Taking the Tasmanian fish case, one could envisage such selective forces operating especially during periodic stress episodes, for example at the end of a hard winter when the spring egging or sealing seasons were for some reason late. Meehan (in press) has documented for the Anbara how a single fresh-water flood out of the mouth of the Blyth River during the 1973-74 wet season wiped out the coastal shellfish beds, which during the previous year had been an important resource for them (see above). After the flood the Anbara were easily able to increase their attention to the other elements of their broad-based foraging pattern—fish, mangrove shellfish and crustacea, land reptiles, and so forth. To have a major category of food proscribed during such an episode might have changed an inconvenience into a calamity.

In the closed system of the Tasmanians, a maladaptation might have a better chance of surviving simply because of the lack of better competing neighboring economies. If fish were not caught for several generations, much of the skill, technology, and ethnoscience concerned with their capture might also be forgotten. The isolated Tasmanians, unlike a group of tribes in a similar-sized portion of a continent, would have had no opportunity of relearning such skills from neighbors even if they had wanted to. That the Tasmanians could be receptive to new ideas once their closed world was breached was shown by the speed with which they adopted dogs and changed their hunting methods to incorporate them when dogs were first introduced on the island by the British in 1803 (Jones 1970).

The Tasmanians—numbering only 4,000 souls, separated into several language groups, and on their own for some 12,000 years—present us with an extreme case of cultural isolation (Jones

1977). In coming to an explanation of the discontinuation of fishing; of the abandonment of bone tools and the other items that they made; of why at the South Australian threshold to Tasmania 10,000 years ago we have wooden boomerangs and barbed spears (Luebbers 1975) and yet none were found in the Tasmanian kit of A.D. 1800; of why again no hafted stone tools and no edge-ground axes were in nineteenth-century Tasmanian technology, and yet both are now known to have had a Pleistocene antiquity on the mainland (C. White 1971; Gould 1973; Jones 1973:280), we may need to draw upon analogues from the biogeography of islands, where pauperation of species, a simplification of the biological matrix, is the inexorable consequence of the sundering of continents into their daughter islands (Jones 1976, 1977; Diamond 1977). Perhaps these historical events in Tasmania constitute a specific case within a general proposition that *the number of ideas in a cultural system is a function of the number of minds interacting within it*. To test this we need to look at other islands, at other histories of isolation, at the evolution or breakdown of other human information exchange systems.

NOTES

1. By one of the many ironic twists of Tasmanian history, this is precisely what happened, against her wishes, to Truganini (Trugernanner), the last full-blooded Tasmanian Aboriginal to die in Tasmania. Her skeleton was placed on display at the Tasmanian Museum between 1904 and 1947, but in 1976, the centenary of her death, the remains were given a state funeral, indeed completing the picture (see the Tasmanian Museum and Art Gallery Annual Report, 1974/75, pp. 2-3 [Hobart]).

2. Van Diemen's Land was the original name for Tasmania.

3. *Callorhynchus milli*—"excellent eating" according to Anderson (30 January 1777). This incident was also described by Midshipman Martin, who said that on being offered a fish, the Aborigines "instantly run away, and seem'd very much terrified at the sight of it, but what their fears can have arose from, I cannot conceive" (28 January 1777 in Beaglehole 1967: 1:54-55).

4. That Robinson was referring to molluscs is clear from the context.

3
Archaeological Ethnography . . . Because Sometimes It Is Better to Give than to Receive[1]

WILLIAM L. RATHJE
University of Arizona

[Archaeologists], shrive yourselves of the notion that the units which you seek . . . must match the units in social organizations which contemporary ethnographers have attempted to tell you exist. (M. Harris 1968a:359)

A POTENTIAL TO "SHRIVE"

For more than a decade, archaeologists have been formally engaged in "ethnoarchaeology." Their goal has usually been to document patterns in the relation between material culture and human behavior in an ongoing society in order better to reconstruct past behaviors from their extant material remnants. In this effort, the ethnoarchaeologist's vision has often been limited to deteriorating huts, dissolving bones, or other data directly relevant to refining archaeological interpretation. Rather than study contemporary societies from the same holistic, processual perspective used in studying extinct systems, the ethnoarchaeologist usually finds that his group is not "pristine" enough for his needs and therefore attempts to reconstruct the way things were done in the past before contact with "Western Civilization." Thus archaeologists have often avoided or ignored opportunities to use their unique skills and perspectives to contribute to a fuller view of the contemporary societies they study. There is good reason, however, to make use of such opportunities.

Archaeologists are doing ethnoarchaeology because most ethnographers, in their analyses of behavior, do not pay sufficient attention to material culture to be useful in reconstructing the past or in analyzing ongoing processes. For decades, archaeologists have "taken" concepts and units of analysis from social anthropologists. It may now be time for archaeology to attempt to offer a few theories, methods, and data sets to the study of contemporary society. Based on this approach, the Garbage Project of the University of Arizona was developed to expand the meaning of ethnoarchaeology to include archaeological ethnography.

It is important to make clear at the outset that I do not claim that contributions from archaeological ethnography will be unique. Anthropologists and sociologists like Sharp (1952), Tumin (1952:84-98), and Lewis (1969) have produced classics using a material-behavior perspective; Rappaport and Marvin Harris, among others, are continuing this tradition. Nor do I claim that archaeological ethnography will replace traditional anthropological and sociological techniques for collecting and analyzing data in ongoing social systems. It is clear that for many problems a material-behavior perspective would be largely ineffective. I do propose, however, that ethnoarchaeologists need not limit themselves to collecting data that are directly relevant *only* to building reconstructions of the past. They can apply their material-behavior perspective to the study of ongoing processes in modern systems. In fact, it is reasonable to suppose that viewing knowledge of both the past and the present from the same perspective will increase the understanding of each.

THE GARBAGE PROJECT AS ARCHAEOLOGICAL ETHNOGRAPHY

The Garbage Project was originally devised, in the spring of 1971, for standard ethnoarchaeological reasons; its goals soon broadened as additional applications for the data became apparent. One new avenue of analysis was based on the limitations of the data-collection techniques traditionally utilized to study behavior in contemporary societies. Modern material culture analyses proved to have enormous advantages in these settings.

The limitations of traditional methodologies are clearly recognized by social scientists who use them:

> Interviews and questionnaires intrude as a foreign element into the social setting they would describe, they create as well as measure attitudes, they elicit atypical roles and responses, they are limited to those who are accessible and will cooperate, and the responses obtained are produced in part by dimensions of individual differences irrelevant to the topic at hand. But the principal objection is that they are used alone. . . . (E. J. Webb et al. 1966:1)

With the publication of this manifesto in 1966, Webb and his behavioral science colleagues formally launched the search for survey alternatives, for unobtrusive measures of actual behavior to supplement and refine the use of interviews and questionnaires. Not surprisingly, sociologists and psychologists soon found themselves plunging into a promising but unfamiliar sea of physical evidence. This interest in studying the material correlates of contemporary behavior raised the possibility that the expertise of archaeologists could usefully be involved in the endeavor.

Of all social scientists, the archaeologist is perhaps the most sensitive to the important role material culture plays in human behavior. Archaeologists have begun to see that detailed analyses of physical evidence can be relevant and helpful to social scientists looking for more accurate methods of recording and analyzing *behavior*. Such analyses are especially useful when material culture can be observed in its production, consumption, or use stages, without the intervention of discard and recycling behavior (see Eighmy n.d.).

The first advantage for the researcher dealing with physical evidence is that the data are *nonreactive*. As long as material artifact data are generated without the knowledge that they will be used in research, they do not exhibit the distortions inherent in methods in which a respondent's awareness of his subject status may itself act as an agent of change. Because the "respondents" are objects, furthermore, the number of measurements that can be taken on sets of associated data depends upon the interest of the researchers and not on the cooperation and attention span of the respondents.

A second advantage of physical data is simply that they are *quantifiable*. Material culture is the product of human behavior; unlike behavior, however, material culture is relatively static and easy to quantify through the use of common "standard" measures. Many measurements can be easily replicated, and data collected by different researchers are often readily comparable, either as they stand or through indexing. In addition, because of the relative permanence of material culture, a basic research setting can often be held constant while a set of items is measured in a variety of ways and at different times to provide data on many diverse research problems.

Physical data can also provide *an independent check on interview methods and data*. It is clear that although interview-surveys are vulnerable to reactive biases, they provide significant data and cannot be abandoned. Therefore, they must be critically evaluated and refined by isolating and measuring reactive effects. Although material-culture studies suffer from distortions, these are quite different in character from the distortions typical of interview data. Thus, because material culture is a quantifiable, nonreactive correlate of behavior, the greatest utility of material-culture studies may be to provide quantitative measures of behavior to compare to interview-elicited data (E. J. Webb et al. 1966:16). Such comparisons could ultimately lead to a quantitative description of the parameters of reactive distortion, which could in turn be used to refine interview-survey techniques and data manipulation.

Material culture provides *an alternative data source*. "Overreliance on questionnaires and interviews is dangerous," as Webb et al. put it, "because it does not give enough points in conceptual space to triangulate" (1966:34). Material culture can provide many excellent alternative sources for measuring behavior; hence it can check the biases inherently possible in any measure used alone. In addition, material-culture studies can supplement traditional measures by providing data that cannot be collected by interview-survey methods.

Totally aside from its advantages as a passive measure of associated behavior, material culture must be studied as *an independent variable* in human behavior.

Putting the idea of simple technological determinism aside, there are obviously aspects of behavior which are influenced primarily by material culture. . . . At a time when the earth is slowly being covered with (man-made) litter, one of the most pressing problems facing man may well be dealing with the global impact of material culture itself. (Eighmy n.d.:5-6)

These characteristics of material-culture-behavior studies—along with a growing concern among researchers over the value of interview-survey data collected without independent checks—may have an exciting effect upon the discipline of archaeology. For over a century, archaeologists have labored in the dirt upon material things. During the same time period, social scientists studying contemporary society chose interview-survey techniques as their primary source of data, almost totally ignoring material culture analogous to the remnants exhumed by archaeologists. Now, as material culture becomes as respectable as verbally elicited data, archaeologists have the opportunity to draw upon their expertise and make a contribution to the study of contemporary society.

For one thing, archaeologists can offer constructive criticisms of the modern material-culture analyses of other social scientists. For example, from an archaeological perspective, many typologies are based on poorly defined criteria that require subjective, nonquantitative decisions on the part of the data recorder. For example, Warner's house typology (cf. Warner, Meeker, and Eells 1960:143-48) has few rigorous criteria for separating houses in "good condition" from those in "medium condition." This sort of vagueness in data recording obviously undercuts the usefulness of material culture studies.

The widespread interest in nonreactive measures, however, offers archaeologists an opportunity more important than the chance to aid their colleagues in social science. It challenges archaeologists to validate their methods of studying the past by applying them to the study of the present. In recent years, several archaeologists have attempted to test their expertise on modern material culture through small pilot studies. One arena of such endeavors is the University of Arizona's Anthropology Department, where several hundred modern material-culture analyses have been conceived and carried out by undergraduate archaeology students since 1971. The subjects of analysis were as diverse as building plans and waterbeds, bumper stickers and book illustrations, church interiors and children's toys. A particularly memorable study used a measure of bathroom decoration to indicate the degree of illicit drug use (marijuana and LSD). It was based on the proposition that "a nothing bathroom can bum you out fast," and it seemed to work (Motz n.d.).

All of these studies, though interesting, are, as yet, in rather crude pilot form. From this array of modern material-culture studies, one promising set of interests was formalized into Le Projet du Garbàge, a concerted attempt by analysts of the debris of the past to address themselves to the present.

LE PROJET DU GARBÀGE

Background

Archaeology pioneer Emil Haury likes to tell his audiences, "If you want to know what is really going on in a community, look at its garbage." The Garbage Project has taken Doc Haury at his word; since 1973, it has been systematically analyzing quantifiable refuse collected in household-level units to describe the social correlates of modern urban resource management.

The Garbage Project is conducted in the city of Tucson, an urban community of slightly more than 360,000 inhabitants located in southern Arizona. Tucson is characterized by rapid growth in population, a large proportion of Mexican-American residents (27 percent in 1973), and a significant proportion of elderly residents (12 percent over age sixty-five in 1973).

The sampling unit for the Garbage Project is the census tract. Tucson's 66 urban census tracts were grouped into seven clusters derived from 1970 federal census demographic and housing characteristics (Rathje and Gorman n.d.). Household garbage samples were collected from 19 census tracts selected as representative of the seven census-tract clusters. A "household" is defined as any autonomous residential unit with a clearly identifiable individual garbage container. Residential refuse is collected twice a week in Tucson, and the trash which a household places out for one city pickup is the Garbage Project's most specific data-observation unit.

Raw data were collected for the project by Tucson Sanitation Division personnel who randomly selected household refuse within each sample census tract, biweekly in 1973 and weekly in 1974 and 1975. Refuse was collected from February through May and in November and December 1973, from February through May in 1974,

54

and from March through May and October through December in 1975.

In order to protect the privacy and anonymity of sample households, addresses were not recorded. Specific households were .not followed over time; a new random selection of households was made each time trash was collected. Individual households were not informed that their garbage was being studied, although there has been local newspaper, radio, and television publicity on the project at frequent intervals, with emphasis upon procedures taken to protect anonymity.

Since 1973 more than 300 student volunteers have sorted, coded, and recorded the items in the refuse, working at tables provided in the Sanitation Division Maintenance Yard. After sorting and recording, all items in the refuse were returned to the Sanitation Division for deposit in a sanitary landfill. Student workers were provided with lab coats, surgical masks, and gloves and were given appropriate immunizations. In three years of formal operation, there have been no illnesses attributed to garbage work.

Items found in the refuse were sorted into more than 150 initial categories representing food, drugs, personal and household sanitation products, amusement and education items, communication media, and pet-related materials (Figure 3.1). For each item the following information was recorded onto precoded forms: (1) item code; (2) type or subcategory ("ground chuck" as a type of "beef"); (3) original weight or volume (derived from package labeling); (4) cost; (5) material composition of containers; (6) brand; and (7) weight of any discarded food (Figure 3.2). The total refuse recorded includes garbage collections from 223 households in 1973, 392 in 1974, and 470 in 1975. This three-year record forms the Garbage Project's Data Base 1.

Garbage and Interviews

For all their usefulness, it is clear that modern material-culture studies cannot and should not stand alone. Just as they can supplement interview data, interview data can supplement them. Despite the limitations of verbally elicited information, such information is essential to developing the full potential of garbage analysis as a social science methodology. Only by discovering and documenting behavior and attitude correlates of household residuals

55

GARBAGE ITEM CODE LIST (F·75)

✳ SEE SPECIAL NOTES ▲ SEE FRUIT AND VEGETABLE PAGE

MEAT · beef only ✳ ······ 001
MEAT · other ✳ ········· 002
POULTRY · chicken only · 003
POULTRY · other ········ 004
FISH · (fresh, frozen, ····· 005
canned, dried) ✳
CRUSTACEANS + MOLLUSKS 006
(shrimp, clams, etc.)
T.V.P. TYPE FOODS ✳ ······· 007

CHEESE · (including ······ 010
cottage cheese)
MILK ✳ ················· 011
ICE CREAM · (also ice milk, 012
sherbet, popsicles) ✳
OTHER DAIRY · (not butter) · 013
EGGS (regular, powdered, · 014
liquid) ✳

BEANS · (not green beans) ✳ 015
NUTS ·················· 016
PEANUT BUTTER ········ 017
FATS : Saturated ✳ ····· 018
Unsaturated ✳ ···· 019

CORN (also corn meal ····· 022
and masa) ✳
FLOUR (also pancake mix) ✳ 023
RICE ✳ ················· 024
OTHER GRAIN (barley, ··· 025
wheat germ etc.)

NOODLES (pasta) ········· 026
WHITE BREAD ··········· 027
DARK BREAD ··········· 028
TORTILLAS ✳ ············ 029
DRY CEREALS : Regular ··· 030
High Sugar (first or · 031
second ingredient)
COOKED CEREALS ······· 032
(instant or regular)
CRACKERS ·············· 033
CHIPS (also pretzels) ···· 034

FRESH VEGETABLES ▲ ·· 041
CANNED VEGETABLES ··· 042
(dehydrated also) ▲
FROZEN VEGETABLES ▲ · 043
POTATO PEEL ▲ ········ 044
FRESH FRUIT ▲ ········ 045
CANNED FRUIT ········· 046
(dehydrated also) ▲
FROZEN FRUIT ▲ ········ 047
FRUIT PEEL ▲ ········· 048
CONDIMENTS (relish, ···· 049
pickles, olives, vinegar
etc.)

SYRUP, HONEY, JELLIES,
MOLASSES ·········· 051
PASTRIES · (cookies, cakes
and mix, pies etc.) ✳ · 052

SUGAR ✳ ··············· 053
ARTIFICIAL SWEETNERS · 054
CANDY ✳ ··············· 055

SALT ✳ ················ 056
SPICES (solid or powdered) 057
BAKING ADDITIVES (yeast, 058
baking powder, etc.)

PUDDING ··············· 061
GELATIN ··············· 062
INSTANT BREAKFAST ······ 063
DIPS (for chips) ········· 064
NON·DAIRY CREAMERS + WHIPS 065

HEALTH FOODS ✳ ······· 066

SLOP ✳ ················ 069
REGULAR COFFEE ······· 070
(instant or ground) ✳
DECAF COFFEE ········· 071
EXOTIC COFFEE ✳ ······· 072
TEA ✳ ················· 073
CHOCOLATE DRINK MIX
OR TOPPING ········ 074
FRUIT (or veg.) JUICE ···· 075
(canned or bottled)
FRUIT JUICE CONCENTRATE 076
FRUIT JUICE POWDER ···· 077
(tang, koolaid)
DIET SODA ············· 078
REGULAR SODA ········· 079
COCKTAIL MIX (carbonated) 080
COCKTAIL MIX (non-carb. · 081
liquid)
COCKTAIL MIX (powdered) · 082
PREMIXED COCKTAILS ···· 083
(alchoholic)
SPIRITS (booze) ········· 084
WINE (still + sparkling) ·· 085
BEER ✳ ················ 086

BABY FOOD + JUICE ✳ ··· 087
BABY CEREAL (pablum) ··· 088
BABY FORMULA (liquid) ✳ · 089
BABY FORMULA (powdered) ✳ 090
PET FOOD (dry) ········· 091
PET FOOD (canned or moist) 092

T·V DINNERS (also pot pies) 094
TAKE OUT MEALS ········ 095
SOUPS ✳ ··············· 096
SAUCES ✳ ·············· 097
PREPARED MEALS ······· 098
(canned or packaged) ✳

VITAMIN PILLS AND
SUPPLEMENTS ········ 100
(commercial) ✳
PRESCRIBED DRUGS ······ 101
(prescribed vitamins)
COMMERCIAL DRUGS :
ASPIRIN (also ······· 102
acetaminophen)
STIMULANTS AND
DEPRESSANTS ✳ ···· 103
REMIDIES (physical) ✳ · 104
ILLICIT DRUGS ✳ ········ 105
COMMERCIAL DRUG
PARAPHERNALIA ······ 106
ILLICIT DRUG
PARAPHERNALIA ······ 107
CONTRACEPTIVES :
MALE ··············· 108
FEMALE ············· 109
BABY SUPPLIES (diapers · 111
etc.) ✳
INJURY ORIENTED ······· 112
(iodine, bandaids etc.)
PERSONAL SANITATION ✳ · 113
COSMETICS ✳ ··········· 114

CIGARETTES (pack) ✳ · 124
CIGARETTES (carton) ✳ · 125
CIGARS ················ 126
PIPE, CHEWING TOBACCO,
LOOSE TOBACCO ····· 127
ROLLING PAPERS ········ 128

HOUSEHOLD CLEANERS
(also laundry) ✳ ······· 131

HOUSEHOLD CLEANING
TOOLS (not detergents) · 132
HOUSEHOLD MAINT.ITEMS · 133
(paint wood etc.)
COOKING + SERVING AIDS ·· 134
TISSUE CONTAINER ······· 135
TOILET PAPER CONTAINER · 136
NAPKIN CONTAINER ······ 137
PAPER TOWEL CONTAINER · 138
PLASTIC WRAP CONTAINER · 139
BAGS (paper or plastic) ✳ · 140
BAG CONTAINER ········· 141
ALUMINUM FOIL SHEETS ··· 142
ALUMINUM FOIL PACKAGE · 143
WAX PAPER PACKAGE ····· 144

MECHANICAL APPLIANCE ··· 147
(tools)
ELECTRICAL APPLIANCE
AND ITEMS ·········· 148
AUTO SUPPLIES ········· 149
FURNITURE ············· 150
CLOTHING : CHILD ✳ ···· 151
ADULT ✳ ··· 152
CLOTHING CARE ITEMS · 153
(shoe polish, thread)
DRY CLEANING (laundry also) 154
PET MAINTENANCE (litter) 155
PET TOYS ·············· 156
GATE RECEIPTS (tickets) · 157
HOBBY RELATED ITEMS ·· 158
PHOTO SUPPLIES ········ 159
HOLIDAY VALUE (non·food) ✳ 160
DECORATIONS (non holiday) · 161
PLANT AND YARD MAINT. · 162
STATIONARY SUPPLIES ··· 163
JEWELRY ··············· 164
CHILD SCHOOL RELATED
PAPERS ✳ ··········· 171
CHILD EDUC. BOOKS (non·fiction) 172
CHILD EDUC. GAMES (toys) · 173
CHILD AMUSEMENT
READING ··········· 174
CHILD AMUSEMENT TOYS · 175
(games)
ADULT BOOKS (non·fiction) · 176
ADULT BOOKS (fiction) ···· 177
ADULT AMUSEMENT GAMES 178

LOCAL NEWSPAPERS ✳ ··· 181
NEWPAPERS (other city, · 182
national) ✳
ORGANIZATIONAL
NEWSPAPERS OR
MAGAZINES (also religion) ✳ 183
GENERAL INTEREST
MAGAZINES ✳ ········ 184
SPECIAL INTEREST
MAGAZINE OR
NEWSPAPER ✳ ······· 185
ENTERTAINMENT GUIDE ··· 186
(T·V guide etc.)

MISCELLANEOUS ITEMS 190
(specify on back of
sheet) ✳

FIGURE 3.1. Garbage item code list.

(FOR OFFICE USE ONLY)

NAME OF RECORDER: Kelly Allen

DATE OF ANALYSIS: Oct. 30

PACK NUMBERS TO RIGHT OF COLUMN, LETTERS TO LEFT (22–68)
WRITE NUMBERS CLEARLY AND USE CAPITAL LETTERS ONLY.

MATERIAL COMPOSITION CODES
CODE (LIST MOST PREVALENT MATERIAL FIRST)

A PAPER	H RETURNABLE GLASS	R COPPER AND BRASS
B FERROUS (STEEL/TIN)	K WOOD	S BIODEGRADABLE PLASTIC
C ALUMINUM	M CERAMICS	T TEXTILES
D PLASTIC (CELLOPHANE)	P LEATHER	V CORRUGATED CARDBOARD
E NON-RETURN GLASS	Q RUBBER	X OTHER (SPECIFY ON BACK)

#	Census Tract	Mo.	Day	Item Code	No. of Items	Fluid Ounces	Solid Ounces	Cost	Waste (grams)	Spoilage Indicator	Brand	Type	Material Composition Code
1	019	10	30	041	001		16.0		70		MARSHBUR	CARROT	D
2	019	10	30	086	003	36.1		.87			SCHLITZ	MALT	C
3	019	10	30	079	002	24.0			282	X	SEVENUP		BC
4	019	10	30	027	001		16.0	.65			NORTHRID	HONEYEGG	D
5	019	10	30	118	002	32.0		.43			CIRCLEK	WHOLE	A
6	019	10	30	086	002	24.0					LITE		C
7	019	10	30	051	001		32.0	1.19	40		WELCHS	JELLY	E
8	019	10	30	041	001				55	X		LETTUCE	
9	019	10	30	048	001				45	X	LONGHORN	CHEDDAR	D
10	019	10	30	181	003				260			BANANA	
11	019	10	30	181	001							CITIZEN	A
12	019	10	30	044	001	25.6		.15	95		ROYALOCC	VODKA	ED
13	019	10	30	084	001		10.7	.65	105		HARVESTO	BUNS	D
14	019	10	30	027	001		16.0	.23			CAMPBELL	TURKEYNO	B
15	019	10	30	096	001			.40			WESTERN	HARDMARG	A
16	019	10	30	124	001						MARLBORO	FILTER	A
17	019	10	30	099	001		12.0	1.73	372				
18	019	10	30	002	001						FOODGIAN	PORKCHOP	D
19	019	10	30	095	001			.15			HARDEES	FRENCHFR	A
20	019	10	30	055	001						REESES	CHOCOLAT	E
21	019	10	30	102	001		1.2				BAYER		A
22	019	10	30	037	001		9.0				CRISPIES	PRETZELS	E
23	019	10	30	001	001		20.0				FOODGIAN	GROUND	A
24	019	10	30	001	001		18.0		85	X	FOODGIAN	SIRLOIN	D

FIGURE 3.2. Garbage Project data recording form.

through small-scale combinations of interview and garbage studies can large-scale garbage analyses become a significant anthropological data source.

Therefore, in order to refine the utility of household residual analysis, the Garbage Project and the University of Arizona Medical School participated in a cooperative garbage-interview operation. The purposes of this study were (1) to record the presence of garbage disposal systems, pets, compost piles, vegetable gardens, and other variables and quantify their effect on garbage data; (2) to compare refuse and interview data related to utilization of resources that might be expected to be subject to reactive bias and/or error in interviews; and (3) to identify specific demographic, sociocultural, economic, cognitive, and behavioral attributes of households that might account for variability in food utilization and waste patterns (Harrison n.d.).

Three sample census tracts were selected to give maximum variability in income and ethnic distribution. The sample was selected to represent approximately 1.4 percent of the households in each tract and was randomly drawn from a list of all households in the tracts that had individual refuse pickup. During late 1974 and early 1975 refuse was collected and analyzed from each of 73 households for a period of five weeks to assure good data on patterning in resource management strategies. An interview took place during the last three weeks of the refuse collection period to identify specific demographic, socioeconomic, behavioral, and attitudinal characteristics associated with variability in the remnants of specific household resource management strategies. The interview schedule was standardized in both English and Spanish, and the single interviewer utilized was bilingual.

To make sure that no bias affected household discard patterns, households were not informed that their garbage was being analyzed. To assure household anonymity, stringent safeguards developed with the Human Subjects' Committee and the Tucson Sanitation Division were put into operation. Address lists for matching interview and garbage identification codes were accessible only to the field director of the Garbage Project and one supervisor in the Sanitation Division during the data-collection phase and were destroyed after all data were collected. At present, all data are totally anonymous except to associate specific interview responses with specific records of household residuals. This record of 551 pickups from 73 households forms the Garbage Project's Data Base 2.

THE USES OF GARBAGE

Using Data Bases 1 and 2, three potential Garbage Project contributions to the establishment of "archaeological ethnography" as a supplement to traditional means of studying our contemporary society can be briefly described: (1) refinement of interview-survey techniques; (2) collection of data beyond the range of interview-survey techniques; and (3) quantification of present behaviors so as to make them more comparable and relevant to past behaviors.

Refinement of Interview-Survey Techniques

In 1966 E. J. Webb and his colleagues reviewed existing techniques for identifying informant bias in interview-surveys; ironically, these measures were almost all in the form of post-test interviews, which were subject to the same types of informant biases as the original tests. "Ultimately, the determination of reactive effect depends on validating studies—few examples of which are currently available. Behavior observed under nonreactive conditions must be compared with corresponding behavior in which various potentially reactive conditions are introduced" (E. J. Webb et al. 1966:15).

Archaeologists have always maintained a healthy lack of belief in the infallibility of language. This results partially from archaeology's role in corroborating or questioning historical sources through the analysis of quantifiable material culture. Based on this tradition, it seems reasonable that archaeology could be used to evaluate modern interview-survey results as far as they claim to predict or represent behavior. Garbage analysis is an especially well-qualified candidate for this job because it largely circumvents the problem of reactive bias. The advantage of refuse in this light is obvious. Interview data are always subject to questions concerning whether they represent what people do, what they think they do, or what they want an interviewer to think they do. In contrast, most garbage is the quantifiable result of what people did. Garbage analysis, to be sure, suffers from biases introduced by garbage disposal systems, household pets, and recycling, but not from the reactive effects typical of interview-surveys.

Thus the Garbage Project seems an ideal medium by which to attempt to establish parameters on the relationship between interview data and the empirical results of behavior. Comparison of data derived by interview-survey and garbage-survey methods may identify areas which are particularly subject to distortion in interview-based procedures and may lead to useful refinements in interview techniques and the manipulation of verbally elicited data.

The first phase of a detailed comparison of interview and garbage data is currently under way in cooperation with Project ECHO (Evidence for Community Health Organization, Pima County [Arizona] Health Department), an interview-survey designed to derive the socioeconomic correlates of health-related behavior. Between February and May 1973, trained personnel conducted interviews with individuals in a random 5 percent sample of the households in the city of Tucson. Results are available in a published report (Bal, O'Hora, and Porter 1973a) of the Pima County Health Department.

Both the Garbage Project and Project ECHO collected data independently in the same census tracts during the spring of 1973. The two resulting sets of data are complementary, if not totally comparable. Only preliminary comparisons of these data bases have been made, but the results are already extremely interesting.

"On the average, how many cans or bottles of beer does _____ have in the usual week?" (Bal, O'Hora, and Porter 1973b:114-16). This question from the ECHO interview was intended to elicit straightforward answers for each household member. If certain members were not present, the head of the household provided an estimate by proxy. Anonymity was guaranteed and "don't know" was considered an acceptable answer. In quantification of ECHO responses, there was only one real problem: is a "can" or "bottle" 8 ounces, 11 ounces, 12 ounces, 16 ounces, or 32 ounces? The distinction is not made in the interview questionnaire. In order to facilitate this preliminary study, all "containers" were assumed to hold 12 ounces.

Garbage beer-consumption data were recorded by counting actual beer containers in the garbage. Where 8 ounce, 16 ounce, or other size containers were found, they were converted to equivalent numbers of 12 ounce "cans." Since garbage sample data represent beer cans or bottles per three and one-half days per household, the figures were doubled to represent a week's consumption. Random refuse pickup throughout a 12-week period was assumed to even out midweek-weekend consumption differences. The discarding of visitors' beer cans in a household's trash is not considered to bias garbage data toward higher consumption than ECHO interview reports because (1) random garbage sampling should even out visited households with the households of visitors; (2) ECHO beer-consumption reports include beer drunk away from home; and (3) in 1973 many beer cans in Tucson were made of recyclable aluminum, and the effect of recycling behavior is to reduce estimates of home beer consumption. Garbage data, recorded by number of ounces, were grouped in such a way as to make them comparable to the intervals used by ECHO.

The beer-consumption comparisons show that "front door" and "back door" information are extremely different (see Table 3.1 and Figure 3.3). Tract 10 is a good example of the divergence in data. According to interview survey data from 60 households, beer was not consumed at all in more than 85 percent of them and *no* households reported drinking more than 8 "cans" a week. Garbage data from 13 households within the same tract identified only 3 samples (less than 25 percent) with no beer containers, but 7 (54 percent) included more than 8 "cans" per week. In those 7 households, in fact, the average beer consumption was two and a half six-packs, or 15 cans, a week. It is important to note that the differences between ECHO and garbage data are all patterned in one direction: heavier beer consumption, in the form of more drinkers and higher rates of drinking, than was reported to interviewers. Garbage data from 1974 and 1975 provide the same pattern of contrasts with 1973 ECHO data as do 1973 refuse results.

The difficulty of obtaining accurate interview data on beer consumption, just at the level of whether or not beer drinkers admit to consuming beer, is also well illustrated by Data Base 2 interview-garbage comparisons. Informants from all 73 sampled households were asked the frequency of purchase of beer, plus many other food and beverage items. The possible answers included: more than once a week, once a week, once every two weeks, once a month, occasionally, and never. Out of 73 households interviewed, 33 informants claimed that beer was "never" purchased for household consumption.

Garbage data from each of the 73 households were collected and analyzed for a five-week period. This record shows that of the 33 households answering "never" only 12 discarded *no* beer containers. Four households produced only one or two beer cans, and these households were considered to have reported their behavior fairly accurately; however, each of the other 17 households over five-week

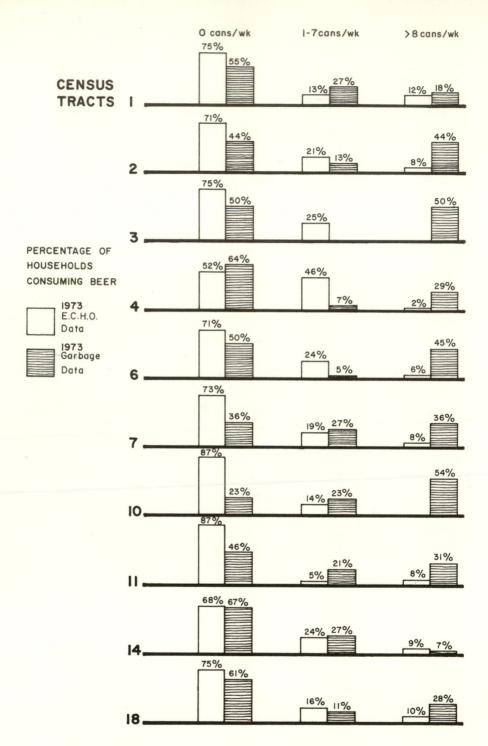

FIGURE 3.3. Household beer consumption data (see Table 3.1) shown as percentages.

TABLE 3.1
A COMPARISON OF PROJECT ECHO AND GARBAGE
PROJECT BEER CONSUMPTION DATA, SPRING 1973

Census Tract	0 cans/week ECHO	0 cans/week Garbage	1-7 cans/week ECHO	1-7 cans/week Garbage	8+ cans/week ECHO	8+ cans/week Garbage	Total ECHO	Total Garbage
1*	6	6	1	3	1	2	8	11
2	47	7	14	2	5	7	66	16
3*	30	5	10	0	0	5	40	10
4	24	9	21	1	1	4	46	14
6	48	10	16	1	4	9	68	20
7*	47	4	12	3	5	4	64	11
10*	52	3	8	3	0	7	60	13
11*	33	6	2	3	3	4	38	13
14	48	10	17	4	6	1	71	15
18	62	11	13	2	8	5	83	18
Total	397	71	114	22	33	48	544	141

* Census tracts in which more than 45 percent of the households were below the poverty level in 1973.

periods averaged a discard of containers which once held a total of about two gallons of beer.

Obviously, some informants either deliberately falsified responses, did not realize how much beer was brought into the household, had extremely bad memories, or had access to large quantities of free beer. Whatever the specific reasons, more than 27 percent of the interviewed sample grossly underestimated the input of beer in their households.

Perhaps the most interesting aspect of these lapses in recall or distortion in reporting is the pattern in relation to the three sample tracts. The middle-income Anglo households of Tract 40.05 provided reasonably accurate information: 10 families claimed they did not buy beer and only 3 of these discarded beer containers; 2 households only discarded one 12 ounce can each (Figure 3.4).

In Tract 38, composed of low-income Mexican-American and Anglo households, 11 of the 12 sampled households that claimed not to purchase beer threw out beer containers representing the input of enough beer to average 134 ounces (almost two six-packs) over each of the 9 households (Fig. 3.5). Nine of the 11 "never purchase" families in Tract 11, an extremely low-income Mexican-American neighborhood,

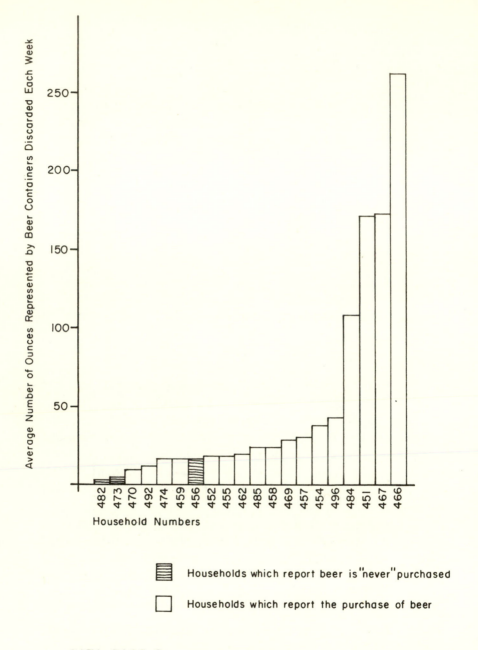

DATA BASE 2
Tract 40.05 Households With Beer Containers In Their
Residuals

FIGURE 3.4. Beer consumption in a tract of middle-income Anglo households.

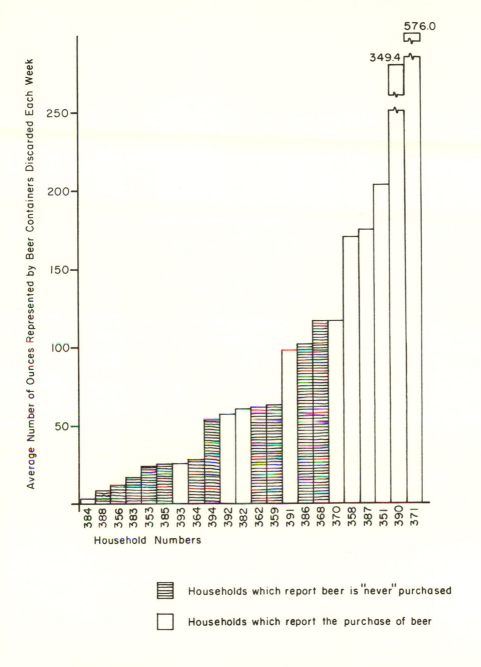

FIGURE 3.5. Beer consumption in a tract of low-income Mexican-American and Anglo households.

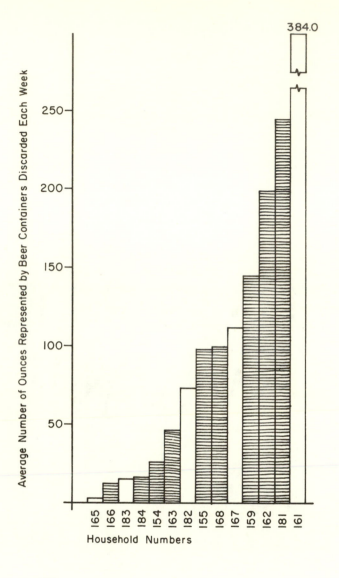

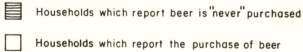

Households which report beer is "never" purchased

Households which report the purchase of beer

DATA BASE 2
Tract 11 Households With Beer Containers In Their
Residuals

FIGURE 3.6. Beer consumption in a tract of extremely low-income Mexican-American households.

discarded beer containers. The volume represented in five-week collections of each household ranged from a low of 60 ounces (five cans) to a high of 1,037 ounces (three and a half cases). In fact, the average for the 9 Track 11 households was three times higher than the average for the 9 Tract 38 households (Fig. 3.6).

The suggestion that there is considerable distortion in interview-elicited data on beer consumption will surprise no one; the interesting implications of garbage-interview comparisons are that we can use such procedures to measure the direction and magnitude of the distortions, and that if the distortions are found to be significantly patterned, they may be subject to correction. For example, it is worth noting that further preliminary studies of both Data Base 1 and Data Base 2 indicate that very-low-income groups tend to distort their behavior simply by reporting no consumption at all, while middle-income groups misrepresent the quantities involved. One possible explanation for these distortions may lie in the fact that many of the very-low-income groups were making use of food stamps issued by the U.S. government (for which beer is not an allowable purchase). It may be feasible, through comprehensive interview-garbage projects, to quantify patterns in reactive distortion of beer consumpon and in many other data realms, some perhaps unsuspected, and thereby to increase the utility of a wide range of interview techniques and data.

Beyond Interviews

It is generally accepted that the results of interview-surveys are efficient for obtaining the social, economic, and moral concepts kept in people's heads which influence their behavior; interview-surveys may not be totally satisfactory, however, for describing the actual resource-management behavior that results from these concepts when they are employed in different environments. For example, it has been noted that attitudes may not be equivalent to behavior; respondents may not be aware, in some cases, that their actual behavior conflicts with their verbalized description of their behavior. Another problem of interviews is simply that desired data may be beyond the reasonable limits of a respondent's recall. Material culture studies can make up for these deficiencies. They can go beyond supplementing interview data by recording significant new data outside the range of verbal elicitation. The Garbage Project illustrates this potential.

The supply, distribution, and utilization of food resources are critical issues, both nationally and internationally. Due to rapidly rising food prices in the United States and urgent problems of food supply on a worldwide basis, the government and the public need as much information as can be made available on food utilization and the ways in which it is affected by economic pressures. It is especially important to identify behaviors and their socioeconomic correlates that result in more or less efficiency in food utilization and to obtain information on how inflation is affecting nutrient intake in low-income segments of the population (those groups most vulnerable to malnutrition).

Too often Americans try to solve their problems by concentrating all their efforts on the development of new technological solutions. Alternative approaches, however, are needed to supplement technological research. To get to the real roots of the problem of household-level resource procurement, utilization, and discard, the socioeconomic correlates of food management must be identified and studied in different contexts. This is not a simple task.

Properly done, a food-consumption survey is a mammoth undertaking involving sizable amounts of money and professional time, numerous trained interviewers, and substantial goodwill and cooperation on the part of the subjects. Thus the U.S. Department of Agriculture surveys household food consumption in the United States only about every ten years. But even when completed, how accurate are the results? When data were last collected by the USDA, for its 1965-66 household food-consumption survey, interviewers used a detailed food list to help the homemaker recall the kinds, quantities, and costs of food used at home the seven days preceding the interview. The obvious problem is that the homemaker may not "recall" exactly what was consumed at some twenty-one meals and untold numbers of snacks. In this case even garbage-based "corrections" for informant bias would be relatively useless; garbage can, however, provide an independent set of quantifiable data on household-level consumption.

Another source of error is the fact that the USDA report is based on "economic consumption" (food purchased), rather than on quantities of food eaten. Thus, because of "discards of edible food, the calorie and nutrient levels of food eaten were probably below the levels calculated" (USDA 1969:2). Past attempts to correct this deficiency in food-discard data are unquestionably insufficient. Few Americans like to admit that they discard food, even when it is spoiled, and mere participation in a study of discard behavior is sure to bias results. As a consequence, only a few food-discard studies have been attempted. For example, in the late 1950s the USDA undertook some small studies of household "waste" using records of weighed food discard kept by volunteer respondents (Adelson, Asp, and Noble 1961; Adelson et al. 1963). The studies utilized small samples, and the authors noted that the behavior of the respondents was changed by their participation in the studies.

Interview and questionnaire methods, then, may record people's attitudes, opinions, and educated guesses about their behavior but often cannot produce accurate quantitative data on actual behavior. The Garbage Project, however, has been used as a nonreactive, quantitative method to extract household food input and discard data (see Harrison, Rathje, and Hughes 1974, 1975; Rathje 1974, 1975).

Garbage Project food input data were derived from packaging; they did not include items, like some fresh vegetables, that come in unmarked wrappers. Discarded food was defined as any once-edible food item, except for chunks of fat, and was recorded by weight. No bone, eggshells, skins (except potato peels), rinds, tops, or other plant parts not usually deemed edible were included in this category. The study of garbage has its own limitations as a measure of food management; however, all the distortions which enter into what is found in the trash—such as garbage disposal systems, household pets, fireplaces, compost piles, and recycling of containers—act in the same direction to minimize the refuse in the garbage can. Thus while data on household-level food input and discard as found in garbage cannot be used as an index of nutritional adequacy, they can be confidently interpreted as representing minimum levels of household food utilization. On this basis, population segments defined by U.S. census and ECHO interview-survey data were compared over time.

Data collected from 1973 to 1975 indicate that approximately 9 percent of the food (by volume and nutrient content) that was purchased by sampled households was discarded in household garbage. Extrapolating to all of the city of Tucson (population 360,000), over 9,500 tons of once-edible food, worth between $9 million and $11 million, probably ended up in sanitary landfills in 1974. Actual food discard is probably far greater, since 21 percent of the households in sampled census tracts have garbage disposal systems. The proportion of food discarded remained relatively constant between 1973 and 1975, but the proportion of food discarded in the form of significant quantities of single items, as opposed to plate

69

scrapings, increased from 60 percent to 70 percent in 1975 (Harrison, Rathje, and Hughes 1975).

At the level of garbage analysis, low-income areas of the city seem to be the most efficient utilizers of food resources; census tracts in which 25 percent or more of the households were below the poverty level discarded consistently less food than the nonpoor census tracts. Food discard in census tracts with no households below the poverty level may run as high as 25 percent of food purchased, and in 1974 over 80 percent of the food discarded in nonpoor tracts was in the form of large quantities of single items (Harrison, Rathje, and Hughes 1974). Although patterns emerged around group means, a great deal of variability cut across these groups. Clearly, an important question was, Are there more general and useful correlates of food discard behavior?

Data from the 1973 beef shortage provided an initial clue. As prices went up and beef became less available, household purchase behaviors changed rapidly and radically—shoppers bought new cuts, they bought in new quantities (either trying to stock up or trying to cut down), and they bought more or less frequently than usual. As this variety came in the front door, an all-time high waste of beef, 9 percent of the volume purchased (not including the weight of bone and fat), spilled out the back.

As beef-purchase behaviors stabilized in 1974 and 1975, however, the quantity wasted decreased drastically to 3 percent of input volume. These data led to a hypothesized "food-discard equation." This simple formula states that regularity in purchase-consumption behaviors varies inversely with the percentage of food input that is discarded. This waste equation is only a hypothesis and must be tested rigorously with our current data; however, we have had success in predicting and retrodicting relative waste rates among different population segments over a three-year time frame for a variety of food commodities. Nevertheless, the formula remains applicable only to Southwest U.S. communities that purchase modern processed foods and prepare and consume them at the household level.

From this formula we were able to anticipate food discard behavior in relation to the sugar shortage. As the variety of purchases increased along with sugar prices and scarcity in the spring of 1975, the quantity of waste of pastries, "kiddie" cereals, candy bars, and even sugar in granular form was double its previous rate.

The formula is also useful in evaluating the waste associated with commonly utilized commodities that do not rapidly fluctuate in price under normal conditions. White bread is an example. Bread discard associated with high-consumption, standard 24 ounce and 16 ounce packages is less than 5 percent of the total input of 24 ounce and 16 ounce loaves. Bread packaged in smaller than 16-ounce-size wrappers occurs in an extremely wide variety of sizes and, as expected, the waste associated with these less regularly utilized breads is high, almost 10 percent of the total input represented by these specialty items (see Table 3.2, Figure 3.7).

Edible food in refuse adds up to as much as 8 percent of the total weight of household garbage, and a considerable quantity of nutrients ends up in dumps and sanitary landfills. To make any kind of dent in this behavior, edible-food discard must be fully documented, the critical-resource-management behaviors associated with different patterns of discard must be identified, and attempts by consumer educators to modify behaviors must be accurately evaluated. The best place to find many of the data necessary to accomplish these goals is in the garbage can. The same data may also lead to the documentation of general regularities or trends in the interaction between human behavior and material culture.

TABLE 3.2
BREAD WASTE IN WRAPPERS
(DATA BASE 2)

	24 oz. loaf	*16 oz. loaf*	*16 oz. bread item*
Total input (in ounces)*	4,464	1,232	1,081
Percent of total bread input	66	18	16
Total waste in wrappers (ounces)	159.4	58.2	101.8
Percent of total waste	50	18	32
Percent discarded in wrappers of the total input volume of wrappers with waste	10.5	11.4	42.6
Percent discarded in wrappers of total input	3.6	4.7	9.4

*From package labeling

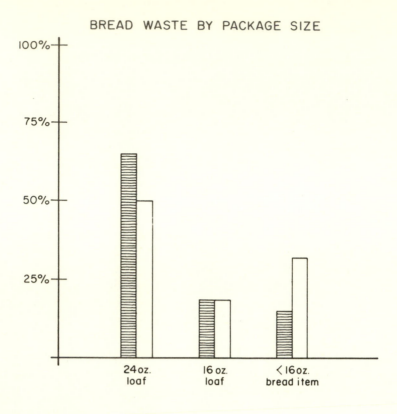

FIGURE 3.7. Bread waste by package size.

A Direct Link to the Recent Past

Analyses of contemporary industrial societies using traditional archaeological methods and measures can make behaviors today comparable to those of the past. This comparability provides a link to the work of other archaeologists in the form of a concluding period for the long time sequences they have reconstructed and produces a unique perspective that relates past to present. To place present types of resource discard into a meaningful frame of reference, for example, long-term data are needed. Without these, modern data are often equivocal or misleading.

Because we have so few comparative data, we often think of ourselves today as ardent recyclers. Coors, Olympia, the Iron and Steel Foundation, Alcoa, Reynolds, and everyone else seem to be recycling metal cans. Until the slump in the building industry, there were incessant newspaper drives. Many Christmas cards are printed on recycled paper. We have little reason for self-congratulation, however, for at present, generally, we are recycling less than we did in the recent past. For example, today only 19 percent of all wood fiber is recycled, in contrast to the 35 percent that was recycled during World War II. (EPA 1974).

Preliminary comparisons with even older data indicate exponential changes in rates of reuse, recycling, and resource discard. Fontana's classic study (1968) of bottles excavated from mid-nineteenth-century trash deposits in Magdelena, Mexico, is an example. Fontana noted that after glass containers were first introduced only broken bottles were found in trash, and where bottle bases were recorded, they were worn almost paper thin from long-term reuse. Even after bottles became more common and the infrequent discard of whole bottles began to appear, both whole and broken bottles continued to show signs of long-term reuse.

Garbage Project data from modern Tucson present a striking contrast to those of Fontana. The average Tucson household discards 500 whole glass bottles each year. Around 50 of these bottles (10 percent) are made of returnable glass and could be reused, ideally, up to forty times if returned to distributors. The other 450 bottles could be turned in to local recycling plants and ground into cullet for making additional bottles. Nevertheless, almost all bottles seem to be discarded as soon as the original contents are emptied; none show traces of reuse.

Another example of time depth in resource discard may be nearer and dearer to the hearts of archaeologists. A change in the discard of ceramics is illustrated by data presented by Deetz and excavated at Plymouth Plantation in New England (1973). The Joseph Howland site was occupied for 50 years, between 1675 and 1725. Deetz's photograph of the ceramics from its trash pits shows eight puny piles of broken pieces spread out on a large lab table. The same table is smothered by a deep layer of ceramics from a century later. The majority of the second collection of pottery seems much less damaged by cracking and chipping, and several complete place settings are discernible in the piles of porcelain. This entire load was produced by a single family in only 5 years, between 1830 and 1835.

Tucsonans today do not often discard serving items; they concentrate instead on high-turnover packaging materials. The average household each year discards 1,800 plastic items, both wraps and containers; 850 steel cans; 500 recyclable all-aluminum cans; and more than 13,000 individual items of paper and cardboard (largely packaging). Altogether, more than 60 percent of Tucson's residential refuse, by weight, is packaging. The United States produced 55 billion pounds of food packaging in 1966, most of it discarded after a single use and disposed of in dumps and landfills at a cost of over $400 million. The majority of this packaging was developed to decrease food discard due to spoilage, and for this purpose it has been effective. Although considerable variability among sociodemographic groups has been identified by the Garbage Project, and although the only other large-scale food-discard data for households were presented almost fifty years ago without any clear statement of methodology of collection, it seems fair to say that packaging (along with other technological changes) has cut household food discard from 20 to 25 percent of total input by volume during World War II (WFA 1943) to between 10 and 15 percent of input by volume today in Tucson (Harrison, Rathje, and Hughes 1975).

However, this technological solution to waste has been bought by a trade-off of nonrenewable resources (iron ore for "tin" cans, oil for plastics, bauxite for aluminum) or slowly renewable resources (forests for paper packaging) in exchange for rapidly renewable resources such as corn, beef, and apples.

It is important to study the development of this trade-off and to quantify various aspects of it now because many ramifications of our material-behavior interactions go unrealized while our possible

74

responses become increasingly limited by the size and inelasticity of our resource demands. This resource-discard trade-off is a good long-term problem for archaeologists to develop because their data base can place resource trade-off behaviors in an extremely useful perspective for modern consumers, as well as provide unique data to test general regularities in long-term man-material interactions.

AN ARCHAEOLOGICAL ETHNOGRAPHY CONCLUSION

These examples of Garbage Project studies are initial attempts to do archaeological ethnography, to contribute to the description and understanding of contemporary societies while we also do ethnoarchaeology to refine our techniques for describing and understanding our past.

Because of the bias of this paper, the contributions of traditional ethnography to archaeology and of contemporary behavioral science studies and interview-survey techniques to the Garbage Project have not been emphasized. In both cases, they have been substantial. I have presented this essay with these past contributions in mind to suggest to archaeologists that once in a while it is better to give than to receive.

NOTE

1. Major portions of the research for this essay were supported by Grant AEN716371 from the RANN (Research Applied to National Needs) Division of the National Science Foundation, by the University of Arizona College of Medicine, and by Biomedical Sciences Support Grant RRO7002 from the National Institutes of Health. Work is continuing through grants from the Frito Lay Company and the Chevron Oil Company.

Appreciation is due to Tom Price, Director of Operations, City of Tucson; Carlos Valencia, Director of Sanitation, City of Tucson; the personnel of the Tucson Sanitation Division; the dedicated student volunteers who have made the Garbage Project possible; Dileep G. Bal, Deputy Director of the Pima County Health Department; Judy O'Hora of the Arizona Regional Medical Program; Wilson Hughes, Field Director of the Garbage Project; Gail Harrison, Nutritionist of the Garbage Project; Sherry Jernigan, Research Director of the Garbage Project; and Marvin "Swede" Johnson, A. Richard Kassander, Jr., and Raymond H. Thompson of the University of Arizona for administrative support.

Many useful ideas considered in this paper were developed in conjunction with Fred Gorman and Jeff Eighmy as well as members of the Santa Fe ethnoarchaeology seminar.

4

Ethnoarchaeological Observations of Natural Processes Affecting Cultural Materials[1]

DIANE P. GIFFORD

Merrill College
University of California, Santa Cruz

INTRODUCTION

Ethnoarchaeological research has thus far focused mainly upon gathering data with which to test hypotheses concerning the relationship between culture process and its direct material manifestations. While cultural factors are the primary agency producing the remains with which prehistorians are concerned, there are in addition noncultural factors which can substantially alter cultural materials as they become part of the archaeological record. These processes have never been described in a way generally useful in evaluating their influence upon archaeological materials. Since these noncultural factors affecting archaeological sites are processes, they can—like cultural processes—be observed in the contemporary world, and their effects clarified by ethnoarchaeological research.

Recently a growing number of archaeologists have recognized the need to define noncultural processes more closely. Ethnoarchaeological observers have commented upon the problem of differential preservation of contemporary sites and the skewed representation of cultural materials in preserved contexts (Gould 1974; Yellen 1974). Other researchers have undertaken experimental work over the last fifteen years in attempts to explicate natural processes of alteration (Isaac 1967; Jewell and Dimbleby 1966).

Consideration of natural processes of alteration should be of primary concern to all archaeologists, especially to those working with sites that lack enduring structures, as do most hunter-gatherer and many pastoralist occurrences. In these cases, behavioral reconstructions have been drawn exclusively from the distribution of materials upon living floors. Wheat's Olsen-Chubbuck work (1972), for example, and Leroi-Gourhan's Pincevent investigations (Leroi-Gourhan and Brezillon 1966), base extremely detailed behavioral inferences upon such distributions. These investigations are notable for the integration of microstratigraphic and sedimentological data with other evidence in drawing such inferences.

In many situations, however, direct behavioral reconstruction from intrasite distributional patterns may be considerably complicated by both cultural and noncultural factors. Schiffer (1972a), in his discussion of primary and secondary refuse, has criticized the assumption on the part of many archaeologists that spatial clusters of artifacts invariably reflect activity loci. He points out that on many sites the primary factor structuring cultural materials as recovered by the archaeologist may be refuse-disposal behavior. Noncultural processes, especially those operant after site abandonment, may likewise alter spatial patterning in cultural materials. In addition, these processes may selectively destroy perishable materials, skewing the originally constituted sample.

This chapter will discuss the more common noncultural processes affecting archaeological materials prior to burial, and the role of these in determining "archaeological visibility." Special reference will be made to the effects of contemporary processes on site preservation in the East Lake Turkana (formerly Lake Rudolf) region, and to the implications of this research for evaluation of regional archaeological sequences.

POSTOCCUPATION PROCESSES

Most human living sites that become archaeological sites undergo some kinds of depositional processes. These may be aqueous or eolian in nature, and can vary tremendously in their effects upon a site. Moreover, the span of time intervening between the abandonment of such a site and its burial can vary considerably; during this period a range of natural processes may rearrange or destroy various cultural materials. The most common of these processes and their effects are represented schematically in Figure 4.1. It must be emphasized that the "stages" in Figure 4.1 actually form a continuum, and that the processes listed for one "stage" may well occur in another. For example, animal disturbances can occur during occupation as well as during later stages. The following cases exemplify specific alterations caused by such processes.

Plant disturbance can cause major rearrangements in materials of all kinds. Treefalls are capable of lifting and reconcentrating artifacts lying in or on their root systems in strikingly consistent and patterned shapes. As the fallen tree decays, it may leave a stain pattern in the soil liable to further misinterpretation. At the Dutch Mesolithic site of Bergumermeer, Newell and Musch (personal communication) have discerned the "ghosts" of treefalls interspersed with those of actual structures. These two features differ in their shape and in the placement and concentration of artifacts within. It is possible that some of the hearthless "huts" and "tent circles" in forested areas of Northern Europe, such as those reported by Rust (1943), are actually the relics of ancient treefalls.

These and other disturbances of the occupation layer can often be discerned through detailed examination of site stratigraphy.

In his excellent ethnoarchaeological research on the Kalahari Bushmen, Yellen (in press) noted that nearly all identifiable bone not trodden into the substrate during occupation was quickly consumed by wildlife. Any marrow-bearing bone was eaten by carnivores, and the ecology of the Dobe region is such that even bovids consume bones, apparently to obtain salts and minerals otherwise lacking in the environment. Yellen observed that the bones remaining on the surface tended to be those of larger animals, especially the diagnostic articular ends, and that subsurface large-animal elements were predominantly nonidentifiable fragments. The resulting selective destruction of large

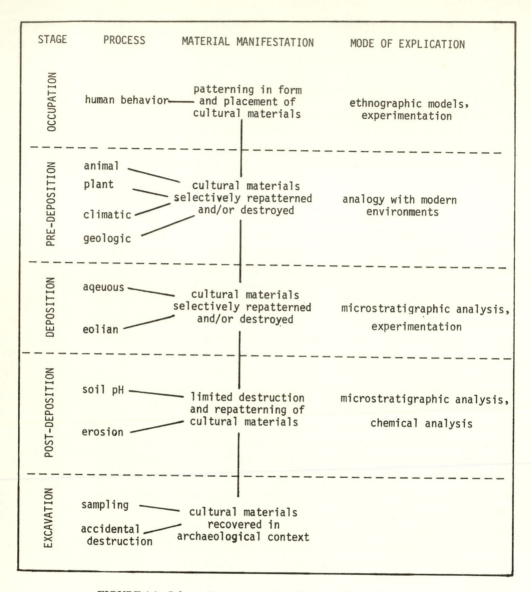

FIGURE 4.1. Schematic representation of stages of formation of an archaeological site, from creation to recovery. Shows processes affecting cultural materials and primary methods of determining their presence and effects.

animals' bones skewed the large-species representation in the recoverable sample by as much as 50 percent.

At Lake Turkana bones on abandoned campsites are not consumed by wildlife. But sites exposed to the elements for upwards of five years undergo a loss of identifiable surface bones through weathering attrition, with the smaller elements of the surface sample decomposing earlier. Ultimately, if all surface bones were to decay, a skew effect similar to that reported by Yellen would occur.

Processes causing differential destruction of cultural materials may leave little evidence of their operation other than that of the structure of the sample itself. Ethnoarchaeological research can describe the distinctive features of assemblages affected by such processes. These data can then be used in much the same manner as studies of distinctive structures resulting from observed geologic processes, at least indicating, if not actually proving, the likelihood of operation of such processes on prehistoric samples. For example, Yellen notes that the preserved subsurface bone samples from his Kalahari sites consist mainly of whole bones of smaller animals, plus small, largely unidentifiable fragments of larger animals' bones. Recovery of a sample in which large animals were represented only by fragments of similar size to small animals' bones may indicate the operation of such processes. Adequate knowledge of regional paleoecology is a basic requirement in assessing the likelihood that certain processes were operant upon an assemblage. Weathering and biological damage to perishable materials vary in nature and rate depending upon local climatological and ecological conditions, and it is imperative to establish whether or not observed destruction phenomena could have occurred under ancient ecological conditions.

While technically not a postoccupation process, trampling of small objects in the substrate by site inhabitants deserves mention here. It may be a site formation process of as yet unrecognized importance. Yellen's and my own observations of newly vacated sites indicate that normal human activity on a loose substrate will result in subsurface migration of most smaller elements. At Site 20, mapped on the day of abandonment and later excavated, I recovered about nine times as many pieces (1,953) from the subsurface layer as had been visible on the surface (200). These subsurface elements averaged three centimeters in maximum dimension, with some long, narrow pieces reaching five centimeters. An occupation of four days' duration was sufficient to effect this size-dependent sorting, with a fine sand substrate.

Trampling may have several important effects upon cultural materials, which can be investigated through both experimental and ethnoarchaeological research. It should be possible to use results of such research to discern trampling effects in archaeological occurrences.

As in Yellen's Kalahari example, trampling of smaller elements into the substrate, if combined with destruction of larger surface elements, can substantially bias the preserved sample. Surface samples of imperishable as well as perishable materials can be skewed, should the surface be modified by geologic processes. Experimental and ethnoarchaeological observations should be directed at ascertaining whether subsurface zones consistently develop with permeable substrates and occupation activities, and whether these zones can be distinguished. Hypotheses which should be tested include the following:

(1) Given a permeable substrate, normal occupation activities on a site ("trampling") will generate a subsurface zone of like-sized items, definable within a given range of maximum dimensions, and a surface zone composed of all items of larger maximum dimension than those in the subsurface zone.

(2) The amount of subsurface migration of pieces due to trampling depends directly upon the permeability of the substrate and the amount of trampling activity.

(3) The greater the median grain size of the substrate, the larger the median maximum dimension of elements migrating subsurface.

There may be a highly significant relationship between trampling phenomena and the preservation of primary refuse. Schiffer (1972a, 1975d, Chap. 9, below) has pointed out the important distinction between primary and secondary refuse. The former consists of materials discarded at their use location, the latter are discarded away from the location of use. On the basis of students' observations of Nacirema discard behavior, Schiffer proposes that size is a major factor in determining whether an item becomes primary or secondary refuse. Elements less than one inch (2.7 cm) in maximum dimension appear highly likely to become primary refuse (Schiffer: Chap. 9, below). This is close to the median size of subsurface pieces recovered from Site 20. A second set of hypotheses concerning this relationship may be proposed for testing:

(4) Elements below 3 cm maximum dimension are highly likely to become primary refuse, while those above this size are less likely to be primary refuse.

(5) Given the conditions described in (1), elements likely to be primary refuse are also likely to migrate subsurface due to trampling.

(6) A subsurface trampling zone will contain a relatively higher proportion of primary refuse than will the surface zone of a site.

I would agree with Schiffer's (1972a) proposition that increasing intensity of occupation (a function of population size and duration of occupation) will be paralleled by decreasing primary refuse and increasing secondary refuse. However, when considering the actual material consequences of the interaction of these variables, I would add the additional variable of substrate permeability. Substrate permeability may be a major factor in primary refuse preservation, acting in a feedback system with cultural formation processes during occupation. A nonpermeable substrate (stone, beaten earth, and the like) will not absorb cultural materials to any degree, increasing the probability on intensively occupied sites that all refuse will become secondary. A permeable substrate, on the other hand, may absorb smaller primary refuse elements, as well as lost items, allowing them to be preserved through an out-of-sight-out-of-mind process.

I am proposing here that trampling by site inhabitants may preserve a certain class of cultural materials from subsequent cultural and natural disturbances. Further, I am proposing that deposits of trampled materials may have diagnostic features. Ethnoarchaeological and experimental research can test these propositions.

With regard to the effects of geologic processes upon cultural materials, archaeologists can profit from a rapidly expanding literature on contemporary processes and their effects in the fields of sedimentology, geomorphology, and paleontology (J. R. L. Allen 1963; Bigarella 1972; Selley 1970; Visher 1972). Of special interest to archaeologists concerned with postoccupation processes is the recent research of vertebrate taphonomists,[2] which has included considerable observation of natural processes and experimentation (Behrensmeyer 1975; A. P. Hill 1975; Voorhies 1969a, 1969b). Since the major concern of taphonomists is closer definition of the processes of alteration intervening between the death of an organism and the deposition of its remains in geological context, these investigators share many of the same interests as archaeologists studying postoccupation processes. The major conclusion derived from these studies, which should be considered carefully by archaeologists, is that attempts at paleoecological and behavioral reconstructions must be based upon a thorough knowledge of the processes intervening between life situation and geologic deposition (A. P. Hill 1975; Voorhies 1969b).

One area of common concern is that of biological alteration processes, and numerous data on bone damage and weathering are available to interested prehistorians (Behrensmeyer 1975; A. P. Hill 1975).

With regard to geological processes, taphonomists have drawn upon and augmented sedimentological process studies. A primary principle is that bones are sedimentary particles which, in the course of deposition, behave according to definable, predictive rules. Since most fossil-bearing deposits are aqueous in origin, most research has focused on defining the behavior of bones in flowing water, at different velocities, with various types of bed load (Behrensmeyer 1975; Voorhies 1969a). The relevance of this research to many archaeological situations is great, as the following discussion of my own research will indicate.

DASSANETCH SITES

Formation Patterns

I worked in northern Kenya among the Dassanetch people who live on the eastern shore of Lake Turkana, immediately south of the Ethiopian border (Fig. 4.2). The Dassanetch homeland extends from the Omo River Delta in Ethiopia down the eastern shore of the lake, as far as fifty kilometers south of the Kenyan border. The Dassanetch have been studied for the first time during the past seven years (Almagor 1971; Carr 1977). They view themselves as pastoralists, keeping cattle, donkeys, sheep, and goats; dogs are rare. They do, however, cultivate millet and maize in the few areas suitable for crops in their arid land. Poorer members of the tribe supplement their diet with animals caught in the lake. At Ileret, where I conducted most of my work, the majority of people belong to the Inkoria territorial section. Raiding by traditionally hostile tribes to the south and east still occurs. Due to these hostilities, the Dassanetch in the region live in defensive settlements, with the house area entirely surrounded by thorn-brush animal pens (Fig. 4.3).

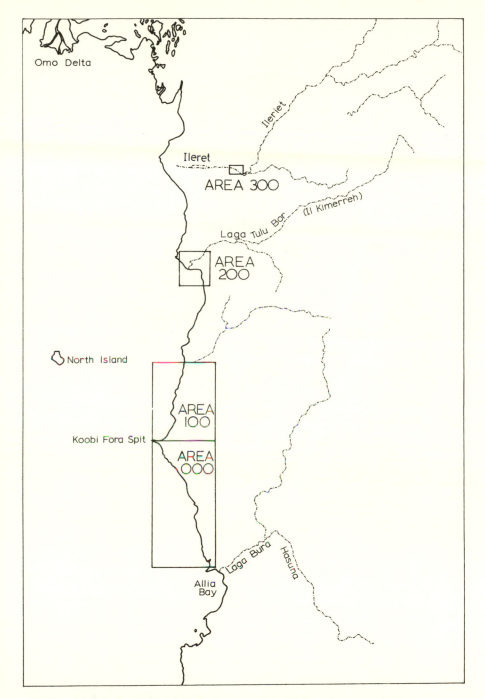

FIGURE 4.2. East Lake Turkana study area. Area 300 contains 15 manyatta and stock-camp sites. Area 000 contains 19 *gal dies* hunting-fishing sites.

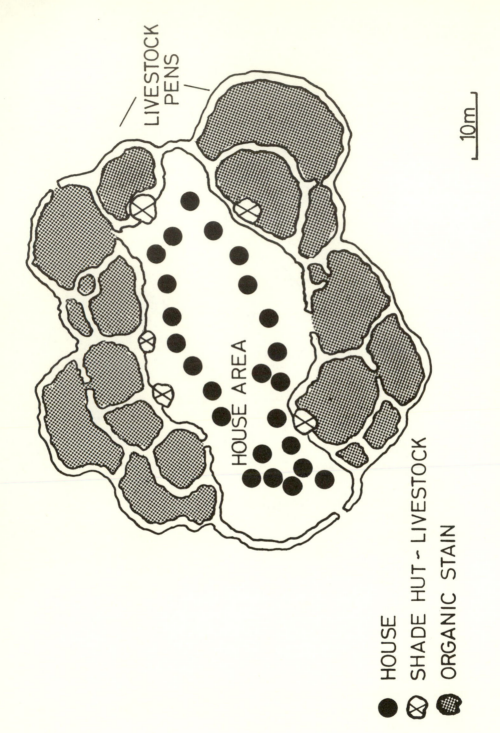

LIVESTOCK PENS

HOUSE AREA

10m

● HOUSE

⊗ SHADE HUT ~ LIVESTOCK

⬢ ORGANIC STAIN

FIGURE 4.3. Plan of a Dassanetch defensive settlement.

Because water is scarce, settlements lie relatively close to the lake. Most are located along the lower reaches of major ephemeral rivers, where wells for subsurface water can be dug. Lake water is used mainly to water stock; it is potable, but somewhat alkaline, and water from riverbed wells is preferred for human consumption. Aerial photographs (1:24,000) of the region clearly show the arrangement of larger settlements along major watercourses. Two types of pastoralist sites exist: large semipermanent ones inhabited by men, women, and children, referred to here by the Swahili term *manyatta*, and mobile stock camps staffed by boys and young men. Manyattas are usually occupied for a span of years, but settlements of a few months' duration may be made in areas where water and forage are temporarily good. Milking stock for the families is kept at the manyattas, but most of the herds are sent to stock camps. Hundreds of head of stock may be kept in these camps, which shift location to take advantage of new vegetation that springs up after scattered showers. In times of scarcity, cattle, sheep, and goats are all herded in separate areas according to their differing forage requirements. During the time I was at Ileret, the land had been very dry for about seven years, and nearly all the cattle had been sent north to better grazing lands near the Omo Delta, leaving only donkeys and small stock in the south. Stock camps are often located inland or along the lake, in areas lacking sufficient water for larger human populations. In the upper reaches of the Il-Erriet River Valley herdboys were expected to live on meat, milk, and whatever water they could obtain from the riverbed.

The manyattas are characterized by a relatively large core living area, with houses arranged in roughly linear order according to the kin relations of the households. Manyattas may contain between 10 and 80 houses (Fig. 4.3). The houses, built by each married woman with offspring, are entirely portable one-room huts of skins and hides, lashed over a sapling frame. They are low (1.5 m) ovals, measuring about 3 by 4 meters. Each contains a hearth, always placed to the immediate left of the entrance. Depending upon local availability of stone, hearthstones may or may not be left in place upon abandonment of the site. The surrounding animal pens are shared by male kin and friends. Small stock and calves are kept in the inner pens, larger stock in the outer pens. Informants agreed that although some areas are habitually reoccupied, it was forbidden to establish a new manyatta directly on top of the visible remains of an old one, although fences and other components could be reused.

During and after occupation, the house area is distinguishable from the pens by its relatively lighter soil color, higher proportion of artifacts, and ash lenses with hearthstones. The manure-stained pen regions show up clearly, even on aerial photographs. The outermost large stock pens are marked by piles of burned manure, up to fifty centimeters high and three meters across, swept up and fired every day by the women. Inner pens are usually marked by deposits of food refuse and ash, formed as women habitually dump household debris into or over the inner pen fences. Household food refuse consists primarily of bones and other inedible parts of caprines; cattle are not normally slaughtered for household consumption, being eaten away from the settlement by older males.

Stock camps during their occupation lack formal structures, other than pens and sometimes an openwork shade hut for newborn kids and lambs. Herdboys do not normally construct shelters for themselves; their actual living space is usually a sleeping area with a hearth, centered under a shade tree, with the pens around it (Fig. 4.4). Herdboys are given few items of any real worth from family stores, and their cultural debris is minimal, consisting mainly of animal bones. Since the camps are inhabited for shorter periods than are the manyattas, manure staining of the pen area is imperceptible. Once the fences of a stock camp have decayed, the site is hard to discern.

A third type of site in Dassanetchland is the hunting-fishing camp. Persons who have, through past misfortunes, lost their herds are known as *gal dies*—with alternative meanings of "poor people" and "fishermen"—and form a distinct class among the Dassanetch. If the loss was suffered several generations back they tend to live in their own settlements, located in areas suitable for cultivation. Younger men and boys conduct fishing and hunting expeditions, traveling as far as 120 kilometers down the lake in their dugout canoes. They lack firearms and are so poor in trade goods that even iron for spear tips is precious; until recently, they had no fishnets. Nonetheless, they manage to procure a variety of fish—including the huge Nile perch, terrapins, soft-shelled turtles, and crocodiles—with their spears and detachable-head harpoons. They occasionally take larger land mammals and hippopotamuses in cooperative hunts. If their catch is large enough, they transport dried meat back to their settlements; if not, the men are at least able to live off the land without drawing upon the family grain

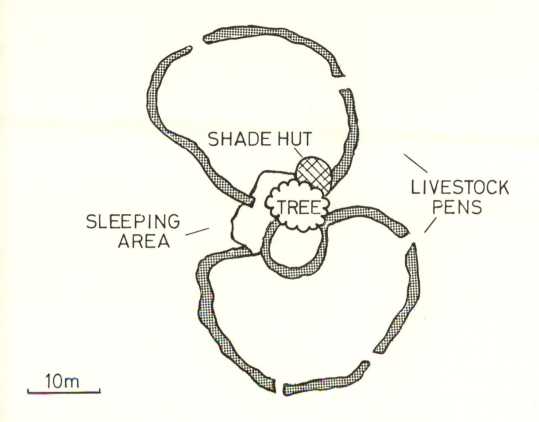

SHADE HUT

TREE

LIVESTOCK
PENS

SLEEPING
AREA

10m

FIGURE 4.4. Plan of a stock camp.

supplies. The *gal dies* are sometimes joined by younger sons of poorer
herding families and by men who have lost their herds in the course of
their lifetimes, but still reside at herding settlements.

Gal dies camps lie along the lakeshore, varying in size from small,
single-occupation "lunch stops" to large, repeatedly occupied sites
near good fishing grounds. Normal occupation debris consists of bone
associated with hearths, plus occasional stone tools; low windbreaks of
stone or thatch sunshades are sometimes constructed. A survey of a
19-by-1.5-km strip of shore south of Koobi Fora (see Fig. 4.2) yielded 22
such sites which, judging from correlation with recent beach levels,
span about fifteen years.

89

It should be noted that the Dassanetch intensively curate nearly all items of their material culture, due to the relative difficulty of replacement, with a resulting low rate of discard. This leaves little artifactual material for potential preservation in the archaeological record. Government restriction of Dassanetch contact with other tribes has severely limited trade, and even wealthy persons cannot readily obtain or replace trade goods. Gourds, pottery and metal containers, metal implements, beads and other ornaments, and cloth all must be acquired through a tenuous set of trade connections into Ethiopia, at vastly inflated prices. Such items are used and mended until completely beyond repair. Among the few locally manufactured household items are wooden milk containers, made by women; even these are intensively curated, since trees of sufficient diameter for use are rare in this arid region. Animal skins are recycled through various functions as shelter components, shoes, or clothing. Observations of abandoned manyattas indicate a relatively low proportion of artifact discards to food refuse and a relatively high proportion of probable loss items (isolated beads, fishhooks, a tin crucifix, and so forth) to actual artifact discards. These sites contrast sharply with Maasai pastoralist settlements about seventy kilometers from Nairobi, where proportions of artifactual refuse are about equal to those of food refuse on abandoned sites.

It is probable that a major shift in refuse patterns occurs when stone implement technology with a high overall discard rate is replaced by metal implement technology with a very low discard rate. While the timing of this shift in the East Lake Turkana area is not yet known, there are in the region large surface scatters of lithic materials with some preserved bone which may represent pastoralist sites of this former phase.

Postoccupation Process

Through informant interviews I was able to arrange abandoned sites in two age-ranked series, establishing a site decay sequence for all three types of occupation. The series, which spanned 15 years, permitted me to isolate various postoccupation processes affecting cultural materials. One area intensively studied was a 0.5-by-0.3-km area in the Il-Erriet Valley, wherein lay 15 abandoned manyattas and stock camps

(Fig. 4.2, Area 300). The oldest site was inhabited in 1957-58, the newest in 1973. *Gal dies* camps were surveyed along a 19-km strip of shoreline between Koobi Fora and Allia Bay (Fig. 4.2, Area 000). Dates of occupation for the 19 sites in the zone ranged from 1960 through 1973. In addition to the intensive studies in these two areas, brief observations were made on site preservation in two other areas (Fig. 4.2, Areas 100, 200).

If a site remains exposed to the elements for 15 years, considerable alteration of perishable elements takes place. On manyattas and stock camps, thorn-brush fences become relatively fragile after 5 years, and have disappeared completely after 15. Manyatta pen areas continue to be set off by manure-stained soil, and piles of burned dung in outer pens, on which plants cannot grow, are easily distinguishable after 15 years. The inner pens continue to be set off by small scatters of bone and ash refuse.

Bone specimens from the surface zone of the oldest site (1957-58) were deeply invaded by weathering lines and were extremely fragile but still identifiable. Subsurface bones were less heavily weathered, although leached of organic content and fragile. It appears from these observations that bones of medium-sized mammals, in this case caprines, can remain on the surface in the East Lake Turkana region for at least 20 years before totally disintegrating.

In the course of 20 years, manyattas, stock camps, and *gal dies* sites lose nearly all perishable materials if exposed to the elements. Once weathering has destroyed the bone component on such sites, very little remains, since the low artifact-discard rates produce little in the way of imperishable materials. I saw a number of manyattas representing this decay stage, on which all that remained were soil stains, hearthstones, and scattered ash lenses, with rare artifacts. Burial relatively soon after deposition will protect cultural materials from further decomposition and, to some extent, disarrangement. But if the geological processes involved in burying a site are sufficiently intense, they can alter the distribution of materials or even completely destroy the occurrence. In order for a site to be preserved as originally constituted, a fine balance must be struck between geological and other postoccupation processes.

The range and intensity of geological processes to which a site may be subject depend upon its geomorphic setting. The Dassanetch are well aware of the relationship between setting and geological process and accordingly locate their semipermanent settlements in areas of minimal disturbance. Stock camps and manyattas are deliberately sited away from areas liable to flooding. Owing to this understandable human preference, abandoned sites are subject to little if any deposition. The main geological processes acting upon them are eolian, with wind deflation outpacing deposition. Deflation exposes formerly subsurface items to surface weathering processes, thereby accelerating site destruction processes.

Nearly all the manyattas and stock camps I observed were located in areas of minimal geologic activity. One short-term manyatta was sited in an environment potentially favorable to aqueous deposition, a large, low island in the main watercourse of the Il-Erriet. It was, however, completely destroyed during severe flood in April 1974. During one flood, a crest of water about four meters high swept over the island, carrying off nearly all cultural materials. Test scrapes of areas formerly rich in bone refuse yielded next to nothing. The two extremes in depositional process observed on Dassanetch sites in the Il-Erriet Valley would have much the same outcomes in terms of archaeological preservation. Whether all the organic materials so valuable in behavioral and economic reconstructions disappear over a 30-year period or within 24 hours, the resultant site impoverishment is the same.

Although lying in a different sort of geomorphic context, the *gal dies* hunting-fishing camps I observed were likewise not in locations favorable to speedy deposition. In the case of lake-margin sites, the situation was not so much the result of human intention to locate sites away from sedimentary processes as of the continuing regression of the lake (Butzer 1971). The important point to note here is that had the lake instead been in a transgressive phase, many of these sites would be covered with lacustrine sediments. It is important to recognize the role that duration of occupation may play in determining the placement and, in terms of geologic process, the sedimentary environment of a site. Hunting-fishing camps are occupied for only a few days at a stretch, are easily occupied, and are just as easily vacated. There is no premium in this case on selective avoidance of certain sedimentary environments, as in the case of pastoralist settlement patterns. Since a number of *gal dies* sites are located in environments with good potential for sedimentation, these short-term Dassanetch occupations have a relatively higher probability of preservation than do longer-term ones. In addition, sedimentary processes in the lake-margin zone, whether lacustrine or deltaic, are considerably gentler than those in the major river courses along which the pastoralist sites lie. The only two sites subject to any kind of depositional processes during my period of observation were short-term *gal dies* sites, one located on the lake margin, the other in a delta.

Site 02 is a hippo-butchery camp created in September 1972. Because of the problems of managing a hippo carcass, the camp was situated close to the kill site, just at the wet interface between lake and shore. The posterior axial skeleton and limbs of the animal were transported to a spot about sixty meters inland from the hippo's head and cervical vertebrae. Two rock windbreaks and a stone-circled hearth were constructed in the inland zone. The lake level was rising at the time of the kill, and within a week the head and neck bones were standing in shallow water, while the rest of the animal's body lay on dry ground. The lake level continued to rise in October 1972 until the outer scatter was totally covered by gently lapping water. The lake level fell markedly in December 1974, exposing the head and neck bones again. About three centimeters of fine silt had built up in and around the bones, which were in relatively better condition than their subaerial counterparts. Had the lake level stayed high, those bones would probably have been preserved long after the subaerial ones had disintegrated. The remaining site would thus probably consist of the head and neck of a hippo, plus two stone semicircles, and a rock-ringed hearth area about fifty meters northeast of the bone. The surviving bones might provide a clue to the actual nature of the site.

Site 20 is another campsite, created over four days in November 1973 by eight men and boys. They made their camp in the shallow, braided distributary system of the delta of a small ephemeral river. The camp was situated about three hundred meters from the shore, in the conjunction of the main stream channel and two side channels. The sandy substrate of the channel was much more suitable for occupation than was the surrounding landscape, which is largely covered with the spike-leaved local grass. The camp consisted of a hearth, with three stones to support a kerosine tin for cooking; a scatter of ash dug out of the hearth; a woodpile; and a sleeping area with a lakeweed "mattress." During their stay, the men procured and ate 40 small terrapins, 4 small-to-medium-size crocodiles, about 14 catfish, and a few small Nile perch and other fish. In addition, they were able to scavenge meat from two lion-killed zebras. The meat of one they cut off the carcass and carried back to camp in their tin; from the other they took an entire hind leg. The zebra meat was laid out to dry about twelve meters up the larger channel from the camp, and the bones of the leg were left there. I mapped the resulting scatter a day after they left the camp (Fig. 4.5).

In the spring of 1974, unusually heavy rains fell in the East Turkana area. The region usually receives about 300 mm per year, but in two weeks that spring it got well over 70 mm (Butzer 1971; East Rudolf Fisheries Research Project: personal communication). I was in the area at the time and observed the stages of the burial of Site 20. The first rains falling in the watershed were light. The runoff dispersing across the delta was gentle and confined largely to the main channel, with slight lateral invasion of the overbank area. Bones in the main channel, including the zebra leg, were swept downstream as much as 25 m. Materials only a few centimeters upslope from the channel in the overbank region were not displaced and were covered in place by 2-5 cm of sand and silt. The silts and sands of the first rain dried to a hard cap over and around these materials prior to a second, heavier rain four days later. Massive runoff from this episode flowed over the entire site, adding another 5-10-cm deposit to the overbank region, completely covering all materials.

In the summer of 1974 I excavated the core area of the site to ascertain the degree to which depositional processes had affected the original distributions. The effects of flooding differed in the main channel zone and the overbank zone. Bones in the main channel had been swept away; a trench eight meters farther down the channel course yielded only a few shell fragments. Distributions in the overbank zone, on the other hand, were preserved nearly intact; even the ash layer remained in place (Fig. 4.6).

Dr. A. K. Behrensmeyer (University of California, Santa Cruz), whose geologic and taphonomic work at East Lake Turkana has received much attention, was very interested in the site and undertook to study its microstratigraphy. She was able to discern in the site's section the two depositional events I witnessed in the spring of 1974. We have subsequently analyzed sediment samples from the depositional phases and facies and also conducted flume and settling velocity experiments with bones recovered from the site. The results have allowed us to estimate the rates of water flow that selectively preserved and destroyed portions of the site.

94

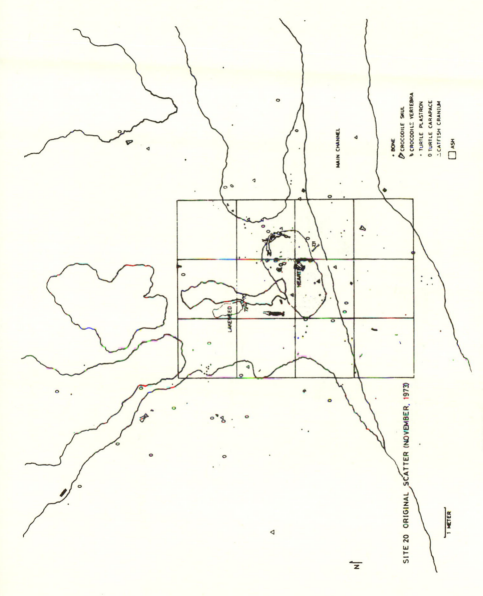

FIGURE 4.5. Site 20: plot of original distribution, November 1973.

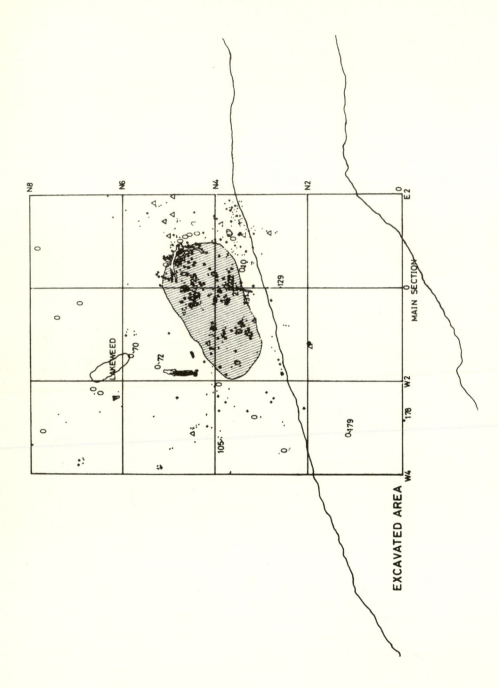

FIGURE 4.6. Site 20: plot of excavated sample, August 1974.

As the largest sedimentary particles on the site, bones were useful in estimating flow velocities. Two experimental approaches to bone transport were utilized. First, bones were subjected to calibrated flow conditions in a water flume belonging to the Department of Hydraulic Engineering, University of California, Berkeley. With a substrate approximating that of the site, we determined that flow velocities of about 40 centimeters per second were necessary to put bones of all sizes into continuous movement, as was the case in the channel. Overbank flow conditions probably did not exceed 10 cm/sec, the point at which all small elements are in motion, for any appreciable amount of time. Second, the same bones and others either too large or small to be placed in the flume were observed settling in standing water. The settling velocity of a bone is very heavily influenced by its shape, as well as by its weight, and two bones of disparate weights may have similar settling velocities. From an element's settling velocity one can calculate the diameter of a round quartz grain with equivalent settling velocity. This nominal quartz diameter equivalence is useful because it allows one to consult the sedimentological literature on transport of regularly shaped materials (J. R. L. Allen 1963; Compton 1962). Nominal quartz diameter equivalences (d_q) from fossil and nonfossil bones may be calculated in the following ways (Behrensmeyer 1975:492-93):

Nonfossil Elements:

$$d_q = \frac{2 \cdot (v_s)^2}{4/3 \cdot g \cdot (\rho q - 1)}$$

simplified to:

$$d_q = .000928 \cdot v_s^2$$

v_s = bone settling velocity

$g = 980 \text{ cm/sec}^2$

ρq = quartz density = 2.65

Fossil Elements:

$$d_q = (P_b - 1) \cdot d_b/1.65$$

d_b = Nominal diameter of the bone $= \sqrt[3]{1.91 \times \text{Volume}}$

ρ_b = Bone density

Table 4.1 shows examples of d_q and flume data from Site 20 specimens. A detailed report on sedimentary processes and effects at Site 20 is currently being prepared by Behrensmeyer and myself.

Generalizing from these observations, I would conclude that Dassanetch site location preferences, based upon knowledge of local geological processes, determine that most pastoralist sites will lie in zones unfavorable to good preservation of cultural materials. These sites reflect the settlement patterns and economic base of about 85 percent of the Dassanetch people. Sites most liable to be preserved are short-term *gal dies* camps, located in zones avoided by the more sedentary pastoralists; the likelihood of aqueous inundation of the sort that would preserve a site is the very reason given for this avoidance. Hunting-fishing camps reflect the protein procurement activities of a small segment of the total regional population and are not typical of the total range of activities of even that group.

Relative degree of sedentism may be extremely influential in determining the likelihood of site preservation. A hypothesis concerning these relationships may be framed as follows: Given a range of geomorphic zones in an inhabited region, increasing duration of site occupation will result in placement of long-term sites in geomorphic zones of minimal depositional activity.

ARCHAEOLOGICAL VISIBILITY

In discussing the effects of postoccupation processes upon sites, the concept of archaeological visibility is potentially useful, but it has not thus far been adequately defined. Here I use the term as an abstract concept that relates ethnographic reality on one time level to its probable material evidences on some future time level. Drawing in part upon Cowgill's (1970) discussion of archaeological sampling problems, I propose that a spatial focus of some human activity must meet three conditions to be archaeologically visible: (1) the human activities must have material consequences; (2) the material consequences must be potentially preservable; and (3) natural processes must act upon these material consequences in such a manner as to preserve them. If an occurrence fulfills all three conditions, it will be archaeologically visible.

Preservation of cultural materials in much their original condition and disposition (fulfillment of the third condition) is often the result of a complex interaction of cultural and natural processes. As indicated in the discussion of trampling, the substrate may interact with cultural processes in determining whether or not primary refuse is preserved on a site. Cultural factors may likewise determine whether or not geological processes capable of preserving a site can act upon it.

Deetz (1968b) discusses the notion of a "threshold" of archaeological visibility, which, he has proposed, most hunter-gatherers do not surpass. According to the definition given here, the prerequisites of ar-

TABLE 4.1
SITE 20, EXPERIMENTAL BONE DATA

| Element | Weight(g) | V_s(mm/sec) | d_q(mm) | Flume Experiment Transport Velocities (cm/sec)* | | |
				Initial	Continuous	Burial
Terrapin carapace	74.7	161.0	2.41	25	45	—
Terrapin carapace fragment	14.3	177.9	2.94	10	20	—
Terrapin plastron fragment	3.8	154.3	2.21	10	20	35
Terrapin radius	1.0	282.5	7.41	8	25	35
Crocodile half-mandible	162.3	500.0	23.13	15	35	50
Crocodile humerus	44.6	378.0	13.25	25	35	50
Crocodile radius	9.1	272.3	6.87	no move-ment	no move-ment	40

* Water depth: 15.2 cm (0.5ft); substrate: well-sorted coarse sand (median dq = 1.3mm).

chaeological visibility have no necessary connection with a particular type of subsistence pattern, but rather with the interplay of cultural and natural factors. Certainly a group of people who habitually erect durable structures on their occupation sites may be more archaeologically visible than those who do not, and certainly this type of cultural behavior is rare among hunter-gatherers. But it is likewise rare among shifting agriculturalists and pastoralists. For the reasons given earlier, some transhumant or seminomadic pastoralists may be even more "invisible" than hunter-gatherers. In such groups low discard rates (first condition) combine with poor preservation conditions (third condition) to limit archaeological visibility. Although the research situation is changing (see Hole: Chap. 6, below), pastoralists' archaeological invisibility may well account for the lack of serious attention given the role of that subsistence pattern in the origins of food production in the Near East.

Regional surveys of archaeological sites have been the basis of recently proposed models of culture change in both the Old and New worlds. These studies all assume that the sites observed are the result of regularities rather than vagaries in human cultural behavior. Another assumption implicit in such studies is that the observed sites are a random sample of the original range of cultural occurrences. But, as stressed earlier, sites of certain types may not be randomly distributed as regards geomorphic zones in a region, and in fact certain geomorphic zones of high preservation potential may be intentionally avoided in location of long-term occupation sites. The interaction of cultural and natural processes will in such cases lead to a skewing in the preserved archaeological sample. In the Dassanetch situation, for example, pastoralist sites will generally be poorly preserved surface scatters, which, unless the cultural and natural processes involved in site preservation are understood, may be avoided by researchers looking for "good" sites.

Only an understanding of the ancient geomorphic processes operating in a region combined with ethnoarchaeological settlement-pattern data can indicate potential skewing of a regional site sample. Construction of a comprehensive regional model of ancient geomorphic environments and processes seems a basic requirement in any regional archaeological survey.

CONCLUSIONS

In assessing the effects of noncultural processes upon archaeological sites, ethnoarchaeological research can do more than simply provide cautionary notes to archaeologists. This paper has presented several testable propositions concerning the operation of such processes upon cultural materials. It has further stipulated probable diagnostic features of one type of affected sample. Further research will undoubtedly yield many more such propositions.

Studies of natural alteration processes in the present, of course, cannot conclusively prove the operation of such factors in any given prehistoric sample. They can, however, be used predictively to improve interpretation of the archaeological record. As Schiffer and Rathje (1973) have stated in their discussion of "n-transforms," a systematic knowledge of natural alteration processes can be helpful in locating abundant and well-preserved archaeological materials. The same knowledge that allows one to locate such samples can permit one to assess how truly representative these samples are of the total range of prehistoric phenomena.

If archaeologists wish to derive detailed inferences regarding prehistoric cultural behavior from patterns in the archaeological evidence, they cannot afford to ignore the patterning effects of noncultural processes upon such materials. Ethnoarchaeological research should encompass all processes, cultural and natural, affecting the material traces of human behavior.

NOTES

1. Equipment and labor expenses for my work in Kenya were provided by National Science Foundation Dissertation Research Grant GS-40206. Living expenses were paid by the final year of an N.D.E.A. (Title IV) Graduate Fellowship. The Wenner-Gren Foundation for Anthropological Research, in remuneration for my analysis of faunal material from the site of Longs Drift, Kenya, during my time in Nairobi, paid my airfare to Kenya.

I wish to thank the Office of the President of the Republic of Kenya for permission to conduct research and the Trustees of the National Museums of Kenya for their sponsorship and aid. Personal thanks are given to my academic advisor, Dr. Glynn L. Isaac, University of California, Berkeley, and to Mr. R. E. Leakey, Administrative Director of the National Museums, for their invaluable advice and material aid. My field assistants, Mr. Jack Kilonzo and Mr. Andrea Kilonzo, receive my thanks for their patience and hard work.

My deepest gratitude, of course, goes to the people of Ileret.

2. Olson (1962) defines taphonomy as the study of the laws of burial, including all aspects of the transference of organic remains from the biosphere to the lithosphere.

5

Ethnoarchaeology and the Study of Agricultural Adaptation in the Humid Tropics

PATRICK V. KIRCH

Bernice P. Bishop Museum
Honolulu, Hawaii

INTRODUCTION

Archaeology is, and has always been, the study of the present. Its ultimate aim may be the reconstruction of past lifeways or the generation of models of cultural process, but its materials are artifacts—in the broadest sense—existing here and now. It is impossible to study the past directly; it can be approached only indirectly through the material patterns of extinct behavior as they are reflected in contemporary patterns of artifacts and other remains. Thus it is surprising that ethnoarchaeology—the study of contemporary behavior in order to draw inferences concerning patterns of extinct behavior—has been so long in coming into its own.

This chapter is an attempt to explore the possibilities of an ethnoarchaeological approach to the study of agricultural adaptation in the humid tropics. Ethnoarchaeology, as a burgeoning discipline, has to date largely been concerned with subsistence patterns of hunter-gatherer and nomadic societies, or with the reconstruction of prehistoric social structure. The present essay thus seeks to expand ethnoarchaeological methodology to the subsistence ecology of tropical horticulturalists.

The areal focus of this chapter is Malayo-Oceania, although the approach espoused here should be generally applicable throughout the humid tropics. A theoretical orientation is developed around the concepts of cultural adaptation and adaptive strategy. A case study in the application of this approach, utilizing recent field data from Western Polynesia, is then summarized. The emphasis of this case study is methodological rather than substantive.

THE HUMID TROPICS

The humid tropics, a circumglobal belt incorporating vast regions of Central America and the Amazon Basin, Central Africa, and mainland and insular Southeast Asia and Oceania, are characterized by warm temperatures, high rainfall, and high relative humidity, as well as by a diverse and generally mesophytic vegetation (Fosberg, Garnier, and Kuchler 1961). Included within the humid tropics are the American, African, and Indo-Malayan rain-forest formations, marked by diverse, evergreen, dominantly arboreal vegetation (Richards 1952). The indigenous agricultural systems of these humid tropics also share certain consistent features, although their origins are probably diverse. Tropical agricultural systems focus on cultigen inventories dominated by vegetatively propagated tuberous or fruity species (D. R. Harris 1972). Among the more important tropical crops are manioc, sweet potato, and *Xanthosoma* (Americas), the *Dioscorea* yams (Africa and Southeast Asia), taro, and bananas (Southeast Asia and Oceania). Harlan (1971) has noted that these indigenous tropical agricultural systems comprise vast "noncenters" of agricultural origins, as opposed to the seed-crop "centers" of temperate regions. The association of such tropical systems with the complex of cultivation techniques that has been termed "shifting cultivation" (Spencer 1966; Conklin 1954) should also be noted. Janzen's (1973) term "tropical agroecosystems" is perhaps the best to describe the close interrelations between agriculture and the natural ecology of the humid tropics.

Tropical agricultural systems, although much studied by anthropologists and ethnobotanists (Conklin 1963), have been neglected in archaeological investigation. Among the cited reasons are the lack of preservation of tubers, corms, or fruit in the acidic soils of tropical sites, and the general lack of structural features (terraces, ditches, and the like) in association with shifting cultivation. Thus the vast majority of archaeological investigations related to agricultural origins and development have focused on the seed-crop "centers," particularly those of the Near East and of Mesoamerica (Harlan 1971). Nevertheless, recent indications of considerable antiquity for the origins of agriculture in the humid tropics (Gorman 1969) have spurred archaeological interest in these tropical agroecosystems.

THEORETICAL ORIENTATION

Cultural Adaptation and Ecology

An investigation of the relations between culture and environment, of which agriculture is a crucial part, is perforce a study of adaptation. Adaptation, whether cultural or biological, may be defined as the continual process an organism or a population undergoes to establish and maintain a relationship with its environment. The concept of "suitability" or "fitness" between organism and habitat is inherent in the term *adaptation*, as may be clearly seen in its etymological origins: from Latin *adaptare*, "to fit" (from *aptus*, "fit"). In other words, adaptation is the process of maintaining a suitable interrelation between organism and habitat, in which "suitable" may be minimally defined as adequate for the maintenance of life.

The adaptation concept in anthropology is largely derived by analogy with the biological concept of adaptation, and it may be useful to contrast these two uses of the same term. Biological adaptation is dependent upon the process of natural selection. In a specific environment, the selection of certain random genetic variations, with differential fitness (defined in terms of reproductive success), favors those variations which result in increased reproductive success. Adaptive information is stored in, and transmitted through, the genetic code.

In Dobzhansky's words (1962:319), biological evolution transcended itself in producing the genetic basis of culture. This genetic basis was in the selection for somatic traits (stereoscopic vision, bipedal locomotion, expansion of the cerebral cortex, and so forth) that favored behavioral, nongenetically determined responses to environment. These genetic modifications produced in man the capacity to store and transmit large quantities of adaptive information through the use of symbolic or cognitive codes, the most important of which is language.

Cultural adaptation, then, is the maintenance of a human population (a group of interacting individuals sharing certain cognitive codes, as well as the same environment) in its habitat by extrasomatic means. Furthermore, shared symbolic codes permit extremely rapid transmission of potentially adaptive information between individuals of a population. It is thus that man has been able, in a few million years, to modify both his behavior and his environment to such an extent that the sphere of his niche encompasses the entire planet. (A recent useful review [Alland and McCay 1973] of the concept of adaptation in anthropology and biology contrasts the differences in usage in the two disciplines in greater detail than is necessary here.)

An inherent problem with the term *adaptation* is that it implies, and may be used in the sense of, either a *process* or a *synchronic relationship* between a population and its environment. The use of the term to refer to a particular "state of being adapted" can be seen, for example, in Cohen's "Culture as Adaptation" (1968). In this paper I specifically restrict the use of the term *adaptation* to the *process of modification* of one or more shared cultural (i.e., nongenetically determined) traits of a human population in order to maintain itself within its environment. For the synchronic relationship between a specific population and its habitat at a given point in time, I propose the term *adaptive strategy*. This term is borrowed from Levins (1968), who has successfully used the concept of strategy in considering biological adaptation. The need for a population to alter its adaptive strategy over time may be necessitated by changes in the nature of the population itself (for example, in its size or density in relation to the environment), by changes in the parameters of the ecosystem (either endogenous or exogenous), or by a combination of these. The effects of other, neighboring human populations may be important in inducing change, but these can be subsumed under the general category of the ecosystemic context of the population in question.

The advantage gained by distinguishing between adaptation as process and adaptive strategies as static relationships is not trivial, for it concerns the basic methodological issues in the anthropological, and

106

especially archaeological, study of man-land relations. At any point in time, a particular adaptive strategy comprises patterned behavior in relation to a specific environment. Ethnographically, it is possible to approach these behavioral patterns either from an etic, operational viewpoint using categories that are meaningful to the investigator, or in terms of indigenous, emic categories that structure the particular activities of the population's members from their own viewpoint. Ideally, an investigator can combine both perspectives in characterizing a particular population's adaptive strategy in a specific ecosystemic context (Rappaport 1971; Vayda and Rappaport 1968).

Archaeologically, a prehistoric adaptive strategy is potentially reconstructable as a patterned set of artifacts and environmental modifications reflecting past behavior. It is assumed, of course, that the patterns reflected in the material traces of human activity are to some degree isomorphic to the actual behavior which produced the archaeological record (Deetz 1965:2). The emic categories and cognitive codes through which the prehistoric population viewed their world and structured their behavior in relation to it exist for the archaeologist essentially as a "black box" (Clarke 1968:59-62). The use of the "black box" permits us to recognize and incorporate the emic or cognitive aspect in our archaeological reconstruction, while at the same time recognizing that, in all probability, we are for operational reasons (except in certain instances of abundant textual or iconographic data) unable to specify its particular content. We may, however, be able to specify input and—especially—output (the patterns of behavior) of the cognitive "black box."

The important point is that for a specific time and place, it is possible (assuming the patterned nature of human activity) to characterize ethnographically or to reconstruct archaeologically a particular adaptive strategy. Such a characterization consists, in essence, of a description of the behavioral patterns by means of which the population maintains itself within its habitat. Technology, settlement patterns, agricultural systems, or methods of marine exploitation are all examples of components of an adaptive strategy. Characterizations of ecosystemic context and of population parameters are further important aspects of an adequate description of an adaptive strategy.

It should be stressed that an adaptive strategy must always be characterized in reference to a specific environmental context. For this purpose, the concept of *ecosystem*, the interaction sphere between the population in question and the other biotic and abiotic components of its environment (Tansley 1935), is particularly useful. The ecosystem construct and its applicability to ecological research are sufficiently well known not to require further explication here.

With regard to the analysis of cultural adaptation, having characterized a set of adaptive strategies $(S_1, S_2, \ldots S_n)$ and their ecosystemic contexts $(E_1, E_2, \ldots E_n)$ for a series of historically related populations $(P_1, P_2, \ldots P_n)$ at specific times $(t_1, t_2, \ldots t_n)$, it is possible to isolate differences in particular parameters or aspects of these strategies (Fig. 5.1). In this fashion, the successive changes (or stability, as the case may be) in the adaptive strategies of these populations may be exposed. Such a series of adaptive strategies would constitute a sequence of adaptation over time. As noted above, a variety of endogenous and/or exogenous sources may initiate such changes in adaptive strategy.

FIGURE 5.1. Graphic model of the relationships between a series of successive populations, ecosystem states, and adaptive strategies over time.

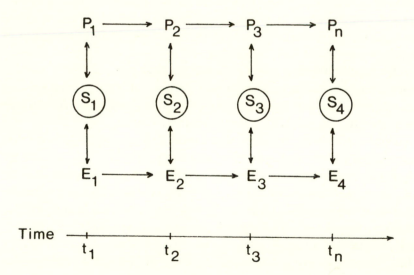

Agricultural Adaptation in the Humid Tropics

It is here that the concept of adaptation as *process* provides a useful analytic framework. While we may potentially characterize a sequence of adaptation for successive populations over time, and isolate the specific changes in particular parameters, the causal explanation of this change as a process involves the use of modeling. A model of a process of adaptation for a series of successive populations over time is a theoretical construct consisting of two or more hypotheses regarding causal or systemic linkages between variables. Such a model may be expressed as a set of potentially testable multiple working hypotheses which may either verify the model in light of the available evidence or suggest alterations in the original model. The continual process of data collection, analysis, modeling, hypothesis testing, model revision, and so on, of course, forms the very core of the scientific method (Medawar 1969).

Ethnoarchaeology and the Study of Adaptation

Within the theoretical framework proposed above, what specific roles may an ethnoarchaeological approach play, especially with regard to the analysis of agricultural adaptation? R. A. Gould (1971:175) demonstrated, in his Western Australian work, that "ethnographic knowledge can be brought to bear on at least three levels of archaeological research." These are (1) the *practical level*, for example, locating sites during archeological survey; (2) the level of *specific interpretation*, for example, the functional interpretation of artifact types based on a knowledge of present use of the same or similar types by contemporary peoples; and (3) the level of *general interpretation*, where "broad interpretations of culture history are attempted." I would equate Gould's third level with the process of model building as defined above.

Gould's tripartite classification provides a useful scheme for examining the role of ethnoarchaeology in the study of agricultural adaptation. First, the practical level of ethnoarchaeological research is virtually a prerequisite for the study of agricultural adaptation. This is particularly true in Oceania, where time depth is relatively short and where contemporary indigenous populations are often the direct descendants of the archaeological populations one wishes to study. Thus, not only are local informants usually able to direct the researcher to known sites of previous cultivation activity, but also observation of contemporary cultivation systems should provide information on the range of microenvironments in which to search for such sites. At the level of specific interpretation, ethnographic knowledge can also contribute significantly to the analysis of prehistoric agricultural systems. For example, the interpretation of carbonized material in pondfields has been of some importance in Oceanic archaeology, as it may derive from upslope burning (whereby carbon is incorporated in irrigation flow) and thus indicate the nearby presence of shifting cultivation (see Yen et al. 1972). In my recent Futunan investigation of contemporary irrigation systems, some effort was directed toward identification of all possible sources of carbonized material in pondfield soils. The result was knowledge of a wider range of possible carbon introduction mechanisms, which in turn suggests caution in the blanket interpretation of this phenomenon as an indicator for swidden activity.

It is, however, at the level of general interpretation or model construction that ethnoarchaeology has the most to offer in the study of agricultural adaptation. I am referring to the coordinate use of ethnographic and archaeological methods to generate a series of multiple working hypotheses, which themselves form the basis for more general models. With regard to the construction of models of agricultural adaptation, ethnography may contribute in several ways to archaeological research. An example is in the analysis of contemporary variation and contrast in adaptive strategies, and how such variation correlates with environmental, economic, social, or political factors. Covariation between several factors may thus provide the basis for proposing one or more hypotheses which may in turn be tested with the diachronic data of prehistory.

The theoretical orientation espoused above provides a framework for a more rigorous structuring of an ethnoarchaeological approach to the study of agricultural adaptation, particularly in the Malayo-Oceanic region, where, as I have noted, some continuity between prehistory and contemporary agricultural systems is evident. Such an approach would entail the following steps: (1) the ethnographic analysis of variation and contrast in contemporary adaptive strategies, and the correlates of such variation and contrast in environment, as well as in other social-cultural factors; (2) the formulation of a set of hypotheses sufficient to explain the range of contemporary variation in terms of temporal process; (3) testing of these hypotheses with the diachronic evidence of archaeology, through the reconstruction of past adaptive strategies; (4) based on the results of Step 3, repetition of Steps 1-3, with revision and alterations of specific hypotheses as suggested by the archaeological evidence, as well as by further analysis of the ethnographic data; and (5) construction of general models for adaptational process in agriculture.

This approach is perhaps best illustrated with a specific case study, in this instance that of agricultural development in Western Polynesia. Rather than attempt a summary of the archaeological findings (see Kirch 1976, Kirch in press), this case study will focus on the use of ethnographic analysis to generate several major hypotheses with significant implications for West Polynesian prehistory.

A WEST POLYNESIAN CASE STUDY

In Malayo-Oceania, the reconstruction of prehistoric agricultural systems has long been a major goal of ethnobotany. Investigators such as MacDaniels (1947), Barrau (1965a, 1965b, 1965c), and Yen (1971, 1973, 1974) have emphasized the implications for prehistory in their researches. Nevertheless, attempts to apply direct archaeological testing to these ethnobotanical hypotheses are a new feature of Oceanic research (see Yen et al. 1972; Golson 1974), one that has yet to realize its full potential.

The decision to undertake an ethnoarchaeological study of indigenous agriculture in Western Polynesia was similarly stimulated by certain ethnobotanical data. Yen (1971, 1973) had proposed that the border area between Eastern Melanesia and Western Polynesia encompassed considerable diversity and variability—in native agronomy, in cultigen inventories, and in methods of food preservation and preparation. The West Polynesian high islands of Futuna and Alofi (Horne Islands) and Uvea (Wallis Islands) were chosen as a research locus not only because they are examples of this East Melanesia-West Polynesia border area, but because their indigenous agricultural systems had not been greatly modified by the effects of Western economic pressures and remained relatively intact (Barrau 1963). Hence these islands offered virtually a model situation in which to undertake an ethnoarchaeological study.

Futuna and Uvea were selected as a research locus for two further reasons: (1) cultural and linguistic data indicated that the contemporary Futunan and Uvean populations were genetically related, that is, they were descended from a common ancestral population; and (2) they occupied two broadly similar yet specifically contrastive ecosystems. This, then, was an excellent "laboratory" for the study of differential adaptation by two daughter populations in two different ecosystems. Furthermore, investigation could proceed both on an ethnographic level, examining variation and contrast on the level of contemporary systems, and on an archaeological level, projecting back two parallel sequences of adaptation. In terms of the theoretical framework developed above, this situation may be graphed as in Figure 5.2.

The Horne and Wallis islands lie midway between the larger and better-known Samoan and Fijian archipelagoes (Fig. 5.3). They are an autonomous French overseas territory, with the administrative seat on Uvea. Futuna and Uvea were ethnographically studied by E. G. Burrows in 1932, and his monographs (1936, 1937) provide a starting point for further ethnographic inquiry. The contemporary population of Futuna is 2,750 persons, that of Uvea 5,950; Alofi has not been permanently inhabited since late prehistoric times, although it is utilized for shifting cultivation by people from the Alo District of Futuna.

Futunan and Uvean agricultural systems are focused on four major, staple, starch-producing crop assemblages: aroids (especially taro), yams, bananas, and breadfruit, supplemented by numerous other secondary cultigens (Barrau 1963). Cultivation techniques include shifting cultivation, in the pattern characteristic throughout Malayo-Oceania (Spencer 1966), intensive water control (irrigation in Futuna, drainage in Uvea) for taro culture (see Barrau 1965a), and arboriculture (centered on breadfruit, but including several nut- and fruit-bearing species). Animal husbandry, particularly of pigs, is closely integrated with the agricultural system.

Knowledge of spatial and temporal variation in the Futunan and Uvean ecosystems is critical to the analysis of agricultural adaptation. Some of these salient ecological contrasts are summarized in Table 5.1. Perhaps the most important spatial contrasts are those of topography (relief) and water regime. The susceptibility of Futuna's exposed volcanics to erosion resulted in a highly dissected topography, with permanent-stream valleys amenable to intensive irrigation. The

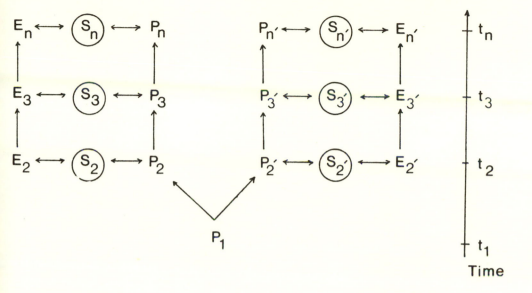

FIGURE 5.2. Graphic model of the relationship between two series of populations where the populations have a common ancestor.

karstic limestone capping of Alofi prevented such dissection, while Uvea has always been too low and gently undulating for significant stream cutting. Uvea's water regime, however, is amenable to an alternate method of control for cultivation. The island's basaltic core is a high-capacity aquifer, acting on the Ghyben-Herzberg principle. This fresh water, existing along the coastal margins, feeds swampy lowlands which may be modified by drainage for intensive taro cultivation.

Temporal variability, also significant in Futunan and Uvean agricultures, includes annual (seasonal) variability, as well as longer-term, more irregular variability in the form of cyclones and droughts. Seasonal wet-dry variation largely controls the scheduling of agricultural activities, because of the trophytic nature of the dominant yam crop. The occurrence of cyclones once every decade or so, on the average, adds another dimension to the patchiness of Futunan and Uvean climate. A cyclone can wreak extensive damage to

TABLE 5.1
ECOLOGICAL CONTRASTS AMONG FUTUNA, ALOFI, AND UVEA

Character	Futuna	Alofi	Uvea
Area (hectares)	6,211	2,906	5,912
Population density (per hectare)	0.301*	......	1.006
Average yearly rainfall (mm)	3,000†	......	2,599.6
Average temperature	26.0†	......	27.0
Average relative humidity	83%†	......	83%
Highest point (meters)	760	365	150
Degree of relief	highly dissected	elevated; not dissected	gently undulating
Permanent streams	20+	-0-	-0-
Geology	tertiary volcanics with some calcareous sediments	tertiary volcanics capped with calcareous sediments	pleistocene oceanic basalts
Fern land (toafa)	prominent	slight	prominent
Marine resources	restricted	restricted	diverse

* Combined figure for Futuna and Alofi.
† Estimated.

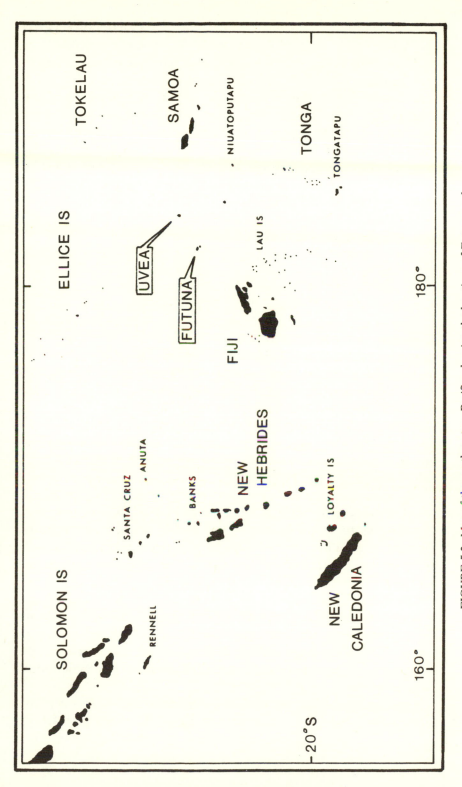

FIGURE 5.3. Map of the southwestern Pacific, showing the locations of Futuna and Uvea in relation to other important island groups.

swiddens, taro fields, and tree crops, and can thus induce a serious food shortage.

As I have noted, the methodology applied in Futuna and Uvea involved the use of ethnographic analysis of contemporary adaptive strategies, especially agricultural systems, to derive several major hypotheses concerning the temporal process of adaptation. For the purposes of this essay, however, the sequence of presentation will be reversed; I will present salient aspects of the ethnographic analysis in the context of four major hypotheses.

Hypothesis 1. The initial Lapita colonizers of West Polynesia were agriculturalists who transferred with themselves a horticultural complex that included crop plants, with attendant technology and agronomic lore.

The attribution of an agricultural technology to the founding population of West Polynesia (S_1 of P_1 in Fig. 5.2) is crucial, since it concerns the "zero point" of cultural adaptation in the region. Such an attribution, however, has by no means been entirely accepted by Oceanic prehistorians. Groube (1971:310-12) had proposed an alternative hypothesis of a maritime orientation ("Oceanic strandloopers") in Lapita economy. Ethnographic evidence supporting Hypothesis 1 includes the botanical relationships of the Futunan and Uvean crop-plant inventories, linguistic data for cultigen names, and the contrastive nature of the contemporary adaptive strategies themselves, as probable endpoints in a process of differential adaptation from a common ancestral strategy (Fig. 5.2).

The linguistic evidence in support of Hypothesis 1 is particularly strong. Pawley and Green (1973:15) remark that "the linguistic evidence shows the contemporary Fijian and Polynesian languages as retaining all the Proto-Austronesian terms for major cultigens, as well as a good many other horticultural terms, suggesting continuity in the agricultural tradition." Table 5.2 presents a few selected examples of Futunan and Uvean reflexes for cultigens and terms relating to agriculture, in which these reflexes are clearly retentions of the ancient Austronesian terms (reconstructed terms are drawn from Pawley and Green 1973). These linguistic data present a strong case for continuity of agricultural tradition, as opposed to later intrusion of an agricultural subsistence base.

Hypothesis 2. Diversity of island environments (and microenvironments) played a major role in the differential adaptation

116

TABLE 5.2
FUTUNAN AND UVEAN REFLEXES OF SELECTED
AUSTRONESIAN TERMS RELATED TO AGRICULTURE

Gloss	PAN	POC	PCP	EFU	EUV
'to plant'	teba	topa	topa	tō	tō
'taro'	tales	ntalo(s)	ntalo	talo	talo
'yam'	qubi(s)	qupi	qupi	'ufi	'ufi
'swidden'	quma	quma	?	'umanga	. . . . .
'fallow land'	wawaw	wawo	wao	vao	vao

Abbreviations: PAN, Proto-Austronesian; POC, Proto-Oceanic;
PCP, Proto-Central-Pacific; EFU, East Futunan; EUV, East Uvean.

of Austronesian agriculture and settlement patterns, the *constraints* of environment being particularly significant.

The importance of environmental variation in cultural adaptation has been recognized for some time (Coe and Flannery 1964). Futunan and Uvean ethnographic data suggested two elaborations on this theme: first, that *temporal* as well as spatial variation may have significant consequences for adaptation; and, second, that the limitations or constraints are highly influential, although not necessarily determining, factors. Two examples may illustrate.

Temporal variability is demonstrated in the ecological wet-and-dry seasonality of Uvea and its influence upon the cultivation of yams. Figure 5.4 plots the cultural scheduling of indigenous yam planting periods (*ta'u*) (1, *ta'u muamua*; 2, *ta'u lahi*; 3, *ta'u muli*) against the ecological rhythms of rainfall, temperature, and relative humidity. Perhaps more significant, however, is the indication that the period from August through October is critical in terms of staple food resources. During this time the earliest yams are not yet mature, and the June-July breadfruit harvest has ended. Dependence must therefore be placed upon the aroids and bananas, which may be insufficient. The Uvean calendar defines this as a time of famine (*hoge*). Pressures exerted by such famine on the process of ecological adaptation may have been considerable. Certainly the extent to which stocks of preserved food (fermented and pit-ensiled breadfruit, *mahi*; arrowroot and sago flour, *mahoā*) were available would determine one's ability to weather the crises. Ethnographic data from other Oceanic groups (Yen 1976) suggest that chiefly control over such preserved food stocks was particularly important in the allocation of these stocks during famine. Such famine might also have contributed

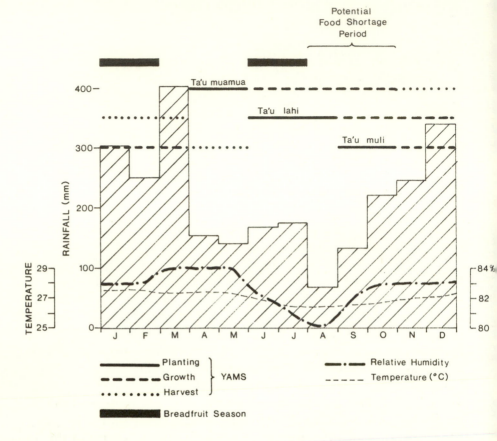

FIGURE 5.4. Annual relationships between ecological cycles and agricultural activities in Uvea.

to intergroup conflict or warfare over food supplies and land. Clearly the implications for prehistory are numerous.

The effect of spatial variability is evident in numerous aspects of the agricultural systems. One of these is the role of hydrologic regime in the intensive cultivation of taro, with irrigation in Futuna, drainage in Uvea, and lack of such intensive cultivation in Alofi (see above, and Table 5.1). A second example, relating to the intensity of shifting cultivation, is well illustrated in the ethnographic data. Shifting cultivation is more intensive in the Alo District (including Alofi) of Futuna, and more intensive in Uvea than in Futuna as a whole. This

118

contrast is perhaps best displayed in folk terminology and in directed-graph representations of land-use categories. In etic terminology, the agricultural subsystem of shifting cultivation involves four major land-use states: (1) swidden; (2) second growth; (3) primary or climax forest; and (4) a fern-desert, terminal vegetative association (*toafa*), largely anthropogenic (a result of overcultivation). These etic categories are closely matched in indigenous linguistic categories, for which the following dyads provide defining criteria:

arable: nonarable $A:\bar{A}$

cultivated: fallow $C:\bar{C}$

herbaceous vegetation:
   woody vegetation $H:\bar{H}$

The Futunan and Uvean emic terminological domains, with componential definitions, are:

FUTUNA (1) *faigasaga* : AC   UVEA (1) *gaue*   : AC
           (2) *lusa*   : $A\bar{C}H$ (2) *vao mui*   : $A\bar{C}H(1)$
                                       (3) *vao lelei* : $A\bar{C}H(2)$
           (3) *vao matu'a*: $A\bar{C}\bar{H}$ (4) *vao matu'a* : $A\bar{C}\bar{H}$
           (4) *toafa*   : $\bar{A}$ (5) *toafa*   : $\bar{A}$

The sequences of land use in Futuna and Uvea may be represented in directed graphs, using indigenous folk taxa as nodes, solid arrows to indicate normal sequences, and broken arrows to indicate culturally undesirable (but recognized) sequences (Fig. 5.5).

The Futunan and Uvean linguistic domains differ principally in the definition of second growth, Uvean making a finer distinction between largely weedy-grassy second growth (*vao mui*) and older herbaceous-to-woody second growth (*vao lelei*). This second category is the pre-ferred vegetative association in which to clear and plant a new swidden (*lelei* = good). Such a distinction might be supposed to reflect a more intensive system, in which a maximum long fallow—while culturally desirable—may not always have been feasible (because of greater population density, environmental restrictions on intensive irrigation or drainage cultivation, or for other reasons). Such intensity in the Uvean case was in fact the observed phenomenon, and was supported in lengthy informant discussions.

The important point is that the ethnographic analysis of con-temporary agricultural systems in Futuna and Uvea was able to

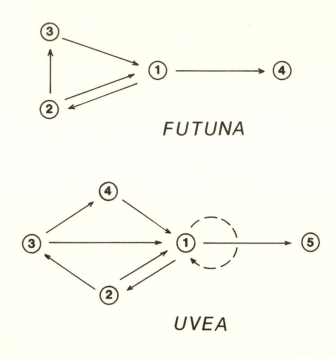

FUTUNA

UVEA

FIGURE 5.5. Directed graphs of swidden cycles in Futuna and Uvea.

suggest that environmental variability—both spatial and temporal—may have had important effects in constraining the directions of agricultural adaptation in the two islands. Such insight, especially with regard to the range of specific constraints involved, would not have been gained through a purely archaeological approach.

Hypothesis 3. Population pressure in a circumscribed environment was a major impetus to cultural adaptation in Western Polynesia—in agriculture and settlement patterns, as well as in sociopolitical organization.

The issue of population as a factor in cultural adaptation, and particularly in agricultural intensification, has stimulated considerable debate (Boserup 1965; Spooner 1972; Brookfield 1972; Zubrow 1972). Contemporary population densities in Futuna and Uvea suggest something of the importance of this factor in relation to agricultural

120

intensity. As demonstrated above, the Uvean system of shifting cultivation is more intensive than the Futunan with respect to the cropping-fallow time ratio, particularly as reflected in the indigenous emic terminology of land-use classification. Relative population densities of 0.301 per hectare for Futuna and Alofi (combined figure) compared with 1.006 per hectare for Uvea indicate that population density on arable land resources is significant in determining intensity of land use.

Again, however, ethnographic analysis indicated that the role of population pressure in agricultural adaptation would be more complex than that implied by a consideration of standard demographic variables (population size, density, carrying capacity) only. I refer to the sociological constraints on population and on allocation of resources. R. C. Kelly (1968), in a classic study, demonstrated the importance of social structure in defining demographic pressure, using data from the New Guinea highlands. A similar situation exists in Western Polynesia, where land-use rights are transmitted through local descent groups with a strongly agnatic core (see Panoff 1970). Thus imbalance in male-female ratios in any successive generation may produce pressure on the allocation of arable land, tree crops, pigs, or other property, even though the size of the society's total population may remain relatively constant.

Hypothesis 4. While demographic pressure is posited to have been a significant factor in determining the direction of agricultural adaptation, other political and socioeconomic pressures were also important in such adaptation.

The role of various social pressures, such as production for ritual and prestation, or of chiefly control of certain economic resources cannot be neglected in a model of agricultural adaptation. Brookfield (1972) has emphasized this point in relation to agricultural intensification, while Sahlins (1972) has pointed out the role of chiefly control in the evolution of Polynesian societies.

Two ethnographic examples from Futuna and Uvea will exemplify Hypothesis 4: (1) production of suids for ceremonial distribution; and (2) descent-group fissioning as a mechanism for population distribution eventually resulting in what Carneiro (1970b) has termed "social circumscription."

The integration of animal husbandry, particularly of suids, with Oceanic agricultural systems, has often been remarked upon (see Yen

121

1973:1; Oliver 1949), and Futuna is no exception. Pigs are regularly fed on agricultural products (coconut, taro, bananas), and considerable effort is spent on preparing foodstuffs for them (rough estimate: ± 1.5 hours per day per household). Pigs are furthermore the most important food item in *katoaga*, the regular village ceremonial food distributions (see Burrows 1936), each household being assessed one or more pigs depending upon the importance of the occasion and upon the household's resources. On April 28, 1974, at the *katoaga* in Kolia Village, approximately 250 medium-sized (six months to one year old) and more than 30 fully mature pigs were consumed, in addition to vast quantities of yams, taro, and other agricultural products. This was the production of a single village. This example gives some idea of the pressures on agricultural output which may be made by a society's high-level demands for ritual and prestation in excess of the normal demands for household subsistence (the "domestic mode of production"; see Sahlins 1972).

Second, we may briefly note the importance of descent group structure in Futuna and Uvea (Burrows 1936, 1937; Panoff 1970), with its proclivity for fission. This fission process provides a mechanism for relatively rapid expansion into new agricultural lands, leading to what Carneiro (1970b) has termed "social circumscription." In such circumscription, each local social group is constrained not only by physical parameters of the immediate environment, but by territorial claims on adjacent land by neighboring social groups. With a burgeoning population growth rate, and in a situation where shifting cultivation is the only feasible agricultural strategy, such social circumscription may have major consequences—for warfare (Vayda 1961) and political evolution (Kirch 1975).

The scope of this chapter does not permit a detailed review of the testing of these ethnographically generated hypotheses in Futunan and Uvean archaeology (one preliminary report on the archaeological work has been published [Kirch 1976] and one is in press [Kirch in press]). Two specific instances may, however, be briefly cited as examples.

In Hypothesis 1, it was posited that the colonizing populations of Futuna and Uvea were agriculturalists, in contrast to Groube's alternative hypothesis of "Oceanic strandloopers" (Groube 1971:310-12; see also Howells 1973:254-55, 260; Shutler and Shutler 1975:82). Direct archaeological evidence of agriculture is scarce in the humid tropics, for several reasons, especially the lack of frequently carbonized seed crops (see above). Nevertheless, indirect evidence such as site location (site catchment analysis), soil modifications, and the nature of the material culture assemblages can be used to build up an indirect case for the former existence of an agrarian economy; such was the approach utilized in Futuna and Uvea. Surface survey for ceramic-bearing sites (attributable to the Late Eastern Lapita horizon; see Green 1972) revealed inland settlements (ranging from 2,000 to 8,000 square meters) in areas favorable to shifting cultivation, but at a considerable distance from the coast and from marine resources. Such a settlement pattern is clearly antithetical to Groube's "strandlooping" hypothesis. Furthermore, excavation in one ceramic-bearing site (FU-11) yielded not only a few plant macrofossils (coconut, pandanus, and candlenut) but a material-culture assemblage suggestive of forest clearance (adzes) and of preparation of vegetable foods (a range of chert core and flake tools). The ceramic-bearing horizon was, in addition, capped with a soil layer interpreted as resulting from shifting cultivation.

What I wish to emphasize here, however, is that without the prior ethnographic analysis which led to the formulation of Hypothesis 1, the archaeological evidence of early settlement might not have been approached as critically. In fact, Groube's hypothesis seems to have been a result of a failure to consider the abundant ethnobotanical, linguistic, and cultural data (Barrau 1965a; Yen 1971, 1973) which strongly suggest that agriculture has been a part of Austronesian economy for five or six millennia at least.

Hypothesis 4 posits that certain political and socioeconomic pressures were, in conjunction with environmental constraint and population growth (Hypotheses 2 and 3), important factors in cultural adaptation in West Polynesia. The example of lineage fissioning leading to social circumscription has been cited above. Hypothesis 4 provided a useful framework in which to examine the later prehistoric settlement patterns of Futuna and Uvea, for it emphasized the sociopolitical, as well as environmental, determinants of settlement patterning (cf. Stanislawski 1973). In particular, two features of these settlement patterns were suggestive of a systemic relationship among environment, agricultural technology, social structure, and political evolution: (1) fortification; and (2) site components related to rank or social stratification (chief's backrest stones, coral slab tombs, large earthen burial mounds, symmetrical special-purpose "pigeon mounds" [cf. McKern 1929]). The dominance and development of these structural features in regions where shifting cultivation is prominent, and their absence in regions of irrigation development, suggested that pressure for predatory expansion in a situation of social circumscription may have been the major impetus to elaboration of social stratification. The exposition of this model of West Polynesian political evolution has been presented elsewhere (Kirch 1975). It is important to note here that only through a coordinate ethnoarchaeological approach could such a model have been generated, for it relies as much on the ethnographic evidence of social structure and of traditional oral history (Burrows 1936, 1937) as on the data of settlement archaeology.

RETROSPECT AND PROSPECT

The use of ethnography in archaeology is not a new phenomenon. In Oceania or North America, for example, obvious continuity between the prehistoric past and the ethnographic present has always favored the utilization of ethnographic data in archaeological interpretation. These applications, however, were usually restricted to Gould's (1971:175) first two levels, the practical level and the level of specific interpretation (or analogy; cf. Ascher 1961a). A theoretically more powerful use of ethnoarchaeology would seem to lie in the generation of whole models, as Gould (1971) has done in his characterization of the Western Desert culture of Australia, or as in the case of West Polynesian agricultural adaptation cited here. Among other things, the coordinate use of ethnography and archaeology should make us more aware of the potential complexity, and range of alternative hypotheses, for any situation. As Stanislawski recently pointed out:

> The real or native settlement world is obviously much more complex than that theoretical or model world of the archaeologist. While cultural factors are difficult to quantify and compute, it *is* often these factors or norms that guide many aspects of settlement variation, or site abandonment and resettlement. We will make many errors of interpretation if we are not aware of the limitations of information in the archaeological record, and of the alternative possibilities known to the ethnographer. (1973:388-89)

124

The increasing use of an ethnoarcheological approach is indeed encouraging, and its continued application should contribute in bringing us closer to the ideal of "archaeology as anthropology."

POSTSCRIPT

In 1976, receipt of a grant from the National Science Foundation (BNS 76-04782) permitted further ethnoarchaeological field investigations in Western Polynesia. Testing of the four hypotheses outlined in this chapter was the central objective of this research, which was carried out on Niuatoputapu Island, at the extreme north of the Tongan Archipelago. Ethnoarchaeological studies were again directed at the indigenous agricultural system, with investigations extended to include traditional fishing and marine exploitation methods as well.

The earlier ethnoarchaeological investigations in Futuna and Uvea had suggested that temporal constraint in local environment—specifically drought and periodic damage from tropical cyclones—was a significant factor in human adaptation to Oceanic ecosystems. This finding was stated in Hypothesis 2. During the period of our 1976 fieldwork, a four-month drought struck Niuatoputapu, and provided an excellent opportunity to test this hypothesis ethnographically. Although our field data have yet to be fully analyzed, Hypothesis 2 was extensively validated in the results of our more recent observations. These ethnoarchaeological data have provided the basis for an ecologically grounded model relating environmental constraint, development of food preparation-preservation methods (e.g., anaerobic pit fermentation of starchy food pastes), and chiefly control and allocation of food reserves. The implications of this model for the development of indigenous Polynesian economic systems are considerable, and testify to the value of an ethnoarchaeological approach to Oceanic prehistory.

6

Pastoral Nomadism in Western Iran[1]

FRANK HOLE

Rice University

INTRODUCTION

The ethnographic investigation discussed here developed in the context of an archaeological project centered in Deh Luran, Southwest Iran. The overall concern of the project is with the origins and development of domestication of plants and animals, both of which have been investigated chiefly through excavations of villages. The origins of pastoral nomadism and their relation to the origins of animal husbandry had not been approached directly in previous work; the present project was designed to rectify that situation.

The study described here has many facets, most of which cannot be discussed in this brief essay, although many of them were raised in the background paper prepared for discussion in the seminar. Here I shall stress general matters: the history and archaeology of nomadic pastoralism; the case study of a nomadic tribe in Luristan, Iran; and some generalizations that result from the study. The themes running through this essay are the nature of transhumant nomadism, and the ways in which we can learn about events that took place more than 8,000 years ago by studying modern people.

What follows is a rigid selection of information that only hints at the volume of detail and, equally important, the impressions that I gained. In doing ethnography an archaeologist, accustomed to working with the leavings in an archaeological site, enters into a fully rounded world of unaccustomed richness.

Among the kinds of information I obtained that are available only through ethnographic study are knowledge of the patterns of movement of nomads in Deh Luran and their interactions with settled villagers, and the composition, variation, and management of herds, information which could then be related to size and composition of cooperative camps. In the most general sense I learned what it takes to live as a transhumant herder and something of the possible range from affluence to poverty that nomads in the area experience.

Nomads were able to tell me the reasons why they migrate at particular times, why they choose certain sites, and how to interpret their leavings in abandoned camps. They could tell about practices, like the gathering of acorns, which I was not able to witness myself, and show me locations of acorn grinders and kilns. They also provided useful data on conditions in the past which helped me visualize the profound effect on the environment of new technology and great rises of population during the twentieth century.

The most useful ethnographic information was about things that are vitally important if we are to understand nomad behavior, but which will leave few, if any, archaeological traces: the number of women required to milk a herd; the reason for the interior arrangement of tents; the amount that pack animals can carry; the differences between pastures; and so on. The nomads also told us things that we could not infer accurately from the archaeological remains alone. For example, we could only have guessed at the use of stone pavements inside tent enclosures. We might have found it hard to visualize the behavior that leads to a scattered ash area, often partly water-laid, outside every tent. Nor might we have realized that the little interior hearths are used for heating liquids or baking bread but that the roasting of meat is done outdoors. And without elderly informants we might never have discovered the meaning of the memorial "houses" of tribal leaders.

These and many other things developed out of the ethnographic fieldwork. That experience has opened our eyes a little wider; it has given a human dimension to pastoralism to round out our archaeological picture of people mechanically marching back and forth across a map in response to shifts in wind, rain, and temperature.

128

Much of what I learned might be called "cautionary tales," anecdotes which tell us that things are not simple, that we may be misled easily in our interpretations of archaeological data, and that there are relatively few certainties in this business. I think we all recognize that we are dealing with probabilities and degrees of likelihood when we make most of our inferences. It is important, nevertheless, to try to make statements that have general relevance— that relate to the deeper structure of human societies and behavior. If this structure can be inferred from ethnographic sources, it can be used in developing general anthropological theory and ultimately can enable us to make accurate interpretations of the behavioral correlates of remains found in archaeological sites. At this stage of our work generalizations remain inadequately tested, but stating them paves the way toward testing and allows them to be used provisionally in making archaeological inferences.

NOMADIC PASTORALISM

Perspectives on Pastoralism

This study developed out of my archaeological interests, a passing personal familiarity with nomads and with ethnographic studies of them, and my sense of what might be important to study. After studying many groups of nomads and one camp of one tribe in detail, I came away with a latent impression which has taken some time to develop fully: the nomads are strongly influenced by the social circumstances of their larger political milieu. What is basic, unchanging, and therefore interesting is not what nomads appear to be, but what they are: poor rural folk who work very hard to make a living and whose only escape from unrelenting toil is death. They are a people to whom catastrophe is a constant threat and for whom diligence, pursued with stoic resolution, is a way of life. They seize opportunity only when it is unencumbering; they see in its absence only a manifestation of expectable fate. Comfort is ordinarily denied them. They revel in it when it is available but see in unrestrained pleasure a cancerous vice. Nomads are inward turned, sustained by self-sufficiency, and wary of intrusion. Historically, they have been pawns in elaborate political charades just as peasant farmers have been fodder for kingly ambitions. In nomad society the elite are a small group who govern by force, patronage, and guile, and prey on the cupidity of their followers. My problem, however, was not to construct new stereotypes of nomads but to see them from perspectives that will help us interpret prehistory.

The term *nomad* refers to a cultural type. Parallel terms are *peasant*, *merchant*, *explorer*, and *astronaut*; similar ones are *Big Game Hunter*, *Formative*, or *Neolithic*. These terms refer to portions of the world's population that are identified by occupation or, in the case of extinct groups, by durable remains from which their principal subsistence activities can be inferred. In short, *nomad*, like *peasant*, *merchant*, and so forth, is imprecise as to ethnic affiliation, geographic location, size of group, social organization, religion, and similar things. Like other terms we use as labels, *nomad* is useful in discourse for the images it evokes, but for precision in discussion its particular qualities in specific instances must be defined.

What do we mean by the term *nomad*? Definitions have included views that nomads represent a type of culture which is opposed to farmers; that nomads are mobile; that they are creatures of environment; that they are apt to be hostile, opportunistic, treacherous, and at the same time generous and hospitable. We also read that nomadic life represents a stage in cultural evolution, and that the role of nomads in the human drama is coming to a close. Nomads are said to depend on the animals they herd but they are also said to have close connections with settled people on whom they depend for grains and goods. Today, nomads are still found in the drier deserts and steppes of the world, but their fortunes are rapidly waning as their way of life succumbs to the assault of technology in the service of industrial society.

Nomads are marginal to the mainstream of civilization. Historical interest in them has been not in the creative forces which they have nurtured but in the terror which they have inspired. Our interests in them, however, are in their role in taming the beasts of nature, and in serving as agents of dispersal of cultural materials and ideas. Our interests are in their mode of subsistence and how it developed. How did it happen that today there are tens of millions of folk whose lives are passed in small camps in the company of animals; people whose abodes are moved periodically in response to the needs of their herds; people whose ties with antiquity seem more profound than their affiliations with the civilizations that buy their products and sell them wares today?

Rightly or wrongly, nomads are typed as a separate breed by historians and anthropologists. The normative, generalizing view emphasizes their distinctive way of life. In early history there was clearly less reason for this differentiation. Early texts from Sumer make mention of herders and describe an amiable debate over the merits of herding (Kramer 1961:203-6). Here the economic role of herders who had their god, Dumuzi, was clearly and rightly acknowledged.

Nowhere in pre-Assyrian texts are there accounts of the relations between herders and city folk. Prior to Assyrian times herding was recorded as an unexceptional component of an integrated economic and social system that Rowton (1973:203, 212) refers to as a "dimorphic chiefdom or state," first demonstrated in the kingdom of Mari in Upper Mesopotamia at the end of the third millennium B.C. Indeed there is evidence that families shifted with relative ease from life in the city to life on the steppe in response to economic opportunities. Such history as we have of ancient times suggests that nomads were little noticed precisely because they were a normal part of life. In archaeological remains we should not expect evidence of a dramatic bifurcation in style of life until mobility was significantly advanced by the use of horses and camels; then the wealth in the cities could be readily acquired and transported. (The specialized camel nomadism of modern Arabia may go back to only A.D. 200 [Dostal 1967:22]).

By 2000 B.C. some nomads had acquired horses (Drower 1969)—which most city folk could ill afford—and the skill to use them, as well as the ethic that sanctioned plundering the prosperous. Eventually, indeed, competitive predation became a way of life for many nomads, and in some instances sanctions were imposed by nomad chiefs to prevent their followers from adopting the encumbrances that civilization would entail.

It is scarcely a wonder, then, that modern observers have emphasized the flamboyant aspects of nomadism as a convenient contrast to the gentler arts and stolid predictability which support the essential qualities of civilization. But to hold such a view is of less avail in helping us understand the nomads than it is in illuminating our own prejudices.

If we wish to gain some perspectives on pastoralism in prehistory we must no longer act as if the nineteenth century A.D. or even the nineteenth century B.C. witnessed the essence of nomadic life. More-over, we must ignore the Bedouin of the desert upon their dromedaries and even the Arabs of Mesopotamia astride their Arabian steeds. Still less would we glance a second time at the donkey-riding Sleb. Rather we might turn to the tribes of the Zagros slopes, who missed most of the glorious episodes of the past just as they stand outside the course of history today. Or we might look at the horticulturalists of the U.S. Great Plains, or even the Apache buffalo hunters of prehorse days. The point is that we should look at the unexceptional nomads rather than at those whose extraordinary exploits have affected history and become the stuff of elaborate legend and myth.

The world's major plains, like the major mountainous regions, have seldom, if ever, seen the density of settlement that is commonplace along the shores and banks of major rivers. Indeed, the remoter interiors of the plains—whether they lie in the moist temperate latitudes or in the arid tropics—have often lacked any permanent settlement. The unrelenting uniformity of the flatlands is a hazard to the exposed, the unwary, and the unprepared. These same lands are a haven to the nomads with their swift mounts, portable equipment, and traditional skills. Their open sanctuary is other men's perdition, but surely it became theirs through slow adaptation rather than by sudden acquisition. As ecologists tell us, man has more opportunities in an ecotone, where environments change abruptly, than he does in the midst of a uniform sea of grass. Thus we should not expect the most "typical" riding nomads who occupy the latter areas to have much, if anything, to tell us about the origins of nomadic life. They are surely a late product of changing technology and historical opportunity.

As Rowton (1973:202) has pointed out, the tribal people of the flanks of the Zagros Mountains are probably the most useful models to guide our reconstructions. These people live in an ecotone, have until fairly recently been effectively self-sufficient, and have been relatively unaffected by the course of history with its attendant sophistication and technology.

In this region one should not imagine herders living in isolation from farmers, because there is enough variety in a typical region of the Zagros to allow, if not demand, considerable mixing of activities. Thus in one area there is more wild grain, in another better soil for planting, while a third has the best stands of oak, or an abundance of game.

Indeed, it is scarcely imaginable that, within the range which would be traversed in the course of a year by any nomadic group, there should not be similar diversity.

The area I describe includes flat lowlands, well under 1,000 feet in elevation, at the margin of the Mesopotamian Plain, where there is enough rainfall to grow grain without benefit of irrigation but in which there is enough variation in precipitation to make crops uncertain. The plain merges abruptly with foothills, some unrelievedly of gypsum, others of more beneficent limestone. Water trickles intermittently down ravines and in the wide gravel beds of seasonal streams. With increase in elevation come the first scrubby oaks, almonds, or pistachios and the lusher grasses which are stimulated by the greater rainfall and lower temperatures. Range upon range of these hills rise, separated by flat-bottomed alluvial valleys where there are major drainages, or by unstable steep-sided valleys where runoff is rapidly dissipated. Eventually one passes above the deciduous trees and enters a zone first of occasional trees, then shrubs, and finally barren rock which seasonally wears a mantle of snow.

In these mountain ranges live the wild relatives of today's domesticates and other animals: deer, gazelle, sheep, goats, cattle, pigs, hyenas, wolves, and bears. Here too are stands of barley, wheat, oats, forests of acorns, some almonds and pistachios, cherries, and other fruit. In the rivers and springs are fish, turtles, crabs, and frogs. These mountains offer the materials to support a comfortable life without excessive effort; they are an ideal habitat for man with a simple technology and the disposition and will to move seasonally. Here families could survive seasonal extremes as well as irregularly spaced natural catastrophes, so long as they could move when the need arose. Nowhere are the advantages of the ecotone and mobility more apparent than in those parts of Southwest Asia which are lush one year and barren the next. These are the upper plains and lower slopes of the mountains that embrace Mesopotamia.

In this region there are no natural incentives to specialize in either farming or herding. Indeed there are powerful natural sanctions against such behavior. Where specialized nomadism has taken hold, it has been a result of political circumstances and an elaborate enabling technology, reinforced with arbitrary sanctions against settling and accumulating wealth.

133

Rowton (1974) takes somewhat the same view by formally contrasting "external nomadism," characteristic of the great deserts and steppes, with "enclosed nomadism," where tribal peoples are in close contact with settled people seasonally or, in some instances, nearly the year round. The tribes of the Zagros fit this latter type, as do virtually all others who practice vertical transhumance. As Longrigg (1953:22) expressed it, "The Kurdish nomads moved among settled folk, the desert Arabs abode in their own empty isolated world." Rowton (1974:27-28) points out that enclosed nomadism is based both on the physical environment, which requires seasonal movement, and on the social and political interaction between the nomads and the settled people. Where the contacts are closest, a symbiosis between the peoples may arise, but when such contacts are tenuous, the political ties likewise may be tenuous.

Within their territory nomads often maintain an autonomous polity, although when circumstances are right they may be part of an integrated tribe or state which has components of nomadism, agriculture, commerce, and so on. The circumstances that encourage political integration are varied ecological zones, with their scattered resources, and the seasonal contact between the nomads and farmers. The stronger the government of the sedentary zone, the greater the likelihood of integration, for nomads have rarely imposed their rule on sedentary peoples.

During most of the era with which we are primarily concerned, peoples who comprise both sedentary and nomadic components were probably integrated socially and economically. In fact, such a pattern is typical today of the region under consideration, in spite of comments by some travelers in the 1920s that the Lurs had no permanent settlements. What is closer to the truth is that the Lurs and others have settlements when the advantages outweigh the risks—that is, in times of reasonable political stability. The last hundred years of history in the Iranian Zagros should make this principle clear.

Bearing these things in mind, we should refrain from speaking of nomads as if they are simply creatures of physical environment and recognize the important role played by social and political circumstances. A form of nomadism has existed from very early times, but it may have differed considerably from what we know as nomadism today, especially from what we recognize as "specialized" nomadism.

134

Origins of Animal Domestication

One of the curious findings of archaeology in the Zagros-Taurus region—that is, the fertile mountain and plain zone wherein conjoin the distributions of all the important domesticates—is that there is no evident continuity between the hunters of the Pleistocene Paleolithic and the farmer-herders of the Recent. In a sense this should not be surprising in view of the changes in vegetation (let alone in life-style) that are thought to have occurred: immediately after the end of the Pleistocene, forests and cereal grains invaded the Zagros habitat in which they are now found (Farrand 1972; Van Zeist 1969; H. E. Wright 1968). One is likewise struck by the dearth of terminal "Paleolithic" sites, and by the fact that we have no certain post-Pleistocene sites of purely hunter-gatherer folk.

Caves and shelters ceased to be primary loci of habitation and activity at, or soon after, the end of the Pleistocene. There was then a shift to occupation of open-air camps of some permanence, with suggestion or direct evidence of either farming or herding or both. None of these sites can presently be demonstrated, in any stratigraphic sequence or through typology, to be related directly to their Paleolithic predecessors in the area. It is as if a curtain fell at the end of the Pleistocene, and, following an intermission, the players commenced an entirely new drama on the old set. It is equally remarkable that nowhere do we have a hint of lingering hunters forced into the geographic wings. For all we know *archaeologically*, their life ceases.

The available archaeological data bear chiefly on the domestication of plants rather than of animals (Flannery 1965; G. Wright 1971). Village sites *older* than most of those of the mountain region are found on the upper Mesopotamian Plain. Both Mureybet (Cauvin 1974) and Abu Hureyra (A. M. T. Moore 1975) have Natufian-like occupations which date to about 10,500 years ago. The evidence at these sites points—although not unequivocally—toward farming (or intensive collecting) along with hunting or herding of gazelles (Legge 1972). The only sites of equivalent age in the mountain region are Zawi Chemi (Rose L. Solecki 1964) and the deposits in layer B1 Shanidar Cave (Ralph Solecki 1963:5). Although grinding stones were abundant at Zawi Chemi, there is some evidence that the site may have been a large camp of herders and collectors of wild plant foods. None of the other excavated open sites in the Zagros is older than about 9,000-9,500 years.

It is interesting, however, that epipaleolithic Kebaran sites in the Levant are as old as 16,000 years (Henry and Servello 1974). These sites contain grinding stones and sickles and seem to develop directly into the Natufian, which has long been suspected of having some relevance to the origins of food production, largely because of the "agricultural" tools and permanence of architecture at some of the larger sites (Perrot 1966). Contemporary with the Kebaran is the Zarzian of the Zagros, a set of late Paleolithic camps in caves and shelters where there are no traces whatsoever of the use of plant foods.

Further suggestions that the Zagros may be marginal to the origins of agriculture comes from Egyptian Nubia, where Qadan sites in the same general technological stage of development as the Kebaran also include sickles and grinding stones and date back some 15,000 years (Wendorf 1968:940-46). Farther south in the Sudan the story is repeated in sites of similar age.

Perhaps most interesting is that some of the Kebaran and Natufian and all of the Egyptian and Sudanese sites are in areas which today cannot support wild grains because there is too little precipitation (Wendorf 1968:946). We are reminded that studies of pollen show a cooler and drier climate in the Zagros during the later stages of the Pleistocene and that wheat and barley were not present. Following the Pleistocene there are scattered but persuasive hints of climatic changes which were great enough to have affected strongly the distribution of plants in the drier parts of Southwest Asia (Blake 1969). Without being able to specify conditions precisely, we can suggest that the present distribution of the wild domesticates may not be very illustrative of their spread at the times we are concerned with archaeologically. The climatic and vegetational history of Southwest Asia is clearly a topic that needs vigorous investigation.

Rather than trying to be too precise, it seems more useful to suggest that, at least as early as the late Pleistocene, some groups of people who lived in the drier parts of Southwest Asia had developed a series of adaptations to grasslands in which the gathering and processing of seeds was an important part of the subsistence activities. Evidence suggests that hunting was a major pursuit as well, and that a pattern of seasonal movement within a circumscribed area was established. There is no evidence in this region yet of food production or of domestication. Rather, we have the oldest evidence of *patterns* of behavior which characterized later peoples who practiced mixed farming and herding. The sickles and grinding tools for the planting and processing of cereals, and the patterns of seasonal movement, were well established and must, in my view, have constituted prerequisites to the final shift to domestication.

Although the early cereal grains may have been more widely distributed than today, there is no evidence that sheep and goats were similarly scattered. These two species have apparently always been either in the mountains or on the steppelands at the verge of the Mesopotamian Plain and the Zagros-Taurus ranges. Elsewhere the most abundant ungulates are gazelles, deer, and antelope, none of which was domesticated (or lasted as a domesticate into historic times). The restricted distribution of sheep and goats relates closely to topography and secondarily to aridity, because both species require water frequently and prefer rolling or rocky topography.

The distribution of sheep and goats suggests the possibility that they were domesticated independently of cereals. We can refer again to the available dates to support this possibility. No domestic animals have yet been identified which even approach the age of Kebaran sites where plant processing is attested, and only Zawi Chemi, where sheep may be domestic, is as old as Mureybet, where only hunting is claimed. Finally, *if* sites in the mountains with domestic animals were found to be of Pleistocene age, there would not (on available evidence) have been any grains in the environment for people to use.

The actual archaeological evidence of pastoralism is meager. Only one excavated site, Tepe Tula'i in Khuzistan, Iran, has been identified as the camp of nomads (Hole 1975). It dates to around 6000 B.C. Contemporary with this site are settled farming villages and some surface scatters of chipped stone and/or ceramics whose location suggests pastoral rather than farming activities. Earlier than 6000 B.C. we have a series of villages at which mixed farming and husbandry were practiced, such as Ali Kosh, Jarmo, and Guran. Possible camps of pastoral peoples of about the same age are at Sarab, basal Guran, and Ganj-Darreh (Mortensen 1972). In Anatolia the somewhat older Suberde is thought to have been a hunter's village, although this seems implausible in view of its size and permanence (Bordaz 1970; Perkins and Daly 1968). At all of these sites there was continuous settlement (perhaps seasonally) as evidenced by the accumulation of debris, if not always by the permanence of architecture. It is also striking that at most of these sites agricultural tools—sickles and grinding stones—are present even though the insubstantial architecture and animal remains suggest that they were pastoral camps rather than villages. On the basis of the limited available evidence we are certainly not assured that there were *any* herders (or settled hunters?) who eschewed agriculture entirely prior to very recent times.

It is apparent that we have not considered vast areas in which nomadism is practiced today; we simply have no useful information on the huge stretches of desert and steppe. On the other hand, as noted earlier, we have no reason to think that pastoralism, separate from farming *or* gathering of plant foods, is anything but a late aberration from an ancient lifeway. The most ancient pastoralists of whom we have evidence seem to have been as closely linked to the availability of plant food for themselves as they were to pasturage for their stock. Although in part this reflects the places where archaeologists have looked, it is probably an accurate picture. Early herders probably preferred those regions where dry farming could be practiced. Thus, by coincidence or not, gathering (or farming) and herding would have been complementary components of their way of life.

In some areas herding might be possible without agriculture (as in Luristan today), and elsewhere collecting and processing of plant foods may have provided the mainstay of the diet. Nevertheless, it appears that when herding was combined with farming (no later than 7000 B.C.) numerous villages of greater size than antecedent camps were established and that from this point onward there was a rapid increase in population, expressed as an increase in the number of villages. One is tempted to see these two dietary components as having had a mutual impact on the history of mankind which one alone would not have had.

It is for this reason, rather than because of any assumption of necessary absolute priority of farming in human history, that we are concerned with early evidence of plant processing. An equally compelling reason is that, as stated earlier, we have no unequivocal data to support the idea that there was domestication of animals during the Pleistocene or that habits of tending them were being developed.

With these things in mind we must question whether we can learn about the origins and early development of domestication if we remain fixed to the post-Pleistocene period. Clearly this span encompasses the establishment of an effective food production and its crystallization as a way of life, but it may tell us little about its origins. Origins should probably be sought in people who developed a technology for the large-scale processing of cereals or other plants, and the means of storage. These developments imply the establishment of base camps and a relegation of hunting/herding to ancillary importance in subsistence, whatever its economic or social role may have been.

The regular eating of meat may have been a novelty for the ancestors of pastoralists; hunters often alternate between feast and famine. Hunters had to anticipate the presence of a herd (of many, few, or only one animal[s]) and then invade it; they must have missed as often as not. What herding did was to keep the animals close by, to bring them within easy range, and to keep them for certain use. This could have been accomplished with or without the farming of crops—all that was required was that sufficient vegetable food be available year round for both man and beast. As we know from Ute Indian history, when men and animals compete for the same food in arid areas, it is the animals who give way. In the Ute case men gave up horses in the more marginal areas, a practice also followed by many other peoples, ancient and modern (including ourselves), who might own livestock more for prestige than for use.

If it is true that man did not require agriculture to provide the resource base to tame and feed animals, it is probably only coincidental that where pastoralism was first practiced (because animals do well there), men can also live well off the same raw foods—the various grains, acorns, and other vegetation. Once the pattern of tending flocks was established, the herding component might have been moved farther from the primary agricultural areas until it eventually came to be identified with desert and steppe zones. The farther these movements, however, the more the lifeway had to be tied to a supplementary food supply which could be ensured through raiding, markets, or symbiotic relations with farmers.

NOMADS OF LURISTAN

The Ethnographic Project

In the spring of 1973 I spent several months visiting nomad camps and carrying out an archaeological survey of their territories. During this time I also joined one camp of Luri nomads while they made their annual migration from their winter to their summer pasture.

The Baharvand are a tribe of Luri-speaking people, about one-fourth of whom still pursue full-time pastoralism. Fifty years ago the tribe was entirely pastoral, but since then it has been largely settled into agricultural villages as a result of government policy. (Efforts are under way to settle the remaining nomads in Iran as quickly as possible.) Today these people occupy terrain which they have used since the tribe was founded, some 425 years ago. The boundaries of the territory are somewhat more restricted and movements more circumscribed now than at the tribe's peak during the nineteenth century, but for practical purposes individual camps follow exactly the same patterns they always have (Amanolahi-Baharvand 1975). Thus in studying the nomads today we have a glimpse into practices that are known to have characterized the area well before modern politics intervened and before modern commodities were introduced. The Baharvand are isolated. They have played minor roles in major events and no roles at all in minor chapters of Iranian history. Their isolation is shared by thousands of similar tribespeople of Luri and Bakhtiari affiliation.

These nomads keep sheep, goats, and cows for subsistence and maintain donkeys, mules, and horses for packing and riding. Significantly, however, all of the subsistence and life-support activities can be carried out on foot; the pack animals carry tents and baggage, and horses are ridden for prestige, but neither is absolutely necessary. In an elementary sense these larger animals are a drain on the resources and an unnecessary, though much prized, luxury.

The territory consists of rugged mountains, relatively small stretches of bottomland plain, and few sources of flowing water; it suffers intense heat during the dry summers and intense cold during the wet winters. The winter pastures are in low-lying valleys where there is shelter from wind, and the summer pastures are at the edge of the snow line. The latter lie amid forests, whereas the winter grounds are barren of trees. Oaks are the predominant species of tree; there are also quantities of wild fruits, shrubs, aromatic plants, and wild cereals. Both humans and herds depend on the oaks for food. Formerly there were many wild goats, sheep, pigs, bears, and gazelles in the territory, but these have been hunted to near extinction since the introduction of shotguns.

Following a wet winter, Luristan turns emerald green and the bottoms of many valleys hold water in lakes for weeks at a time. Cold years will see the entire territory blanketed with snow, sometimes to considerable depth in the higher valleys. In dry years the green never overcomes the brown, and dust obscures the rows of mountain ridges. Overly wet or overly dry years occur with ominous regularity. A "normal" year is hard to describe and harder still to find.

Environmental Aspects of Animal Husbandry

In western Iran weather is highly variable from year to year. Although weather records are not available for long periods in most of the area occupied by the nomads, in Khuzistan, the winter territory, precipitation may vary fourfold from one year to the next. Equally important is the month of its onset and its spacing through the ensuing months. The variability is such that one cannot predict accurately whether it will rain in a given month, let alone in any week. People who live in the area assume that two or three out of five crops will either fail outright or be so poor as to make the work and cost of planting hardly worthwhile.

To a similar degree, but possibly with lesser effect, precipitation in the mountains varies. There, however, snowfall is an added complication which can cause as much suffering and death if it is too heavy as it can if it fails to soak the ground sufficiently. In general, conditions are better in the mountains than on the Khuzistan Plain. That means that one or two crops out of five may fail.

Weather statistics are measures of amounts but not of effects. Rarely have persons reported the annual variations in terms that relate them to actual life instead of to bushels of grain or head of sheep. From the notes of one archaeologist who has done so during several seasons' work in an environment very similar to Deh Luran, we can take the following comments.

The winter of 1970-71 was one of total drought. Rain, in the form of torrential thunderstorms, came in April. All the villages were abandoned. (Kirkbride 1972:4)

The 1972 season at Umm Dabaghiyah took place under vastly different conditions from the first year. An exceptionally good spring turned the countryside into a comparatively green and flowery land. Without a single dust storm and with thunder and rain only during the evenings and nights, we were able to work without interruption. (Kirkbride 1973a:1)

The 1973 season at Umm Dabaghiyah took place under weather conditions different from those of the two preceding ones. The exceptionally good spring of 1972, and subsequent heavy dew, enabled the scrub vegetation to come up and thus to hold the surface soil in place despite high winds and a practically total drought. In 1973, we had neither rain, apart from a few sparse drops, nor a single thunderstorm, while the real dust-storms started only late in May despite the high winds that were a constant factor. (Kirkbride 1973b:205)

The start of the fourth and final season at Umm Dabaghiyah was seriously delayed by yet another variation in the Iraq weather pattern. In this case torrential and long-lasting late spring rains not only caused wide-spread flooding throughout the country, but also brought down the bridges across Wadi Tharthar. . . . Once the camp was established the weather relented and we were able to work almost without interruption. The delay did mean that we had to work in ever-increasing heat. Let it suffice to say that the June shade temperatures, taken under a tent flap as no shade is available at the site, kept steadily in the upper 40°s C with a maximum of 49°C (c. 126 F). It may be worth recording while memory is fresh that during this hot period the flies, of which we had over-many, simply lay still on the tent floors apparently incapable of flying. (Kirkbride 1974:3)

From the nomads I also got information on really bad years, years that are used as relative dates for other events. These are years that everyone knows about, thanks God if he lived through them, and dreads that the future will inevitably bring another. Oldsters often referred to *barf sal*, the year of the snow. Few are now alive who remember this tragedy, which occurred in approximately 1911 (Amanolahi-Baharvand 1975:41). More recently, there were two years of famine, 1941 and 1948, which brought appalling mortality.

The year after we did our study, extremely heavy snows and temperatures below zero in the mountains resulted in the deaths of huge numbers of livestock and of many of the nomads too. The following spring meltwater caused heavy flooding, thus adding to the general misery, especially in the lower valleys, where there is extensive agriculture. (This is 1974, which Kirkbride documents as a year of heavy rains and flooding.)

The nomads see these fluctuations as just another of the ills that

142

beset them. If one had only to worry about rainfall, life would be relatively secure. In the "normal" course of events nomads should prosper even when farming is unprofitable, because with mobility they can and do seek out the remoter pastures which are "banked" against time of dire want and not used at all in good years (a practice of Bedouin Arabs also). What are as distressing to nomads as variations in rain are the animal diseases and, formerly, the raids, attacks by wolves, and so on to which even the most prosperous were vulnerable.

I was able to collect much information on diseases, although I have not accurately identified all of them in medical terms. My information comes from interviews with nomads who described symptoms and effects, and with veterinarians assigned to a research project in Khuzistan.

There are two noteworthy findings. First, all informants agree that disease has increased since nomadism has been curtailed and nomads have been settled as farmers. Second, disease decimates herds every few years, evidently largely independently of the rainfall cycle and the fate of crops. In this connection it is useful to review some statistics on sheep and goats. Both species are able to reproduce by their second year and, if conditions are good, to give birth twice a year. They continue to breed until they are 9 to 10 years old. Thus an animal can have as many as 16 offspring in its lifetime. Under these conditions one would expect herds to increase dramatically even if all but a few males are sold or killed for food. As Barth (1964) has pointed out, herding potentially allows one to go from rags to riches in a few years. However, one seldom sees a rich nomad.

The reason is that there is great variation in the actual increase of herds as a result of environmental, pathological, and economic factors. For example, although my informants all said that sheep and goats will breed twice a year if pastures are good, Jacob Black (1972:626) heard that double lambing is unknown and twinning rare among the Lur flocks. Since he studied people only a few miles from where I was working, his information is suspect, but it may reflect the fact that the group he studied is sedentary. He also reports that "a single ewe is not likely to produce in her life more than *one* female lamb which will survive to reproductive age." Although I have no numerical data to contradict the last statement, none of my informants found it credible. It is true, however, that sheep raised by Arabs on the Deh Luran Plain produce only once a year. This is clearly a result of the lack of green

143

pasture coupled with extreme heat for half the year and it is probably true of stock kept in southern Mesopotamia throughout history.

In full recognition of the inherent uncertainty in applying averages, ideals, and typical figures, it is still instructive to see what *could* happen under ideal conditions with a herd of sheep and goats. Table 6.1 shows how a herd might increase and reveals some interesting factors that bear on the strategy of building and using a herd. In spite of the fact that the table does not reflect actual (modern) conditions, herders act in accordance with its underlying logic.

The table shows that during the first four and a half years there is no substantial addition to the *breeding* crop. Once new breed ewes start coming into the system at the rate of two or more a year, the population begins to grow rapidly. Since the first two years in the life of an animal are unproductive but costly, it makes economic sense to kill or sell lambs and yearlings and to buy breed stock. Considering the hazards of raising animals, there is a relatively low probability of their reaching maturity, so they are cheap. It is an inexpensive gesture to use lambs and kids for sacrifice, gifts, and so on, and it may even represent a savings because of the costs of raising animals. It also follows that the strategy in raiding should be to capture breed ewes, whereas one should pay a hired herder with lambs and sell only aged or infertile ewes on the market.

According to one Deh Luran informant, disease will kill one-third to one-half of a herd every three to seven years, but sometimes it will strike two years in a row. When this happens a herd of 200 can be reduced to a few animals. The same informant also said that in dry years, when there is not enough grass, the mortality may be worse than when there is disease. When we recall that at least a mild drought occurs three out of five years in Deh Luran, we can quickly recognize that without mobility there is limited potential for economic growth. Even though nomads can take herds to good pastures, the livestock must also have sufficient water. Depending on the heat and moisture in the grass, the animals may require drinks one to three times a day. This requirement effectively prevents use of certain pastures except in wet years, when they are probably not needed. Thus, although mobility reduces certain hazards, it does not eliminate them.

Herders also fear predators, especially during hard years, although most suffer relatively small losses from wolves today because numbers of wolves have been greatly reduced. However, one informant in

144

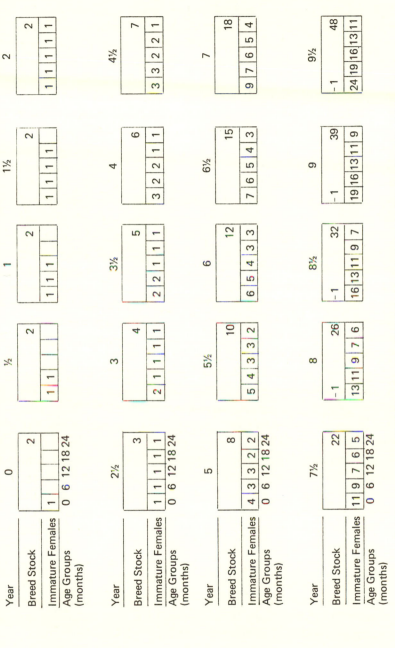

TABLE 6.1 EXPECTED MAXIMUM GROWTH OF A HERD OF SHEEP OR GOATS, based on the following assumptions: Each breed animal (age 2 +) gives birth twice a year. There are no mortalities other than the male animals which are all killed for food (except for a few stud animals). At year 0 there are two breed stock and each is expected to produce one female each year. If half the birth are males, only half of the total births are contributing toward the future growth of the herd. In this example .5 is always rounded to the lowest whole number. The original breeding stock begins to die in year 8.

Saimarreh said that he lost all but 5 of a herd of 90 animals in a raid by wolves just before NoRuz (spring equinox) one year.

Since informants agreed that today's circumstances are not typical of past conditions, we tried to elicit specific information on what nomads consider to be ideal and what conditions were like in former times.

We have already noted that disease is more prevalent today, but we have not commented on the relatively small herds held by most individuals. To give an example, the group that I traveled with was composed of five households, including an elder tribal leader, with a total of about 20 persons of all ages. The entire camp held fewer than 200 head of sheep and goats: specifically, 53 ewes, 1 ram, 112 she-goats, and 5 billy goats. Lambs and kids were not counted in these totals, nor were the breed stock separated from younger animals. The important point is that informants agree that a family needs about 200 animals to ensure a reasonable standard of living. This size herd can be managed easily by the herders and the women who must milk them. More animals are difficult for a typical family to manage, although wealthy persons sometimes have herds several times that large. Clearly most nomads today live at a lower standard than they would like.

Formerly, we were told, the nomads were fewer, sedentary farmers in tribal territory scarcely existed, and herds were much larger. Then, nomads told me, they ate meat every day. As we learned, the members of a camp traditionally share meat. If the camp of about 20 people held in the neighborhood of 1,000 animals, there would have been more than enough meat if they had killed just the males and aged females even with natural attrition of the herds. The situation, today, where tribal people eat meat only once every month or two, is due partly to the small size of herds and partly to the high cost of meat. The nomads can get more for their animals than they are worth to them as meat. "Who is the man who can afford to kill a goat?" is the way one man put it.

Historical Perspective on Pastoralism and Luristan

With so much emphasis in archaeology on trade, interaction networks, sustaining areas, and symbiotic regions, it is surprising to learn how isolated many of the Luri nomads were until this century, in spite of the caravan routes that crossed their territory and the sizable

146

towns that were near either end of their migration route. The oldest informants (in their eighties) provided information that will startle those who may think that people will automatically head for the market when there is the opportunity and that they will be informed whenever goods are available. Atawak, the oldest among the Baharvand informants, recalled how in his youth there was no cloth for sale in the stores. Clothing was made by the women from coarse spun wool, goat hair (it scratches!), or felt. The clothes for people were the same as the blankets and pads used today on animals. Atawak said that he had never heard of anyone using animal skins for clothing. He also said that the tribe went barefoot. This was surprising because early travelers reported the use of *givas*, ubiquitous footware until the advent of the cheap molded-rubber shoes that are sold today. Atawak said that an entire family of seven might have one pair of *givas*. The shoes were made in town but had to be ordered six months in advance, as the shopkeepers did not maintain a stock. (Six months reflects the migration schedule.)

The people had more animals in the past, but they rarely sold them, because markets were inaccessible and the prices of animals were too low. For example, I once heard that a lamb sold for 15 rials (20 cents). At those prices it was not worth selling them except for absolute essentials. Today, whatever the cost, the Lurs feel that they must obtain tea and sugar, but in Atawak's youth tea was unknown and sugar was used only once a year, at the feast of the dead. The people drank only milk or water. Since tea is a universal drink in Iran, I was startled at this information. Subsequent questioning of other elderly informants elsewhere in western Iran, however, confirmed that only those who were near cities or directly on migration routes drank tea.

Atawak also informed us that formerly the population was smaller, herds were larger, and wild game abounded. He said he ate meat every day, often hunting wild game rather than consuming his own herds. Nevertheless, since animals were not sold, half of each year's crop was available for slaughter. He said that it was the modern shotgun which did in the game; the old single-shot muzzle loaders were not as effective.

Atawak said repeatedly that in his early days it was not the habit of nomads to farm. He recalls subsisting chiefly on meat and acorn preparations, although occasionally he would have rice (a product which was obtained in the market) and chicken.

It was interesting to learn his impressions of changes in the environment. Formerly, he said, the forests were much more extensive; in many places it was difficult to walk because of the density of vegetation. This corresponds with my own impressions based on the vestiges of forests now and the rate at which they are being cut. When the forests were more extensive there was less grazing land, but there would have been more acorns and wild game. Atawak also recalls greater rainfall and snows in his youth. This recollection is probably incorrect if our weather records are at all informative; however, the decimation of the forests and heavy erosion has certainly reduced the effective moisture available in the ground.

Formerly the nomads used wooden vessels made by gypsies who live in tribal territory, and they made occasional purchases of metal pots in the bazaar. Little has changed in this pattern of acquiring utensils. Atawak stressed that nothing basic in the pastoral way of life has changed. What has changed, he says, is that people have become more acquisitive and they are now burdened on migration by excessive baggage which requires more pack animals and labor. These problems, coupled with the decline in cooperation, make nomadism more difficult.

All nomads agree that conditions today are much worse than formerly, chiefly in that there are too many people, too few animals, and not enough land. When there was little farming, all land that was not heavy forest was available for grazing, and when there were fewer nomads, each family had herds large enough to provide self-sufficiency.

North of Khorramabad is a small plateau on which there are numerous archaeological sites. While we were surveying there we questioned some old informants who gave us some totally unexpected information. Although the plateau is now settled, in the memory of our informants it was not. It was farmed, however, by people who lived in Khorramabad. (Incidentally, only in the valley around Khorramabad were there settled villages in Luristan in the nineteenth century.) These people used no draft animals in plowing; men drew the plows. Moreover, when they harvested the grain they did not use sickles; all of the grain was hand stripped. Each harvester had a cloth bag slung over each shoulder into which he dropped the heads of grain. The straw was simply left in the fields. Finally, threshing was done by men walking on the grain or using flails. If there is an ethnographic description of

148

farming practices closer to what we might infer for the incipient stages of domestication, I do not know of it.

Mobility

Although the reason for seasonal movement is well known, the means of movement has not been much considered. At issue is whether it is possible to be nomadic without pack animals or equipment which would not have been available in prehistoric times. The answer to both parts of the question is a decisive "yes." There is nothing in the vertical transhumance which characterizes much of Southwest Asia that would not have been possible without pack animals.

Today transhumance is almost unthinkable without donkeys, horses, or mules to carry the tents, bedding, and other gear. Nevertheless, if the movements are relatively slow, much gear can be packed by people even today. However, one would expect that shelters were not carried from one site to another in prehistoric times. Assuming that vegetation was no sparser than today, it would be feasible for people to have built shelters at each stop where they were needed. During clement weather they may have eschewed roofs entirely as nomads do now during migration.

If we leave tents out of the picture, we are left with bedding, utensils, and various tools to move. Even today bedding is likely to consist chiefly of a ground cover (a rug or mat), one's clothes, and a blanket of some sort. In warm weather, of course, bedding is scarcely needed. There is nothing necessary for warmth that cannot be carried by an adult, although bedding today is often bulky because of pillows, spare blankets, and rugs. With judicious movements that avoided climatic extremes, little bedding would have been necessary. The pastures that are subject to snow may not have been used in early times except perhaps as hunting grounds.

Nomads are usually thought not to have pottery. None of the people I traveled with had any bowls or jars, although they did have metal or porcelain tea pots and glasses. The functional equivalents to ceramic containers are copper bowls and jugs, and skin bags. Even villagers use essentially the same utensils, although they may have ceramic jugs for cooling water. In western Iran pottery is little used for domestic utensils; today all cooking is done in metal pots or on spits over an open fire.

149

Formerly wooden vessels were widely used. These utensils, made locally, go back an undetermined time into the past. Recently they were made on lathes, and their precursors may have been made with adzes. Metal vessels probably have as long a history in Luristan as the lathe-made wooden bowls. We should expect, however, that the nomads used pottery. Since the pastoral people of the Zagros typically stay in one place for months at a time, there is no reason that they should not have made and used pots. The main problem is that ceramics would not hold up well under the strains of migration if pack animals were used. Because of the techniques of packing, the rugged terrain, and the movements of the animals, baggage suffers greatly when it is packed on animals. We know from Mexican examples, however, that pots are carried routinely by human porters over great distances to market. Thus, until they began to use metal vessels, there is no obvious reason why nomads should not have had pottery.

Knives and some kind of weapon—arrows, spears, or clubs (maces)—are about the only other tools that would be needed. Anything else might be made on the spot and would probably not be carried on journeys.

One would imagine that early pastoral peoples had little baggage, and that if they had more than could be carried at one time, it was moved in stages, as is the custom today when people have too few pack animals. As Atawak said, today life is harder because people have too many things. He was voicing the same idea that was expressed first in Latin (and later in English) by the term *impedimenta*, which refers to baggage, especially that which was carried by soldiers on the march (in Caesar's Gallic wars).

Nomad Sites and Facilities

The tent is the characteristic nomad dwelling, but the summer *coola*, a structure of poles and branches, is also typical of the people of Luristan. Elsewhere in Iran, insubstantial houses or shelters are made of reeds. Many peoples of western Iran today live in mud houses in a village and migrate with their herds to summer pastures where they may use either tents or *coolas*. Even nomads who live the year round in tents are likely to have different kinds of camp sites in the different seasons. Thus the appearance of nomad camps changes with the season.

150

The Baharvand pass the winter in Chin-i-Zal, a valley where there is seldom snow in winter, although strong cold winds from the west and rains from the east regularly rake it. Winter tent sites are always placed with the long axis running east-west so that wind will hit an end rather than the longer front or back. In addition, fieldstone walls are piled up around three and sometimes four sides of the tent to screen out the wind. Such tent sites are used for about three months during the coldest part of the year. When the weather permits, nomads move away from the stone-enclosed sites to others which allow freer passage of wind. The latter may be only a few hundred meters away.

At a minimum, whether the tent site has walls or not, it will include a pavement of stones along the back wall so that bedding can be kept dry; usually another pavement at the front where skin bags are kept; a small fireplace toward the center; a ditch or line of stones or small postholes marking the perimeter; large midline postholes; and an ash-disposal area in front of the tent. A summer *coola* has essentially the same features, although the fireplace may be outside.

Within a campsite, the tents will be clustered together rather closely—around ten meters apart. The tents are often arranged in two rows, sometimes on either side of a corral. The position of the tents depends on a number of factors: availability of level land, size of herds, season, and relationship of the people living in the tents. All informants agree that the tents in any camp always have the same relative spatial relationship to one another. However, because of other factors noted above, the *actual* spatial relationships may differ greatly from one camp to another. What is constant is that in any camp the tents are clearly clustered so that none is exposed in isolation. In descending order of importance, the requirements for tent sites are: level land, pasturage, water. Men pick the sites and herd the animals; women fetch the water.

During the season when young are born, the baby animals are kept inside the tents at night. One end of the tent is reserved for these animals, who are usually provided with a floor of branches to help reduce the mud and dust. Needless to say, this practice of penning the animals inside results in a consolidation of dung, a fact which enables one easily to tell when a site was occupied.

The older animals are kept in an area among the tents. Sometimes the space between tents is enclosed with a low brush fence and the animals are kept penned there overnight. Again, this results in a concentration of dung and tightly compacted earth. For the most part, however, the nomads whom I observed did not make much use of corrals. In some areas, however, corrals are built out of fieldstones and seem to be used chiefly for baby animals.

In the winter, animals are sometimes kept in caves or rock shelters. When we were digging Paleolithic sites we often found as much as a meter of dung and ash resulting from this practice above the Pleistocene deposits. The nomads of Chin-i-Zal sometimes use small shelters along the river as pens, although they are more often used for storage of straw. In Iraqi Kurdistan, Ralph Solecki found that Herki nomads live in Shanidar Cave during the winter, setting up a tent camp much as they would outdoors in the summer. In prehistoric deposits at Kunji Cave we found small circular areas outlined with rocks which may have been tent sites.

Another kind of buildinglike structure is sometimes found in nomad sites. This is an open shelter, consisting of three walls, at some distance from the tent sites. Such a shelter is oriented, like the tents, against the prevailing winds, but its open side catches the morning sun. The side and back walls reflect the heat and create an ovenlike effect inside which makes the shelter pleasant on chill mornings. In warmer weather the back wall shields the interior from the afternoon sun and thus makes the shelter cooler than outside. These structures, used by men as lounges and meeting places, contain no evidence of domestic activities.

Throughout western Iran one sees analogous structures in villages, where men erect a simple mud wall in an open area. Depending on the temperature, they sit on the sunny or the shady side. In villages where such walls are not to be found, house walls serve the same purpose, and one sees men lined up along them as they while away the day.

Another kind of structure, which I have seen only once, is a den dug into a hillside for a bitch with pups. The nomads' guard dogs are normally fierce, but with pups they are said to be too dangerous even for owners to approach. Nomads thus provide a place for them some distance from camp. In the instance which I observed, a small cave was dug into the hillside about a hundred meters from camp.

Where nomads do some farming, they usually have buildings or bins in which to store the grain while they are away. Since grain ripens in the winter pasture about the time the nomads must leave, and it does the same in the summer pasture, it is stored until the people return. In

Chin-i-Zal some bins were dug into an ancient archaeological site, another was a dry sinkhole with a small opening, and some standing buildings in a Sasanian site were also used. Grain bins are variable in size but tend to be on the order of 2.5 to 5.5 cubic meters (they hold about 70 to 150 bushels of grain). In shape, the bins tend toward the rectangular, although right angles are not emphasized. The walls are of mud or of stone plastered with mud, and the contents are sealed with mud mixed with straw. Bins are altered as necessary to accommodate the size of the crop.

Although the bins are left untended, there are usually few people around to bother them, and in times past when there was constant conflict there was no farming anyway. Bins are close to fields and threshing floors rather than alongside tent sites. Tent sites are placed for reasons of shelter and the like, rather than for proximity to fields, which are moved from year to year to allow for fallowing and to take advantage of local moisture.

In addition to grain, nomads cut straw, which is stored for use as animal fodder when they return during the fall. The herds at that time will need both straw and barley as supplementary food unless there are unusually early rains. In Chin-i-Zal, straw is kept in some of the vaulted buildings still standing in the Sasanian site and in natural rock shelters along the river. The latter, which are difficult of access, have dry-laid stone walls in front.

During our travels we occasionally found grain bins along migration routes and near arable land. We also found one cave in which bins had been carefully made of stones which were entirely plastered over, inside and out. These bins made use of the ceiling and back walls of the cave and could be entered only through small openings near the top. Probably of relatively recent age, the bins had been vandalized in the last year or so.

Nomads go to little effort to improve their territories; however, with water as scarce as it is, a number of springs have been altered. In most cases seeps have been cleaned out, sometimes lined with stones, and provided with stock troughs at the overflows. In numerous places in Western Iran, nomads have dug wells, usually in the bottoms of wadis. Most of these are shallow, and they are usually accompanied by stock troughs.

Although I have not seen or heard of instances where nomads irrigate natural stands of grass, nomads who farm often make use of ancient canals and terraces. Today's farmers, however, are doing little to improve the deteriorated condition of these facilities and in many instances are causing damage to them.

Throughout the migration areas we found mills. Most of these probably date back to Sasanian times originally, although many have been in use recently. Until power mills became available in towns and villages, the nomads depended on water power to grind their grain. I saw no instances of the use of manos and metates and have never heard of their being used, although stone mortars and pestles are still used. The mills are alongside streams where sufficient water can be channeled to turn a large stone wheel. James Neely excavated one of these in Deh Luran which was in use only a few decades ago. It seems unlikely that nomads were responsible for building the mills. In some cases they are demonstrably of ancient age; in others they were said to have been operated by persons from town who took a proportion of the flour from the nomads as payment.

More representative of the way many of the Luri nomads lived are the acorn smashers and kilns. For the bulk processing of acorns it was necessary to roast them and grind them into flour. The roasters are simply rectangular stone structures about a meter and a half on a side and of a similar height. These roofless buildings will be found in the mountains where there are oaks; there will not necessarily be campgrounds in the immediate vicinity. Nearby is likely to be a large rock on which another large rock sits. These are crushers, very large "manos and metates." One that I photographed has a boulder base and an upper stone which was simply rocked back and forth, as it is too large to pick up. The size of all the acorn smashers I saw greatly exceeds that of manos and metates in archaeological village sites, although there is no reason why this should always be the case.

Nomads also leave piles of rock atop passes and sometimes alongside trails which pass by important shrines. The stones are added one by one by passersby who are thankful for having made a safe ascent or who are hopeful of favors. Women in our group made prayerful offerings at a number of such places in the hope of conceiving male babies. At some of these sites there are hundreds of piles of rocks, testifying to hundreds if not thousands of years of passage and prayer. In a type of such shrine which I have noticed only in Luristan, sticks are pounded into the ground although stones are readily available. I was unable to determine any difference in expectation; apparently it

154

was simply customary at some places to place sticks rather than stones. Finally, we may mention that today pilgrims and supplicants often tie bits of clothing or hair to bushes, trees, rock cairns, and so on. One sees this also in mosques and shrines in towns, where padlocks, cloth, and locks of hair may be attached to gates and doors.

Finally we may consider structures for the dead. Today nomads usually bury their dead in a simple grave in the nearest convenient spot. Formerly there was a practice in some areas, possibly exclusively in southern Kurdistan, of constructing a "house" for a tribal leader who died without male heirs. Quite by accident we ran across a number of these while on survey and later learned from informants that the practice has died out but was formerly quite common. It is so old in some places as to defy the memories of today's inhabitants (Edelberg 1966-67:397). The "houses" in these sites consist of carefully made outlines in stone, with fireplaces and doorways. They never had walls or superstructures, they were never lived in, and there are no artifacts in association with them. Some that we visited were accompanied by stone cairns with memorial plaques set into them, but in no instance was the body put either in the cairn or near the site. The "houses" were placed in traditional tribal territory in places which were thought to have been favored by the deceased, especially on hills overlooking pastureland.

Although nomads are thought to leave few tangible remains, we can see that this is not necessarily the case. Of course, some of the things which they use—storage bins, shrines, and mills—may be used by farming people too. What makes them recognizably nomad remains is their location. Much nomadic terrane is now and always has been far removed from settlements.

CONCLUDING GENERALIZATIONS

Social Factors in Modern Nomadism

Transhumance is an adaptation which allows the keeping of livestock in areas of marked seasonal changes in pastures where farming is practiced little, if at all. Two distinct patterns of pastoralism are recognized—vertical and horizontal, or enclosed and open. The former pastoralists encounter and may be surrounded by settled people as they migrate through their territory. The latter encounter settled people only by choice and are more likely to exist as distinct polities. The enclosed nomads are often integrated into administrative systems which include city as well as tribal folk. The enclosed nomads most often herd sheep and goats, whereas horses and camels are the preferred stock of the open-plain nomads. We have dealt in this paper only with enclosed nomads who live in lands where agriculture can be practiced and who are in close contact with farming people. Today all these people do some farming and the majority of people in most tribes are settled in villages.

The circumstances today are not typical, if we believe oral tradition and the little historical information at our disposal. Formerly a much larger proportion of people lived the year round in tents, and some nomads never came into contact with settled people. Today's situation is instructive, however, because it illustrates what nomads do in times of stress and thereby gives us some clues about how certain social factors shape the way of life itself.

One way to express the importance of social factors is to begin with the basic fact of nomadic life and see what its implications are: herds must move seasonally so that they can obtain sufficient forage and fodder. This can be accomplished most easily when there are relatively few livestock, because then it may be necessary to move only very short distances to secure fresh forage. When the number of animals exceeds the capacity of pastures to support them, however, nomads may respond by taking the herds to more distant pastures, forcing them to endure on less forage, or allowing them to strip damaging amounts of vegetation from the pastures. Only the first alternative has long-term viability, although the second may leave the animals only in poor rather than in grave condition. An entirely different kind of solution is for people to raise fodder and feed it to livestock during months when the pastures near home are poor. This practice is routine among farmers who cut straw from their fields and raise barley for the animals in addition to wheat for human consumption. Thus a single set of circumstances may lead to quite different responses: increased nomadism or increased sedentism. Both kinds of solutions have been and continue to be employed in as many combinations as one can imagine.

A third response to overcrowded pastures might be to reduce the size of herds. This implies a kind of control which might be employed by an individual, but probably not by whole groups because of the inherent

156

uncertainty in herding. Large herds are a much better hedge against disaster than small herds, and they can regenerate more quickly. In the psychology of a herder, "more is better."

Assuming that people opt to expand herding territories rather than reduce their standard of living and expose themselves to unnecessary hazards, they will seek virgin lands and, when necessary, compete with other groups for good pastures and for the routes to them. Thus a simple need to move will set in motion activities that require a flexible social structure which can expand or contract as the need arises. Manpower is required during long moves to handle the animals and provide security for flocks and people. Once dispersed, however, smaller groups are advantageous.

Tribal history is largely one of conflict among neighboring tribes over grazing lands. The tribes who command the greatest number of fighting men have an advantage, but the arts of politics, especially when they are backed with the threat of force, often serve as well as the sword or gun.

In Luristan we are seeing today what has happened before on a smaller scale: farming people are spreading at the expense of herders. In this regard, there are a number of factors to consider. First, any land that can be farmed is potential pasture, and extensive farms thus remove extensive areas of pasture from pastoralist use. Second, settlements may block routes of migration and prevent free use of resources other than grass. Water and fuel (trees) may be either depleted or protected as a result of heavy use by settled people. Settlements also imply that people stay in an area all year, and insofar as they hunt, cut wood, graze the land, and so on they deplete the resources much faster than transitory nomads would. The wholesale stripping of forested mountainsides in the last two decades is evidence of this, as is uncontrolled erosion resulting from farming on too-steep slopes. In the end both nomads and farmers suffer, although the former suffer first because the weight of authority is usually in the hands of the settlers, who are able to live in the midst of the nomads.

As game and forests are depleted, and the settled population grows, so does the demand for livestock, whose value thus rises. Therefore we find nomads competing to sell their stock rather than eating it, and being forced in return to buy agricultural products to supplement their diets. In extreme situations, like that prevalent today, we find a tightly integrated symbiotic relationship between farmer and herder. The nomad consumes most of the milk products, but otherwise he is now as reduced to eating bread alone as his sedentary brethren.

Nomads caught in these straits often try for greater mobility through the acquisition of riding stock and pack animals, but they may also launch predatory raids to get what they are otherwise deprived of by circumstances beyond their control. Today, of course, nomads leave their tents in droves for seasonal wage labor, and many never return to the mountain camps.

It is interesting that nomads historically have been an important source of manpower and population for cities where mortality is often so high as to preclude biological continuity without immigration. Paradoxically, nomad psychology emphasizes fertility and high rates of reproduction for both man and beast, yet overpopulation is the bane of nomadism and contributes directly to the forces in the cities that impinge on pastoral vitality.

To carry the cruel paradox still further, there are only enough persons to do the necessary tasks in the nomad camps when the overall population of nomads is relatively low. When populations are too high, the holdings of livestock by each family drop too low to support persons whose labor is not needed daily. A family with 200 head can easily support several strapping sons, daughters, and some elderly relatives. In these camps, whenever heavy work is required there are plenty of hands. But the wretched nomad with 25 head can hardly afford to keep one son and daughter, and he will not have enough labor to handle pack animals and herds when his camp is moving. Things are especially cruel now that each family has more possessions and consequently needs more otherwise unproductive, expensive animals to carry them.

The nomads' "golden age" was the mid nineteenth century. Then the Baharvand controlled many times as great a territory as they do today. Perhaps four to five thousand tents dotted the hillsides and provided manpower to control a major caravan route and keep both the central government and the forces of the Wali of Pusht-i-Kuh at bay. None of the surrounding tribes could withstand the Baharvand in direct confrontation. The Baharvand had as much as they wanted and as much as they needed. There was no worry either that the population would rise out of control. Young men were born to die in battle, and enough of them did so that this attrition was as much a drain on the population as emigration to the cities and factories is now.

Then there was an equilibrium enforced by strength of arms. The nomads fought for what they could get and kept what they had. The system was closed to outsiders and self-sufficient within.

Another Look at Origins

In spite of much archaeological work, the hindsight of history, and some ethnographic studies, the genesis of pastoralism remains an enigma, although now that we have recognized its complexity we have learned to avoid asking what *the* origin is. In retrospect it seems clear that there must have been many origins, many routes which eventually converged in the patterns of pastoralism that we see today. The diverse origins and paths resulted from the many environmental factors that have determined the limits of viability of the men and herds; the men, in turn, grasping for the competitive edge in survival, have converged in forms of tribal society, which is itself born in strife.

Although the tribal societies of nomads may be rather late inventions, mobile economies which feature a mutually beneficial relationship between men and animals are theoretically very old indeed. They may have been much more widespread than generally thought and may have involved animals like deer and gazelles which are ordinarily assumed to have been left untamed (Higgs and Jarman 1972; Saxon 1974). In view of the restricted focus of this chapter, however, we cannot deal with these matters.

My project dealt with a particular locale among the possible array because I was chiefly concerned with how sheep and goat pastoralism developed in the area of my archaeological research. There, I conclude, pastoralism may be as old as agriculture and may have arisen quite separately from it in some favorable locations. The valleys which I examined in the Zagros, and their counterparts in the Taurus range, seem especially suitable to a herding economy without a supplementary diet of cereal domesticates. The oaks in this region provide modern nomads with acorn flour, and wild cereals can also be harvested and used in combination with or separately from acorns. Although as yet we have no direct evidence that acorns were used in antiquity, they were available, and even today they provide a nutritious substitute for cereals.

The principal differences between sheep and goat herding now and when we first have evidence of it are in the amount of baggage and in the presence of pack animals. In most of the region under discussion, seasonal movements with flocks, family, and baggage could be made on foot, without pack animals. The use of donkeys or mules encourages the nomads to build inventories of equipment, simplifies housing, and perhaps makes longer migrations possible, but pack animals are not essential to the way of life.

Herding in early prehistory was probably not clearly distinguished from settled agriculture, on the one hand, and migratory hunting and gathering, on the other. The evidence then, as today, suggests that people took advantage of local circumstances and retained a great deal of flexibility in their adaptation year by year and generation by generation. Specialized forms of pastoral nomadism which involve long treks through chiefly grazing land, and consequently require inputs of agricultural products, are probably a relatively late development whose origins have yet to be documented. These specializations probably depended on a combination of social, demographic, and technological factors.

Considering the environment in which the Baharvand live, there would have been no obstacles to the development of pastoralism independently of farming, except perhaps the most important ones: the idea and then the decision to implement it. In my view the greatest obstacle was psychological. Persons who lived in the area as hunters and gatherers would have followed a seasonal round which would have been little different from that followed by herders. Moreover, essentially the same diet could have been maintained. The animals might even have been husbanded through selective culling so that their numbers remained large enough to support small bands of hunters. The principal changes with domestication would have been in deliberately tending animals by taking charge of their movements, and in putting their milk, hair, and wool to use as harvestable resources which could be converted to multiple human uses. These shifts would have entailed a change in the social organization such that routine labor could be performed daily. They also would entail an organization that could fit milking, spinning, weaving, herding, and so on into a daily pattern and an annual cycle. In all these respects a degree of commitment and cooperation uncharacteristic of hunters and gatherers may have been necessary. Finally, ownership of animals and the things that result from them became important. Man's relations to his fellow man, as well as to his animals, underwent

160

profound changes when domestication as we know it today became established.

If, like most nomads, we see today's pastoralism as a "free" life in comparison with that of the peasant farmer, we would have to concede that the nomad is a veritable prisoner compared with his hunter-gatherer predecessors. Thus the transition from one style of life to the other was not necessarily inevitable or welcome (cf. Higgs and Jarman 1972:12).

Farmers around the world will probably agree that keeping livestock is a chore. Animals make incessant demands on their owners that planted crops never do. It is a myth, therefore, that nomads are free. What is nearer the truth is that nomads' mobility enables them to escape taxation and other onerous demands of more powerful people. They are free of taxation, but they are slaves to their herds. The whole psychology of nomadism that argues the opposite is thus exposed as a creation of social factors which have nothing basic to do either with farming or with herding. The psychology stems from unwarranted meddling in tribal affairs by powerful people. The nomads' reaction to such meddling is to become supernomads and to create a myth of basic differences between themselves and farmers which serves to perpetuate the viability of pastoralism by denying the worth of its opposite. At the same time the settled meddlers define the nomads as barbarians so that any atrocities perpetrated on them can be done in good conscience.

Pastoralists are indeed creatures of their environment. But the environment has its geographic *and* its social components. In their interaction lies the transition from mobile hunters to transhumant herders.

Archaeological Implications

We may look at pastoralism archaeologically from two points of view: as a style of life that is different from that of contemporary sedentary agriculturalists, and as a contrast with the life of hunters and gatherers who would ordinarily be antecedent historically. The former view concerns subsystems of economic enterprise within a region, whereas the latter concerns the historical succession of types of economy. First I shall briefly discuss the archaeological evidence that might relate to the behavior I recorded ethnographically.

For reasons previously stated, early forms of pastoralism are unlikely to parallel closely any modern patterns. Obviously no aspect of prehistoric economy was fully developed in its incipient stages, and specialization in the economic and social sense is not to be expected for any early tenders and keepers of domesticates. Nevertheless, pastoralism has some fundamental implications, whether it is an early or a late form. Among these are the following. Transhumant pastoralism is characterized by

(1) a seasonal pattern of movement from pasture to pasture with domestic flocks;

(2) a tendency to follow the same pattern annually;

(3) a style of dwelling which can be discarded or carried;

(4) a subsistence based upon meat and milk from wild or domestic stock, and wild or domestic cereals, acorns, or other storable plants;

(5) a social organization which allows for the changing composition of cooperative work groups and for corporate or individual ownership of herds;

(6) a sense of territory (albeit somewhat indefinitely delimited) with resources "held" in common; and

(7) a systematic effort to increase the number of livestock by means other than improvement of the territory.

These criteria describe pastoral nomadism in its own terms, rather than in reference to other modes of production to which it exhibits differences or similarities. This kind of description has the advantage of removing from consideration the variety of historical and technological factors that have impinged on nomadism and especially on our conception of it. It also helps us to focus on those characteristics which may leave identifiable archaeological remains.

We should expect to be able to find some information on most of the characteristics. For example: (1) Sites should be situated with respect to seasonal pastures routes of migration rather than with regard to arable land or close proximity to water. (2) Sites should show repetitive occupation at the same seasons. (3) The sites should show evidence of impermanent shelters or tents and of repeated, though discontinuous, occupation. (4) Faunal remains should include a high proportion of sheep and goats, and perhaps some wild animals. Tools for processing plants may be present: mortars and pestles, and manos and metates. There may be sickles for the cutting of grains or reeds which would be used for fodder, bedding, reed screens, baskets, and so on. There may be facilities for storing grain or acorns, and perhaps there may be ovens. These facilities may be some distance from camps and have no datable artifacts in or around them. (5) Sites should show evidence of groups of shelters or tents. Camps tend to comprise four to six family shelters arranged formally or informally, but the distance between shelters is unlikely to exceed 10 meters. Camps of different sizes may be found in different pastures as evidence of the fluctuating size of cooperative groups. (6) It would be difficult to determine territorial boundaries, although not necessarily impossible if there were sufficient numbers of sites because tribal groups display their distinctiveness in subtle physical arrangements. (7) The territories should show few if any improvements (terraces, check dams, and similar structures), although there may be corrals and other facilities.

These are the kinds of evidence that might tell us whether transhumance was being practiced in an area such as the one I have been studying. Looking at the problem historically, however, we would like to know when and how pastoralism developed. Consequently, we would like to be able to distinguish among sites of the following kinds of people: (a) pastoral nomads, (b) hunters and gatherers, (c) settled farmers who keep livestock, and (d) nomadic farmers who have no livestock.

All evidence points to the fact that settled agriculturalists have distinctive villages with permanent architecture and facilities. There seems little problem in distinguishing such sites from those of mobile people, although on occasion the latter may reside in villages alongside agriculturalists. The major problems lie in differentiating between mobile people with and without domesticates, and between settled people with and without domesticates. The latter problem is not addressed here, nor are we concerned with nomadic farmers, chiefly because such a style seems distinctly disadvantageous by comparison with others in the area under question (R. Adams 1974b:7). At the moment we dismiss them as possible but highly improbable. We are left then with one basic issue: how can we tell a nomad camp from the camp of a group of hunters and gatherers?

Such a question drives deeply toward whatever fundamental structural differences there may be between the two ways of life because it is immediately apparent that each way has its own impressive range of variation. For example, the kind of pastoralism

163

differs depending on the territory, climate, kinds of animals herded, pressure from or intercourse with peoples of different economic orientation, sizes of populations, uses to which animals are put (whether they are used for food or as cash crops), and so on. Social, technological, and environmental factors are all relevant and help shape the patterns and style of pastoral nomadism. Clearly one would not expect sites of reindeer herders in Scandinavia to be the same as those of Yak breeders in Tibet, horse herders in Kazakstan, goat herders in Luristan, camel Bedouin in Arabia, or cattle keepers in East Africa. But in all these areas, and with such diversity of livestock, there must be differences between the local antecedent hunters and gatherers and the nomads. Some of these differences should be inherent in the fact of domestication. What then, does this "fact" entail?

Basically it entails this: *Herders have a commitment to the livelihood and perpetual maintenance of particular groups of animals*. There are a number of corollaries to this proposition.

1. People orient their principal movements and activities the year round in accord with the habits and needs of one or more species of animals.

2. People alter the balance among species of animals by enhancing the reproductive potential of some species through reducing natural hazards and by eliminating competition.

3. People may modify the natural environment for the well-being of herds by building shelters, corrals, trails, and so on.

4. People may intervene directly in feeding livestock through cutting fodder or raising grains.

Activities of these kinds will have unpremeditated effects on the natural environment, especially as regards the vegetative cover and the distribution of species that use it. These effects will probably culminate in an equilibrium among species different from that which characterized the area in days when hunting and gathering were the main activities.

Let us consider the way these matters might be expressed in sites of pastoralists as opposed to those of hunters.

1. *The locations of sites*. There are basic human requirements, such as the need for water, which affect the location of sites, but these are likely to be masked by other factors. Pastoralists place their camps where the needs of both the people and the herds are met. My study

164

suggests that flat land, pasture, water, and fuel are all considered. The specific location of a camp depends mostly on human needs, because herds feed in the vicinity and can walk considerable distances from the campsites. We can assume, therefore, that most camps are sited to accommodate the needs of humans who are herding animals. Sites will naturally be in or near pasture and water, and they may be located so as to take advantage of passes, fords, and other features that allow for the passage of animals and laden people. Whereas herders' camps are sited in relation to the needs of one or two species, hunters may be more eclectic and consequently their camps may be more dispersed and less predictable in location.

2. *Duration of sites*. There are basically two patterns: herders in many areas tend to remain in camps for prolonged periods at certain seasons, but during the transitional seasons, when they are on the move, the sites are occupied only briefly. The sites with prolonged occupation will be at the elevational and territorial extremes of the seasonal round. Hunters' sites probably tend to be of shorter duration unless food is stored, because game in any one locale might become depleted. Although we do not know whether this is the case, it seems likely that hunters were usually less numerous, more eclectic in their diets, and moved more frequently than herders. Under these circumstances their sites may have been used for shorter times, and favorite sites may have been selected for different reasons than would have been the case with herders. Clearly the sizes of human populations and the capacity of an area to support free-moving (nonherded) animals are crucial.

3. *Uses of sites*. There is a fundamental difference between the ways hunters and herders use sites. The former are concerned with sheltered focal points from which to forage. To be sure, herders also use sites as base camps, but additionally they use them to accommodate their herds. Nomad sites are readily recognized by the concentration of dung, trampled ground, and stripped vegetation. Moreover, seasonally the young may be kept inside houses or tents, and there may be corrals among the dwellings.

4. *Contents of sites*. Remains of structures may be at either hunters' or herders' sites and in both cases would most likely be of impermanent construction. I see no reason why the same shape and size dwelling might not have been used by both groups. Further, both groups tend to live in family-size units, and to require only one "room."

The structures themselves are not necessarily different, and the household debris in them may be similar, too. Herding as such requires no tools; if hunting, butchering, and preparation of hides were not carried out at nomad camps, there might be no stone tools. It is hard to imagine, however, that hunters could get by without them, and actually most herders need such tools at least seasonally, but they might not show up in all camps. Herders frequently require sickles for reaping, axes for cutting wood, and knives when they do butcher animals or shear them. In the same locales these tools might also be necessary for hunters. The situation is thus ambiguous. It would be hard in many cases to tell on the basis of stone tools only whether one were dealing with hunting or herding peoples.

The bones found in sites could be the most useful clue. In the early stages of domestication, one cannot tell on morphological criteria whether an animal was wild or domestic. This particularly difficult problem has been approached from various angles without unanimous agreement on the implications, partly because it is not clear how one should define domestication. What is safest to say now is that when one species is heavily represented there exists the possibility of herding. If the proportions of species more nearly approach those found in the natural environment and include many relatively unproductive species, the chances of domestication of any one seem less. Recent studies of the ages and sexes of animals found in archaeological sites suggest that selective culling, a kind of husbandry, may considerably antedate transhumant herding (Higgs and Jarman 1972; Jarman 1972; Saxon 1974). One immediately recognizes the problems in making all of these inferences, which need not be belabored here.

5. *Historical patterns.* When we look at the history of domestication in most of Southwest Asia as we know it archaeologically, there is a point at which sheep and goats become the major faunal component of most sites. In some instances the shift may have been gradual; in others it may have amounted to a rapid replacement of species. The points made by Higgs and his collaborators concerning the behavioral implications of hunting in comparison with herding are apposite and bear serious further investigation. Selective culling of hunted animals was very likely a kind of primitive husbanding of resources which made possible an enduring stable way of life long before the patterns of transhumance which I have investigated were developed. I would maintain, however, that even considering certain behavioral

similarities between some hunters and herders, the fundamental difference between the two lies in the fact that herders literally live with their animals and intervene in all aspects of their life. Careful studies should reveal archaeological evidence of this pattern.

As well as learning when these changes occurred, in the future we must examine the reasons for this shift in commitment. Are the factors to be found in changes in the biological or climatic environment? Are they in man's sudden acquisition of new skills? Do they have to do with the synergistic effects of combining animal and plant husbandry? Do they stem from the opportunity to control uncertainty more efficiently in an unpredictable environment? These and similar questions can now be raised as a result of multidisciplinary studies in the last few years. This ethnoarchaeological project contributes to both the specific and the general aspects of the problem.

NOTE

1. The ethnographic study was facilitated by Sekandar Amanolahi-Baharvand, a member of the Luri tribe and a Ph.D. candidate in anthropology at Rice University. His dissertation, "The Baharvand, Former Pastoralists of Iran" (1975), provides much supplementary information on Luri history and cultural practices.

The project described here was funded by National Science Foundation grant GS-35818 to Rice University. Previous archaeological work described here was funded by NSF grants GS-67 and GS-2194.

7

Experimentation, Ethnoarchaeology, and the Leapfrogs in Archaeological Methodology

RUTH TRINGHAM

Harvard University

INTRODUCTION

The methodology of science can no longer be conceived as "empirical" in the traditional sense of the term. . . . the presuppositions of inquiry have become far more complicated than early experimental science dreamed. (Churchman 1948:vii)

This statement referred to scientific research in general; it was an appeal to the philosophers and practitioners of the natural sciences. Such a sentiment, however, seems equally appropriate to the archaeology of the 1960s and 1970s, in view of the present conflict between the traditional "empiricist" archaeology and the "New Archaeology." The main thrust of this essay is that observation of and experimentation with archaeological materials cannot be separated from hypothesis building and testing, and, as a corollary, that basic research in archaeological materials is as much an integral part of

169

archaeological question answering as the philosophical model building of Binford, Plog, and Clarke.

The two aspects of archaeological research discussed here— ethnoarchaeological and experimental archaeology—both manifest many of the attributes of traditional empirical investigation and have been spurned and belittled by the philosophers of archaeology as peripheral to the New Methodology, as unscientific, and as having only specific time-space utility. This chapter examines the methodological procedures by which these two aspects of our discipline may be transformed to play an integral part in hypothesis testing and in the formulation of probability statements in archaeological research.

We can define ethnoarchaeology as the structure for a series of observations on behavioral patterns of living societies which are designed to answer archaeologically oriented questions. "Experimental archaeology"—that is, experiments as part of archaeological investigations—on the other hand, comprises a series of observations on behavior that is artificially induced. Both may involve more or less rigorously controlled conditions and recorded results.

Both are important aspects of a materialist study of behavior, pertinent to the study not only of past behavior but also of that of the present and the future. Theoretically, both ethnoarchaeological and experimental observations should provide valuable resources for testing hypotheses concerning archaeological data. Ethnoarchaeological observations are not in competition with experimental observations in providing valuable data on behavior; their information is of a different kind, and this distinction should be made self-consciously when using these data, since it affects conclusions and the confirmation of hypotheses.

The stress in this chapter falls on the side of experiments in archaeology, since my own research has been directly concerned with this aspect of archaeological testing. But my argument will emphasize that both sources of information, although separate, increase their value in interpreting archaeological data when one recognizes and takes advantage of their close interrelationship and interdependence.

Experimental tests made by archaeologists vary enormously along a continuum from rigorous control to complete lack of control of variables. At the rigorous end, we find the experiments carried out in

170

the laboratory and under other highly artificial conditions (Steensberg 1955; Jewell and Dimbleby 1966; Sarayder and Shimada 1971; Tringham et al. 1974) and those using ethnographic operators (White and Thomas 1972; Yellen 1974). At the less controlled end, the Good Life of the Past is relived under the guise of happy experiences referred to as "experiments" (O'Kelly 1954; Ryder 1969).

There is an important distinction between the "ethnographic experiment" and the experiments which have been carried out in artificial laboratory or "field laboratory" conditions in which, ideally, all aspects of the experiment—including the operator—are tightly controlled. (In some cases the operator is a machine, such as the Hydraulic Semenov [Tringham et al. 1974] or the Stainless Steel Indian [Bonnichsen and Morlan 1974].) In ethnographic experiments the operators carry out activities in their own social context in patterns familiar to them or to their immediate ancestors (White and Thomas 1972; Yellen 1974; Godelier and Garanger 1973; Franke and Watson 1936). Ethnographic experiments are distinct from ethnoarchaeological observations in that behavior in experiments is manipulated; for example, actions are repeated and isolated, and in some cases are carried out many years after they have ceased to be a normal part of the operator's way of life. The value of experiments for archaeological interpretation does not necessarily increase with a change from ethnographic to laboratory procedure in the design, execution, and interpretation of the experiment.

I shall argue that experiments in archaeology have for the most part been justifiably ignored because of (1) their lack of a strong theoretical base and a resulting lack of general applicability in testing archaeological hypotheses (this is also true of many ethnoarchaeological observations), and (2) their lack of rigor and of attention to scientific experimental procedure in design, execution, recording, and analysis. In 1957, the great exponent of microwear studies in the USSR noted that "the amateur nature of the experiments and doubts about the results is the reason why the majority of archaeologists [carrying out experiments] leave their work unpublished" (Semenov 1964:2). This, however, is not to say that testing by controlled experimentation should not be an integral part of archaeological investigation. Quite the contrary; it is my belief that experimental testing is as essential in archaeology as it is in most other scientific disciplines (and not only natural sciences), in the same way that material (archaeologically)-oriented ethnographic observations are essential.

Most historians of science would agree that

> Science as we know it today may be said to date from the introduction of the experimental method during the Renaissance. Nevertheless, important as experimentation is in most branches of science, it is not appropriate to all types of research. It is not used, for instance, in . . . observational ecology. . . . However, investigations of this latter type make use of many of the same principles. The main difference is that hypotheses are tested by the collection of information from phenomena which occur naturally instead of those that are made to take place under experimental conditions. . . . (Beveridge 1961:13)

The difference between experimental tests and ethnographic observations in archaeological investigations is very clear in this context. Archaeology, like biology and ecology, covers many directions; there is no doubt of the appropriateness of both experimental and observational testing in archaeology, but the value of the former is nullified if the boundaries of appropriateness are not made explicit. In fact, most scientists would be appalled if they knew that gap existed in our investigatory procedures.

LEAPFROGGING IN ARCHAEOLOGY

In the current milieu of the popularity of the hypothetico-deductive basis in archaeological investigation (with which I may say I have no quarrel), a corollary has been a stress on adopting the "procedures of science," comprising both scientific inference and scientific practice (Wisdom 1952:1). There are certain cardinal principles involved in scientific procedures, such as the fact that hypotheses should be testable—that is, confirmable or falsifiable (Wisdom 1952:37)—and that they should be tested by observational or experimental data. There are suspicions, however, in my own mind and in the minds of others (Redman 1974; Bonnichsen 1973; Clarke 1973) that, although we have developed theoretical bases and statistical means of measuring significance of variation, "we have not developed adequate means of observation and measurement . . . in recognizing relevant attributes and functional artifact identification" (Redman 1974: 249-50).

172

Bonnichsen notes that "very little effort has been devoted to testing the validity of archaeological inferential methodology" (1973:277) and that "if as most frequently happens a cultural reconstruction is based on intuitively-derived interpretations a sequence of errors . . . reflect the fact that mistakes made at the identification level are frequently carried over into each succeedingly higher level of interpretation" (1973:286). Bonnichsen's statements were made in reference to an experimental excavation and interpretation of a recently abandoned site. But we can see many instances of the problem he cites even in the most recent, supposedly most progressive literature. In David Clarke's masterful analysis (1972) of socioeconomic systems at the Iron Age site of Glastonbury, England, with all the sophisticated analysis of data in the upper level of inference, his low-level analysis was sometimes incredibly weak—for example, in reconstructing the sexual dimorphism of residence units on the basis of what he assumed (not what he had proved) were male- or female-associated artifacts. Another investigator, Robert Whallon (1974), used sophisticated nearest-neighbor proximity analysis of stone tools to reconstruct activity areas; at the most basic level, however, the use and function of his stone tools were never identified (Tringham et al. 1974), and the cultural processes involved in the deposition of artifacts (Speth and Johnson 1976) were never taken into account.

Glynn Isaac introduced his systematic experimental and observational testing of the processes of the deposition of archaeological debris in East Africa with a succinct statement:

> The eager archaeologist frequently finds himself tempted, or even obliged, to invoke evidence from site features, for which the determining processes have never been investigated; in this situation archaeologists must either run the risk of dependence on *a priori* reasoning and untested assumptions, or they must undertake the investigations of the relevant processes by experiment of systematic observation. (Isaac 1967:31)

Isaac diplomatically attributes to enthusiasm and eagerness the archaeologist's tendency to leapfrog the tedious basic-level testing of things like depositional processes in favor of investigating more interesting upper-level problems such as population dynamics. In my skepticism, it seems to me that this phenomenon may be another manifestation of the basically unscientific nature of many archaeological investigations, in spite of loud claims to the contrary.

Lewis Binford, who has certainly played no mean part in shaping the present character of archaeological investigation—that is, its basis in the explicit formulation and testing of hypotheses—has also tended to concentrate on the investigation of upper-level problems, but perhaps this can be excused on the grounds that his work is really a series of charismatic manifestos (Binford 1972). Nevertheless, I am tempted to draw attention to the fact that in 1966, he and Sally Binford pleaded the cause of a "functional outlook" on variation in Mousterian lithic assemblages, arguing that the sites should be seen as functionally specific on the basis of functional identification of the stone tools by their macromorphological attributes (Binford and Binford 1966). In spite of the fact that Semenov's book on microwear and identification of usage had been brought to the Western world two years before, they made no mention of this method of low-level testing of usage of the tools (Semenov 1964). Since that time Binford has backed down from his 1966 position, but not on methodological grounds:

> I would like to suggest that what has been summarized by my critics as the "functional argument" is really an appeal to archaeologists to explain their observations. This means addressing themselves to the difficult task of determining what our taxonomies are measuring and what demonstrated patterning refers to in the organization of past human systems of adaptation out of which these patterns derived. (Binford 1973:253)

Thus he is suggesting that his original statement was intended not to express any ultimate truth, but to act as a catalyst to encourage necessary low- or basic-level testing. This seems to me a legitimate cause as long as it is explicitly stated in such terms.

A later instance of the same kind of thing is his discussion of Tretyakov's reconstruction of prehistoric residence patterns in the Volga Basin (Binford 1968). Tretyakov (1935) argues that it is possible on the basis of fingerprints on prehistoric pottery to identify the sex of the potter, and that in the Volga Basin all potters are female. On the basis of this conclusion Tretyakov is able to make further propositions of residence patterns. Far from refuting Tretyakov's primary identification on the basis of its notoriously poor sample and hastily drawn conclusions, Binford accepts the assumption that "females were potters" and aligns it with a similar assumption made by archaeologists in the U.S. Southwest (Longacre 1964b). The difference is that the statement "females were potters" is an assumption rather than a testable hypothesis in southwestern archaeology, but it is at least made with some justification on the basis of assumed cultural continuity to historically known societies. In the USSR, however, the assumption is made on a quite unacceptable basis.

Scientific research is necessarily long-term, tedious, lonely, and often boring. Patience and imagination are necessary to see the worth of such labors. This applies to the basic testing of hypotheses on the mechanical properties of materials (stone, clay, and so forth) as much as it does to the retrieval of data through excavation, or to upper-level analysis. "Each stage of the investigation must be established beyond reasonable doubt before passing on to the next, or else the work may be condemned, quite properly, as being 'sloppy' " (Beveridge 1961:16). As I have indicated, however, many archaeological investigations consistently fail to build a firm base of confirmed hypotheses for their higher-level hypotheses, with the result that their "facts" are easily refuted.

"SCIENCE IN ARCHAEOLOGY"

In fact, of course, archaeologists *do* use scientifically deduced information derived from series of tested and confirmed hypotheses when they call in the Magical Specialist, the Scientist, the metallurgist, the nuclear physicist, the zoologist, and so on. The fact that these investigations tend to be grouped under such titles as "Science in Archaeology" indicates the existence (in the minds of the archaeologists) of other sets of investigations outside the range, parameters, and procedures of "science." From this point of view, archaeologists are like police detectives, who have their own Magician, the Forensic Scientist, whose information is drawn from countless series of carefully tested and confirmed hypotheses. Like detectives, not many archaeologists have any idea, or *want* to have any idea, what those tests are as long as they can just use the "facts." I am not advocating that all archaeologists should *know* the procedures by which it became possible to identify the technique of manufacture of metal objects. There is a tendency, however, for techniques of identification to be adopted by archaeologists as established "facts" before adequate testing is complete. For example, the use of optical emission spectroscopy to identify the source of metal artifacts (Junghans, Sangmeister, and Schroeder 1960) was thought to be the answer to every archaeologist's prayer. Artifacts were sampled and analyzed by the Stuttgart Laboratory and exchange and resource-exploitation patterns were confidently reconstructed on their basis. A few years later it was shown that in their eagerness and

175

impatience the archaeologists had seized upon a method which, when subjected to further testing, could be interpreted in quite different ways (Waterbolk and Butler 1965). With some knowledge of the specialist's procedures of research, it is possible for the archaeologist to evaluate the Magician's "facts" and understand to what extent they are subject to changing hypotheses and tests.

In addition, as Brothwell and Higgs have pointed out,

> there are not—and never have been—enough of these tame "specialists" to go around. Moreover, the situation looks like deteriorating, not improving. In the fields of zoology and physical anthropology, for instance, interest has swung away from osteological work. . . . The answer, whether archaeologists like it or not, is that they . . . must adapt to the need for scientific research within their own discipline. (Brothwell and Higgs 1969:23)

This does not mean necessarily that archaeologists will have to do basic theoretical and experimental physics research themselves (although as Sir W. Hamilton, a noted physicist, said, "In physical sciences the discovery of new facts is open to any blockhead with patience and manual dexterity and acute senses" [quoted in Beveridge 1961:149]). What the statement of Brothwell and Higgs implies is that the testing of basic hypotheses on the mechanical properties of materials, and especially on the effect of human modification on them, has to be done by archaeologists; such questions, for example, as the osteological results of varying diets in domestic animals are not likely to be tested by zoologists at this stage, not only because of their lack of interest in osteology, but also because research into meat and soft parts has more commercial applicability.

Archaeologists tend to avoid doing the basic analysis and testing of the properties of archaeological materials themselves; they are willing to "leave it to the experts" and to believe the specialists' conclusions as "proven facts." They also tend to regard those engaged in this basic research as "technicians" whose function is to service archaeological investigations. I would suggest, however, that research into the basic properties of archaeological materials, whether by a natural scientist or by an archaeologist, cannot be carried out productively without attention to cultural implications. Neither systematic ethnographic observation nor experimentation can be carried out meaningfully unless it is constantly related to the more general cultural applicability

176

of the test, with a constant awareness of what is being tested and why, and of the logic surrounding the confirmation of the hypothesis. Experimentation into the formation of microwear on flaked stone tools, for example, means very little if it is not related to theories on cultural variability of stone tools on the one hand, and to theories on the principles of fracture of conchoidally flaking materials on the other (Tringham et al. 1974). At the same time, observations on pottery manufacture and use in a modern village mean much more when related to general hypotheses on socioeconomic implications of ceramic traditions (see, for example, David and Hennig 1972). This may seem an obvious statement, but it is surprising, when one reviews the literature on ethnoarchaeological and experimental observations, how particularistic and caught up in time-space specifics the majority of studies are.

THE PROCEDURES OF EXPERIMENTAL RESEARCH IN ARCHAEOLOGY

The procedures of scientific research do not encompass mystical practices available only to an initiated few. Straightforward sets of rules are readily available, stated sometimes in very practical terms (Wilson 1952), sometimes from a more philosophical point of view (Wisdom 1952). A strong awareness of the theoretical and philosophical basis of the investigation is a prerequisite of any scientific research, whether observational or experimental. Many other "rules" in scientific procedure apply equally to experimentation and to systematic observation. The discussion that follows, however, concerns the procedures that relate to experimentation.

Ascher, whose 1961 article "Experimental Archaeology" remains the most, if not the only, theoretical statement on the use of the experimental method in archaeology—as opposed to a bibliography (Graham, Heizer, and Hester 1972) or a descriptive history (Coles 1973)—makes the statement: "At first glance, the imitative experiment appears so unlike experiments in other disciplines, that it becomes suspect" (Ascher 1961b:807). I see the lack of similarity as resulting from the differences in *procedure* by which scientific experiments and archaeological experiments are carried out. Ascher, on the other hand, sees it as the result of the fact that "the kind of order (pattern) with which imitative experimentors are concerned is cultural, not natural" (Ascher 1961b:807). He adopts the term "imitative experiment," whose aim is "testing beliefs about cultural behavior." Such experiments "entail operations in which matter is shaped, or matter is shaped and used in a manner simulative of the past" (Ascher 1961b:793). His argument, which has been adopted by all subsequent experimenters, seems to state that since archaeologists are testing cultural behavior they do not have to follow the rules of the natural sciences. It is difficult, he explains, in the presence of so many unknown variables, to systematize the execution and quantify the results of archaeological experiments.

Both Ascher (1961b) and Coles (1973) list basic procedures which should be followed in archaeological experiments:

(1) Convert limited working hypothesis into verifiable form.
(2) Select experimental materials, preferably those available to the society about whom the experiment is being run.
(3) Operate experiment, preferably with as many alternative sets as possible.
(4) Observe results.
(5) Interpret results as an inference.
(6) Find corroborative evidence, such as direct contact traces of inferred activity or behavior in archaeological data (or in the ethnographic record).

This is a logical order in which to carry out an investigation, but one finds rather more sophisticated and significant discussions of procedural details in the manuals from the natural sciences (Wilson 1952).

Detailed suggestions for the improvement of procedures in the design, execution, and interpretation of archaeological experiments have been put forward elsewhere (Tringham in press c). Here these suggestions may be summarized as a need for greater explicitness in stating the theoretical basis of the experimental program, in stating the hypothesis that is being tested by the experimentation, in stating the variables that are being manipulated and the basis of their selection, and in publishing the records of the operational procedures of the experiment and its results. In addition it was suggested that those carrying out experimental research in archaeology might profitably be more aware of and utilize objective measurements in the recording and interpretation of their results. Statistical tests of significance, and the application of logic, which are regularly utilized by materials scientists, are rare features indeed in the general sphere of archaeological experimentation.

Following Ascher's lead (1961b:807), archaeological experimenters operate on the assumption that rigor in quantification of results and in the procedures of interpreting the results through logical deduction are not appropriate to archaeological experimentation. Sarayder and Shimada (1973:344) have recently discussed the limitations engendered by Ascher's definition of experimentation in archaeology. They argue in particular that the results of archaeological experimentation can and should be quantifiable in a manner which allows them to be subjected to statistical tests of probability. In interpreting the results of experiments in archaeology, one most frequently finds answers to questions such as, Does it work? and, Is it a reasonable proposition (because it works)? Ascher argues that from the answers to these questions it is possible to formulate inferences of the following nature:

> If an operator achieves B by behavioral set A, and only A, an inference may be formed that B could have been achieved by A. On this basis it is possible to infer with enough tests that B may be achieved by two or more equipossible sets of behavior. An inference cannot be formed on the basis of B being achieved by none of the tested behavioral sets. (Ascher 1961b:810)

The emphasis here is on forming a *positive* inference, that is, on trying to produce positive results in the test. We must try to produce B by A, and if not by A then by $A_{1, 2}$, and so on. In general, once B has been produced by A, the experiment stops. In scientific experimentation, on the other hand, the emphasis is rather different. Wisdom (1952:55) has called the testing of a hypothesis "an endurance test." In other words, to confirm a hypothesis, a scientist must subject it to the most stringent possible tests in order to try to refute it. Thus if an archaeologist proves that B is possible by A, the only way he or she can make any progress toward verification and applicability to archaeological data in the form of an inference is by carrying on, testing other behavioral sets which produce B, until he or she begins to find behavioral sets which do *not* produce B, that is, which refute the hypothesis. This is the basis of Popper's (1963) main argument that progress in knowledge comes only as one refutes hypotheses.

Translated into archaeological terms, this would mean that when Semenov (1964) hypothesized that certain actions would result in a certain pattern of damage on the edge of a flaked stone tool, and that

179

this pattern of damage would be identifiable as resulting from this action on a prehistoric flake, it was not sufficient for him to have shown in an experiment that this action did cause this damage pattern. To have confirmed his hypothesis, he would have to have shown that the same damage pattern could *not* have been produced on an edge with the same characteristics (spine-plane angle and so forth) by any other action. Our own experiments started off with rather a similar hypothesis. We hypothesized that damage patterns of certain kinds were the result of specified action of the edge on specified worked material; we have tried to test the tools on as many materials as possible that would have been available and modified by flint edges (Tringham et al. 1974). By proving that certain materials were not the agents of a specific kind of damage, we can confirm our hypothesis with a greater degree of certainty.

It is probably fair to say that the majority of experiments described by Coles (1973), Ascher (1961b), and others are really not "scientific experiments" in that their results cannot be used with any measurable confidence to make statements on the nature of materials and their relation to human behavior. Procedures whereby the experiments *could* have been used in such a way have not been followed explicitly. This is not to say that the mass of human endeavor which these experiments represent has been wasted. As a means of gathering information on the parameters of the test, which variables to select, and the construction of hypotheses to be tested, this vast majority of experiments is invaluable. They should, however, be regarded as the first stage in the inquiry, not as the successful conclusion of an experimental test of a hypothesis in archaeology.

THE SIGNIFICANCE OF EXPERIMENTATION FOR ANTHROPOLOGICAL RESEARCH

In further modifying Ascher's aims and strategies for archaeological experimentation, I would suggest that, among experiments appropriate to archaeological research, there is not *one* basic category (Ascher's "imitative experiment") that forms the "cornerstone of archaeological experiment" (Ascher 1961b:793), but *two* kinds of experiment (see Fig. 7.1). Each of these has a different potential degree of confirmability inherent in its results; therefore different levels of inference and different kinds of interpretation are appropriate to each. We may

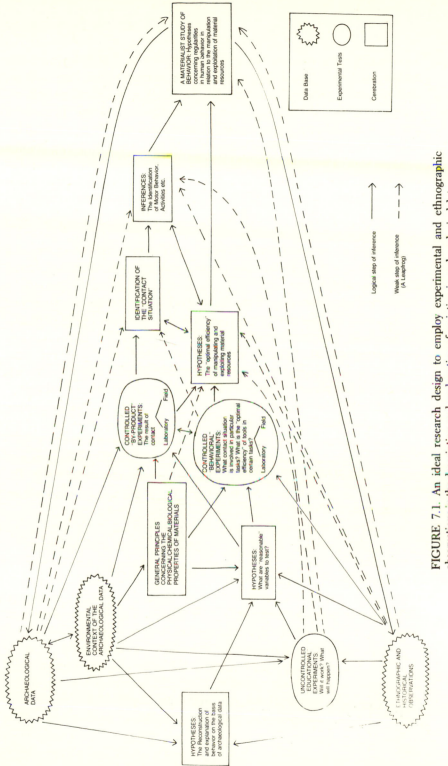

FIGURE 7.1. An ideal research design to employ experimental and ethnographic observations in the description and explanation of variation in archaeological data.

describe the first category as *experimentation on the by-products of human behavior*, including what the paleontologists refer to as "taphonomic" testing (Isaac and McCown 1976:78-79). This kind of experiment amounts to basic-level investigation of the nature of materials that have been modified through human agency. The second category is *behavioral experimentation*, the more risky testing of upper-level propositions about activities of which there is no direct archaeological evidence.

Experimentation on the By-Products of Human Behavior

These experiments test the processes by which the direct data of archaeological sites—the modified natural phenomena of stone, earth, dust, clay, and organic substances—acquire the characteristics they manifest when the archaeologist discovers them. The natural scientists have already contributed a great deal to the understanding of these phenomena, through sedimentology, ceramic analysis, metal analysis, human and animal osteology, lithic analysis, and so on. The intended aim of this kind of experiment is the reconstruction of the human and natural agents responsible for the modification, "contact traces," damage, wear, breakage, deposition, and decay of materials before, during, and after deposition in the archaeological record.

In addition such "by-product" experiments test the nature and properties of materials with a view to understanding their potential for human exploitation. Much of this information is provided by the theoretical and experimental bases of the material and biological sciences. In the case of some materials, however, particularly those no longer commercially viable, such a base does not exist or is very weak. Such is the case, for example, in understanding the structure of conchoidally fracturing stone, such as flint, in which the basic research is only now being carried out by, for lack of more qualified experts, archaeologists! (See Speth 1974, in press; Faulkner 1972; Tsirk 1974.) In providing information on the minimal morphological requirements of given activities, such as the melting point of copper in different situations, the relative resistance of different woods, and so on, basic materials experiments are a necessary prerequisite to the understanding and reconstruction of the relationship between materials and human behavior in both the past and the present.

If these experiments are carried out according to scientific procedure, the results can be used to make statements in which it is possible to put a great deal of confidence, for, as mentioned above, "by-product" experiments are testing *natural* phenomena, whose variables are relatively controllable.

Behavioral Experimentation

Most of the experiments described by Ascher, by Graham and his colleagues, and by Coles constitute the first stage in behavioral experimentation. These are designed to test (1) the relationship of human operators to material, in such terms as the efficiency of energy input–production output ratios, and (2) the factors of social organization that contribute to variability in the materials. Most frequently, the results of the tests have not been put in any quantifiable terms but have answered the question, Will it work? Sarayder and Shimada (1973) have shown (see p. 179), however, that it is quite possible, as well as desirable, to express the results of behavioral experiments quantitatively in a way which can be used, for example, as the basic testing for mathematical simulation models. For example, "efficiency" can be broken down into not only speed and amount of production, but also the oxygen output during human energy expenditure.

We might refer to behavioral experiments as an "upper-level analytical testing mechanism." As with much social-sciences testing, there are problems in controlling the human variables in these tests.

Coles (1973:16) warns against not taking into account the lack of skill and practice of modern operators in techniques. Godelier remarks on the effect of age, skill, and strength differences of his New Guinea operators in testing the efficiency of steel versus stone axes (Godelier and Garanger 1973:211), and on the difficulty in predicting the results of this variance. The problem of subjectivity of human subjects and objects is, of course, not restricted to such "behavioral" experimentation. There are many worrisome stories told of the effects of subjectivity and bias (often quite unconscious) in, for example, medical experimentation (Wilson 1952:44-45).

The archaeological data themselves, if subjected to the kind of basic-level materials tests described above, may be used with confidence in formulating and testing hypotheses on prehistoric modes of behavior. Without the basic-level analysis, however, the upper-level behavioral investigation, whether experimental or observational, will be much less conclusive. For example, when Iversen and Steensberg tested by experiment the relative efficiency of stone and bronze axes in felling trees (Iversen 1956; Steensberg 1955), their conclusions would have been far more significant for hypotheses on forest clearance in prehistoric Denmark and much more appropriate to the archaeological data if they had first tried to confirm that the prehistoric implements whose efficiency they were testing had actually been used in felling trees. Steensberg and Iversen, however, reconstructed the function of the prehistoric implements on the basis of their morphological similarity to European medieval metal axes and ethnographic stone axes from New Guinea. The axes' function, however, could have been reconstructed more objectively by an analysis of the "contact traces" on the prehistoric tools themselves. Further study of the materials involved in the behavioral ("efficiency") test of Steensberg and Iversen—investigation, for instance, of properties (such as resistance) of the wood of the trees which were to be felled, or the relative mechanical properties of the materials used in the manufacture of the chopping tools—would have given a much greater depth and significance to their conclusions.

In summary, therefore, the basic-level materials and "by-products" testing provides the necessary "theory and background of the situation" (Wilson 1952:36) on which the behavioral tests can be based. Because of the complexities of the human variable, and the absence of direct evidence of the behavioral set to be tested, the inferences which can be made from behavioral experiments are inevitably more dubious than the conclusions drawn from lower-level testing. This degree of doubt may, however, be somewhat decreased by the use of a basic-level experimental and observational study of the materials (either hypothetical materials or those for which there is direct archaeological evidence) involved in the behavioral set in the design, operation, and interpretation of the behavioral experiment.

In addition, observation of the modification of the material during the behavioral experiment—for example, modification of the plowshare observed during plowing experiments (Reynolds 1967), edge damage of stone tools which were being tested ethnographically (J. P. White 1968b; Gould, Koster, and Sontz 1971; Nissen and Dittemore 1974), or the formation of butchering marks in an ethnographic experiment (Yellen 1974)—allows the results to be tested back directly, and thus more conclusively, against the archaeological data.

184

EXPERIMENTATION AND
ETHNOARCHAEOLOGY

It has been pointed out in a number of places (see, for example, Donnan and Clewlow 1974) that the role of ethnographic observation in archaeological interpretation has traditionally been to provide analogical situations from which the archaeologist tries to find the "best fit" or "best fits" to his hypothesized prehistoric situation. It was also traditionally advocated that the "best fit" would come from ethnographic or historical contexts with a strong tradition of cultural continuity from the prehistoric situation or at least with environment and economic strategy analogous to that of the prehistoric situation (Childe 1956:48-51).

The most widespread and most confidently used method of incorporating ethnographic data into archaeological interpretation—a method which is especially prevalent in ethnoarchaeological studies and experimentation in archaeology (see Sarayder and Shimada 1971; Franke and Watson 1936; Puleston 1971)—has been that which assumes in the relations of materials to their human manipulators in a particular society a continuity through time from a prehistoric to a present-day or historical context. This is the method referred to as the "direct historical approach" in the New World, the "folk-culture approach" in the Old World (Fagan 1975:330).

More recently Ucko and others have suggested that, since "it is not true to say that either the environment or the economy determines the rest of a particular people's activities" (Ucko and Rosenfeld 1968:156), it is not necessary to be so restricted when looking for analogies in ethnographic behavior. This attitude, which many archaeologists seem to find quite shocking, is especially associated with a point of view which states, "My job is to come up with general statements, and I should be explaining variation ethnographically as well as archaeologically if I am dealing with human behavior and variability" (Binford quoted in Orme 1974:210). This statement reflects a rather more positive attitude to the use of ethnographic observations in archaeological interpretation than that of the writers of "cautionary tales" for ethnographic relations with archaeology (Ucko and Rosenfeld 1968; Heider 1967). It suggests that the aim of ethnoarchaeology and the use of ethnographic sources is to seek regularities in human behavior which can be tested against the archaeological data, rather than to provide analogical situations which can be "fitted" to the data. As mentioned above, the ethnoarchaeological investigations at present extant appear to have been carried out with a primary aim of illuminating the immediate prehistoric ancestors of the same area. Those which have been designed to seek generalizations, or which are applicable to human behavior in general, are the exception (for example, David and Hennig 1972).

Whichever method is deemed the most valid and valuable for uniting present observation with past data, the problems remain. What are the actual procedures involved in testing ethnographic observations against archaeological data? On what basis can we measure the "best fit" among a large number of analogical situations? By what means can we arrive at a meaningful statement of probability in testing a generalization based on a living population against the remains of a dead one? Clearly there are no simple answers to these problems, but I would argue that the combination of ethnoarchaeological observations and experimental testing mechanisms suggested in this paper is an essential step in bridging the gulf between the living and the dead.

If the purpose of "by-product" and basic material experiments is the reconstruction of the process of modification of materials through the agency of human behavior, then these experiments and observations may be regarded as providing the *direct evidence* of hypothesized behavior patterns in the archaeological data, and the *direct link* between these data and ethnographic observations. Information on the process of modification of materials and their natural properties becomes significant, however, only when it is considered in the context of the hypothesized living behavior. The source of the hypothesized behavior and the selection of testable variables lies in the ethnographic and historical data. Behavioral experiments, on the other hand, are most appropriate as a mechanism to test the relationships of human behavior to material—energy input-output relationships, for example—noted in the ethnographic data.

Behavioral experiments thus take on the role of testing the regularities hypothesized in ethnographic or historical behavior, and hence are as important for social anthropological studies of materialist inclination as they are for archaeological investigations. Godelier, for example, has shown this in his comparative studies of stone and steel axes in New Guinea (Godelier and Garanger 1973). The circle of investigation is complete when the regularities observed in ethnographic behavior, along with the controlling experiments, are tested against the archaeological data by direct observation, and by experimentation with the by-products of behavior. Two examples will be given to illustrate this combination of ethnographic observation, behavioral experimentation, and by-product experimentation: first, the classic case of the Smudge Pits, brought up by Lewis Binford in another article to provoke action; and second, lithic analysis.

The Use of Analogy in the "Smudge Pits" Problem

In "Smudge Pits Revisited," Lewis Binford, remarking on the fact that Munsen's alternative hypothesis on the function of "smudge pits" was as valid as his own, states:

> The presence of a valid alternative proposition based on ethnographic analogy is not sufficient to refute an equally valid but different proposition. A valid proposition can only be refuted through hypothesis testing. However, when faced with valid alternatives one can evaluate in probabilistic terms the relative strength of alternatives and make decisions as to how to invest time in hypothesis testing. (1972:57)

Theoretically, this is a valid statement, but its application to the interpretation of the smudge pits of the Mississippi Valley is frustrating.

There seems an inherent weakness in both Binford's and Munsen's argument in their selection of "relevant ethnographic descriptions" for analogy (Binford 1967; Munsen 1969). They limit themselves to a search of the Southeastern United States and the Great Lakes region in the period immediately following the archaeological situation. Binford explains his selection on the grounds that "the relatively late archaeological documentation for the use of the smudge pits . . . would make continuity between the archaeological and ethnographic periods reasonable" (Binford 1967:8). Thus the "direct historical approach" is used to justify the assumption that the relation between form and function in the ethnographic situation was directly analogous to the relation between form and function in the archaeological situation. Having found a "convincing correspondence between the formal attributes" of the archaeological features and the ethnographic features (which finding is itself questionable), Binford makes a leap and assumes that the function is also the same. Although in the revisitation he suggests that "the accuracy of a proposition can only be determined by the testing of deductively drawn hypotheses against independent data" (Binford 1972:56), he has to admit that "this has not been done thus far for either proposition." As Sabloff, Beale, and Kurland (1973:111) noted, "The arbiter of the smudge-pit function is not a deductive model but merely the feature's documented ethnographic associations, which, it develops, have been variable in the case cited." In fact Binford, in his frustration at having failed to resolve the function of smudge pits (because of lack of testing), is forced to fall back onto a more general proposition: "the observed archaeological features were smudge-pits as distinct from lighting fires, roasting pits, etc." (Binford 1972:57). This more general proposition does *not* solve the problem since it is also no more than an untested proposition. It has not been shown convincingly that the archaeological features in the Mississippi Valley were caused by no process other than that associated with smudging. Instead of subjecting their proposition to the strictest possible tests in trying to *refute* it, both Binford and Munsen have in a positivist way accepted the first interpretation that would fit the observed features.

This attitude manifests itself in the suggestions made by Binford with regard to testing the propositions concerning the smudge pits: "The only method for determining the truth value of a proposition, and hence refuting it, is to devise deductively reasoned hypotheses regarding expected relationships between phenomena in question and other classes of remains" (Binford 1972:53). The procedure suggested includes examining (1) spatial correlates, (2) temporal correlates, and (3) formal correlates and associated activities of the hypothesized ethnographic activity, in this case hide smoking, and also observing the presence or absence of the same correlates in the archaeological data. It seems to me, however, that the archaeologist carrying out these tests is likely to assume, however subconsciously, that the identification of smudge pits as (1) for smoking and (2) for smoking hides or possibly smudging pottery is basically correct. Hence any positive correlations between archaeological and ethnographic features will be taken immediately as *positive* support of the hypothesis. One other test which Binford suggests, however, would afford the opportunity of refuting and more rigorously testing the hypothesis: one should "determine if there are any other activities which employed facilities which shared the same formal attributes as observed in hide-smoking pits" (Binford 1967:8). I suspect, however, that "other activities" would be searched for *only* in the "relevant" ethnographic literature, in this case the immediate successors of the prehistoric occupants of the eastern United States.

I have no basic objection to the suggested observations in the ethnographic and archaeological data. They are obviously an essential step in linking hypothesized behavior of a living society to its material remnants on an archaeological site. I would suggest, however, that some of the built-in bias could be minimized and a greater degree of confirmation in the hypothesis obtained if the observations were made from a slightly different direction.

Binford refers in passing (1967) to generalizations about the relationship of human behavior to materials which may be made on the basis of the recognition of minimal morphological requirements of a particular activity, and the recognition of the factors contributing to the form and features of materials associated with these activities. Ucko has argued the advantages for archaeological investigations and material culture research in general of this kind of ethnographic study (Ucko 1969b). He also points out that a relatively large cross-cultural sample of ethnographic examples is necessary if the generalizations are to bear any weight. I would suggest that control behavioral experimentation would also add value to the conclusions. Many of the arguments between Munsen and Binford could have been resolved by examining the different minimal morphological requirements of hide smoking and pottery smudging by means of basic experimentation and observation of the properties of the materials involved in such behavior.

As mentioned above, such tests also link the ethnographic behavior to the archaeological data by examining and testing the processes which could on a mechanical level have produced the phenomena observed in the archaeological features, in this case smudge pits. In the smudge-pit case, it was already established that the corncobs were burned in a reducing atmosphere (although there is no mention of how), but what about the differential coloring of the pits themselves? In a situation where one is not relying on the "direct historical approach," the observation and testing of the by-products of hypothesized behavior would seem a logical first step in the confident identification of the mechanical process which could have been involved in the manifestation of the archaeological data. As mentioned above, the investigation of the by-products of behavior through observation and experimentation does not proceed by groping in the dark for random information, but by a systematic procedure of testing deductively drawn hypotheses from ethnographic and other sources. The information established at this level may then be used along with ethnoarchaeological sources to generate testable hypotheses on efficiency, energy input-output, seasonality, specific location, and so forth of the given activity.

In summary, therefore, the difference between the testing method suggested in this chapter and that suggested by Binford is as follows: the testing mechanisms Binford suggests are designed to identify a specific activity in the archaeological data, in this case hide smoking, in order to verify an analogy from an ethnographic situation. The investigator having by positivist means confirmed this hypothesis (i.e., that the pits were for smoking hides), many other hypotheses follow, some testable, some not, on such matters as the social relations of hide smoking and so on. The testing mechanisms offered in this essay, on the other hand, approach the problem from a different, more generalized direction. On the basis of the identification of the by-products of the behavioral set, one can hypothesize that the pits were involved in a process which required the fuel to produce smoke. One does not assume, however, that smoke was being produced for any reason known to the historic occupants of the eastern United States. Instead, behavioral sets involving the production of smoke may be selected by means of a cross-cultural study, and through observation and experimentation their minimal morphological requirements and material by-products may be defined in different environmental, economic, and social contexts. The ideal would then be to test the generalizations resulting from such a study against the data of the smudge pits of the eastern United States for the identification of both the by-products of behavior and the behavioral corollaries of the material remains. At present, however, not only has such a cross-cultural study of these behavioral sets not been attempted, but the ethnographic and historic evidence which would make such a study possible is generally not available (which is, of course, where the need for ethnoarchaeological "materialist studies of behavior" becomes especially vital).

190

Ethnoarchaeology, Experimentation, and Lithic Analysis

The second case study is the analysis of flaked stone tools, a problem with which I have been directly concerned on the experimental side (Tringham et al. 1974; Tringham in press c). With the exceptions of work by some nineteenth-century optimists (Nilsson 1868; Evans 1872) and of the research mentioned below, the function of flaked stone tools has until recently been treated summarily. The traditional criteria used in classifying flaked stone tools have been such macromorphological characteristics as hypothesized method of manufacture and modification of the flakes' shape by deliberate retouch. In some cases these characteristics have been quantified by sophisticated statistical tests that plot inter and intrasite variability and reconstruct changing cultures and traditions (see, for example, Binford 1973; Bordes 1973; Collins 1973; Mellars 1973).

Bordes (1971), Crabtree (1973), Semenov (1964), and others recognized that classification on the basis of shape and technology called for experimental tests on the manufacture of flaked stone tools. "Unwittingly, the inquirer is aware that he must understand the mechanics of percussion, indirect percussion and pressure to be able to recognize these differences and that the answer lies in verified experiment" (Crabtree 1973:10). Their experiments are designed to reconstruct the steps in the manufacture of tools by replicating the ultimate shape of cores and flakes.

> My replications are based on actual experiments—rejecting and accepting various stages of manufacture until simulation of the aborginal artifact is acquired. . . . If the finished product is a true replica, then it is safe to assume that the primary and intermediate stages are parallel to those of the aboriginal. For, if the experimenter allows extreme deviations in the initial stages, then the finished product will be aberrant in form and technique and, therefore, not a true replica. (Crabtree 1973:12)

For his starting point, namely, the primary stages of manufacture, Crabtree relies on manufacturing debitage flakes found on archaeological sites. Semenov started from a rather different direction; he identified damage marks on cores and flakes as the by-products of manufacture. Semenov's attitude to experiments is more equivocal than Crabtree's:

> As an auxiliary method to confirm or make more precise deductions from the traces left by wear, experiment is undoubtedly useful. . . . Experiment is important (apart from testing the mechanical properties of ancient tools) for the physiological experience of really assessing the nature of the working skill of prehistoric man, of the live sensation of the expediency of form of a stone tool, and so on. (Semenov 1964:2)

He thus places much more weight on the damage traces themselves, both damage from manufacture of the flake and damage through its usage. Throughout his book *Prehistoric Technology*, Semenov does not specify whether he tested experimentally (1964:28) his interpretation of the damage pattern. He remarks, for example, "After establishing that the traces of the cores had been produced by a very hard presser we turned our attention to the study of the platforms on the blades themselves" (1964:50). Semenov's approach is inherently more productive for the identification of methods of manufacture and usage of stone tools, since it takes as the starting point for research the direct by-products of the behavior. As others have pointed out, however, this virtue is somewhat undercut by the fact that when his interpretation of the traces is tested by experimentation (as many of them are), the tests are rarely repeated. Moreover, as his statement quoted above implies, his experiments are of a positivist nature, that is, they are designed to *confirm* his identification rather than refute it, which means that he is reluctant to test alternative hypotheses on the formation of a certain damage pattern.

The experiments of Speth and Faulkner on the nature of conchoidal fracture and the properties of conchoidally fracturing rocks have contributed considerably to bringing experimentation in lithic analysis onto a higher plane of respectability and confidence (Speth 1974; Faulkner 1972; Tsirk 1974). Their experiments have tested the mechanical properties of natural phenomena, and in this way have confirmed hypotheses on the basic mechanical principles of flaking which can be applied at a macrolevel to the manufacture of flake tools, and at a microlevel to modification by retouch and the like and to the formation of edge damage through usage.

Damage of flaked stone tools through usage is manifested in several ways, including microflaking and various forms of abrasion such as striations, gloss, and polish (Semenov 1964:14). In reconstructing usage from, for example, striations, Semenov relies heavily on the principles of kinetic theory (1964:16-21), which have been tested as yet much less thoroughly on the use of stone tools than the principles of conchoidal fracture and flaking. For this and other reasons (see Tringham et al. 1974:175), our own reconstructions have relied most heavily on the criterion of microflaking.

Our experimentation on the formation of edge damage in flaked stone tools during usage constitutes essentially what I have termed "by-product" experiment, in that it tests at a basic level the mechanical processes of damage to the edge of a flake during its contact with the worked material (Tringham et al. 1974). "Tool usage" was broken down into its most basic variables, which may be expressed in a statement such as: "Edge contacts a surface of given resistance in a given direction at a given angle to the surface."

The constant variable throughout the whole series has been the raw material of the flakes, which is a European chalk flint. Variables tested include those of (1) the edge of the flake (spine-plane angle, curvature, modification by retouch to varying degrees, and so on); (2) worked or contacted material (of varying degrees of resistance); (3) action (angle of work, direction). The variables have been tested and replicated in a number of combinations, although by no means all the possible ones. We have been as honest as possible in trying to refute our hypotheses concerning the agents that caused the damage patterns of different kinds, but we could, no doubt, have been even more strenuous in our attempts.

The sources for the hypotheses we tested in the series and for the variables we selected are threefold:

(1) the archaeological data themselves (European lithic assemblages from a post-Pleistocene temperate forested environment);

(2) a hypothesized ecological situation in which materials were available to the prehistoric societies and might have been worked by them with flaked stone tools; and

(3) ethnographic and historical sources that suggested which of these possible materials were more likely to have been worked by flaked stone tools (they suggested, for example, that we not select mushrooms as a suitable variable, but might do well to select *Chenopodia* and fish) even when the materials were not found on the archaeological sites in question; these sources also suggested which actions should be simulated (suggesting, for example, that it would be useful to include "chopping" even

though no "ax-shaped" flaked stone tools had been discovered in the sites and it was assumed that the only "chopping" tools were those made of polished stone); we tended to reduce the action of a living society, for example, "cutting," to simple variables such as "longitudinal action, at varying angles to the worked material," rather than simulate whole behavioral patterns.

These experiments have to be looked at as a series; they cannot be seen in isolation. They were designed to aid in the confident identification of used vs. unused edge, or used vs. accidentally damaged edge, and the action and, if possible, worked material of the tool. It was hoped that these tests for the identification of usage, along with those testing the identification of methods of manufacture, would contribute to the credibility of statements that use lithic analysis in the explication and explanation of cultural variation and change.

The intellectual reasons that prompted our experimentation have been discussed elsewhere (Tringham et al. 1974; Tringham in press c). It is sufficient to say that our work formed part of the strategy to add an extra dimension to lithic analysis (in addition to those traditionally employed), in order to include the assemblages as an integral part of the study of East European Neolithic society. This extra dimension was the selection of the edge of the flake, rather than the whole tool, as the main unit of analysis. Such a strategy may be seen, for example, in the analysis of material from Divostin, Banja, and Anzabegovo in Yugoslavia, Bylany in Czechoslovakia, Sitagroi in Greece, and some of the more recent studies of Mesolithic and Neolithic assemblages in western Europe. These analyses involve a descriptive coding of the edge of each flake in terms of which part was broken, which part was used and how, which part was modified by retouch, and so forth, and an analysis of the correlation of usage with modification and with the selection of flakes of certain dimensions, and so on (Tringham 1973, in press a, in press b; Odell 1974, in press; Voytek 1974, in press; Whitman and Voytek in press; Elster 1976).

Inherent in this strategy is the hypothesis that retouch of flakes is a function of the maintenance and usage of the flake rather than attaining a morphologically ideal type (J. P. White and Thomas 1972; Gould, Koster, and Sontz 1971). Our experiments were designed to facilitate the testing of this hypothesis directly against the archaeological data by making possible the confident identification of the used, as opposed to the unused or accidentally damaged, edge.

194

Traditionally, with a few exceptions (see Tringham et al. 1974:171-72), the usage of stone tools either was ignored as irrelevant for monitoring culture change or was reconstructed halfheartedly on the basis of the philosophy that "form follows function." Unlike many other forms of archaeological data—such as house structures, ceramics, or metals—flaked stone tools have been minimal in or absent from the material culture of most societies in the world for 2,000 years or more. There has been less temptation, therefore, to reconstruct their manufacture and usage by invoking continuity of tradition from prehistoric into historic and ethnographic societies. Nevertheless, ethnographic examples of stone tools have been used to provide analogies in reconstructing the function of prehistoric stone tools. For example, the relation of the form to the function of Eskimo end scrapers has been a frequent source of analogy in reconstructing the function of distally retouched blades found in the Upper Paleolithic assemblages in Western Europe (Semenov 1964:85-93). Ethnographic descriptions and subsequent microwear analysis (Nissen and Dittemore 1974) indicate that in the Eskimo examples the retouched edge did in fact coincide with the used edge. On the basis of a study of the microwear traces of Neolithic prehistoric distally retouched blade tools, however, it would seem that to make such a correlation is a dangerous assumption (Tringham in press a).

My decision to take the edge as the main unit of analysis and revolve the analysis around (1) usage–flake selection and (2) usage–flake modification correlates was, I am afraid to say, completely intuitive and based mostly on a gut reaction against the constructions of the traditional typologies of Paleolithic and Mesolithic lithic studies in Europe. It was only later that I became familiar with the observations made in present-day New Guinea and Australia on the use of flaked stone tools (J. P. White 1968b; White and Thomas 1972; Gould, Koster, and Sontz 1971):

> Flakes without any secondary retouch are used as tools, and they constitute the only category of flake tools: no secondary retouch with the aim of shaping flake tools has ever been observed among the New Guinea highlanders. . . . The two most important features—namely edge type and size—are functionally determined. . . . Functional limitations, however, set only broad formal limits. . . . Occasionally, if a sharp edge interferes with a comfortable grip on the stone, then the edge will be blunted. . . . (White and Thomas 1972:278-79)

195

Associated with these phenomena, the methods used to apply the ethnographic classification to the archaeological materials in New Guinea are

> based on making the altered (i.e. used or retouched) edge on an artifact the prime unit of analysis, and treating each piece of stone as the record of a series of discrete processes acting on it, rather than as a functional whole in the normal archaeological sense. (White and Thomas 1972:282)

In an ideal world, with a Utopian order to research procedures, these ethnoarchaeological observations would have been available before I started my analysis of East European assemblages, and would have provided a source for generating hypotheses on the relation of tool use to tool shape which could have been tested against the East European data. As it turns out, I had already intuitively decided to examine in the East European assemblages and by experimentation those variables which the studies of Gould and White would have prompted anyway.

On the basis of the ethnoarchaeological observations and control "ethnographic experiments" made by White in New Guinea, and by Gould, Hayden, O'Connell, and others in Australia, it is possible to make various generalizations that may be formulated as a set of hypotheses testable against *any* lithic data; the tests are not restricted to the lithic assemblages of the immediate prehistoric ancestors of the inhabitants of New Guinea and Australia. One such hypothesis is that variation in the flake usage–flake modification correlate reflects variation in the exploitation of the flake raw material, variation in the care given to the manufacture of certain flake tools, variation in the "curation" and maintenance of flake tools through repair, resharpening, recycling, and reuse, and variation in methods of handling and hafting, rather than variation of social norms and traditions of morphological categories. If on the basis of microwear studies it is possible to identify the usage of the tool (single or multiple), as well as modification which has served to resharpen the edge, modification which has served to blunt the edge, and damage to an edge through hafting and handling, points of accidental breakage of the tool, and so on, then it is possible on the basis of direct archaeological evidence to reconstruct—or begin to reconstruct—the life history of a flake.

With this kind of information confidently established, the spatial distribution of the flakes takes on some significance in terms of reflecting the cultural processes involved in their deposition, for example in localizing activity-specific areas on a site.

The importance of the factor of individual variation in the manufacture and usage of tools was demonstrated (it is questionable how successfully) by the ethnographic experiment carried out by White (White and Thomas 1972:289). However much one may argue with the results, the experiment was certainly important in suggesting ways in which one might devise tests of hypotheses concerning (1) the integration of lithic tools into the rest of the material culture of society, and (2) lithic variation reflecting "cultural variation," small- and large-group interaction, and social organization (Sheets 1975).

Without any recourse to continuity of cultural tradition in a historic period, therefore, or to the use of random analogies for the "best fit," it is possible, with a little optimism, confidently to use generalizations formulated by ethnoarchaeologists as testable hypotheses in the interpretation of archaeological data. One will not find the truth, but the risks one takes with statements on prehistoric societies are rather more calculable. From the point of view of ethnoarchaeological research and controlled experimentation, lithic studies are far ahead of most kinds of archaeological investigations. Much of the fundamental testing of the mechanical properties of the raw materials, techniques of manufacture, modification, and usage has already been carried out, and the possibility of the identification of these properties in the archaeological data is relatively assured. It is interesting in this respect to note that the majority of Old World archaeologists dealing with lithic assemblages, sometimes as their only source of information, have not taken advantage of the results of this research.

CONCLUSION

I would like in conclusion to draw attention to a recent paper by David Clarke, who discusses the emergence of General Theory in archaeology, especially in the "New Archaeology":

> . . . the rising interest in archaeological philosophy naturally leads to necessary metaphysical theories of archaeological concepts, epistemological theories of archaeological information and classification and logical theories of archaeological reasoning. Here is certainly a body of necessary but *unfulfilled* theory which overlies and permeates a series of other levels of archaeological

theory that translate and explain the relationships between classes of archaeological phenomena; it is these unspecified steps which underlie the *critical leaps in archaeological reasoning*. Without such a body of theory these critical leaps do indeed take-off and become a free-flight of creative fancy—an irresponsible art form. (Clarke 1973:16; italics added)

The General Theory that Clarke proposes includes five "other levels of archaeological theory," which, he feels, with some justification, have been ignored and leapfrogged.

Predepositional and depositional theory relates hominid activities and behavioral patterns to "the sample and traces which were at the time deposited in the archaeological record." Ethnoarchaeological and experimental (both behavioral and by-product) research is essential in this body of theory, in formulating testable hypotheses.

Postdepositional theory relates the traces of behavior in their original deposition to subsequent disturbance by human, animal, plant, and geological agents. This is "largely a microgeomorphological and statistical theory," but it must include theory on human debris-dropping and garbage-disposal patterns.

Retrieval theory, the theory of sampling and retrieval and excavation strategies, relates what is actually retrieved of the behavior by archaeological research to the surviving sample which was available for recovery.

Analytical theory identifies and reconstructs behavior through information retrieval, analytic techniques, quantification, and by-product experimentation.

Interpretive theory relates information gained by direct observation, testing, and analysis of the archaeological data to "predictions about the directly unobservable ancient behavioral and environmental patterns." This is the theory of the formulation and testing of hypotheses generated by ethnographic, historical, and other generalizations and behavioral experimentation. This is the "upper-level testing" referred to in this paper as opposed to the lower level of analytical theory.

In my detailing of Clarke's steps in archaeological General Theory, I have stressed the relevance of ethnoarchaeological and experimental information in each step. I should say that this is purely my own interpretation of Clarke's scheme, and may very well not meet with his approval.

It has, I hope, helped to emphasize the three main themes of this chapter. First, although the study of material culture may not be synonymous with archaeological research, it is nevertheless essential in archaeology to understand the theory and identification procedures of the relationship of human societies to materials in order to understand the relationship of one human individual or group to another.

Second, ethnoarchaeological and experimental research in archaeology are not romantic adjuncts to understanding the nature of human-material and human-human relationships, but play a consistently important and integral role at all levels of the analysis and interpretation of these relationships in past societies.

Third, and most important, we recognize in archaeological research that speculation and game theory provide the bulk of our working hypotheses. I also recognize, however, that, at all levels of this research, explicit attention to the interplay of theoretical issues and scientific procedures in the analysis and interpretation of data, whether one is rummaging in other people's garbage or constructing Paleo-Malthusian simulation models, gives a much clearer picture of how far we are along the line from fairy tale to reality.

8
If Pots Were Mortal[1]

MICHAEL B. STANISLAWSKI
Museum of New Mexico

*One day Nasrudin lent his cooking pots
to a neighbor, who was giving a feast.
The neighbor returned them, together
with one extra one—a very tiny pot.
"What is this?" asked Nasrudin.
"According to law, I have given you
the offspring of your property which
was born when the pots were in my care,"
said the joker. Shortly afterwards
Nasrudin borrowed his neighbor's pots,
but did not return them. The man
came around to get them back.
"Alas!" said Nasrudin, "They are dead.
We have established, have we not, that
pots are mortal?"
—A Sufi Parable (Elizabeth Hall 1975:54)*

INTRODUCTION

Archaeologists often assume that pots can multiply, types are born and die, and ceramic traditions, like lineages, can be classified into "families" or clans. We also assume that particular ceramic types, wares, or schools of design are tightly linked to other aspects of culture, as if they were part of a family. These assumptions may occasionally be true, in a general sense (see Newton 1974, who shows a clear relationship among some Brazilian hammock-weaving styles and tribal boundaries). But our goal as ethnoarchaeologists should be to step outside these assumptions, to learn those technological ideas, behaviors, and end results of members of other ongoing traditional societies; and then to base our statements concerning the relationships among artifacts (such as pottery) and other parts of the Institutions of Culture, on those beliefs, actions, and patterns of material remains that are actually observed. (For indications of lack of relationship among artifacts and other cultural institutions see Robbins and Pollnac 1974 and Stanislawski in press.) By the comparative study of artifact clusters in several such societies we may finally be able to discover regularities in association of specific artifact groups, social units, and social processes (such as trade, cultural contacts, stimulus diffusion, innovation, assimilation, and acculturation). This is the same problem that other anthropologists face and study in similar ways (for example, Spicer 1952, 1962; Foster 1973); and they point out that it is often the differential assumptions, rules, and ideas of people in varying social systems that determine whether an object will be accepted or rejected. For example, Foster (1973) stresses the different social, cultural, and psychological barriers or stimulants to change which may affect the acceptance or use of an otherwise efficient tool. Spicer (1952) provides examples of the meaning, use, and function of tools in specific practical situations, as well as a set of suggested questions concerning their systemic relationships.

Whether quantifiable or not, human choices, as modified in specific situations and given specific social system restraints and stimuli, do alter the possible artifact patterns. The work of cultural geographers demonstrates this; for example, Kniffen (1974) discusses the differences in land use and other natural resources, housing, tools, and other material culture items in the southwest Louisiana area, according to Native American, French, Spanish, and Anglo lifeways. It may be taste and feel, both literally and figuratively, that will determine whether a new variety of corn is accepted or rejected in a Hispano village of northern New Mexico, regardless of its superior yield per acre, growing season, or disease resistance (Apodaca 1952: 35-39). In short, quality is often more vital than quantity.

Definitions of Culture

There is a developing emphasis among social and cultural anthropologists on a behavioral adaptive definition of culture. For example, Roger Keesing (1974: 74-77, 82-89) defines culture as follows (emphasis added):

1. Cultures are systems of socially transmitted behaviors, a set of concepts that each individual *thinks* other people know, believe, and mean; i.e. concepts that relate human groups to the natural environment; and thus includes technology, settlements, social groups, and economic systems. They are shared behavioral systems which provide adaptation, i.e. ways of "playing the game";
2. Cultural change involves natural selection of the best adaptive system or parts of systems including artifacts [see Clark 1970 for a Darwinian and genetic process model of natural selection of ideas and "best fit" technologies] and thus can be modeled in terms of self-regulating systems factors, i.e. positive and negative feedback [see Flannery 1968].
3. Technology, economic systems, subsistence systems, and all the production systems of adaptation are central to the problem of where change begins.
4. Ideational components of cultural systems, and the conflicts within them, have vital adaptive consequences [e.g., Foster 1973; Spicer 1952].

In short, there are patterns of life typical of communities, which Keesing calls "sociocultural systems" or "social realizations of ideational designs for living." In such a behavioral definition, one cannot separate the ideational and technological realms, for they are always integral parts of the human behavioral set.

Modern archaeologists are also reconsidering the definitions of their goals and aims, and a similar behavioral definition of archaeology is becoming increasingly popular (for examples, see Spaulding 1973:35; Redman 1973; Rouse 1973; Streuver 1968; Schiffer 1975c; Deetz 1968a, 1971). For example, Spaulding states, "Human cultural behavior exhibits properties not found in other living systems, and it is precisely this *peculiarly human way of behaving* that is our subject" (1973:34; emphasis added). Charles Redman has defined archaeology as "the systematic (i.e., scientific) study of the nature and cultural behavior of human beings through the examination and analysis of the material remains of their past activities. I think the main focus of archaeology is human behavior instead of artifacts" (1973:6).

Ethnoarchaeology

I have previously defined ethnoarchaeology as "the participant or direct observation field study of the form, use, meaning, and function of artifacts within their institutional settings in a living society" (Stanislawski in press). It can also be defined as "a concern for the relationship of man's visible and measurable modification of his environment and his invisible and less easily measured social and ideological life" (Deetz 1971:3). Our basic goal is to link artifacts and their behavioral correlates in such a manner that archaeologically testable propositions may ultimately be made and tests of archaeological propositions may be attempted. Since our particular focus is on collecting ethnographic data of archaeological interest, archaeological testing "must form the controlling factor by which the evidence from ethnography can be organized to form relevant models" (Rowlands 1971:210). In other words, our purpose is to render ethnographic evidence strictly comparable to that from excavated sites (Gould 1971:145), and, in turn, to use archaeological data to lead to an understanding of ethnographic systems in dynamic change (Van der Merwe and Scully 1971:194). While a focus on participation or direct-observation fieldwork among nonindustrial peoples is not essential (see Brown 1973), ethnoarchaeology will often stress such studies, for several reasons. First, such studies will make our evidence more applicable to prehistoric behavioral situations and are not now generally being done by other historians or cultural anthropologists (see Fenton 1974). Second, the field requires a knowledge of, and training in, the techniques of classification and analysis of archaeological data in order to make archaeological and ethnographic data comparable. Third, our understanding of the form, manufacture, distribution, meaning, and use of artifacts in an integrated system, as well as in their institutional setting, can really only be attempted in the analysis of the smaller, more isolated, and more homogeneous societies which resemble those of the prehistoric past. This is a particularly vital point, for, as Ascher notes,

> the import of this shift [from hand to machine production] extends far beyond the materials and machines themselves. They are different worlds; and the humble objects . . . have shaken our mode of living to its very roots. Modest things of daily life, they accumulate into forces acting upon whomever moves within the orbit of our civilization. (Ascher 1974:8)

Change in recent machine-made, mass-produced artifacts is thus very fast, widespread, and noncontinuous, producing a record distinctly different from that of the slowly changing, continuous tradition of the folk culture which would have been characteristic of the nonurban prehistoric societies we excavate. Finally, we must study these folk societies quickly, before they cease to exist as functioning individual systems, leaving only isolated members. Also we must do the studies while participant-observation or direct-observation field techniques are still possible, for we must attempt to discover what people do rather than what a few informants say they do, or did; how the physical remains are actually left; and what is the range of variation and activities (such as difference in individual and subgroup performance in stone chipping or pottery making). This is distinctly different from the problems of sociologists or ethnographers, who sample fragmentary cultural patterns in complex, large, modern or historic industrial societies, where many different ethnic groups, castes and classes, ranges of literacy, and different cultural and individual ways of doing things are found competing for success as specialties, alternatives, or universals (Ascher 1974; Linton 1936).

In this vein, Margaret Mead has recently argued that our knowledge of ourselves, of our unique characteristics, requires both a humanistic (direct-observation) and a physical-science (hypothesis-testing) approach to study, and comes

> from our capacity to explore human responses to events in which we and others participate through introspection and empathy, as well as our capacity to make objective observations on physical and animate nature. . . .
> Human beings have the capacity to understand their feelings because they are sufficiently like themselves so that attention to their own internal states provides information about the internal states of others. (1976:905)

Questionnaires and their quantification, she believes, artificially "evoke" fragmentary human behavior, giving anthropologists the illusion of science. Participant or direct-observation techniques, however, are a type of "peculiarly intensive" apprenticeship training which provides data "derived from time consuming shared experiences that cannot be replicated" (1976:907). The human scientist thus uses a "natural history approach" to record parts of nonreplicable events in a particular social and ecological setting, and particularly emphasizes

205

behavior (as in the complementary field of animal ethology).

Raymond Firth shares the same philosophy concerning the major emphasis of modern ethnographic field work. He says:

> The essence of the social anthropologist's field approach is his combination of verbal enquiry with direct field observation. . . . Formal interview and questionnaire both have their place, but adapted to the conditions of lengthy residence; the direct observation of behavior is not merely a corrective to verbally acquired data but an indispensable complement. . . . The emphasis on direct observation is not fortuitous. It is linked with a theory of social controls—a classification of rules and their sanction; a conception of differential conformity to them, with distinctions between the ideal of conduct, imputed conduct and actual conduct. In any given society the anthropologist is always concerned with practice as well as principle, and with the relations between them. (1975:16)

Most significantly, he notes,

> Impressive displays of model building or dazzling analyses of the meaning of vernacular terms may be no more than ritual exercises or aesthetic constructs unless they are latched into some body of data relating to an identifiable society. (1975:18)

A major key to fieldwork and data collecting in ethnoarchaeology, then, must be an emphasis on the direct- or participant-observation technique in specific and individually described ongoing societies, whose sociocultural systems are still relatively intact and which thus allow the observation of variations in behavior leading to variations in material culture or other changes in the natural landscape. We otherwise run the risk of artificially "evoking fragmentary behavior" which, out of context, will skew our understanding. We will have partially *created* the cultural facts we record!

Two fine recently published ethnoarchaeological accounts exemplify these points. Lewis Binford (1975) describes his work in a village of the Nunamiut Eskimo near Anaktuvuk Pass in northern Alaska. He particularly wished to study their caribou-hunting techniques so as to make possible analogies with the similar techniques used by Western European Neanderthal reindeer hunters in sites some tens of thousands of years old. At first, he was, however, horrified by the modern houses, clothing, speech, and other behavior of the villagers. Even the famous "chief informant" of the village (Simon Paneack) seemed to know more anthropology than traditional Eskimo life. Nonetheless, Binford attempted "salvage ethnography" (oral history studies), particularly stressing hunting and butchering techniques; but even when using villagers to help dig their own kill sites and asking them on the spot to identify and explain artifacts found, he received disinterest, unusable information, or highly variable results due to age, sex, and "value" variations. It was only when he participated directly during the spring hunt season that he saw the old hunting ways acted out; patterns of land use and variability in actual hunting activities leading to the production of "traditional" kill sites were revealed. Observation was his only valid source of information; "historical accounts were mute and even the men who produced the patterns were unaware of their existence and meaning" (1975:30).

This is also the set of points explicitly made by Richard Nelson in his fine Eskimo study, *Hunters of the Northern Ice* (1969), wherein he details his learning in tool-making and snow- and ocean-ice-hunting techniques in villages of the Wainwright Eskimo of northeastern Alaska. This is an area where mistakes are costly and theories must be consistent with reality: "the Eskimos must perform in an arena which has many high-level constraints on behavior and which offers little guiding information. Penalties for mistakes are prompt and drastic. Death in cold water is assured in minutes. . ." (Laughlin 1969:xiv-xv). Nelson participated with several hunting groups in all of their stalking, killing, butchering, and traveling activities for more than a year. He learned by doing, by rewards of the hunt, and by ridicule—the traditional education techniques of the Eskimo. Nelson believes that attempts to amass data by scientific experimentation or questionnaires alone would almost certainly have failed. He learned (as I have done in working with Hopi potters) that instruction and learning for the Eskimo is a matter of copying the actions of good hunters, listening to elders in a group, and mimicking their series of interlocking procedures, many of which are unverbalized and invisible (like, for example, the almost impossible-to-describe process of learning to steer a car, or ease out the clutch). He stressed that one learned little or nothing by asking formal questions. His was thus a field study focused on direct participation in human activities on floating sea ice, and because he was so thoroughly trained, he provides us with a tremendous amount of necessary information for successful survival and exploitation of this difficult eco-niche, even to emergency procedures for safe passage over breaking ice, where death is near. We could not have a better demonstration of the most necessary focus of ethnoarchaeology fieldwork.

A second factor indicating the relevance of ethnoarchaeology is the question of the origin of the hypotheses we, as scientists, wish to test archaeologically in order to attempt prediction or explanation. It is only with such testing of alternative multiple working hypotheses, and the elimination of unsatisfactory ones, that we may attempt to state "laws" (Chamberlin 1965; Platt 1964). I have discussed elsewhere some of the problems in the use of inference and analogy in ethnoarchaeology and archaeology (Stanislawski 1974, in press). Basically the point is that we always must move from the known to the unknown—for example, from the known systemic relationships of economic trade networks in Australia involving stone axes (Sharp 1952), from the mechanism of the New Guinea Kula ring (Malinowski 1922), from the complex patterns of historic and recent trading relationships among southwestern plains raiding, Pueblo farming, and southwestern herding societies (R. I. Ford 1972), or among African metal-working groups (Rowlands 1971) to the vastly more complex problems of inferring and testing such tightly integrated non-Western systems in similar societies of the past. (See R. Adams 1974a and M. Webb 1974 for lucid discussions of other such complexities and the need for such data as emphasized in ethnoarchaeology.) Since every object also contains its own built-in information in the sense of its indicative qualities, contextual relationships, and possibilities for testing (see Thompson 1958), the related subfield or discipline of experimental archaeology may thus also profitably be used in conjunction with ethnoarchaeology (see Tringham: Chapter 7, above; Watson 1975).

Direct historic analogies based on direct historic continuities may even be possible in some world areas such as Australia, where Gould (1973) sees more than 10,000 years of relatively unchanged aboriginal tradition; the Near East (Watson 1975); and perhaps, for shorter lengths of time, the American Southwest (Stanislawski in press; Steward 1937). Even where such direct analogies may not be possible, as in most of Western Europe (Clark 1957:171-72), a general technical and environmental analogy (or "folk cultural" analogy) may be applicable (see, for example, Clark 1952; Ascher 1961:318-19). In each case, there are problems of levels of reliability, which in time must be meshed with the varying levels of inference or analogy attempted (Ascher 1961a; K. Anderson 1969; Gould 1973; Stanislawski in press).

For example, our methods and levels of conclusions must vary depending on whether we are working with multiple informants and observations in an ongoing society, isolated informants, documentary records, or museum pieces. In addition, because of variability in the sharing of prehistoric and modern cultural norms, differences of opinion, or mistakes in understanding, such direct connections would be tenuous at best (for archaeology problems in understanding cognition, see Kehoe and Kehoe 1973; Ucko 1969a; Wallace 1962; Sturtevant 1964). The important point, as many processual or systems archaeologists have said (Binford 1965, 1968; Freeman 1968), is that the analogy proves nothing by itself; it must be independently tested as but one of a number of *multiple* working hypotheses. Since none of us could imagine the form, use, meaning, or systemic artifact relationships of a prehistoric Pueblo kachina dance (for example, those early Hopi styles indicated by the Awatovi murals [Smith 1952]), it is clear that we must start with observed behavior patterns of the ceremonial dances and present patterns of artifacts and social groups, and work backward. While Binford has criticized the casual use of direct-analogy models, he has also said, "It may often be more impressive or scientifically more efficient in obtaining high levels of confidence to make such tests with ethnographic data" (1968:270).

While there are as yet no machines which can turn out valid testable hypotheses, Spaulding (1973:351-52), Mayer-Oakes (1974), Watson (1975:5-6), Stanislawski (in press), and others have pointed out that if we wish to study human behavior of the past, all of our hypotheses and inferences must be made by some sort of analogy. As Spaulding puts it, "Our only way of connecting objects interpreted as relics of the past with human behavior is by analogy with directly observed behavior" (1973:352). In these cases it is again clear that man's ideas of expected patterns of behavior (i.e., norms) are as important in his adaptation as are his basic and unconscious biological forms of adaption. Mark Leone, in a detailed description of Mormon architecture and settlement pattern, has stated:

> . . . despite overwhelming changes in Mormon culture there is an unchanged relationship between a key set of artifacts and a set of religious symbols. . . . Mormonism could not exist without the spatial representations and technological devices that allowed its populations to exist. Here we see that mental processes are as much a product of the use of tools as the way that the tools are used is a product of mental rules. (Leone 1973:148-49)

Clearly there are some limits to human variability, and there are shared patterns in production, trade, use, and abandonment of artifacts in different cultural traditions, at different levels of technology, and in different environmental niches. The works of Coon (1958), Steward (1955), Leslie White (1959), and Wittfogel (1957), among others in social anthropology, are classic reflections of this philosophy. Any science of prehistoric material culture thus depends upon the use of ethnographic observation, the study of behavior which results in observable and standardized changes in the landscape. One author has called such artifact relationships "The Human Mirror . . . the fullest expression of man's efforts to objectify his concepts" (Richardson 1974:4). It becomes our problem as archaeologists to show that any particular variant of the possible applies to a specific site. Even this can be reversed, for the explanation of any one situation is also the test of the "covering law" which is used in explanation, and hence a test of the general again (see Trigger 1970, 1973). All ethnoarchaeological analysis is thus based on the concept that artifacts are not to be treated as things in themselves, or as individual works of art, but are always to be related to a specific social system and a specific type of behavior. This is not to say that material remains always "mirror" human activities equally in all domains or institutions. One recent study (Robbins and Pollnac 1974) indicates that the people over the age of forty in Buganda, East Africa, had the most traditional religious and political beliefs, but also had modern artifacts in their homes. Several ceramic studies have demonstrated little material evidence of the Tewa migration to the Hopi mesas in A.D. 1700 (Ellis 1961), or of the Spanish invasion of Mexico (Charlton 1972) or Peru (Tschopik 1950); these events are not reflected in ceramic evidence for more than a century after the fact. Karl Heider (1967) and Nicholas David (1971) have also discussed the serious problems of calculating population and family structure from the archaeological analysis of highly variable and often misunderstood settlement remains.

In short, we are only beginning to learn what we need to know about the interrelationships of tools and human behavior, but clearly ethnoarchaeology, like cultural anthropology and archaeology, should have a general behavioral definition and focus. We may also focus on certain sites as keys underlying specifically different aspects of human behavior (Gould 1973:17; Yellen and Harpending 1972; Binford 1975). This does indeed help forge a tie between ethnoarchaeology and settlement archaeology, the latter being a field in which, as Jeffrey Parsons notes (1972:146), there has long been a need for cooperation between archaeologists and ethnographers. But it seems to me that this is but one possible subfocus of the discipline. The major question must continue to be, What behavioral patterns and relationships among specific tools, social groups, and religious and moral ideologies, for a specific type or level of society, in a particular environment, at a particular time produce similar "behavioral chains" and similar sets of artifact remains?

Finally, archaeologists will have to do this work, for most ethnographic and ethnological technology studies tell us only of the production phase, and not the distribution, consumption, and reuse or abandonment phases of activity involving the artifact. We know how the artifact was made, on the average, but not why individuals differed, the ideal shape, the actual result, what variations are allowed, or what innovations are permitted (see White and Thomas 1972); the native's concept of type as compared with the archaeologist's; the actual use, meaning, and function of the artifact in the ongoing society; or the final behavior that results in the artifact's becoming part of a site.

DATA EXAMPLES

The balance of this chapter will focus on ethnoarchaeological fieldwork among the Hopi and Hopi-Tewa of northeast Arizona. My wife and I began the project in 1968, and worked at the First Mesa villages of Walpi, Sichomovi, and Tewa, and at the nearby government settlements of Polacca and Keams Canyon, as well as at several new small farm settlements on Antelope Mesa, south of Keams. During our seven summers of fieldwork, we were able to observe and talk with more than 40 principal informants; in addition we observed a number of other men and women more briefly. We never used questionnaires, nor did we take notes in front of informants. We studied trading-post collections and the research collections of the Museum of Northern Arizona, including more than 600 pots, as well as the museum's annual Hopi Craftsman Exhibition records, accession files, and photographs.

The Hopi of Walpi and Sichomovi villages speak Hopic, a variant of Shoshoni, which is in turn related to other Uto-Aztecan languages from as far south as the Valley of Mexico and beyond. Similar peoples have lived in the Mesa area since at least A.D. 1000-1100, and can be identified as ancestral Hopi by at least A.D. 1250-1300. The Hopi-Tewa,

211

who founded Tewa Village (Hano), are originally an Eastern Pueblo Tewa-speaking group who probably migrated to First Mesa in the winter of 1700-1701. There are many cultural similarities between the two groups, including similar social structure, housing, material culture, and subsistence. However, variations in religious observance, kinship terminology and clan groups, political structure, and particularly language and personality traits still reflect some differences between the two societies (see Dozier 1954).

At the present time, the population of the Hopi mesas is about 6,600, of which approximately 600 are of Tewa clans. First Mesa has about 1,500 people, of whom about 600 are Tewa. Of these, 225 live in Tewa Village, about 220 in Sichomovi, and 80 in Walpi; 650 live in Polacca, about 100 in Keams Canyon, and a small number in farms and settlements nearby.

Much of our work was initiated in order to examine specific ethnographic hypotheses in southwestern archaeology (J.N. Hill 1970a, 1970b; Longacre 1968, 1970). The study was first designed to consider the possible relationships of pottery styles and traditions to specific social organization units such as clans, lineages, marriage locality, and sodalities. However, the project soon was expanded to include a wider range of topics such as (1) how artifacts became part of developing sites; (2) networks of ceramic learning models and the spread of new ceramic innovations such as identification marks on pottery; (3) the meaning of Hopi and Hopi-Tewa ceramic types and attributes to the natives themselves; (4) the processes and causes of technological innovation and change since the 1870s (the earliest period from which we have photographs and manuscript material that discusses pottery); and (5) the problem of defining a "culture" from archaeological remains alone.

In correlation with recent remarks of Redman (1973), Rouse (1973:23-28), and Deetz (1968a) on the organization of archaeology, I believe we can study ethnoarchaeological data in a series of hierarchical levs. We can consider a minimum of 10 problem areas in terms of five social levels; the problem areas range from consideration of form, types, modes, and production techniques to questions of abandonment and processes, systems, and function. The levels range from the individual craftsman to cultural and cross-cultural comparisons. In short, we will have at least 10 problem areas which can be' considered in terms of various types and sizes of social groups (see Table 8.1). The field and ceramic data which follow are arranged

TABLE 8.1
PROBLEM AREAS IN ETHNOARCHAEOLOGY

	SOCIAL LEVELS				
Problem Areas	*A. Individual*	*B. Subgroup*	*C. Village*	*D. Culture*	*E. Cross Culture*
1. Form/Design (modes, emic-etic types)					
2. Production					
3. Social Time (daily, seasonal)					
4. Distribution (trade, ownership)					
5. Use and Storage					
6. Meaning (to native society) and Networks of Learning					
7. Reuse and Recycling					
8. Abandonment (discard, breakage)					
9. Processes of Change and End Results					
10. Systems and Function (to anthropologist)					

in this general framework, which I hope will allow for better data comparisons, serve as a fieldwork checklist for data collection, and allow a rapid survey of the strengths and weaknesses of our current knowledge of various practical and theoretical areas.

These problems will be discussed in four convenient categories: technology (production, use, and distribution); learning (meaning and networks of communication); site development (reuse, recycling, abandonment, and discard); and technological systems (processes and cultural change).

213

Technology (Table 8.1, 1-5)

There are currently about 125 active potters in the Hopi region, about 75 of whom are Hopi and 50 Hopi-Tewa. There are few if any discernible differences in their pottery production or learning techniques, and few differences in forms, wares, or decoration of pottery. The Hopi-Tewa apparently learned their pottery techniques from the Hopi, and are an indistinguishable part of their tradition. Except for changes in some forms sold to tourists, few technological or artistic innovations occurred between 1870 and 1970 (see Stanislawski 1974); larger or smaller forms are produced at the order of the customer, but until the 1973-74 period, the Hopi—with the rare exception of a few Anglo-trained potters—would not change colors, decorative motifs, firing, or other production techniques.

Most Hopi and Hopi-Tewa potters are female, although males occasionally paint designs, as Lesou painted for Nampeyo. Detailed production techniques are discussed elsewhere (Stanislawski in press; Stanislawski and Stanislawski 1974). The traditional women potters make seven or eight technological wares, including a plain unpolished brown or gray cooking and storage ware, and decorated and polished yellow, red, and white wares. These wares are based on the choice of clay and firing techniques. Incised, molded, and appliqued designs are occasionally found; an ovoid pumpkin-seed impressed decoration is traditional on redware, and a new triangular can-opener-impressed decoration is currently popular. Most decoration, however, is painted in red, black, white, and occasionally brown. All of these colors are derived from local clays and iron ores. Both molding and coiling techniques are used.

Discussions of ceramic production elsewhere in the Southwest, such as in the Huichol area, indicate that two different persisting methods of manufacturing pots may be simultaneously in use. One Huichol method of making pots involves coils; the other involves making tortillalike discs of clay, which are then pinched together (Weigand 1969:38-41). Maricopa pottery also may be either coil or paddle-and-anvil (Harvey 1964:59). These cases cause confusion for the archaeologist, for we have always assumed that such divergent production methods were cultural markers.

Temper may be diagnostic, as Arnold (1971:38), for example, demonstrated in Ticul. Hopi, Papago, and San Ildefonso potters use a variety of tempers, and Hopi utility forms have a different temper from Hopi serving ware (Stanislawski in press; Fontana et al. 1962; Chapman

1970:24); Acoma, Zuni, and Maricopa pottery tends to have potsherd temper; Taos and Picuris has micacious clay; and San Ildefonso has sand or crushed rock (Chapman 1970:16; Bunzel 1929; Harvey 1964). Clays are generally mined near the villages in the Southwest, but several Acoma and Zuni potters are now bringing their clay to the San Francisco Bay area, and one Hopi potter who lives in Zuni brings Hopi-area clay there (Maxwell Museum 1974). Raw clay is also carried from village to village in Highland Peru (Donnan 1971:465).

The various Hopi color wares, because they involve different choices of clay and firing and production techniques, are considered different in difficulty and technology by the makers. Potters who specialize in yellowware often say that the new whiteware is too difficult because they frequently burn it, causing yellow fireclouds. Some forty-five or fifty Hopi decorative types (in the archaeological sense) could be calculated at a minimum; but they do not mean much, in behavioral terms, to the Hopi, who consider such technological factors as coiling, molding, scraping, smoothing, and firing to be vital, but see decoration, rim form, and the like as relatively unimportant matters of personal choice. To the Hopi, ware, size, and final form are vital. Most of the pottery used in the villages or traded to other Native Americans is in traditional shapes such as the piki and mutton stew bowls, canteens, or ceremonial jars. It will generally be plainware, or decorated with the older Zuni school of design in black on red, or black on yellow. It is rarely signed or marked. Tradeware, on the other hand, is generally decorated and painted in Sikyatki Revival school of design, and may be marked or signed. Only after 1973 did we see whiteware given as gifts and being openly used in native ceremonies and affairs.

In the Hopi ceramic tradition, then, we have found that there are functional correlations of design styles with certain form and use types (e.g., Zuni school of design with mutton stew bowls); there are individual choice of attributes of rim form or design and individual differences in painting quality and technology, but village or cultural group sharing of major elements of form, decorative types, designs, and technology (Stanislawski in press; Stanislawski and Stanislawski 1974; Bunzel 1929:60-65). Bunzel stated that in 1925 nearly any potter could identify another potter's larger painted works in the trading post by technological factors and painting variations. She, too, particularly noted that the Hopi potters stressed their individual styles (Bunzel 1929:52). Fontana et al. (1962) also state that Papago potters share basic forms and designs, but have individual variations in rim form, temper, slip, smudging, and elements of design style. This is also true of the Seri (Bowen and Moser 1968:116-33). However, Chapman (1970: 14-15) notes that Tewa-speaking San Ildefonso potters could not identify makers of most pots, which implies less individual choice.

Theoretically, each special work group, guild, or craft union, or age, sex, class, or caste group, might have its own ways of doing things, leading to style variations or spatial-material correlates. Much of the work in tribal societies is done by informal, ad hoc groups; for example, at Hopi First Mesa, ad hoc neighbor ceramic work groups are particularly common. The same pot may be molded by one woman, and then passed from one to another to be scraped, polished, smoothed, slipped, or painted. Finally, any woman may be willing to sign that pot (Stanislawski in press). Hopi potters feel strongly that they should share their skills and designs, and should aid one another. It is common for a younger woman to paint for her mother, aunt, or neighbor of a different clan, as Nampeyo used to paint and mold for her nonclan neighbors. A Santa Clara potter was also said to have molded for Maria of San Ildefonso; in turn, Maria molded for others, and would sign others' pots as well. Such work groups are thus common in the Rio Grande pueblos as well (LeFree 1975:6; Marriott 1968).

Recent hostility directed toward the Nampeyo family (Qua'töqti 1974) indicates that the Hopi and Hopi-Tewa still do not recognize any family claims to designs or forms of pottery. We observed this to be true in our analysis of the spread of design elements, which crossed lineage and clan borders (Stanislawski and Stanislawski 1974). A Hopi potter may produce as many as twenty or more "types" during a year, and any woman can make any "type" she wishes (Bunzel 1929:58; Stanislawski in press). A woman's preference for colors and forms will change as she grows older, experiments more, or begins to become blind. This indicates that age certainly affects craft production in any culture, as well as style for each individual. But since much Hopi pottery is made in ad hoc work groups, and each pot may be worked on by five or six women in a kind of pottery "bee," there is not even a necessary correlation between one artifact and one maker.

There are clearly some culture-wide styles of artifacts associated with large groups. However, as any student of Southwest ceramics knows, major styles are borrowed or traded every generation or two, so that new classifications must be devised. For example, Acoma potters are now using the "typical" Zuni deer with red lifeline to the heart, and Zuni potters have long favored Hopi styles, just as the Hopi, since

1850, have used Zuni designs and layouts on locally used painted pottery. In fact the most minute differences in style or technique, often unconscious and unverbalized, may be the most vital. For example, Newton (1974) gives a quantitative analysis of hammock styles among Ge tribes of Brazil and demonstrates that the hammocks of two similar Timbira tribes can be distinguished by the ratio of direction of twist of their cotton cordage and twining styles alone.

Learning (Table 8.1, 6)

Some archaeologists today distinguish two different emphases in archaeology: that of the traditional or "normative" approach, which sees artifact types as reflecting the ideals or norms of the homogeneous society of their makers, and that of the systems approach, which sees artifact types and social traditions as highly variable units, not evenly shared by all specific groups or their members (Longacre 1970:2; J. N. Hill 1970b:17-20; Flannery 1968). Like Aberle (1970) and Hole and Heizer (1973:314), I believe that this is a false dichotomy. Processual and systems archaeologists seem to be talking about those idealized artifact types still used by some archaeologists, rather than about general cultural norms as used by modern social anthropologists. We all may be guilty of this. For example, Longacre and J. N. Hill talk about "patterns" of material remains and the "structure" of archaeological sites resulting from "patterned behavior" of members of extinct societies. They clearly believe that people behave in such orderly ways that artifact types at sites precisely reflect these patterns, and thus allow us to reconstruct social groups such as clans, marriage residence units, or corporate sodalities. What arc such concepts but reflections of "ideal" behavioral norms? In any case, James Ford (1954) has long since indicated that both archaeologically and ethnographically known attributes, modes, or types must be discussed as falling within normal patterns of distribution; and we emphasize the center points of the distributions simply for convenience.

Some of the most frequently cited works in systems archaeology, which stresses such a dichotomy, were done in the Southwest. One well-known hypothesis is that in the prehistoric Pueblo Southwest the women were the potters; that they lived near their mothers in a matrilocal residence pattern; and that they had a matrilineal descent system (J. N. Hill 1968, 1970a; Longacre 1964a, 1968, 1970). These inferences were based on analogies with published ethnographic

GROUP 1: In-Clan Models (27 cases)

O = X
  O

a. Mother (14)

O O = X
     O

b. Mother's sister
(5)

O = X
  O = X
    O

c. Mother's mother
(1)

O = X
O→O

d. Sister
(5)

same clan
O = X O = X
  O—→O

e. Clan's sister
(1)

O O = X
    O

f. Sister's daughter
(1)

GROUP 2: Nonclan Models (17 cases)

O = X O
O

a. Father's sister
(O)

O = X
X = O
  O

b. Father's mother
(1)

O = X X = O
    O

c. Father's brother's wife
(1)

d. Husband's mother
(3)

O = X O

e. Husband's sister
(2)

O X = O

f. Brother's wife
(1)

O = X X = O

g. Husband's brother's wife
(2)

O = X O = X
X   = O

h. Son's or daughter's
mother-in-law (2)

i. Nonkin
(5)

X = Father
O = Mother

FIGURE 8.1. Learning models of Whiteware potters, Hopi Mesas, Arizona.

research reports dealing with the Hopi and Zuni. It is then inferred that mothers would teach their daughters pottery-making techniques, and that the design elements and other features of the pottery style would reflect this matrilocal training model. Localized clusters of design elements found on potsherds in different areas of a pueblo would verify the existence of this pattern.

The problem is that of the "fallacy of affirming the consequent." At the time of these studies, none of the basic premises had been tested. One quoted authority for ethnographic statements was Ruth Bunzel (1929); however, she clearly states, "It is therefore of particular significance not that all women mention their mothers' teachings, which is natural, but that *practically all recognized other sources of inspiration as well*" (1929:54; emphasis added).

Recent research of my own indicates that at least four common models of pottery teaching are emphasized in modern Hopi and Hopi-Tewa villages: mother-daughter; mother-in-law–daughter-in-law; aunt–niece of different clan; and neighbor-neighbor. At least eight other teaching model situations can also be identified (see Figure 8.1). Many mothers do teach their daughters, but the teacher may also be the grandmother in another clan, an aunt, or a mother-in-law. All

FIGURE 8.2. Learning networks of Whiteware potters, Hopi Mesas, Arizona.

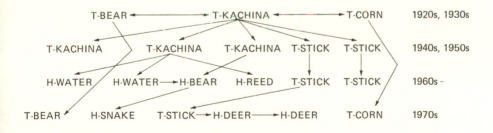

of these models may be involved at different stages in the life of one individual, and indeed, one should expect this, for some mothers do not make pottery, are busy with younger children, or are blind by the time the prospective potter needs instruction.

Analyzing one specific tradition of pottery, Hopi-Tewa Whiteware, I have found that the style is now shared by women of at least 12 different Hopi and Hopi-Tewa clans, living in five villages and two settlements, and of two different linguistic and ethnic groups (see Figure 8.2). Nonclan teaching is an old pattern; for example, the most famous of the Hopi-Tewa pottery makers, Nampeyo, was taught her craft by her paternal grandmother in the Hopi Snake Clan, sometime before 1870. Thus not only do women learn a great deal from nonclan relatives, but they continue to learn and to change styles throughout their lifetimes, ultimately making several different types of pottery. Painting by a nearly blind woman differs from what she did as a young woman, and someone else, such as her daughter or husband, may do detailed work for her. Since pots may not even be the result of a single individual's work, there is almost always considerable difficulty in tracing a single individual's lifetime work by art style alone.

TABLE 8.2
SPREAD OF CLAN IDENTIFICATION MARKS
ON HOPI AND HOPI-TEWA POTTERY

T-Kachina (9)*	H-Sand (1)	T-Corn (2)	H-Water (1)		1930s
H-Coyote (1)	H-Deer (1)	T-Stick (2)	T-Corn (1)		1940s, 1950s
H-Bear (1)	T-Sand (1)	T-Tobacco (1)	T-Corn (2)	H-Water (1)	1960s
T-Bear (1)	T-Kachina (1)	T-Corn (5)	H-Water (2)		1970s

*Numbers in parentheses represent the total number of people in each clan using the marks.

In fact, there do not appear to be any learning networks confined within a single Hopi village; all networks seem to cross village lines, and sometimes mesa lines. Even the distant pueblo villages of the Rio Grande Valley are artistically related to Hopi centers, and potters frequently borrow designs from other villages in the Southwest (Bunzel 1929:57-58). Network analysis of the use of identification marks on pottery indicates the same principles of clan and cross-clan learning (Table 8.2).

Finally, a few words about the placement of clans within a village. To the best of our knowledge, clans have not been localized in one area of the village for a long time; as early as the 1880s they were not localized in Hopi villages (Mindeleff 1900). All Hopi houses go through cycles of building, use, abandonment, trash fill, and reclearing. They may be sold, traded, or left vacant for a time. Clans also fluctuate in size through time. In the last 70 years at least two Hopi-Tewa clans have disappeared, and one more is seemingly about to die. In any town, clans are developing, splitting, or dying. Their housing needs are rising, falling, or disappearing. Land or houses near relatives constantly fluctuates in availability. New rooms for one clan may be needed when the remainder of the village is decreasing in population. New construction, then, is not an indication of general population increase. Clustering of ceramic design units, types, or traditions probably results from other social units or processes, perhaps ad hoc neighborhood ceramic work groups, rather than from localization or training within female marriage and descent groups.

Site Development (Table 8.1, 7, 8):
Reuse, Recycling, and Abandonment

The study of artifacts is a vital type of ethnoarchaeological work, for reuse of artifacts shifts their meaning and function. It is particularly critical in the Southwest, for southwestern archaeologists too often assume that the artifacts are in their original positions, as left by their makers and users; that loss and abandonment occurred at about the same time; and that there has been no mixing, disturbance, or reuse of the artifacts since that time. Often, no change is assumed to have occurred for periods of 100 years or more (Longacre 1968:91, 1970:37).

Recent work of my own among the Hopi suggests that the above conditions are unlikely. Many Hopi potters collect, stockpile in their homes, and reuse both modern and prehistoric potsherds in a variety of ways (Stanislawski 1969b). The sherds may be built into the window or door frames of houses; used as chinking material in walls or bread ovens; used to scrape and finish pottery during molding, and to protect other pots during firing so that fuel does not touch the pots; or placed in shrines and used in divining the future. They are also used as "templates" from which designs are copied, resulting in the maintenance of a traditional ceramic school of design. Huichol potters also reuse broken pots and potsherds. Weigand (1969:23-24) stated that there are as many reused pottery pieces as new ones in an average rancho. A cracked water jar will be used to store food, while large bottom sherds may be used as scoops, as water bowls for animals, for wax melting and candle dipping, as food ladles or spindle whorl weights, or as lids on other jars.

On the Hopi mesas, individual potters often trade with other individuals, thus building up collections of each other's pottery. What a confusion for the archaeologist! For the ethnoarchaeologist, however, this practice allows the understanding of friendship groups and networks of communication. For example, Hopi-Tewa women trade with particular potters in Acoma or Zuni. These long-lasting individual ceremonial trade partnerships are similar to those of the Yir Yoront (Sharp 1952) or the Kula relationships of the Trobrianders (Malinowski 1922; Lauer 1970, 1971). But in the Hopi area, subgroups are also interrelated through trade. Members of a Tewa kachina clan of First Mesa trade pottery for basketry made in a Second Mesa village by their Hopi kachina clan "relatives," and Navajo clan members will stay with and trade with their corresponding Hopi clan members.

Potters also frequently reuse materials and tools. Harvey reported that Maricopa women collect prehistoric potsherds to grind for temper. The Hopi do this frequently from such sites as Sikyatki and Awatovi, and also use sherds for pottery scrapers and for protecting pots during firing (Stanislawski 1969b). Potters at Acoma, Zuni, and several Rio Grande pueblos do the same (Bunzel 1929). Stone tools such as prehistoric pestles of the Hohokam period are collected and reused by Maricopa women (Harvey 1964:58), just as Hopi potters frequently visit Awatovi ruin and collect mortars and pestles, polishing stones, paint grinders, and local clay from mines used in the seventeenth century. New Mexico area potters may even collect whole pots made by deceased potters in some Rio Grande pueblos. By chipping the rim, they feel that they have satisfied the spirit of the former owner (Harvey 1964:64).

We are thus beginning to understand some individual factors of reuse and recycling and can perhaps begin to state some rules of reuse of pottery. But we do not yet have a real idea of how such material is commonly reassorted by native peoples, and how this must affect archaeological stratigraphy (what Schiffer calls "C Transforms").

Obviously the recycling of potsherds and their reuse in modern situations badly confuse the stratigraphy of the sites. Recycling and reuse have long been practiced in Hopi, Zuni, Acoma, and other Pueblo societies (Bunzel 1929), and A. J. Lindsay has noted similar reuse of potsherds in prehistoric sites in the northeastern Arizona area (personal communication). Such a factor may also help to explain the occasional double-bodied vases and Anasazi mugs found with painted styles typical of two or more phases.

Breakage, abandonment, and burial are also critical factors resulting in the formation of site units. For example, Robert Burgh (1959) and Watson Smith (1971) have described such factors affecting the complexity of stratigraphy in Western Pueblo (Hopi) sites. They state that parts of the same pot were found as much as a meter apart in depth, and as much as twelve rooms apart in horizontal distance. Moreover, they found that statistics based upon typologies of sherds differed markedly from those based on typologies of whole pots, and there were also major differences in numbers of sherds per unit of volume in room blocks. Burgh concluded that this "indicate[s] the necessity for judicious evaluation of so-called objective analysis of ceramic data. . . . No infallible rules can be said to govern the order of deposition or the composition of trash deposits within the walls of large Pueblos" (1959:198). Cosmos Mindeleff's (1900) architectural descriptions of Hopi pueblos in the late 1800s and my recent work at First Mesa also reveal that frequent abandonment, trash filling, clearing, and reuse of rooms constantly take place, actions which also disturb the stratigraphy, and constantly affect the redistribution of social groups in the pueblos.

Weigand (1969) made house-by-house counts of ceramic artifacts in use of Huichol camps, and described the breakage rates and life expectancy of individual types of pottery. In most cases, the pots were broken during cooking, although many were broken by children; one was broken by a chicken, one by a drunk, and one when a woman fell during a religious procession (Weigand 1969:24). Weigand also summarized the history of each sherd of two individual broken pots. Part of one was first cannibalized for use as a comal, and then a table top; part of the second was used first as a water jar; then the unused portions were taken to the kitchen wall, where children found some of them and threw them onto the outside trash pile, parts of the same pot landing as much as 100 meters apart. However, several sets of rim

223

sherds of this pot also remained for more than five months leaning against the front wall of the house. Later one of these remaining sherds was reused as an artifact; and finally a set of 38 small sherds remained in place for three more days and were then thrown onto the trash pile, where, after three weeks of farming activity, only 2 pieces remained visible. Weigand (1969:25) also provides us with a table which allows calculation of breakage rates by type during a one-year period for five different ranchos in the Huichol area. Nearly 100 percent of the comal type were broken, while only 1 to 10 percent of other types were broken.

Pastron (1974:101-2) summarizes the Tarahumara situation, where about 2 to 4 cooking pots are made per year, while larger storage pots are made about 1 every two years. Each family owns 7 to 19 pots; only 7 or 8 will be in each of their two or three houses. A cooking pot lasts for one to two years; a storage pot up to five years; 2 to 3 pots will be replaced each year after breakage. When discarded, pots are thrown outside the door of the house, landing within five to ten meters (Pastron 1974:108-9).

Foster (1960), describing Tarascans of Mexico, provides numbers, types of pottery, kitchen and cooking habits, life expectancy of types, and breakage rates for four individual kitchens. Cushing (1920:615) described the annual New Fire Ceremony, held in Zuni in the 1880s, in which pots were thrown from the rooftops as the kachinas passed, and then stamped into the ground. Any other pots seen were likewise broken by the kachinas, and all baskets were thrown down and burned.

In the Mesa area, we have observed potsherds placed in Hopi shrines. Apparently these were remains of pots which broke in firing, suggesting bad luck, and were thus ceremonially offered. Other pots, more normally broken, were simply thrown over the cliff, used around the firing pit to keep the flames from breaking new pots, or reused in other ways (Stanislawski 1969b). Large piki bowls, bean pots, canteens, or stew bowls seem to last for long periods, sometimes passing from one generation to another.

Technological Systems (Table 8.1, 9, 10)

A professional ceramics teacher, Frank Applegate, tried to introduce new temper, clay, paint, and other technological features to the Hopi in 1922, but with no success. However, local native innovators, such as

Nampeyo, followed the traditional ceramic practices of the area, and through their own experimentation revived older traditional styles. Maria of San Ildefonso (Guthe 1925; Marriott 1968), with her husband Julian, experimented with copying old pots and potsherds and developed a revival black-on-black style; the Hopi-Tewa potter Garnet Pavatea accidentally developed a new brownware style. All of these women were traditionalists in their own cultures, and each, in following her own individual interests, also extended that tradition somewhat, while never going so far outside of it that she was considered abnormal by her peers.

We have already mentioned the origin of whiteware pottery and identification marks among the Hopi; both were developed by several women working together who were neighbors, but in different clans. We have also traced the spread of the techniques to families and clans at their various places of residence, thus outlining the way in which networks of learning operate, and innovations spread (Stanislawski and Stanislawski 1974). (See Fig. 8.2, Table 8.2.)

The reasons why so many southwestern Pueblo villages, including many of those of the Hopi, were specialized in craft production by 1850-1900 are not yet well understood. The Spanish attempted to stimulate Mexican village specialization after 1540, but this probably would not have affected the Hopi Mesa region, where there were no Spanish women and never more than a dozen Spanish men at any time. On the other hand, we do have some evidence of borrowing of songs, kachina figures, dances, and pottery designs among the Pueblo villages during the last 100 years (Chapman 1970:48; Bunzel 1929:56-57), although technologies were not borrowed here or in the Pima-Papago areas (Fontana et al. 1962:82-83). Hopi pottery in the last half of the nineteenth century was basically Zuni in design, perhaps because at least one Hopi village population lived with the Zuni for ten or twenty years following a smallpox epidemic in the Hopi area in 1854. In short, relatively frequent intercultural contact followed by considerable fusion of styles was common among the pueblos.

Finally, one of the basic problems for all archaeologists is that of defining a culture from archaeological remains alone, particularly given the variability and differential sharing of norms that may be present. The Hopi and Hopi-Tewa may serve as a case in point. These two groups have lived side by side in three virtually contiguous villages for 275 years. Yet they still maintain different languages and have some

225

different religious and ceremonial patterns and characteristics of social structure and personality (Dozier 1951, 1954). They make identical pottery wares and types, however, and have done so for at least 100 years. Similarly, Charlton (1972:109-11) and Tschopik (1950) have shown that there is little evidence of the Spanish conquest of Mexico or of Peru in ceramic collections alone. Elsie Clews Parsons (1940:218-20) has indicated that archaeologists studying ceramic remains might conclude that the Taos Indians were Apache. Clearly, different classes of archaeological remains do not equally mirror cultural patterns, and their stability or change in style may not reflect other major changes in the same social networks.

CONCLUSIONS

I have attempted to argue in this chapter that ethnoarchaeology should allow better development of inference and analogy models for use in reconstructing behaviors or "behavioral chains" in prehistoric societies. All such chains are composed of individuals or groups of people with specific norms and goals, doing things in prescribed ways, in social time units, at certain localities, using and/or producing artifacts which they ultimately break or abandon, and thus producing archaeological sites. I argue that we must follow some sort of ethnographically based, archaeologically directed behavioral analysis, for it is human behavior and its results which we, as archaeologists and anthropologists, are uniquely trained to study.

It is particularly a method of field research, the participant-observation method, that I advocate, for the archaeologist, like a detective, must treat the specific case and its remains as he or she finds them—that is, often disturbed, out of place, and dead. Ethnoarchaeologists, however, have the advantage of studying the living society before it becomes a corpse. It is this unique and specific set of behaviors and material culture products that we must interpret and model. A major goal of ethnoarchaeology must be to analyze the real as well as the ideal, the possible range of variations allowable at different levels and situations. We must be aware of the alternative ways in which the same sorts of remains are produced; we must pinpoint those qualities of each surviving element which may indicate the particular process of death or discontinuity.

I suggest that we study these factors in terms of a series of 10 problem areas (Table 8.1), which in turn could be subdivided into five levels of social groups, each of which affects site formation in different terms. Such a scheme may allow us to compare our data with those of others; may serve as a fieldwork checklist; and may point out to us the problems which have been well discussed, and those which yet need more work. I have used as my major examples samples of what I and other Southwestern anthropologists interested in ceramics have so far produced in these different realms. All of this, I hope, will indicate some of the directions in which ethnoarchaeology should go, and where the new work needs to be directed. Scientific work is, after all, a very frustrating experience, and we must not expect frequent proof or other rapid advances. As H. L. Mencken once said, "The prototype of the scientist is not the liberator releasing the slaves, or the good Samaritan lifting up the fallen, but a dog sniffing tremendously at an infinite series of holes" (quoted in Smith 1972:103). The sweet smell of success will come but rarely; but the intellectual challenge to understand human behavior and material culture, and the understanding we achieve of alternative ways of surviving, are perhaps of equal importance.

NOTE

1. The work for this paper was done at the School of American Research between October 1975 and March 1976, while I was a Weatherhead Resident Scholar. My thanks are given to Dr. Douglas Schwartz, Director; the seminar participants; and particularly Richard Gould.

9

Methodological Issues in Ethnoarchaeology[1]

MICHAEL B. SCHIFFER
University of Arizona

INTRODUCTION

Ethnoarchaeology seems at last on the verge of becoming a respectable field of endeavor within archaeology (see Donnan and Clewlow 1974). Although most prehistorians acknowledge that their inferences depend in some way on the availability of specific or general kinds of ethnographic information, only within the past decade or two have we begun to realize that ethnographers are not likely to supply such information, and that it must be obtained in the field by archaeologists themselves. Thanks to the dedicated efforts of a handful of investigators who have recognized this need and undertaken sustained ethnoarchaeological research (for example, Ascher 1962, 1968; Gould 1968, 1971; Stanislawski 1969a, 1969b, 1973, 1974; Peterson 1968, 1971, 1973; J.P. White 1967, 1968a; White and Thomas 1972; David 1971, 1972; David and Hennig 1972), we are now poised on the threshold of an enormously fruitful era of discoveries. Already, modern ethnoarchaeological findings, which stand apart from the scattered results of earlier decades, are appreciably affecting analytic

229

methods and leading to revised interpretations of the archaeological record. Despite this rapid and widely welcomed progress, ethnoarchaeological studies are nowhere near stating or approaching their full potential.

My purpose in this chapter is to raise several methodological issues that must be addressed if ethnoarchaeology's potential is to be realized in future investigations. I begin by defining ethnoarchaeology and its subject matter and move on to a critical review of ethnoarchaeological studies, with suggestions for remedying what I perceive as major difficulties in current research. Finally, to illustrate several of the general points, I discuss briefly recent ethnoarchaeological studies carried out by my students among the "Nacirema" (Miner 1956).

THE NATURE OF ETHNOARCHAEOLOGY

Ethnoarchaeology is the study of material culture in systemic context for the purpose of acquiring information, both specific and general, that will be useful in archaeological investigation. Ethnoarchaeology differs from experimental archaeology (with which it is often lumped) because it involves pursuit and study of an actual situation in which specified behaviors can be observed, rather than fabrication of situations in which such behaviors can be simulated (Schiffer 1976). Ethnoarchaeology and experimental archaeology together constitute Strategy 2 of behavioral archaeology, wherein present-day material culture is investigated in order to provide information needed for studying the past (Reid, Schiffer, and Rathje 1975). The broad subject matter of ethnoarchaeology is the relationships between human behavior and the material-spatial-environmental matrix in which it takes place. Admittedly, all the above definitions and distinctions are likely to break down if pushed too far. Some investigators have, for example, undertaken hybrid ethnoarchaeological and experimental studies either by conducting experiments in an ethnoarchaeological setting (Shimada n.d.; White and Thomas 1972) or by experimentally creating a settlement or behaviors that can be studied ethnoarchaeologically (Callahan 1972; Woolsey 1973). Even so, as I define it here, ethnoarchaeology has a coherence that other formulations deny it (for example, Stanislawski 1974; Oswalt 1974). This should become evident as the implications of the present formulation are developed below.

It should also be noted at the outset that ethnoarchaeologists are not limited to studying primitive, nonliterate, or nonindustrial societies. All sociocultural systems are within the province of ethnoarchaeology (see Leone 1972, 1973; Salwen 1973; Deetz 1970; Ascher 1974; Brown 1973).

Material objects are said to be in systemic context when they are participating in a behavior system (Schiffer 1972a, 1976). It is this feature of ethnoarchaeology, the study of ongoing behavioral systems, that gave rise to the concept of "living archaeology" (Gould 1968). Living archaeology is an apt designation, but lacks the generality of ethnoarchaeology (Gould [1974:29] concurs). Ethnoarchaeology can easily subsume situations, for example, where items are studied in archaeological context after having previously been observed in systemic context (for example, W. H. Adams 1973; Ascher 1968; Boshier 1965; O'Connell 1974; Longacre and Ayres 1968; Lange and Rydberg 1972; Clark and Clark 1974; Rathje 1974). Such studies, it is acknowledged, merge imperceptibly into historical archaeology.

The study of material items in systemic context allows the derivation of both specific and general types of information and statements. *Specific* statements describe one or just a few cultural groups. An example is provided from recent ethnoarchaeological work among the Hopi and Hopi-Tewa by Stanislawski and Stanislawski (1974:9):

> Learning of Hopi and Hopi-Tewa pottery making is thus much more complex than is usually stated. It appears to be based on learning from those good potters who are frequently seen, whether relatives or not.

Although this statement describes a large number of potters, it is limited in applicability to the recent Hopi and Hopi-Tewa from which it was obtained. All specific statements take the form: behavior y is found in culture x at time t.

Specific statements, tied to single points in time and space, are traditionally employed in some version of the direct historical approach. In fact, it is often said that use of specific information for interpretative purposes must be limited to archaeological cultures that are historically related to the ethnographic group. Other archaeologists (for example, Binford 1967; J. N. Hill 1970b) have countered that these limitations are unnecessary—that is, that specific ethnographic statements may be applied to any situation—if rigorous testing of inferences is performed on independent archaeological data. These

231

extreme positions both have merits and can be readily reconciled by drawing upon some of Salmon's (1975, 1976) ideas.

It seems hard to deny that inferences obtained from observations of descendant peoples simply possess a greater degree of a priori probability than inferences acquired from just any group. (This is not to say, of course, that such inferences are necessarily true; at present it is difficult to measure their strength [see Peterson 1971 for an attempt to construct criteria of assessment].) For example, early southwestern archaeologists, who were often intimately familiar with contemporary Pueblo Indians, frequently interpreted their excavated artifacts directly in ethnographic terms. Although inferences like Pepper's (1920) about the "prayer sticks" of Pueblo Bonito remain untested, few archaeologists would assign a higher a priori probability of truth to other inferences for the use of these cylindrical wooden objects. On the other hand, because most archaeologically studied cultures have no modern descendants, and because the behavior and organization of descendant cultures may differ substantially from the prehistoric situation, we must provide for the ability to acquire hypotheses (that is, potential inferences) from any source. In such cases, thorough archaeological testing is generally required to establish high probabilities of truth.

General statements are those relating two or more variables without regard to time or place. They are called *laws*, and take many forms. Every law includes a term or boundary condition that delimits its domain (in C, . . .); some laws apply to complex systems while others pertain to hunter-gatherers, households, or biface reduction. For example, after studying patterns of hut use within a Fulani village in North Cameroon, David (1971:117) offered the following lawlike statement:

> The less the capital outlay or labour required to construct a building or complex of buildings, the greater the fit between it and its personnel over the useful life of the building. Conversely, the more permanent the building, the less the degree of fit.

Although this generalization is imprecise and probably inaccurate, it does convey the structure of a law. Another law, perhaps applicable to all settlements, was offered by Yellen (1974: 192, 196–200) after study of the !Kung Bushmen in the Dobe region. He found that the longer a camp was inhabited, the greater was the probability that a given maintenance activity (for example, tool repair or manufacture) would be carried out. From that principle an important corollary can be deduced: to wit, the diversity of maintenance activities performed at a settlement varies directly with the length of occupation (see also Schiffer 1975e). Other examples of general statements offered in the context of ethnoarchaeological studies are rare, a point which I shall take up again below.

Some investigators would restrict the use of general statements to groups having similar technologies or occupying similar environments (cf. Gould 1974; Orme 1974). This is spurious methodological advice. It is based on the assumption that the boundary conditions of most laws consist of very general parameters like environment and technology. Although some laws do have environmental or technological boundary conditions, the latter are or should be spelled out in terms of particular variables, such as rainfall pattern, primary productivity, or energy-processing capability. Most laws, however, have boundary conditions that relate to specific processes, subsystems, or components—many of which are universal. It should be emphasized that boundary conditions are law-specific and that no a priori, independent limitations, other than their boundary conditions, govern the applicability of laws. David's law, for example, would seem to apply wherever architecture is present; thus it should be useful in state-level as well as tribal systems, regardless of technology or environment. Certainly, like other general statements, it ought to be tested in a variety of ethnographic contexts before it is used for interpretive purposes anywhere.

Laws serve a wide range of purposes in archaeological research (Schiffer 1975b; Reid, Schiffer, and Rathje 1975). It is now becoming clear that they play a fundamental role in, for example, designing data retrieval strategies (Schiffer and Rathje 1973; Reid, Schiffer, and Neff 1975), constructing artifact classifications (Schiffer 1976), building subsistence-settlement models (Schiffer 1975a), and justifying specific inferences (Schiffer 1972b, 1976). As research continues on the nature and functions of laws in archaeology, it is becoming apparent that without laws, description and explanation in archaeology would be impossible (see Reid, Schiffer, and Rathje 1975; Salmon 1975; Schiffer 1972b, 1976).

The specific and general kinds of information produced by ethnoarchaeologists may be used in a variety of ways, including analogical reasoning. However, neither class of information contains statements that are, by themselves, analogies. Since all sciences use analogical reasoning, it seems desirable to dispense entirely with the word *analogy* in archaeology, where it connotes a uniquely archaeological process having special characteristics. *Model* or *hypothesis* will usually provide a better fit to the contexts in which the term *analogy* is most frequently used.

SOME BASIC ISSUES

Techniques of Data Collection

As archaeologists began to do ethnography in the service of archaeology, they unaccountably adopted many ethnographic techniques of gathering data. I say "unaccountably" because techniques such as informant interviewing (which emphasizes emic kinds of information) were devised to answer questions posed within the framework of various mentalist ethnological theories. To paraphrase Marvin Harris (1968a), there is no reason to believe that techniques ethnographers find useful are in any way appropriate for obtaining ethnographic data to answer archaeological questions. Techniques developed by other behavioral scientists and by archaeologists themselves may be far better adapted to the efficient achievement of archaeological goals.

Some of the problems inherent in informant-produced data can be easily illustrated. In a recent study O'Connell (1974) obtained several hundred stone tools from the surface of sites in central Australia. He then took these specimens to local Aljawara informants and made inquiries about their names and functions. One particular class of tools, called *yilugwa*, was discussed at length. *Yilugwa* are

> medium to large blades, with straight to slightly convex lateral edges and straight to very convex distal edges. . . . They range from slightly plano-convex to domed in section, with dorsal surfaces often marked by parallel longitudinal flake scars. (O'Connell 1974:189)

In addition, *yilugwa* are made of granular quartzite flakes and, as can be seen from O'Connell's Figure 1, exhibit remarkably variable patterns of retouch. According to the Aljawara, *yilugwa* are used as spoons for eating cooked roots and tubers (O'Connell 1974:192).

234

However, upon close examination of the tools' edges, O'Connell also noted patterns of wear characteristic of scraping, and other damage not readily explained by the activity of spoon use.

O'Connell's purpose in writing the paper was to provide archaeologists of the central Australian desert with some possible functional interpretations for *yilugwa*, and he succeeds admirably in this aim. One can also take O'Connell's findings and, from the standpoint of methodology, formulate a more general question: Why was there a discrepancy between informant statements about tool use and tool use as inferred from patterns of edge wear? This question leads to consideration of the conditions under which informants can be expected to provide reliable generalizations about their own behavior.

I would argue that the participants in any behavioral system simply do not encode in their memories an amount of detail about all events and activities sufficient to form the basis of sound behavioral generalizations. Any system that selected for such abilities would rapidly become extinct from a trivia overload. Scientists, however, are trained to screen irrelevant from relevant observations and document the latter, often in astonishingly precise detail. Let us not forget that we, not our subjects, must exercise this discretion. At present, it is difficult to make definitive statements about the reliability of informant statements regarding any class of behavioral questions that are of current interest. Fortunately, ethnoarchaeological research on this very subject is now being carried out by the Garbage Project at the University of Arizona (Rathje and Hughes 1975). Preliminary findings lead to a sobering view of the accuracy of informant responses on a wide range of subjects (Rathje, personal communication). In view of this uncertainty, it seems prudent for ethnoarchaeologists to rely as completely as possible on observations of actual behavior.

In some instances, of course, it will be necessary to gather informant data, as in the Aljawara case, when it is no longer possible to observe the ongoing behavioral system. When informant data must be relied upon, it is important that ethnoarchaeologists give careful attention to the design of their eliciting techniques, in full awareness of the situational determinants of speech behavior. For example, the native may well categorize the ethnoarchaeologist as "naïve" or "untutored" and answer his questions as if they had been posed by a child. This example is certainly oversimplification, yet how would the same ethnoarchaeologist respond to a subject's query about the function of a screw-driver? I suspect that the situation favors the production of abbreviated and overgeneralized answers, such as "tightening and loosening screws" rather than the more accurate but complex "tightening and loosening screws, opening cans, smoothing putty, testing whether electrical connections are hot, chiseling wood, punching holes. . . ." One way to ameliorate this difficulty, which is frequently to be expected—especially when multi-functional or reused tools are of interest—is to contrive questions that lead the informant to recall his own sequences of activity in different situations. For example, O'Connell might have inquired of his Aljawara informants, "Under what circumstances do you make *yilugwa?*" This might have led to the recollection that formerly when a scraper was needed a *yilugwa* was fashioned, though it may have been used subsequently as a spoon. Different types of questions may elicit statements on different sequences of activity, which the ethnoarchaeologist can then attempt to synthesize.

If the most time-honored and frequently used ethnographic method of data gathering, the informant interview, is often inappropriate for ethnoarchaeology, then how are we to gather our uncompromisingly behavioral data? Fortunately there is a broad range of scientific techniques available for obtaining such data at minimal expense, few of which have ever been employed by ethnographers. In all fairness it should be acknowledged that at least one ethnologist, Marvin Harris (1964), has been concerned with acquiring behavioral data directly. Harris's etic descriptive system is only now receiving thorough ethnographic trials, although it is perhaps too cumbersome for general use. Even so, I have already adapted it for some archaeological purposes (Schiffer 1975c), and it probably can be profitably employed in specialized ethnoarchaeological projects. Having noted this principal exception, we return to other sources of potentially viable techniques. A number of sociologists have devised nonreactive or unobtrusive measures of behavior, some of which may be useful to ethnoarchaeologists (E.J. Webb et al. 1966). Architects, spurred by studies such as those of Amos Rapoport (1969) and Edward Hall (1966), are now becoming concerned with, among other topics, examining the relationships between the intended and actual uses of their creations (see, for example, Perin 1970). In their investigations of space-use behavior, architects are beginning to devise techniques of potential applicability to ethnoarchaeology; this is because their questions are

236

sometimes quite similar to those of ethnoarchaeologists (recall, for example, David's 1971 space-use study among the Fulani). It is instructive to examine more closely one of these architectural studies.

David Saile and his associates under contract with the Rockford Housing Authority have employed a nonreactive technique to acquire data on the use of extramural space in a suburban Illinois community (Saile et al. 1972). Observers with recording sheets walked predetermined routes throughout the housing tract at hourly intervals, sampling on weekdays, weekends, and during different seasons. They noted the activities carried out, their locations, social and biological characteristics of the participants, the distribution of material culture, and other factors of special relevance to their project. Quite clearly, this technique can provide behavioral data of high quality; more important, they are the sort of data that can be standardized and compared cross-culturally. This technique is only one of many available that could readily be adapted for ethnoarchaeological use in order to provide an empirical basis for behavioral generalizations.

Borrowing of techniques from sociology, architecture, and other behavioral sciences will provide for a greater measure of flexibility in data gathering for future ethnoarchaeological studies. Even so, the most useful techniques, those firmly integrated with archaeological questions and hypotheses, will probably be devised by ethnoarchaeologists themselves. Longacre's Kalinga study (1974, 1975) can provide an example of one such technique. Like other ethnoarchaeologists, Longacre is determining the use life of various types of pottery. But unlike past investigators, who have relied on informant recollections as to when they last obtained various vessels (DeBoer 1974; David 1972; David and Hennig 1972; Pastron 1974), Longacre is measuring use life by the far more accurate method of tagging pots in the system and recording their use life directly. I expect that in some of the other ongoing ethnoarchaeological studies similar innovations in technique are occurring; if they are not, one should be rightfully disappointed. Beale and Healy (1975:895) offer some provocative suggestions on the use of ethnoarchaeological films for gathering behavioral data.

For some kinds of ethnoarchaeological study the costs of gathering relevant behavioral data by archaeological and other social scientific techniques may be prohibitive—in terms of time, money, or interaction effects with the system being observed. In such cases, one will of necessity come to depend appreciably on interview data. In order to assess the biases and omissions in informants' statements, one should also obtain a limited number of carefully selected behavioral observations. I suspect, however, that in the majority of studies it will be possible to acquire observations of relevant behavior.

Time Depth

Whenever an investigation is carried out using informant data or behavioral data, or both, the ethnoarchaeologist (like the ethnographer) is bound primarily to data from one point in time. The temporocentric perspective of ethnography, if uncorrected, can seriously distort the view one obtains of the dynamics of an ongoing system. This can occur when some events in a behavioral system, though important, are infrequent and may not be observed at all during a research period. These could include the construction or abandonment of a house, the procurement of a raw material available only at a great distance, and burial of the dead. If the etmnoarchaeologist is interested in, let us say, patterns of grave-good accompaniment, it may be necessary to enlarge the size of the research universe by looking at other communities to ensure that mortuary and burial events are observed in quantities sufficient for sophisticated analysis.

In many instances, clearly, expansion of the universe will not be possible, and other solutions will have to be found. At the very least, the investigator should extrapolate his synchronic statements from a time period long enough to reveal any processual anomalies or inconsistencies. It was by this method of working out the diachronic implications of structural descriptions that the famous Natchez Paradox was uncovered. Examination of the marriage rules in Swanton's 1911 reconstruction of the Natchez social system disclosed that, after several generations, demographic imbalance among the classes would have destroyed the system (Hart 1943). Swanton's reconstruction has since been modified several times to eliminate the paradox (see D. R. White, Murdock, and Scaglion 1971). Ethnoarchaeologists should check their observations frequently for potential inconsistences. Missing (that is, unobserved) activities can be discovered in this way, and additional information about them can then be sought through other channels. Although errors as conspicuous and far-reaching as the Natchez Paradox are likely to be rare, more mundane anomalies may be encountered frequently.

The next two problems I treat are more general in scope and more profound in their implications. The first of these concerns the conspicuous lack of ethnoarchaeological studies attempting to discern or test general laws. The second, which is ultimately related to the first, is the narrow range of problems chosen in current research.

Insufficient Emphasis on Laws

It is hardly necessary to document the particularist orientation of ethnoarchaeology. Fewer than a dozen major studies stand out clearly as exceptions: Longacre's (1974, 1975) ongoing work among the Kalinga; Binford's (1973, 1975, in press) recent investigation of the Nunamiut; David's (1971, 1972; David and Hennig 1972) work among the Fulani; Ascher's (1968) investigations among the Seri; the Arkansas Archaeological Survey's research on current farming practices in the Lower Mississippi Valley as they relate to patterns of site destruction (J. L. Ford and Rolingson 1972; Medford 1972; Schiffer and House 1975); and, of course, Thompson's (1958) pioneering study of archaeological inference using Yucatecan Maya pottery manufacture. Other ethnoarchaeologists sometimes have stumbled inadvertently on general principles, but they are afforded no special prominence in the write-ups and would go unnoticed except by someone looking for laws. The majority of studies, perhaps 90 percent, make no pretensions to general significance and, predictably, achieve none.

In voicing my criticism of the particularistic emphasis of ethnoarchaeology, I want to make it abundantly clear that I do not advocate abandoning the study of interesting and useful specific kinds of ethnographic information. My aim is simply to stimulate ethnoarchaeologists to investigate in addition various general questions. The ethnographic present is a fertile and appropriate laboratory for acquiring the laws needed to reconstruct the past from archaeological evidence (Schiffer 1976; Reid, Schiffer, and Rathje 1975). Unfortunately, few archaeologists—and, consequently, fewer ethnoarchaeologists—have been trained to pursue studies which aim to originate or test general principles. This perhaps stems from the Boasian legacy in anthropology of glorifying the unique and eschewing the search for regularities. Regardless of its historical basis, at present there is still widespread reluctance to accord the search for laws its long overdue high priority (also see Harris 1968b). It is now possible, however, to sketch out some of the considerations which can justify and direct the ethnoarchaeological pursuit of laws.

The use of ethnoarchaeology to derive laws for the study of the past requires that one accept some version of uniformitarianism. A statement of this doctrine which seems particularly useful is that *the laws of nature are constant*. Thus, whenever or wherever the same process is operating, it is subject to the same law or laws. This approach differs from the view that "the processes found operating today also operated in the past" in ways that make it better suited for anthropological research. Quite clearly, the processes of urbanization and state formation observable today were not in operation 10,000 years ago; whenever and wherever they *are* found, however, some laws will apply (laws that specify in their boundary conditions that certain processes, like urbanization, must be present). Our notions of uniformitarianism must take into account the fact that not all processes are distributed uniformly among all sociocultural systems. Let us also note that where laws can be applied, they can also be derived.

The realization that laws vary greatly in their applicability because processes and thus boundary conditions are differentially distributed has one exceedingly important and perhaps even startling implication: although some laws are derivable from only a limited number of ethnoarchaeological situations (for example, those dealing with pastoral nomadism), many laws can be obtained from study of any ongoing behavioral system. The laws of storage behavior, many laws of tool use and manufacture, and laws of space use within activity areas can be examined in virtually all ethnographic settings because the relevant boundary conditions are present universally. Thus it should even be possible to derive laws applicable to the Paleolithic from study of Nacirema behavior. For example, some of the principles that apply to nonsedentary social units, such as hunter-gatherer bands, may be acquired from study of backpackers, campers, and migrant farm workers.

Most ethnoarchaeological studies will, of course, require data on a host of laws and processes, the boundary conditions of which may be found only in some distant and primitive community. Longacre, for example, is presently studying several Kalinga villages of Northern Luzon in an attempt to test several laws regarding ceramic design (Longacre 1974, 1975). The boundary conditions of matrilocal residence, pottery made for local use, and sufficient design variability dictated that only the Kalinga could provide appropriate data. The ethnoarchaeological study of simple systems will continue to expand, for the reason that not all relevant boundary conditions for law testing can be met in a modern industrial society. However, when the last native dies or bars his door to the omnipresent anthropologist, ethnoarchaeologists will still have ample opportunities available in complex systems to obtain laws useful in the study of the past.

Although many ethnoarchaeologists are sympathetic to the nomothetic aspirations of ethnoarchaeology, they seem to have difficulty in acquiring lawlike statements for testing; the absence of readily available hypotheses is a serious stumbling block to nomothetic research. During the past several years I have culled many lawlike statements from archaeological writings, some of which are presented elsewhere (Schiffer 1975b, 1976). Although archaeologists act as though these laws are true, few of them have ever been rigorously tested. Compendia of such lawlike statements thus can serve easily as a source of suitable hypotheses for ethnoarchaeological testing. Aside from my earlier studies, however, I can think of only a few pieces of archaeological literature in which more than one or two laws of potential interest to ethnoarchaeologists can be found (see Read 1971; Griffin 1956; Wauchope 1966; Semenov 1964). Much additional background research is required before we can adequately take stock of and evaluate the many laws presently used by archaeologists.

Narrow Range of Subject Matter

In addition to its almost exclusive preoccupation with specific phenomena, ethnoarchaeological research to date is unduly narrow in its range of subject matter in ways that make it impossible to cope with the wide range of relationships among behavioral and material phenomena needed for reconstructing the past. Although it will come as a surprise to few investigators, it is still worth noting in support of the narrowness proposition that the most commonly treated subject in ethnoarchaeology is the manufacture and use of various objects. Within that class, ceramic manufacture (for example, Lister and Lister 1972; Van der Merwe and Scully 1971; Varner 1974; Lauer 1970; Coutts 1967; Friedrich 1970; Ellen and Glover 1974) and lithic production and use (for example, J.P. White 1967, 1968a; Gould 1968, 1971; Gould, Koster, and Sontz 1971; Peterson 1968) have received disproportionate attention. In the American Southwest, ethnoarchaeological interest in pottery manufacture dates back to around the turn of the last century

241

and continues almost without interruption until the present with the work of Stanislawski and others (for example, Cushing 1886; Guthe 1925; Colton 1939, 1951; DiPeso 1950; Hayden 1959; Fontana et al. 1962; Bowen and Moser 1968; Stanislawski 1969a, 1969b, 1974). Another, more recent emphasis in ethnoarchaeology has been a concern with abandonment phenomena. These studies seek to reveal the relationships between the material-culture inventory in use in a village or dwelling and what remains archaeologically after abandonment (for example, L.H. Robbins 1973; Bonnichsen 1973); there are, of course, many variations on this basic theme (see Stanislawski 1973, 1974). Some studies, to be sure, have ventured beyond traditional confines (for example, Rathje and Hughes 1975; Arnold 1971; Leone 1973; Binford 1973; Lyon 1970; Salwen 1973; Stanislawski 1974; Peterson 1973; Price et al. 1975), but they are few and far between. Another group of studies, conducted by ethnoarchaeologists and ethnographers, have used documented instances of various behaviors and processes to alert archaeologists once again to the obvious fact that reconstruction of the past is not always easy (for example, Heider 1967; Bowen and Moser 1968; L. H. Robbins 1973). (I am becoming rapidly weary of the "cautionary note" format of these presentations with its conspicuous absence of methodological insights into how such specific knowledge can be used.) If the particularist bias of most ethnoarchaeological studies is overlooked, then perhaps they will not seem as restricted in subject matter as I maintain they are. After all, one can study the manufacture and use of an almost infinite number of artifact types. It is likely, however, that the two defects in ethnoarchaeology are causally related; an unnecessarily circumscribed domain springs from a preoccupation with specific questions.

If we adopt the generalist position advocated in the previous section, then it is possible to expand the present conception of ethnoarchaeology's subject matter. Because archaeologists seek to offer diverse inferences about past behavioral systems, they require a correspondingly varied set of laws which cover all aspects of the functioning of sociocultural systems as they impinge upon or relate to material phenomena that are potentially present in the archaeological record. Thus, not only must we acquire laws governing manufacture, use, and even discard of particular artifact classes, but we must also obtain more basic principles relating to the general functioning of material culture. Perhaps this line of argument can be clarified with a concrete example.

In a masterly work, long neglected by anthropologists, George Zipf (1949) offered a series of cogent hypotheses regarding general relationships between material and spatial variables of tool use. For example, he suggests that

> the most frequent[ly used] tool . . . which tends to be the lightest, smallest, oldest, most versatile and most thoroughly integrated tool in the system, will also be the most valuable tool in the sense that its permanent loss would cause the relatively greatest cost of redesigning and of retooling. Hence it is most economical to conserve that most frequent[ly used] tool. . . . we see that the value of conserving any given tool is directly related to its relative frequency of usage. (Zipf 1949:73)

This is just one of the many provocative principles he presents, all of which have numerous archaeological implications. Were this principle verified independently in different sociocultural settings, it would have considerable value in explaining prehistoric artifact changes. If ethnoarchaeologists set about testing this or any of the dozens of other principles that Zipf presents, they would be led to examine a collection of diverse phenomena, all united by potential correspondence to one or more laws. Ethnoarchaeologists will find Zipf's work an unending source of interesting hypotheses. I have already initiated this testing process using material culture of the Nacirema (Schiffer 1971, 1973b), and, in so doing, I have been led to examine the diversity of contents of storage facilities and also to classify activity areas in a small community and monitor the movements of individuals between them.

As the need to focus on general principles in ethnoarchaeological research becomes more widely accepted, it is likely that many new dimensions of sociocultural behavior and material culture will come under scrutiny. It would seem that the trend toward an expanding subject matter is a necessary concomitant of our catholicity of prehistoric interests. If we are sincere in our desire to describe and explain diverse prehistoric behavioral changes, then we must not hesitate to investigate the large set of laws which makes this possible in the variety of ethnographic situations where we can observe interaction of the relevant variables.

ETHNOARCHAEOLOGY AMONG THE NACIREMA

To this point, my arguments have been general ones. Thus my purpose in presenting the following examples, drawn from my

243

well-worn collection of undergraduate student papers, is to illustrate three of the major points made above: (1) that the formulation and testing of general laws should become an important component of ethnoarchaeological research orientations; (2) that concern with general questions will inevitably lead to examination of variables and subjects not previously considered to be within the realm of ethnoarchaeology; and (3) that important ethnoarchaeological studies can be done in modern industrial sociocultural systems, particularly among the Nacirema. (In terms of data-gathering techniques, the undergraduate studies break little new ground; therefore I cannot really illustrate my earlier point regarding the design or borrowing of more behaviorally oriented methods.)

Sipe (1973), in an examination of the relationship between permanency of occupation and nature of refuse disposal, studied nine campgrounds in the Tucson area. He attempted to test the hypothesis that there should be systematic variations in the refuse deposited in camps used for varying lengths of time. The data for the study consisted of observations and inferences on duration of encampments and an inventory of materials discarded at the campsites. One of Sipe's findings, consistent with a general principle widely (if implicitly) used by many archaeologists, is that the amount of investment in facilities and the extent of modification of a campsite is directly related to the length of occupation. It is from such principles that archaeologists infer degrees of sedentism and residential stability. In addition to providing support for this principle, Sipe also found that the greater the degree of permanency of occupation, the more "domestic" the refuse became. That is, the longer the stay, the more likely it is that a greater variety of maintenance activities will be carried out and corresponding refuse discarded. This latter formulation should call to mind the law proposed by Yellen (1974) based on his observations of Bushmen camps. I think it is significant that the same principle has been arrived at independently by the study of groups which differ as much as the !Kung Bushmen and the Nacirema.

In another project relying on data from modern campgrounds, Wall (1973) examined relationships between artifact size and method of disposal (that is, primary or secondary refuse production). She found that while small objects (under an inch in diameter) were much more likely to become primary refuse than large ones, a finding corroborated in another study by McKellar (1973), proximity of the activity area to the secondary-refuse container and the nature of the camping activities also had a measurable effect on refuse disposal patterns. If archaeologists had more principles like these, they would be less likely to undertake sophisticated multivariate analyses of occupation floor data on the assumption that all refuse is primary (see Schiffer 1974). It should also be clear that other variables affecting refuse disposal patterns need to be elucidated and more complex relationships tested against a variety of ethnoarchaeological data. Campgrounds and picnic areas (Depner 1972) seem to be a fruitful place to study refuse disposal patterns in ways that will provide these usable general principles.

Many types of material culture will be, in the course of their systemic context, subject to various reparable failures. Sinew or resin bindings may loosen up, allowing projectiles to separate from their hafts; this and countless other familiar examples raise general questions about the relationships between loci of artifact use and loci of artifact repair. Nettles (1972) tested a hypothesis closely related to some of Zipf's (1949) principles: "as the mass of an element increases, there will be a decrease in the functional distance between the use and repair locations" (Nettles 1972:1). That is, as objects increase in size, the repairman tends to come to the object rather than vice versa. The test focused on one class of material objects, clocks, which vary in mass but perform roughly the same function. She collected data on availability of repair and loci of repair for several brands within 10 classes of clocks (arranged in order of increasing mass): wristwatch, alarm clock, stopwatch, cuckoo clock, mantle clock, wall clock, school or office clock, time punch-in clock, grandfather clock, and outside building clock. Her results provided evidence which tended to support the hypothesis: the average repair distance for clocks of each type was found (in miles) to be 387, 1,455, 1,322, 1,279, 605, 304, 98, 0, 15, and 0. She also attempted to explain deviations from the expected linear relationship and discovered that abundance of a clock type in the community can affect repair distance. These types of relationships, when refined further and tested in other ethnoarchaeological situations, can become part of a more comprehensive set of laws for explaining differential repair behavior.

Recent archaeological research is beginning to suggest that artifact use life is one of the most important variables determining discard frequency, extent of curate behavior, and other variables related to assemblage formation (Schiffer 1972a, 1976; David 1972; DeBoer 1974; Binford 1973). It therefore becomes imperative that we find measures of use life independent of the other variables we are attempting to estimate. One variable potentially related to use life is replacement cost. Larson (1972) investigated this relationship for several types of items. Her sample was stratified into the three categories of technomic, sociotechnic, and ideotechnic artifacts. She gathered actual use life data on several artifacts, such as candles and crayons, by experiment and used more indirect measures for other artifacts. Although this particular study is beset by some methodological difficulties, the general relationship between use life and replacement cost was confirmed for several artifact types where function was held constant. Refinement of the experimental design would go a long way toward providing more satisfying results. Even so, the results are provocative, for they suggest that by experimental means in an ethnoarchaeological context estimates of use life can be obtained for many types of object. In future studies, one could also investigate possible overall relationships between artifact use life and basic subsystem function (that is, technomic, sociotechnic, and ideotechnic), and perhaps test hypotheses I have put forward (see Schiffer 1972a).

Other studies, concerned with status symbol distribution and change, have been carried out by undergraduates (for example, Swan 1972) and are reported elsewhere at length (Schiffer 1973a, 1976). One result of these studies has been development of a model to explain some instances of complex system growth. Known as the "Status Symbol Model," this formulation leads to exciting implications concerning the nature and distribution of reuse mechanisms (activities involving the circulation of used material culture). I have also described a number of these studies previously (Schiffer 1973a, 1976; see also Claassen 1975), and will not repeat those accounts here. In the near future I will be initiating a long-term project among the Nacirema to study the principles of reuse behavior (Schiffer n.d.). Based on the results obtained thus far, it seems quite likely that in the not-too-distant future we shall be able to explain various circulation patterns of used material culture. Such principles will assume an important role in explaining many facts of the archaeological record which are now viewed as anomalies.

This brief overview of several ethnoarchaeological studies conducted among the Nacirema should provide ample evidence of the untapped potential of ethnoarchaeology. To be sure, these studies are not models of rigor, but they are indicative of the fruitful results that can be obtained if general questions are asked and appropriate data are sought, when possible in situations close at hand. If these studies presage future trends, then surely the day cannot be far off when ethnoarchaeology will begin to supply the steady flow of laws needed for archaeological explanation (Reid, Schiffer, and Rathje 1975; Isaac 1971).

CONCLUSION

With the growing realization in archaeology that successful description and explanation of past behavioral systems depends on the availability of a broad range of laws, ethnoarchaeology is finding itself in the position of having to adapt its questions, data-gathering techniques, and range of relevant data in order to become (with experimental archaeology) the principal source of these laws. It seems likely that as the nomothetic role of ethnoarchaeology increases, many investigators will acquire the specialized skills needed for this research and will concentrate their efforts primarily on ethnoarchaeology. This specialization would be a welcome development, for, quite clearly, an individual free to pursue the study of laws wherever it leads will be far more productive than one who feels the need to break the soil periodically in order to reaffirm his status as archaeologist.

Ethnoarchaeology has come a long way since the pioneers of southwestern archaeology firmly bound the study of the past to the study of the present. Even in the short span of time since the call for "action archaeology" (Kleindienst and Watson 1956), the practice of ethnoarchaeology has expanded at a staggering rate, principally in the last decade. And, while progress has been made, the real frontiers have yet to be reached. I hope that in this sympathetic critique I have provided at least the impetus to define those frontiers.

NOTE

1. I thank J. Jefferson Reid, William L. Rathje, David Saile, and especially Alan Sullivan for critical reviews of this paper. Scott Rushforth contributed ideas on how to improve the quality of informant data, and David Saile was instrumental in providing bibliographic material and insight into recent developments in the field of architecture.

Beyond Analogy in Ethnoarchaeology

RICHARD A. GOULD
University of Hawaii

The archaeologist who uses ethnographic evidence is sometimes in the position of Mark Twain's Connecticut Yankee in King Arthur's Court when he was challenged by a rival magician:

> How easy and cheap it was to be a great magician on this fellow's terms. His specialty was to tell you what any individual on the face of the globe was doing at the moment; and what he had done at any time in the past, and what he would do at any time in the future. He asked if any would like to know what the Emperor of the East was doing now? . . . The fraud went through some more mummery, and then made grave announcement:
>
> "The high and mighty Emperor of the East doth at this moment put money in the palm of a holy begging friar—one, two, three pieces, and they be all of silver."
>
> A buzz of admiring exclamations broke out, all around . . . and with each new marvel the astonishment at his accuracy rose higher and higher. . . . I saw that if this went on I should lose my supremacy, this fellow would capture my following, I should be left out in the cold. I must put a cog in his wheel, and do it right away, too. I said:
>
> "If I might ask, I should very greatly like to know what a certain person is doing."
>
> "Speak, and freely. I will tell you . . ."
>
> "Then tell me what I am doing with my right hand."
>
> "Ah-h!" There was a general gasp of surprise. It had not occurred to anybody in the crowd—that simple trick of inquiring about somebody who wasn't ten thousand miles away.

In making archaeological interpretations, we run the risk of being taken in, too. The prehistoric past lies "ten thousand miles away" in time, to use Twain's metaphor, so how can we presume to know what happened then? More specifically, does ethnoarchaeology provide an objective basis for evaluating archaeological evidence about past human behavior and not merely a conjuring trick that leads us to assume the very things we should be trying to find out?

THE PROBLEM OF ANTHROPOLOGICAL UNIFORMITARIANISM

Tuggle, Townshend, and Riley (1972:5) recently pointed out that the idea of explaining past human behavior and events through the application of laws, as proposed by Fritz and Plog (1970:405), rests upon uniformitarian assumptions. Wilmsen expressed a similar view when he stated, "Archaeologists must assume that, other things being equal, those processes which structure the ethnographic record have also structured the archaeological record" (1970:1). Uniformitarian arguments are well suited to fields like geology, where laws of nature are observable and repeatable in laboratory experiments. Not only can one observe gravity or erosion in action in nature, but one can also replicate these forces in a controlled manner and with predictable results. In doing this one assumes, of course, that the laws governing these forces have always operated in a uniform manner in the past. But the social sciences do not readily yield laws in the manner of the natural and physical sciences. As Collingwood pointed out long ago, causality in human affairs is a product of *both* external events and final causes, on the one hand, and free will and efficient causes on the other (Collingwood 1940:290-95). Uniformitarian laws in the sense used by natural and physical scientists explain the patterned behavior of natural phenomena in the aggregate, but, Carneiro's arguments notwithstanding (1970a:494), such laws do little to account for unique events that tend to occur in the historic and prehistoric record of human behavior. The archaeologist, unless he arbitrarily chooses to limit himself, is concerned with explaining both regularities and unique occurrences in past human behavior, and the inferences archaeologists use to make their data "speak" should be appropriate to these dual concerns.

As Tuggle, Townshend, and Riley point out, a systemic paradigm offers an effective way of avoiding explanations that depend upon unilineal causation or general laws (1972:9). One can model a cultural system by perceiving the interrelationships between various sub-systems without worrying about which way the causalities proceed. Furthermore, one can simulate changes in such a model by altering variables in a controlled manner and observing the effects of such alterations throughout the total system. By doing this, an archaeologist can infer processes by which changes occurred in past cultural systems. Extinct cultural systems need not have resembled any that exist in the present or recently documented past, but the starting point for inferences of this sort is still the ethnographic present.

Perhaps at this point I should distinguish between the concepts of *law* and *process*, since these terms are used often and frequently confused. Each term refers to a different order of relationship. Hempel (1965) defines a law as a stated relationship between two or more observed or operationally stated variables that is invariable in terms of time and space. A process, on the other hand, while it also posits a relationship between variables, does not lay claim to invariability in time or space. A process can change, whereas a law cannot. In the study of past human behavior I shall argue that we are better off to avoid the use of laws, with their uniformitarianist implications, in favor of processes, in which altered states of the relationship between variables may be observed. This is because man can alter and amend the relationships that exist between different aspects of his total cultural system by applying values to symbols and manipulating them to a degree not found in any other species. As Leslie White puts it:

> . . . let x equal three pounds of coal and it does equal three pounds of coal; let removal of the hat in a house of worship indicate respect and it becomes so. This creative faculty, that of freely, actively, and arbitrarily bestowing value upon things, is one of the most commonplace as well as *the* most important characteristic of man. Children employ it freely in their play: "Let's pretend that this rock is a wolf." (1949:29)

Given this ability, the archaeologist is faced not only with discovering laws that determine certain aspects of human behavior (Yes, an unsupported person will fall to the ground if he loses his balance, thanks to the invariable operation of gravitational forces) but, more important, with discovering the processes of manipulation that allow people to adapt these laws to their purposes (for example, the ingenious use of gravity to sort railway cars in a marshaling yard). Thus the discovery of invariable laws is only a small part, and in some respects a rather trivial part, of the study of past human behavior compared with the discovery of processes of human adaptation. What we may be doing, in fact, is confusing laws with propositions or hypotheses. One can always propose that certain processes occur invariably, but until this invariability is demonstrated one still has only a proposition, albeit a useful one. In archaeology we constantly consider and test propositions of varying degrees of generalization about past human behavior, but we have yet to determine whether or not laws of human behavior exist.

To discover processes that explain adaptive variation and change, the archaeologist needs a starting point, that is, a model, based on both empirical observation and a logical approach derived from general systems theory. From such a model, one may proceed to make predictions (akin to some of the "law-like propositions" proposed by Schiffer [1972b] or the notion of "predicting the past" advocated by Thomas [1974:57-72]) about the patterns of artifacts, features, and nonartifact remains that should occur in prehistoric sites.

If, as will probably happen in most cases, the actual patterns of occurrence found by the archaeologist do not conform to the predictions, then it should be possible to specify in a controlled manner just what the points of difference are from the "baseline" model. These differences or contrasts from the anticipated results then must be explained by positing alterations in the model to account for them. For example, an ethnographic model of pastoral transhumance could lead to the prediction that an archaeologist should expect to find sites reflecting differing subsistence activities correlated with different reconstructed habitats. If, however, the archaeologist finds a pattern of sites reflecting similar subsistence activities in varied habitats, he will need to modify his model. How the model will be modified depends upon the nature and interaction of the particular subsystems involved. If one finds that grassland conditions occurred to varying degrees on a seasonal basis in each occupied habitat, then the stage is set for positing an adaptive model based upon true pastoral nomadism of the sort defined by Barth (1956).

Although this hypothetical example was assisted by a knowledge of general world ethnography, it should not be taken as an open invitation to ransack ethnographic sources in search of analogues. The

252

ethnographic literature furnishes many useful cases that provide alternative explanations, but it may be necessary in many instances to go beyond such cases by using logical inference. There are virtually no ethnographic analogues to a pedestrian big-game-hunting way of life of the sort inferred archaeologically for many Paleo-Indian and Upper Paleolithic cultures. The Eskimos, because of their heavy emphasis upon sea-mammal hunting, tend not to be a strong analogue, although a possible exception to this argument may exist in the case of Eskimos who depended more or less heavily upon caribou hunting (Birket-Smith 1959:104-9; L. Binford, personal communication). Aside from a few fleeting references by Casteñada in 1541 (Winship 1896) we know little about Great Plains Indian bison hunting before the acquisition of the horse. We do know, however, that the horse was the focus for processes of rapid and profound changes in Plains Indian adaptations (Ewers 1955) that make reconstructions of prehorse adaptations on the Plains difficult and somewhat conjectural. So pedestrian big-game hunting appears to lack straightforward ethnographic analogues. In a situation like this it does no good to go on multiplying bad or inadequate analogies, since none of the possibilities will achieve a satisfactory fit with the pattern of archaeological evidence.

This case will have to be approached indirectly by means of the contrastive approach suggested here. A detailed model of the adaptive system of a group like the Eskimos of the Anaktuvuk Pass region, currently being studied by Lewis Binford and his associates, may provide a baseline for reconstructing this wholly extinct way of life, even though these particular Eskimos today make extensive use of rifles and snowmobiles. How mobile are modern Eskimo hunters, and how is this mobility patterned? How does this patterning compare with specific patterns reflected in ancient Eskimo sites and in sites belonging, for example, to ancient Clovis or Magdalenian hunters? Any differences between the patterning of material remains by modern Eskimo caribou hunters as they move in search of game and the patterning of prehistoric big-game-hunter materials will have to be explained. The primary purpose of the modern Eskimo model, then, is as a baseline for comparison. This general approach may be conveniently termed the *contrastive* as opposed to the analogous method in ethnoarchaeology.

The contrastive method overcomes the principal methodological difficulties discussed earlier. It avoids any assumptions concerning the application of uniformitarian laws of human behavior. By using the cultural system as the basis for comparison, it draws attention to processes of interaction between subsystems rather than to any kind of unilineal cause and effect. And a contrastive model is just as useful for identifying and explaining unique events as it is for dealing with regularities in past human behavior.

ANALOGY REVISITED

Ethnographic analogies are by no means without value in archaeology, but they suffer from an inherent limitation—they cannot inform us about prehistoric behavior patterns that have no modern counterpart or analogue. Yet we should remember that the archaeologist's knowledge of existing ethnographic cultural systems is often incomplete, so by broadening his ethnographic background the archaeologist can become aware of alternative modes of behavior that would have been difficult to arrive at by logic alone. Who would have thought that the chipped stone endscrapers called *yilugwa* by the Aljawara Aborigines of Central Austrialia were used as spoons for scooping out the edible meat of the wild "bush potato" (*Ipomoea costata*)? Yet recent observations and interviews by O'Connell (1974:189-94) suggest that this was the primary function of these tools prior to their replacement by European implements. "Unexpected" interpretations like this are fairly common, and humbling, occurrences for the archaeologist who makes an effort to search for ethnographic analogues. As Stanislawski (1974:15) points out, ethnographic models can provide hypotheses for testing that are relatively free of ethnocentric bias. Thus my preceding comments are intended to argue that a contrastive approach to ethnoarchaeology should not replace but, rather, should supplement and extend beyond analogy.

Some models arrived at by analogy are better than others for archaeological analysis, depending upon how the archaeologist relates these to the materials he is studying from his excavations or surveys. The use of ethnographic models based on analogy always represents a compromise between validity and the availability of ethnographic materials for comparison with the archaeological evidence. The less

254

the archaeologist must depend upon uniformitarian assumptions to infer past human behavior, the more valid his explanations will be.

Elsewhere I have distinguished between continuous and discontinuous models in ethnoarchaeology (Gould 1974:37-40), building on an earlier concept of the "new analogy" proposed by Ascher. According to Ascher, the archaeologist must "seek analogies in cultures which manipulate similar environments in similar ways" (1961a:319). This idea would describe a *discontinuous model*, that is, a model applied in areas where the ethnographic or historic people no longer lead traditional lives and where the ethnographic literature is incomplete. Here the archaeologist must derive his interpretive model from ethnographic studies made in an area in which the basic ecology, resources, and technology are similar to those in the area in which he is excavating, but the two areas may be widely separated in time and space. Sometimes, however, this type of model has been abused, mainly owing to poor control of data bearing on the ecological and cultural context and to an overdependence on uniformitarian assumptions. How far should we go in assuming that past human responses to problems of ecological and cultural adaptation resembled solutions by present-day people of similar problems? Did processes of human adaptation really remain uniform throughout the prehistoric and historic past, or is this a proposition that itself requires testing? As yet I can point to no convincing reason for adopting such a uniformitarian view of past human behavior.

Continuous models, on the other hand, depend upon situations in which the living, ethnographic society upon which the model is based can be demonstrated to be historically continuous with the prehistoric culture being excavated in the same region. Situations like this are less common than the long-distance analogies discussed above, but they rely much less on uniformitarian assumptions and thus offer an inherently higher degree of probability in interpretation. The more strongly one can show both continuity and conservatism between the prehistoric and ethnographic cultural systems in a particular area, the greater is the probability that the model derived in the present is applicable to the past in that region. Elsewhere (Gould 1971, 1974) I have reported on the archaeological sequence at the Puntutjarpa Rockshelter site as an example of a situation where a continuous model existed. That is, a stable and nonseasonal hunter-gatherer adaptation to an undependable and impoverished physical environ-

255

ment along lines closely similar to that of the present-day Western Desert Aborigines appears to have characterized this region throughout the post-Pleistocene period for at least the last 10,000 years. Strong analogies like this are, admittedly, uncommon, but they should be sought out by archaeologists whenever possible.

The question now is, Can contrastive and analogous methods in ethnoarchaeology be unified within a single framework that will avoid making these two approaches seem like "either-or" propositions to the archaeologist searching for models upon which to base his interpretations?

THE SEARCH FOR ALTERNATIVE BEHAVIORS

Collingwood's (1946: 266-302) sleuth, Detective-Inspector Jenkins of Scotland Yard, had the right idea. He knew that past events—in this case the murder of John Doe—were truly past and over with. He knew, further, that all the facts he could gather about the events surrounding the crime would remain just that, facts, and nothing more, until he applied processes of logical inference to them. By imagining himself in the situation of the killer, the detective was able to visualize each suspect in terms of variables like motive and opportunity, and the facts concerning only one suspect "made sense" in terms of these variables. Thus the killer was identified.

This exercise of what Collingwood called the "historical imagination" lies at the heart of all successful detective work, history, and archaeology. Binford would probably agree with Collingwood's statement that "You can't collect your evidence before you begin thinking . . . because thinking means asking questions . . . and nothing is evidence except in relation to some definite question" (1946:281). But what kind of thinking does this process of historical imagination involve? Collingwood goes on to comment that "the historian must re-enact the past in his own mind. . . . he must see the possible alternatives, and the reasons for choosing one rather than another" (1946:281-82). To repeat, the past is over. What we aspire to in archaeology is an idea of the past, and that idea is based upon the selection of alternative behaviors that can most economically account for the facts. If one accepts this philosophy of science, then one also must agree that the awareness of alternative behaviors is the cornerstone of convincing archaeological interpretation. It is the fundamental task of ethnoarchaeology to heighten the archaeologist's awareness of alternative human behaviors that could have occurred, in order to explain the patterning of archaeological facts.

It is this dedication by the archaeologist to seeking out alternative behaviors to explain any given set of archaeological "facts" that gives unity to the diverse interests covered by that conceptual umbrella we call ethnoarchaeology. Here is where experimental studies in lithics, butchering, refuse disposal, ceramics, architecture, and other archaeologically visible phenomena join with observational data on these topics to present us with a view of the widest possible array of alternative behaviors. For example, Crabtree (1966) used an experimental approach employing no less than 11 distinct alternative techniques or combinations of techniques to attempt to replicate Folsom fluted points of the type found at the Lindenmeier Site. Two of these techniques, indirect percussion with an anvil or rest, and direct pressure with a clamp and anvil, produced acceptable replicas, and thus both techniques were viewed as reasonable alternatives. Crabtree favored the direct pressure technique with clamp because it seemed more reliable in producing the desired results, but this preference was expressed only after the other possibilities had been tried, especially when it came to removing the channel flake that gives these points their fluted shape.

It is this same idea of alternative behaviors that unites the contrastive and analogous approaches described earlier. Although these two approaches differ significantly, they are both valid ways of expanding the range of possible alternative behaviors that might bear upon past archaeological events. Whether or not we choose to label all of these efforts "ethnoarchaeology" or cut the cake of concept differently matters very little if we can agree about what it is we are trying to do, namely help us imagine the greatest possible number of ways in which particular patterns of archaeological phenomena may have arisen. It is this informed use of the imagination that can make archaeology a kind of prehistoric anthropology, regardless of the specific experimental or ethnoarchaeological approaches used.

MODELS AND ASSOCIATIONS IN ARCHAEOLOGY

If the foregoing arguments are accepted, then the next step is to consider ways in which the archaeologist should imagine or conceive of the alternative behaviors that might apply in any given situation. Every effort must be made at this stage of analysis to avoid ambiguities, and for this reason some archaeologists have been attracted to formalized, systems-oriented approaches. These approaches are particularly useful in the way they compel one to use a disciplined approach to the data and also in the way they reveal quantitative as well as qualitative relationships. This can be viewed as the modeling stage of the analysis, in which the systematic interrelationships among different components of a cultural system are delineated.

Whether one uses an analogous or a contrastive approach in applying ethnographic observations to archaeological patterns, the role of the model is crucial. First, to be of use, a model must be based on empirical observation. Perhaps this is restating an obvious proposition, but the fact is that most ethnographic observations in the existing literature are framed in terms of normative behavior or a normative concept of culture. I shall refer to this as the "so-and-so do such-and-such" school of ethnography, and such generalizations do have a legitimate place in anthropology. But for archaeology such generalizations without the empirical observations upon which they were (presumably) based are of little value. For example, if one wishes to understand how faunal refuse is disposed of in and around the habitation camps of a particular society, one way to find out is to observe directly how game is butchered, consumed, and finally discarded and, further, to observe any processes that may affect the remains after discard (such as scuffing or trampling underfoot by the site inhabitants, crushing and dispersal due to dogs, and so forth). Such observations involve mapping and plotting the spatial occurrences of refuse in relation to other site features like hearths, structures, and artifact remains. Such mapping is not routinely done by ethnographers, and, indeed, the same can be said for controlled collecting and other empirical techniques for recording the patterning (and especially disposal) of material remains.

So the model, however framed, consists of a statement of the interrelations of different subsystems or components that are empirically observed. Schiffer (1972a) has proposed a useful scheme for assembling ethnographic observations into a flow chart to permit one to visualize the chain of events leading to the final discard of particular categories of material remains. Stanislawski (1969b) and

258

Heider (1967:62) have also emphasized the importance of the archaeologist's paying attention to the ultimate context in which various kinds of artifacts come to rest after use. We cannot simply assume, as many "normative" ethnographers have done, that all broken or discarded materials ultimately find their way into the midden or refuse heap. Pottery, stone flakes, shell fishhooks, and other items may be recycled, curated, or otherwise redirected into contexts that differ from our commonsense expectations. Where do various material objects finally go, and how do they get there? One can assume they do not go to heaven. By monitoring the whole chain of events from manufacture to final discard of material objects we can sometimes discover unexpected relationships. At first glance the absence of bonito fishing hooks, which are distinctive in appearance and relate exclusively to bonito fishing, in the midden deposits of ethnographically known bonito fishing camps on the shores of San Cristóbal in the Solomon Islands appeared contradictory. Yet when M. Kaschko (personal communication) observed the actual chain of events leading to the discard of these implements, he found that these fishhooks either disappeared out to sea with the fish after the line broke or else that broken fishhooks were simply thrown overboard while still at sea, and new ones were attached to the line. Thus empirical observations led to recognition of the systematic disappearance of this class of artifacts from the total artifact inventory, suggesting that the last place to look for bonito hooks would be a bonito fishing camp. Whether such observations are pursued and presented in a formal, systematic fashion in the manner proposed by Schiffer (1972a) and Thomas (1973), or presented in an orderly descriptive fashion is less important than that they appear in relation to their ultimate context of disposal—that is, in a situation that can be related to a predictable archaeological context. That context appears in the form of consistent associations of material remains and site features that either resemble or contrast with the model-derived predictions. To a large extent, ethnoarchaeology is the ethnographic study of processes of human discard.

To demonstrate how one can arrive at ethnographic observations that can be related to predictable archaeological contexts, I would like to turn now to the problem of modeling the relationship among different lithic raw materials and artifact classes of the Western Desert Aborigines of the Warburton Ranges region of Australia.

RICHARD A. GOULD

LITHIC RESOURCES OF THE WARBURTON RANGES REGION, WESTERN AUSTRALIA

As part of an archaeological project at Puntutjarpa Rockshelter in 1969-70, a systematic survey was carried out to locate sources of usable lithic material within a 25-mile radius of the site. Our efforts were aided by Aborigines at the Warburton Ranges Mission, many of whom continued to visit some of these localities to obtain stone for toolmaking. We were also assisted by the Western Mining Corporation, Ltd., then in the process of carrying out a survey for copper ore in this region. The Western Mining Corporation's coverage of the area was complete, with teams on motorbikes and other vehicles inspecting literally every square foot of ground. These teams notified us of any outcrops or other occurrences of potentially usable stone, thus extending the completeness of the survey beyond the limited means available to our archaeological field crew.

In the course of this study, a total of seven classes of usable lithic raw material was noted to occur within this area:

1. Warburton porphyry. A hard, dark bluish-gray stone with pronounced granular inclusions but with little tendency toward internal planes of cleavage.

2. Quartz. Hard white or semitranslucent stone with pronounced internal planes of cleavage.

3. Quartzite. A variable category of stones with noticeable fine granular texture and few, if any, internal planes of cleavage. Color varies from pale yellow to dark red and reddish-brown. Most specimens collected were hard, with a semisilicious surface shine, but some specimens tended toward a dull surface and were rather "sugary" in texture.

4. Red chert. A hard, fine-grained dark red chert with some tendencies to fracture along internal planes of cleavage.

5. Opaline. White stone with shiny outer surfaces but soft internal texture, tending at times to crumble into a white powdery consistency.

6. White chert. Hard white-to-semitranslucent stone with no internal planes of cleavage. Varies in surface texture from dull to smooth. Rough cortex often present, and some pieces show a partial slight pinkish to dark reddish-brown coloration.

7. Agate. Hard, brown-to-semitranslucent stone, sometimes with pronounced internal banding. Smooth texture with few internal planes of cleavage. Few large pieces of this material were seen.

260

All of these lithic materials have natural sources occurring within a 25-mile radius of the Puntutjarpa Rockshelter, and no other kinds of potentially usable lithic materials were found within this area. These natural sources take two forms: localized quarry sites and nonlocalized surface occurrences. Localized quarry sites in the vicinity of Puntutjarpa are summarized in Table 10.1. These occur as modest outcrops (often nearly flush with the ground surface), although at some localities—especially those containing white chert—some shallow digging is necessary to extract usable, unweathered material. The quarries for red chert and Warburton porphyry are no longer used by the local Aborigines, but sources for white chert are still visited and used from time to time. Nonlocalized surface occurrences are mainly scatters of quartz, quartzite, and agate on extensive flats and gibber plains that lie in the area between the Brown Range and the Warburton Ranges and immediately to the north of the Warburtons. Another important nonlocalized source consists of creek beds lying between the Brown and Warburton ranges. Hughes Creek, which passes within 1,600 feet of Puntutjarpa, contains many usable pieces of quartzite and opaline as well as redeposited Warburton porphyry. Thus copious supplies of quartz and quartzite as well as modest quantities of agate and opaline were available to the ancient inhabitants of Puntutjarpa Rockshelter within a half-mile of the site.

TABLE 10.1
LOCALIZED QUARRY SITES
IN VICINITY OF PUNTUTJARPA

Location	Approx. direct-line distance and direction from Puntutjarpa	Lithic Material
Spring Granite (Kunapurul)	20 miles northeast	white chert
Quarry 3 miles W. of Spring Granite	20 miles north	white chert
Warburton Range (immediately S. of Mt. Talbot)	6 miles northeast	Warburton porphyry
The Sisters	10 miles southeast	dark red chert
Mulyangiri	14 miles north	white chert
Quarry 1 mile S. of Wanampi Well	20 miles east	white chert
Quarry ½ mile N. of Mulyayiti	15 miles southeast	white chert

LITHIC RAW MATERIALS REPRESENTED AT PUNTUTJARPA ROCKSHELTER

A general account of the stratigraphic and cultural sequence at Puntutjarpa has been given elsewhere (Gould 1971), and a detailed site report is currently in press, so only certain basic information needs to be given here. Trench 2 at this site contained a total of 77,484 stone tools, cores, and waste flakes in the context of a cultural sequence extending continuously over the last 10,000 years. All of the locally available varieties of stone mentioned above are well represented throughout the sequence at Puntutjarpa in more or less constant frequencies, as shown in Table 10.2, and, in addition, we find a low but more or less constant percentage of raw materials termed "exotic," a residual category consisting of lithic materials known not to occur within a 25-mile radius of the site. These vary greatly in terms of color, texture, and hardness, with mottled and banded cherts in colors such as black, gray, purple, red, yellow, brown, and orange, to mention a few. The source of only one of these lithic materials is known—a bright-to-pale-green semitranslucent chrysoprase from the Wingellina Hills about 180 miles east of the Warburton Mission. Only two pieces of Wingellina chrysoprase were found in the Trench 2 fill at Puntutjarpa. Only 2.6 percent of the total lithic materials excavated in Trench 2 consisted of these exotic materials, with frequencies by stratum ranging from a high of 6.7 percent to a low of 1.0 percent of the total. Table 10.2 provides a more detailed picture of the relative percentages for each class of raw material by excavated stratum and in relation to radiocarbon dates.

The general pattern presented in Trench 2 at Puntutjarpa Rockshelter is one of 10,000 years of continuous and more or less unchanging reliance upon the seven classes of locally available lithic raw materials. Constant, too, however, is the low-level but pervasive use of exotic cherts and chrysoprase. Given this situation, what we need are explanations that will help us to understand the total pattern presented by the data and not just the general pattern represented by the aggregate or statistically dominant trend in the Trench 2 lithic data. In other words, why did the Western Desert Aborigines try consistently and for at least 10,000 years to obtain small amounts of lithic raw materials from areas beyond the site locale, even when suitable materials for toolmaking were abundantly available close at hand?

Of course the question of suitability of lithic raw materials takes in more variables than simply ease of procurement. It is also important to consider the properties of each lithic material in relation to the particular tasks or range of tasks inferred for each class of stone tool found at the site. This is no easy question to handle, since it involves several levels of inference. We must first attempt to establish the functional role or roles for each artifact class, and then we must see what, if any, correlations exist between these artifact classes and the different raw materials. Finally, given certain probable uses for certain tools, we must arrive at some basis for evaluating the suitability of the available raw materials for these uses.

ARTIFACT CLASSES IN RELATION TO LITHIC RAW MATERIALS

Several descriptions exist of ethnographic Western Desert Aborigine stone tools (Thomson 1964; Tindale 1965; Gould, Koster, and Sontz 1971), and a systematic classification of the stone artifacts from the Puntutjarpa Rockshelter excavations is currently in press with the site report. Table 10.3 summarizes the major flaked stone artifact types as they occurred by stratum in Trench 2 and in relation to radiocarbon-dated levels of the site. Each of these types is distinguished from other types by several qualitative and metrical attributes, and each type except for the last two includes several subtypes that are distinguished from each other on the basis of a single qualitative or metrical attribute. This is essentially a formal classification, with a reliance upon readily observable attributes for differentiation. It is intended only as a "first step" classification, since there are many other attributes one could select and measure as a basis for differentiation. But it does provide a basis for discussion of possible tool uses and the relationship of particular raw materials to these uses.

Adzes

Of special interest are the tools classed as *adzes* and *micro-adzes* (subtypes 3a-3i). The use of the term *adze* to describe these artifacts follows current Australian usage and should not be confused with the way this word is used to describe tools of a very different sort from New Guinea, Polynesia, and other parts of the world. Australian Aborigine

TABLE 10.2. RELATIVE PERCENTAGES OF LITHIC MATERIAL BY STRATUM, TRENCH 2, PUNTUTJARPA.

ZONES	STRATA	WARBURTON PORPHYRY		QUARTZ (including quartz crystal)		QUARTZITE	
(DATES BASED ON C–14)							
<185 Years	AX	4.4%	34	50.0%	396	8.8%	68
	BX	5.7	93	52.8	865	6.7	113
	CX	7.1	187	52.0	1363	7.9	208
A	DX	8.0	246	54.5	2073	6.7	256
	EX	5.7	269	53.7	2434	7.2	327
1500 AD	FX	6.2	253	51.0	1899	8.4	313
	GX	9.1	438	48.7	2333	10.9	523
	HX	10.3	400	47.5	1751	12.5	462
UPPER ROCKFALL ZONE	IZ	14.7	457	41.2	1285	16.8	524
	JZ	13.6	181	45.7	610	16.3	218
	KZ	19.8	318	43.1	725	14.6	234
	LZ	15.7	100	50.2	319	13.1	83
	M5	14.3	1168	46.7	3803	19.9	1622
B	N5	11.1	1093	54.0	5321	16.7	1645
4700 BC	O5	10.1	885	55.1	4835	15.4	1353
	P5	11.3	696	52.8	3241	15.7	974
	Q5	14.3	665	46.8	2181	18.5	862
	R5	15.7	596	40.4	1530	20.9	792
	S5	15.7	299	39.4	751	19.2	366
8000 BC	T5	14.5	205	35.8	505	15.7	222
	U5	12.3	56	28.7	131	12.1	55
C	V5	10.5	8	34.2	26	9.2	7
	X5			22.2	4	5.6	1

TOTAL Actual Number of specimens)   8,647   38,381   11,228

TOTAL %   11.2   49.5   14.5

RED CHERT		OPALINE		WHITE CHERT		AGATE		EXOTIC (including Wingellina chrysophase)		TOTAL (actual no of specimens)
.5%	4	.8%	7	24.2%	186	3.1%	24	6.6%	51	770
.5	8	.7	11	22.3	365	4.3%	71	6.7	111	1637
.5	14	.2	21	21.2	557	4.4	115	6.0	157	2622
.3	11	.9	33	20.5	782	4.6	176	6.0	229	3806
.4	17	.8	36	23.2	1050	3.6	163	5.3	239	4535
.3	10	1.2	45	23.7	882	4.3	162	4.4	163	3727
.3	16	1.1	51	20.1	962	5.2	250	4.6	219	4792
.1	5	.9	32	21.5	791	3.2%	117	3.5%	129	3887
.0	1	.5	16	21.4	667	3.5	109	1.8	57	3116
		.4	5	19.2	256	2.6	35	2.2	30	1335 / 6693
.2	3	.2	4	16.6	267	2.2	15	1.2	20	1606
.2	1	1.6	10	16.4	104	1.4	9	1.6	10	636
.0	3	.3	25	16.5	1343	1.2	101	1.0	81	8146
.1	6	.4	38	15.7	1542	1.0	103	1.0	97	9845
.1	7	.3	22	16.3	1429	1.5	134	12	103	8768
.0	3	.2	13	16.9	1038	1.7	107	1.1	68	6140
.0	1	.2	11	16.8	784	1.5	72	1.7	81	4657
.2	6	.2	6	19.1	725	1.4	53	2.2	82	3790
.3	5	.1	2	21.2	404	1.8	35	2.4	46	1908
.2	3	.5	7	26.4	372	2.1	30	4.7	67	1411
		.4	2	40.4	184	2.7	13	33	15	456
				46.1	35					76
				72.2	13					18

124		397		14,738		2,055		77,184
.2		.5		19.0		2.5		2.6

TABLE 10.3. STONE TOOL TYPES BY STRATUM, TRENCH 2, PUNTUTJARPA.

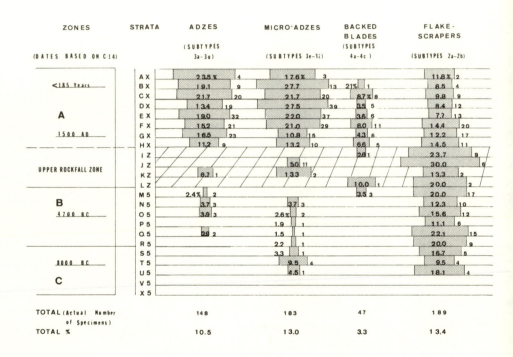

ZONES (DATES BASED ON C14)	STRATA	ADZES (SUBTYPES 3a-3o)		MICRO-ADZES (SUBTYPES 3e-3i)		BACKED BLADES (SUBTYPES 4a-4c)		FLAKE-SCRAPERS (SUBTYPES 2a-2b)	
<185 Years	A X	23.5%	4	17.6%	3			11.8%	2
	B X	19.1	9	27.7	13	21%	1	8.5	4
	C X	21.7	20	21.7	20	8.7%	8	9.8	9
A	D X	13.4	19	27.5	39	3.5	5	8.4	12
	E X	19.0	32	22.0	37	3.6	6	7.7	13
1500 AD	F X	15.2	21	21.0	29	8.0	11	14.4	20
	G X	16.5	23	10.8	15	4.3	6	12.2	17
	H X	11.2	9	13.2	10	6.6	5	14.5	11
	I Z					2.6	1	23.7	9
UPPER ROCKFALL ZONE	J Z			50	11			30.0	6
	K Z	6.7	1	13.3	2			13.3	2
	L Z					10.0	1	20.0	2
B	M 5	2.4%	2			3.5	3	20.0	17
	N 5	3.7	3	3.7	3			12.3	10
4700 BC	O 5	3.9	3	2.6%	2			15.6	12
	P 5			1.9	1			11.1	6
	Q 5	2.9	2	1.5	1			22.1	15
	R 5			2.2	1			20.0	9
	S 5			3.3	1			16.7	5
8000 BC	T 5			9.5	4			9.5	4
	U 5			4.5	1			18.1	4
C	V 5								
	X 5								
TOTAL (Actual Number of Specimens)		148		183		47		189	
TOTAL %		10.5		13.0		3.3		13.4	

LARGE CORES (SUBTYPES 1a-1c)		MICRO-CORES (SUBTYPES 1d-1e)		HAND AXES (PROV. TYPE 5)		RETOUCHED FRAGMENTS PLUS UTILIZED FLAKES (PROV. TYPE 9)		TOTAL (actual no of specimens)
11.8%	2					35.3%	6	17
2.1%	1	8.6%	4			31.9	15	47
4.3	4	4.3	4			29.3	27	92
9.2	13	4.9	7			33.1	47	142
8.9	15	7.3	12			31.5	53	168
6.5	9	5.8	8			29.0	40	138
18.0	25	12.3	17			25.9	36	139
19.7	15	11.1	8			23.7	18	76
18.4	7	21.1	8			34.2	13	38
25.0	5	20.0	4			20.0	4	20
26.7	4	33.3	5			6.7	11	15
		40.0	4			30.0	3	10
16.4	14	25.9	22			31.8	27	85
16.0	13	34.7	28			29.6	24	81
28.6	22	22.0	17			27.3	21	77
37.0	20	22.2	12			27.8	15	54
16.1	11	23.5	16	1.5%	1	32.4	22	68
28.9	13	22.2	10			26.7	12	45
23.3	7	16.7	5			40.0	12	30
19.1	8	11.9	5			50.0	21	42
27.3	6	13.6	3			36.3	8	22
		40.0	2			60.0	3	5
								0
214		201		1		428		1411
27.6		14.2				30.3		

adzes and micro-adzes are unifacially retouched discoidal stone scrapers ranging in width from 4.6 cm to 0.6 cm; in thickness from 2.0 cm to 0.3 cm; and in weight from 32.1 grams to 0.5 grams. The angle of the working edge of these tools, as measured at the midsection, ranges from 96° to 28°, with a mean of 70.4°. The distinction between adzes and micro-adzes rests solely upon differences in size; in all other respects these two artifact classes are identical. Each of these artifact classes is represented not only by complete and relatively unworn specimens but also by slugs, representing varying degrees of wear and resharpening. These slugs show a characteristic macroscopic pattern of stepflaking that undercuts the working edge, and this pattern sometimes occurs on more nearly whole specimens as well. Microscopic edge damage commonly occurs in the form of step fractures visible at 36x magnification along the bulbar face of the working edge of each tool and slug, although the actual number of such microscopic step fractures varies considerably from one specimen to the next. In general, adzes and micro-adzes are the most readily recognizable and regularly patterned flaked stone artifacts in the Western Desert, both in their complete and "slug" aspects.

Adzes (though not micro-adzes) continue to be made and used by many Western Desert Aborigines, including some who reside in the Warburton Ranges area. Ethnographically, these tools function as hafted woodworking scrapers for shaping artifacts of hard mulga wood (*Acacia aneura*), and it is this use that leads progressively to the characteristic "slug" along with stepflaking (the result of resharpening) and microscopic step fractures. In terms of general appearance and qualitative attributes the prehistoric adzes and adze slugs from all levels at Puntutjarpa are indistinguishable from those produced by the present-day Aborigines of the Western Desert. T-test comparisons of metrical attributes of adzes excavated at different levels of the site with those produced ethnographically support the interpretation that this class of tools has not changed at all in the last 10,000 years. A total of 331 adzes and micro-adzes were recovered in Trench 2 at Puntutjarpa, representing 23.5 percent of the total flaked stone inventory there. On associational grounds Puntutjarpa Rockshelter is inferred to have been a habitational base camp throughout nearly its entire history, and, on ethnographic grounds, this is indeed the kind of situation in which one would predict the occurrence of adzes and adze slugs. When all of

268

these lines of evidence are considered together, the probabilities are high that chipped stone adzes were made, used, and discarded in the past at Puntutjarpa in much the same way as they are today among the living Aborigines of this region.

Flakescrapers

Flakescrapers (subtypes 2a-2b) are less regularly shaped than adzes and tend to vary widely in size, though still with certain qualitative and metrical attributes in common. Although produced on flakes of irregular size and shape, all flakescrapers have one or more working edge showing unifacial retouch. Spokeshaves (subtype 2b) have concave working edges with retouch resulting from use wear rather than manufacture. Flakescrapers vary in width from 7.3 cm to 2.3 cm; in thickness from 3.5 cm to 0.5 cm; and in weight from 108.2 grams to 2.0 grams. The angle of the working edge at midsection ranges from 95° to 37°, with a mean of 70.5°.

As in the case of adzes, flakescrapers are still made and used by the Western Desert Aborigines, mainly for heavier wood-scraping tasks than can be done with adzes. Like adzes, they are used exclusively to shape mulga wood (*Acacia aneura*), but, unlike adzes, they are hand-held when used, rather than hafted. Because of this they do not become worn down far enough through use and resharpening to form slugs. In Trench 2 at Puntutjarpa, 189 flakescrapers were found, representing 13.4 percent of the total flaked-stone assemblage there. Their occurrence along with adzes and adze slugs in a habitational context agrees closely with the present-day ethnographic pattern of discard for this class of artifacts. As in the case of adzes, the presumption is strong that flakescrapers served as hand-held woodworking implements in the past in this region much as they do in the present. In passing it should be noted that none of the adze or flakescraper specimens excavated from Trench 2 at Puntutjarpa showed any signs under the microscope of gloss and/or striations of the sort reported by Hayden and Kamminga (1973:4-5) as a result of edge wear arising from working softwoods. Use of these types of stone tools for working softwood was not observed ethnographically in this region and would have to be regarded, on present evidence, as unusual behavior among present-day Western Desert Aborigines.

Backed Blades

Backed blades (subtypes 4a-4c), like micro-adzes, were an important part of the lithic assemblage in the past but went out of use shortly before the time of first contact with Europeans. At Puntutjarpa these ranged in length from 3.0 cm to 1.1 cm; in thickness from 1.0 cm to 0.2 cm; and in weight from 4.3 grams to 0.3 grams. In Australia no ethnographic Aborigines were ever observed making and using backed blades, although Mulvaney (1975:229) argues strongly for their use as hafted cutting edges for composite knives and as inset spear-barbs on the basis of archaeological evidence from sites in southeastern Australia. In Trench 2 at Puntutjarpa we find backed blades appearing sometime around 4,000 years ago and remaining popular almost until the time of European contact, although they never accounted for more than 10 percent of the total lithic assemblage there at any time.

Hand Axes and Large Cores

The provisional type labeled "Hand Axes" (Provisional Type No. 5) is represented by only one specimen from Trench 2 at Puntutjarpa, from contexts dated between 10,000 and 7,000 years ago. This artifact, while it generally resembles the ethnographic Western Desert Aborigine hand axe described from the Warburton Ranges by Tindale (1941), could also be regarded as a Large Core (Type 1). Indeed, large cores sometimes showed signs of attrition and edge damage close to the edge of the striking platform, suggesting the possibility of secondary use as choppers or scraper planes for woodworking and perhaps other tasks as well. However, these signs of edge damage are ambiguous, since our experiments have shown that direct percussion too far in from the edge of the striking platform during flake removal can produce edge damage similar to the attrition caused by scraping hardwoods. Given the generally coarse texture of the stone these large cores were fashioned from, it is presently impossible to be sure of anything except these tools' primary function as cores. Hence I prefer at this time to refer to such implements as large cores and put aside any further inferences about their presumed secondary functions. The class "Provisional Hand Axes" is really intended to alert archaeologists to the fact that possible secondary functions for these large cores may well have been important—a reasonable presumption in light of numerous ethnographic observations (Tindale 1941; Thomson 1964:413; Gould, Koster, and Sontz 1971:156-57; Hayden, personal communication 1974). Large cores, including the so-called horsehoof core, range in weight from 472.9 grams to 15.0 grams, with the provisional hand axe from Stratum 0.5 in Trench 2 at Puntutjarpa fitting on the high side of this range. On the basis of ethnographic observations one would predict that hand axes and large utilized cores would not be discarded in the context of a habitation campsite but would be more likely to occur in dispersed, task-specific sites where woodworking was the primary activity (Gould 1977). The low and rather ambiguous occurrence of such implements at Puntutjarpa tends to conform to this prediction.

Micro-Cores

While representing the same range of forms observed among large cores, these nuclei (subtypes ld-le) are smaller, ranging in size from 14.9 grams to 1.6 grams. These cores served, at least in their final stages of reduction, as sources for small flakes that were used to manufacture micro-adzes, backed blades, and other relatively small implements. Unlike large cores, these micro-cores show few signs of edge damage or attrition suggesting possible secondary use.

Retouched and Unretouched Flakes

Ethnographic Western Desert Aborigines frequently use un-retouched stone flakes with naturally acute edges as hand-held knives for cutting meat, sinew, and fibrous materials. These items are often discarded immediately after use, usually in the context of a habitation camp, where they may be trampled or otherwise affected after deposition. Some items show signs of regular, intentional retouch, and a number of these items from the Trench 2 deposit at Puntutjarpa may be regarded as fragments of what were once larger tools. So far no systematic attempt has been made to classify these materials in terms of form, although such a classification is desirable. Attempts to identify patterns of use wear or edge damage have so far been unsatisfactory in the sense that no unambiguous relationship can presently be shown to exist between observed ethnographic functions for unretouched flakes and the artifacts found in the excavations. Ethnographic specimens show minimal patterns of attrition from cutting tasks, since such flake knives are generally discarded after a single use. No patterns of abrasion or striation were observed on these flakes during microscopic examination at 36X.

Tables 10.4-10.8 present the correlation of different types of lithic raw material with different classes of flaked stone artifacts. Certain materials stand out, which enables us to ask specific questions about the procurement and use of lithic materials by the ancient Western Desert Aborigines:

1. As shown in Table 10.4, white chert was overwhelmingly preferred at all times for the manufacture and use of adzes and micro-adzes. Is this raw material superior for use in shaping implements of hardwood when compared to other, locally available types of stone? To what extent can the same be said for exotic stones, which account for 26.5 percent of the total raw materials used to produce this type of artifact?

2. White chert, Warburton porphyry, and quartzite together account for 71.6 percent of the raw material used to produce flakescrapers (Table 10.5), in roughly equal proportions, throughout the history of human occupation at Puntutjarpa. Thus flakescrapers reflect a greater dependence upon locally available raw materials than did adzes, despite the presumably comparable uses of these two artifact classes. Should this difference be interpreted as in any way reflecting the more regular preparation and prolonged use (thanks to hafting) of adzes as opposed to flakescrapers?

3. More backed blades were produced from exotic types of stone than from any other single kind (Table 10.6). This is a unique pattern at Puntutjarpa, and it compels us to ask, Is there a relationship between the relatively late appearance of backed blades in the Puntutjarpa sequence (sometime around 4,000 years ago) and the fact that this is the only class of tools at Puntutjarpa in which exotic raw materials predominate?

4. In the case of large cores and hand axes, coarse lithic raw materials like quartzite, quartz, and, to a lesser extent, Warburton porphyry predominate throughout the sequence (Table 10.7). Could this pattern perhaps reflect secondary uses for these artifacts, over and above their primary function as cores?

5. Quartz predominates as the lithic raw material for micro-cores, with white chert running a poor second. Quartz is the most intractable of all of these lithic materials for making good flaked stone tools, and at the same time it is the most easily obtained lithic raw material in the

272

TABLE 10.4
LITHIC RAW MATERIALS USED IN MAKING ADZES AND
MICRO-ADZES (SUBTYPES 3a-3i), TRENCH 2,
PUNTUTJARPA ROCKSHELTER

	Stratum	Warburton Porphyry	Quartz	Quartzite	Red Chert	Opaline	White Chert	Agate	Exotic
ZONE A	AX no.						2		5
	% of total						28.6		71.4
	BX no.		1				16	1	4
	% of total		4.5				72.7	4.5	18.2
	CX no.					1	20	4	16
	% of total					2.4	48.8	9.8	39.0
	DX no.		1	3		3	37	1	16
	% of total		1.6	4.9		4.9	60.7	1.6	26.2
	EX no.			3		2	42	4	19
	% of total			4.3		2.9	60.0	5.7	27.1
	FX no.	1	1	1		1	36		13
	% of total	1.9	1.9	1.9		1.9	67.9		24.5
	GX no.	1	5	3		1	19	3	7
	% of total	2.6	12.8	7.7		2.6	48.7	7.7	17.9
	HX no.						16	1	4
	% of total						76.2	4.8	19.0
UPPER ROCKFALL	IZ no.								1
	% of total								100.0
	JZ no.						1		
	% of total						100.0		
	KZ no.						2		1
	% of total						66.7		33.3
	LZ no.								
	% of total								
ZONE B	M5 no.						1		1
	% of total						50.0		50.0
	N5 no.			1			4		1
	% of total			16.7			66.7		16.7
	O5 no.			1			4		
	% of total			20.0			80.0		
	P5 no.						1		
	% of total						100.0		
	Q5 no.		1				1		1
	% of total		33.3				33.3		33.3
	R5 no.			1					
	% of total			100.0					
ZONE C	S5 no.						1		1
	% of total						50.0		50.0
	T5 no.						3		1
	% of total						75.0		25.0
	U5 no.						1		
	% of total						100.0		
	V5 no.								
	% of total								
	X5 no.								
	% of total								
	Total	2	9	13		8	207	14	91
	% of total raw materials	0.6	2.6	3.8		2.3	60.2	4.1	26.5

TABLE 10.5
LITHIC RAW MATERIALS USED IN MAKING
FLAKESCRAPERS (SUBTYPES 2a-2b), TRENCH 2,
PUNTUTJARPA ROCKSHELTER

Zone	Stratum	Warburton Porphyry	Quartz	Quartzite	Red Chert	Opaline	White Chert	Agate	Exotic
ZONE A	AX no.	1	1						
	% of total	50.0	50.0						
	BX no.		1						
	% of total		100.0						
	CX no.		2	2			1	2	2
	% of total		22.2	22.2			11.1	22.2	22.2
	DX no.	2	2	3			1	2	2
	% of total	16.7	16.7	25.0			8.3	16.7	16.7
	EX no.	2		4			5	2	
	% of total	15.4		30.8			38.5	15.4	
	FX no.	3	3	2		1	7		4
	% of total	15.0	15.0	10.0		5.0	35.0		20.0
	GX no.	2	2	4	1		4	3	1
	% of total	11.8	11.8	23.5	5.9		23.5	17.6	5.9
	HX no.	2		3			5	1	
	% of total	18.2		27.3			45.5	9.1	
UPPER ROCKFALL	IZ no.	1		4			2	1	1
	% of total	11.1		44.4			22.2	11.1	11.1
	JZ no.	1		1			2	1	1
	% of total	16.7		16.7			33.3	16.7	16.7
	KZ no.	2							
	% of total	100.0							
	LZ no.	1		1					
	% of total	50.0		50.0					
ZONE B	M5 no.	6	2	6			1		2
	% of total	35.3	11.8	35.3			5.9		11.8
	N5 no.	2	1	5			2		
	% of total	20.0	10.0	50.0			20.0		
	O5 no.	2	3	1	1		5		
	% of total	16.7	25.0	8.3	8.3		41.7		
	P5 no.		1	2			1	2	
	% of total		16.7	33.3			16.7	33.3	
	Q5 no.	7	1	5			2		
	% of total	46.7	6.7	33.3			13.3		
	R5 no.	2		4	1		2		
	% of total	22.2		44.4	11.1		22.2		
ZONE C	S5 no.	1		2			1		1
	% of total	20.0		40.0			20.0		20.0
	T5 no.	2		2					
	% of total	50.0		50.0					
	U5 no.	2					1	1	
	% of total	50.0					25.0	25.0	
	V5 no.								
	% of total								
	X5 no.								
	% of total								
	Total	41	19	51	3	1	42	15	14
	% of total raw materials	22.0	10.2	27.0	1.6	0.5	22.6	8.1	7.5

Beyond Analogy in Ethnoarchaeology

TABLE 10.6
LITHIC RAW MATERIALS USED IN MAKING
BACKED BLADES (SUBTYPES 4a-4c), TRENCH 2,
PUNTUTJARPA ROCKSHELTER

	Stratum	Warburton Porphyry	Quartz	Quartzite	Red Chert	Opaline	White Chert	Agate	Exotic
ZONE A	AX no.								
	% of total								
	BX no.		1						
	% of total		100.0						
	CX no.		3				2		3
	% of total		37.5				25.0		37.5
	DX no.		2				1		2
	% of total		40.0				20.0		40.0
	EX no.		1	2			1		2
	% of total		16.7	33.3			16.7		33.3
	FX no.		2				2	2	5
	of total		18.2				18.2	18.2	45.5
	GX no.			2		1	2		1
	% of total			33.3		16.7	33.3		16.7
	HX no.			2		1	1		1
	% of total			40.0		20.0	20.0		20.0
UPPER ROCKFALL	IZ no.								1
	% of total								100.0
	JZ no.								
	% of total								
	KZ no.								
	% of total								
	LZ no.		1						
	% of total		100.0						
ZONE B	M5 no.		8			1	1		
	% of total		33.3			33.3	33.3		
	N5 no.								
	% of total								
	O5 no.								
	% of total								
	P5 no.								
	% of total								
	Q5 no.								
	% of total								
	R5 no.								
	% of total								
ZONE C	S5 no.								
	% of total								
	T5 no.								
	% of total								
	U5 no.								
	% of total								
	V5 no.								
	% of total								
	X5 no.								
	% of total								
	Total		11	6		3	10	2	15
	% of total raw materials		23.4	12.8		6.4	21.3	4.3	31.9

275

TABLE 10.7
LITHIC RAW MATERIALS USED IN MAKING LARGE CORES
AND HAND AXES (SUBTYPES 1a-1c; PROVISIONAL
TYPE 5), TRENCH 2, PUNTUTJARPA ROCKSHELTER

Stratum	Warburton Porphyry	Quartz	Quartzite	Red Chert	Opaline	White Chert	Agate	Exotic
AX no.		2						
% of total		100.0						
BX no.			1					
% of total			100.0					
CX no.	1	3						
% of total	25.0	75.0						
DX no.	2	6	2	1		1	1	
% of total	15.4	46.1	15.4	7.6		7.6	7.6	
EX no.	1	12	1			1		
% of total	6.7	80.0	6.7			6.7		
FX no.		4	2				3	
% of total		44.4	22.2				33.3	
GX no.		18	2			3	1	1
% of total		72.0	8.0			12.0	4.0	4.0
HX no.	2	6	3			1	1	2
% of total	13.3	40.0	20.0			6.7	6.7	13.3
IZ no.			6				1	
% of total			85.7				14.3	
JZ no.		1	4					
% of total		20.0	80.0					
KZ no.	3		1					
% of total	75.0		25.0					
LZ no.								
% of total								
M5 no.	2	9	3					
% of total	14.3	64.3	21.4					
N5 no.	1	7	2			2	1	
% of total	7.7	53.8	15.4			15.4	7.7	
O5 no.	3	10	5			3	1	
% of total	13.6	45.5	22.7			13.6	4.5	
P5 no.	3	10	5			2		
% of total	15.0	50.0	25.0			10.0		
Q5 no.		5	5				1	1
% of total		41.7	41.7				8.3	8.3
R5 no.	2	5	4			2		
% of total	15.4	38.5	30.8			15.4		
S5 no.	1	3	2				1	
% of total	14.3	42.9	28.6				14.3	
T5 no.	2		4			2		
% of total	25.0		50.0			25.0		
U5 no.	2	3	1					
% of total	33.3	50.0	16.7					
V5 no.								
% of total								
X5 no.								
% of total								
Total	25	104	53	1		17	11	4
% of total raw materials materials	11.6	48.4	24.7	0.5		7.9	5.1	1.8

Zones (left margin labels): ZONE A, UPPER ROCKFALL, ZONE B, ZONE C

276

TABLE 10.8
LITHIC RAW MATERIALS USED IN MAKING MICRO-CORES (SUBTYPES 1d-1e), TRENCH 2, PUNTUTJARPA ROCKSHELTER

		Warburton					White		
	Stratum	Porphyry	Quartz	Quartzite	Red Chert	Opaline	Chert	Agate	Exotic
ZONE A	AX no.								
	% of total								
	BX no.		3				1		
	% of total		75.0				25.0		
	CX no.		2	1		1			
	% of total		50.0	25.0		25.0			
	DX no.		5				1		1
	% of total		71.4				14.3		14.3
	EX no.		5				3	3	1
	% of total		41.7				25.0	25.0	8.3
	FX no.		2	1			4	1	
	% of total		25.0	12.5			50.0	12.5	
	GX no.		10		1		1	2	3
	% of total		58.8		5.9		5.9	11.8	17.6
	HX no.		5				3		
	% of total		62.5				37.5		
UPPER ROCKFALL	IZ no.		7						
	% of total		100.0						
	JZ no.		4						
	% of total		100.0						
	KZ no.		2	2					1
	% of total		40.0	40.0					20.0
	LZ no.		3	1					
	% of total		75.0	25.0					
ZONE B	M5 no.		17	1			4		
	% of total		77.2	4.5			18.2		
	N5 no.		21	1			3	1	
	% of total		80.8	3.8			11.5	3.8	
	O5 no.		14	1			1		
	% of total		87.5	6.3			6.3		
	P5 no.		9				2		1
	% of total		75.0				16.7		8.3
	Q5 no.		15	1					
	% of total		93.8	6.3					
	R5 no.		4	2			4		
	% of total		40.0	20.0			40.0		
ZONE C	S5 no.		2				2		1
	% of total		40.0				40.0		20.0
	T5 no.	1	3				1		
	% of total	20.0	60.0				20.0		
	U5 no.		1				1	1	
	% of total		33.3				33.3	33.3	
	V5 no.		1				1		
	% of total		50.0				50.0		
	X5 no.								
	% of total								
	Total	1	135	11	1	1	32	8	8
	% of total raw materials	0.5	68.5	5.6	0.5	0.5	16.2	4.1	4.1

vicinity of Puntutjarpa. Could these facts somehow be related to the importance of quartz in the production of both large cores and micro-cores throughout the Puntutjarpa sequence?

In short, having established correlations indicating certain preferences for particular lithic raw materials for producing certain kinds of artifacts, we must attempt to move beyond these correlations into the realm of inference. Can we relate these correlations to behavioral models and reach some kind of judgment about their cultural significance? The archaeological correlations themselves only provide the basis for questions—not answers. We must turn now to experimental and ethnographic evidence for models that can be related to the correlations observed for stone tool types and lithic raw materials at Puntutjarpa.

EXPERIMENTAL OBSERVATIONS

A series of experiments was designed and carried out at the American Museum of Natural History to deal with a variety of problems related to the lithic industries at Puntutjarpa, and these have been reported in detail elsewhere (Bronstein 1977). Certain aspects of these experiments are relevant to the discussion here. A variety of lithic raw materials was obtained from the Warburton Ranges area and other localities in the Western Desert to provide a sample for experimental evaluation of these materials for hardwoodworking, in a manner identical with that of the present-day Western Desert Aborigines. These raw materials were collected from the same localities mentioned in Table 10.1, with some additional "exotic" stones coming from the Lake Throssel region (multicolored cherts) about two hundred miles southwest of the Warburton Mission and the Wingellina Hills (chrysoprase). From these materials, a total of 25 adzes was produced by means of direct percussion with a small hammerstone. These adzes were hafted, in turn, to a Western Desert Aborigine club that had once been used ethnographically in precisely this manner. The adzes were attached with spinifex (*Triodia* sp.) resin adhesive, also produced by ethnographic Aborigines. The adzing operation consisted of the operator drawing the hafted adze toward himself, in exactly the manner described by Gould, Koster, and Sontz (1971:152). The angle of the bulbar face of the adze was held as constant as possible between 30° and 45° throughout the experiment, and a large piece of fairly fresh mulga (*Acacia aneura*) wood was used as the item to be worked. These strokes continued with pressure applied as evenly as possible until the working edge had dulled to the extent that it no longer removed wood shavings, whereupon the adze was resharpened in its haft using direct percussion with a wooden percussor to allow the work to continue. Table 10.9 records the number of useful strokes of woodworking wear obtained from each class of lithic raw material during this experiment. Each experiment ended when the adze (now reduced to a slug) became so narrow that it could no longer be held in its haft when subjected to the forces involved in this kind of woodworking. It should be noted that these experiments, in addition to supplying information about processes related to use wear and resharpening of stone adzes, also furnished replicas of adze slugs identical to those found archaeologically and ethnographically in the Western Desert, even down to the step-flaking and microscopic step fractures on opposite sides of the working edge.

A look at Table 10.9 provides some obvious patterns that can assist in the interpretation of some of the correlations noted above. White chert is by far the best material of those tested for scraping hard mulga wood. The preferences shown by Western Desert Aborigines, both past and present, for making adzes out of white chert are most economically understood in terms of both the efficiency and the availability of this type of stone. One is tempted to follow this line of argument further by noting that exotic cherts rate second in efficiency to white chert for this type of task, which might seem to explain the fact that 26.5 percent of the adzes and micro-adzes at Puntutjarpa were fashioned of this kind of raw material—that is, exotic cherts were second in popularity to white chert. This argument is reasonable but does not fully account for the extra effort and planning that were required to transport this raw material to Puntutjarpa. At the bottom of the scale we find opaline, representing a raw material with an efficiency of only 1.03 percent that of white chert. The wonder is that any Aborigines used opaline at all for wood-scraping tasks, yet we find a total of eight adzes and micro-adzes from Puntutjarpa that were made of this stone. While our experimental results point clearly to a mechanical explanation of preferences by the ancient Aborigines for white chert in making adzes and micro-adzes, they are increasingly ambiguous in explaining the relative preferences as one moves down the scale of technical efficiency for each class of lithic raw material.

TABLE 10.9
COMPARISON BY LITHIC RAW MATERIAL OF USEFUL STROKES IN WORKING HARDWOOD
(ACACIA ANEURA) WITH EXPERIMENTALLY PRODUCED ADZES

Material	N	0-500 strokes	500-1,000 strokes	1,000-1,500 strokes	1,500-3,000 strokes	3,000-5,000 strokes	5,000-8,000 strokes	8,000-10,000 strokes	10,000-15,000+ strokes	Average no. of strokes
White Chert	7			1			4	1	1	7,555
Exotic Cherts	9		2	2	2	1		1	1	4,073
Warburton Porphyry	3		1	1		1				1,602
Quartz	1			1						2,072
Quartzite	3		1	1			1			2,659
Opaline	1	1								78
Chrysoprase	1					1				3,369
Total Population	25	1	4	6	2	3	5	2	2	

When experimental data are applied to flakescrapers, the same sorts of problems arise. While it is easy to see how white chert, with its superior edge-holding properties, would be a desired raw material for making this class of tools, it is less easy to use this argument to understand why coarse-grained stones like quartzite were preferred over white chert. And it is harder still to know why 7.9 percent of the flakescrapers at Puntutjarpa were made of exotic chert. In the case of backed blades, the heavy preponderance of exotic materials needs explanation. Since we can assume that the use of backed blades was different from that attributed to adzes and flakescrapers, we cannot use our experiments as a guide to interpretation. Perhaps experiments to measure relative efficiency of different lithic materials in terms of manufacture and for various cutting tasks can be designed to do this, and such efforts should be encouraged. There is nothing in the archaeological evidence itself that explains why we find a three-way correlation between the appearance of backed blades at Puntutjarpa, the heavy dependence upon exotic cherts for backed blade manufacture, and the small but nonetheless noticeable increase in the overall percentage of exotic lithic materials in the total raw material assemblage there. Adzes and micro-adzes (and even some flake-scrapers) raise the problem of explaining the pervasive tendency of the ancient Aborigines at Puntutjarpa to obtain and use exotic cherts and other stone materials (like opaline) when mechanically more efficient lithic raw materials were available in close proximity to the site. The case of backed blades echoes this same question, although without the force of experimental data on edge-holding efficiency. Though statistically of less importance than white chert, exotic cherts constitute a subpattern that is of equal or greater anthropological interest. Both patterns require explanation in terms of human behavior, and a further comparison with alternative ethnographic behaviors affords the best approach to the whole problem presented by the Puntutjarpa data.

ETHNOGRAPHIC ALTERNATIVES

What kinds of predictions can we derive from the ethnographic Western Desert Aborigine model concerning the procurement and use of different lithic raw materials for different classes of stone artifacts? This question is best answered by looking at a series of alternative considerations involved in the selection process as observed among the Aborigines living in the Warburton Ranges area in 1966-67 and 1969-70.

Procurement Efficiency

By far the greatest amount of time and effort in the stone toolmaking process occurred during quarrying and transport. Not only did this involve visits to specific localities where stone can be quarried and collected, but it also included transport of the stone back to camp for further shaping and use. These visits were often planned ahead of time, since quarries seldom occur in close proximity to waterholes where Aborigines might otherwise camp in the normal course of their hunting and gathering routine. Special efforts were made by Aborigines to visit quarry localities, but only when the lithic raw material had something special about it. White chert was always collected in this manner, from localities known to lie within a day's walk of a habitation base camp. Individual men or small groups of men made such trips whenever their supplies of this type of raw material ran low. Since these trips were made on foot, the amounts of material they collected and carried back were limited. In the Warburton area this collecting was made easier by the use of cloth bags, tin billycans, and other mission-introduced carrying devices, but in other parts of the Western Desert I have observed previously uncontacted desert Aborigines carrying one or two large cores of stone by hand and numerous stone flakes tucked up inside their long hair. These flakes were kept apart to reduce dulling caused by the edges bumping together on the trip back to camp. The flakes and cores were carefully selected at the quarry, and, in nearly every case observed, they were used for making adzes and flake knives (mainly knives for circumcision and for cutting fibrous material in making dance paraphernalia rather than for ordinary domestic cutting tasks).

Whenever possible, heavy-duty woodworking tasks like preparation and removal of mulga-wood slabs (for making spear-throwers and throwing-sticks) or mulga branches (for digging sticks) or acacia roots (for spear shafts) were performed away from the habitation base camp at various specific localities where appropriate wood is naturally available. Because certain kinds of stone occur widely scattered on the surface in this region in the form of "gibber" plains, it is often possible to find usable quartz, quartzite, porphyry, or agate close to the place where the woodworking task will be carried out. This was a great convenience to the Aborigines, since it meant they did not have to carry large pieces of stone over long distances. These hand axes and pounders were abandoned beside the tree where the work was performed.

Many other tasks involved this same decentralized pattern of stone procurement. Men and women often picked up sharp stones from the ground surface to use for butchering or cutting plant fibers in the place where the task was performed, far from the habitation base camp. Even such small stones were usually discarded where the task was performed. In other words, given the relative ease of procurement afforded by the widespread occurrence of coarse stone materials on the surface, Aborigines made extensive use of these materials when the need arose.

Thus a twofold process of selection took place before any stone materials reached the habitation base camp. First, only specific, preferred stones like white chert were obtained from quarry localities in the context of special trips planned in advance. These raw materials tended to be allocated for special uses—mainly adze making. Second, large pieces of stone occurring on the surface were almost always used and discarded away from the base camp, in task-specific contexts. So really large pieces of coarse stone usually did not get to the base camp at all unless there happened to be some of this material lying about nearby. Thus one would predict the relatively low occurrence of large hand axes or choppers made of coarse stone material in the context of the habitation base camp, while in the same locality one would expect to find a high proportion of adzes and adze slugs made of quarried stone.

The readiness with which Aborigines pick up and use stones lying about on the surface could also be important if large amounts of stone occur close to the habitation base camp. Any potentially usable stone occurring close to the camp was used, generally for tasks that did not require a carefully shaped tool. Thus one would expect to see flakescrapers (including spokeshaves) and stone knives being made of such readily available raw material for widespread use within the habitation base camp. Although the Aborigines removed flakes by means of carefully prepared cores when obtaining raw material from localities where the material was not abundant, in cases where large amounts of stone were readily accessible they made little or no effort to economize with the material. Random, block-on-block-type percussion occurred in such cases, with tremendous numbers of irregular flakes being produced. Such materials, when carried back to camp, were similarly treated, since there were plenty more close by. Thus we should also expect to find considerable wastage of such immediately available lithic raw materials in the form of cores and flakes discarded within the habitation base camp.

Mechanical Efficiency

It was almost impossible to get Aborigines to express verbal preferences with regard to specific kinds of lithic raw material for certain tasks, despite their observed tendencies to manifest such preferences in their behavior. This may have been due to the Aborigines' casual attitude toward stone toolmaking and everyday tasks performed with stone tools. In the Warburton area, at least, the preference for white chert for adze making was virtually absolute, the only exception being specific pieces of chert brought in or traded from distant, named localities. That is, aside from such "imports," the preference for white chert could be assumed to reflect this material's superior mechanical efficiency in terms of tasks involved with hardwood scraping. In the Laverton area, on the southwestern fringe of the Western Desert, a similar tendency was noted in 1966. There, Aborigines regularly made special visits to a large quarry containing dark bluish-gray chert, located on Mt. Weld Station, about fifteen miles from the Laverton Aboriginal Reserve. Other experiments have shown this material to have almost the same edge-holding properties as the white chert found near Warburton when used to shape mulga wood, and at Laverton this material was used exclusively for adze making and for manufacture of some circumcision knives. At Laverton, too, tasks like removal of the slab of mulga wood for making a spear-thrower were performed with immediately available stones taken from the surface where the woodworking activities took place—at least when no steel axes were available for this purpose.

Flakescrapers (including spokeshaves) were treated even more casually by the Aborigines. These were produced in the habitation camp area as needed for particular wood-scraping tasks, then discarded after use. At Warburton, the fact that white chert was often used for making hand-held flakescrapers did not reflect any inclination on the part of the Aborigines to seek out this material for this purpose. Rather, most pieces of white chert used in making flakescrapers were simply collected off the ground when needed from among debitage accumulated through previous adze manufacture. That is, trips made to quarries to obtain white chert were mainly carried out with reference to adze manufacture, with flakescrapers as a secondary product. Most stone for flakescrapers was obtained from the surface gibber plains and from the creekbeds close to the Warburton Mission area. This same pattern occurred at Laverton in 1966, where Aborigines used blue-gray chert debitage for making flakescrapers along with locally collected stones off the surface, like quartz and quartzite.

It should be borne in mind that in both situations the Aborigines were using increasing numbers of steel axes and chisels for these woodworking tasks. I found it interesting that stone tools were made and used as much as they were on these Aboriginal Reserves, considering the ready availability of metal tools. Not surprisingly, it was the more traditionally oriented Aborigines, both old and young, who tended to persist in making and using stone tools.

Sacred Associations as a Factor in Stone Procurement

As mentioned earlier, some adzes and circumcision knives of unusual stone were observed in use at both Laverton and Warburton. These artifacts were made of various brightly colored chert, and interviews showed that these items came from specific localities far distant from either Aboriginal reserve. In every case, the Aborigine possessing such "imported" stone artifacts was able to name the exact locality where the material was collected and give its totemic affiliation (that is, he was able to name the ancestral Dreaming character connected to that place), even though the man being interviewed might not himself have gone to the place to collect this stone. In other words, these cherts had been collected from various sacred sites, where they occurred in close proximity to landmarks of totemic significance. Adzes of such chert (and a few of Wingellina chrysoprase as well) were not regarded as sacred objects themselves, and they were carried openly in camp where women and children could see them. When I inquired about these items, the response was always one of pride, not in the craftsmanship of the tool (which was often quite poor) but in the raw material. Moreover, the patrilineal Dreaming affiliation of the man being interviewed was always the same as that of the site from which the stone material was collected.

In other words, what I was seeing in these tools of "imported" stone were *relics* that had acquired importance in the eyes of the owner and his associates because of their close physical proximity to some important sacred event. It was almost like a pilgrim showing off a piece of the True Cross or some other souvenir of sacred importance. The stone had been collected at or near the particular sacred site and carried away by a member of the patrilineal cult lodge affiliated with that site, in many cases then to be passed on to other members of the same cult lodge as a token of their mutual affiliation. Thus it was that these items came to rest in habitation base camps, often hundreds of miles from their points of origin. Unlike adzes, circumcision knives were treated as sacred objects in themselves and were concealed from women and children. However, it was not the raw material that was regarded as sacred but, rather, the use to which this particular tool was put. Nevertheless, the sentiment was expressed that it was somehow appropriate and desirable to use such sacredly affiliated stone for this operation in preference to more ordinary, locally available stone. I should note that exceptions to this preferential behavior did occur several times, when I observed circumcisions performed with knives made from local stone. In the case of neither adzes nor circumcision knives were the stones kept after final use. Worn circumcision knives were secretly disposed of far from camp, while worn adze slugs were simply discarded in the habitation camp area. No attempt was made to curate these items beyond their normal use life.

To what extent should this behavior, observed as it was mainly in the context of Aboriginal reserves where contact with Europeans has been intense, be regarded as reflecting traditional values or behavior? When visiting previously uncontacted Aborigines in the Gibson Desert in 1970 I observed behavior exactly like this, so we can be assured that such behavior was a feature of traditional life among the Aborigines. But I strongly suspect that this behavior on reserves and in other contact situations may reflect an increased desire by the Aborigines in these places to reassert and maintain their ties to distant Dreaming places that are simply too far away for them to visit regularly. It is entirely possible that Aboriginal traffic in relics of this sort has increased since these people have left the desert and settled in close proximity to Europeans, and this interpretation would fit in well with general tendencies for increased ceremonialism often observed on Aboriginal reserves. Moreover, motor transport now enables Aborigines to carry these relics farther than was probably true in the past. I have seen adzes of Wingellina chrysoprase atover 800 miles southwest of the Wingellina Hills, where several important Dreaming sites are known to exist (Crawford and Tonkinson 1969). This widespread distribution of such materials may be in part due to post-contact factors, although evidence exists for far-ranging, Kula-like trading networks over much of the Western and Central deserts in early contact and precontact times (McCarthy 1939: 425-29). At Laverton in 1966 I observed trade of this kind. Sacred objects like incised boards and stones, decorated and incised pearl shells, emu-feather bundles, and other items were exchanged between male members of different totemic cult lodges in a formal, ritualized manner. Certain incised stones were clearly churinga of Central Desert origin, while the pearl-shell objects came ultimately from the Kimberley District of northwestern Australia. Unlike the exchange and transport of lithic raw materials, this trade occurred between patrilineages (that is, totemic cult lodges) rather than between members of the same patrilineage. So while there is good evidence for a traditionally active and widespread transport and trade of lithic materials and artifacts, there is also evidence to suggest that present-day traffic in these items under modern, "reservation" conditions may be even more intense and widely ramified than in the past.

Both of these kinds of trade and transport of lithic raw materials reflect the importance of long-distance contacts in traditional Aboriginal desert life. Along with widely ramified kin-sharing networks, the rule of preferred second-cross-cousin marriage, and the eight-subsection system, we find exchange behavior that serves to maintain the widest possible range of social contacts over the largest possible area. These social contacts serve as important risk-minimizing mechanisms by allowing socially adult males and their families to gain access to resources and share food in regions distant from their own in times of extreme drought. Social networks, with their associated obligations of food sharing and access to resources, may extend as much as 350 to 400 miles in any one direction from a particular person's own Dreaming sites, encompassing a radius of direct contacts of up to around 800 miles, with indirect contacts extending even beyond that distance.

CONCLUSIONS

There is nothing about the archaeological data from Puntutjarpa Rockshelter that, by itself, inevitably leads to a particular interpretation of prehistoric Aboriginal selection processes for particular kinds of lithic materials. For such an interpretation we must adopt an ethnoarchaeological perspective that incorporates alternative considerations based upon experimental and observational evidence.

Experimental observations are more compelling than ethnographic observations in explaining the dominant correlation between white chert as a raw material and adzes as a class of tool. Yet the ethnographic and experimental evidence do not contradict one another on this point, and one should bear in mind, too, that assumptions in this argument about the functional use of adzes arose initially from ethnographic observations. This mechanical efficiency argument, however, cannot fully explain the persistent use of less efficient, imported stone for making adzes. Perhaps there was a kind of "efficiency threshold" for the Aborigines that made these exotic cherts acceptable—after all, the experiments showed that exotic cherts were hardly the worst raw materials for woodworking tasks of the sort being posited. But it is at this point that considerations of procurement efficiency must be weighed against those of mechanical efficiency. White chert, in fact, possessed an ideal combination of attributes for the Aborigines of the Warburton (and Puntutjarpa) area. It was the most mechanically efficient material and the second most easily obtained. Exotic cherts, however, were only the second most efficient raw material for adzing tasks, and they were by far the most difficult to obtain. Was the efficiency of exotic cherts great enough to lead the Aborigines to make the extraordinary efforts needed to obtain them for adze making? I very much doubt that it was, especially in light of the more than adequate supplies of superior white chert at known quarries in the nearby area. Exotic cherts, then, were mechanically efficient enough to be acceptable for adze manufacture, but we can reasonably infer that some other consideration led the ancient Aborigines to make the extra efforts needed to obtain them. While the ethnographic Western Desert Aborigines provide us with a ready model for explaining this pattern, through their beliefs concerning sacred totemic sites and the significance of stone materials associated with these sites, we must bear in mind that other, logical possibilities may exist. Perhaps the Aborigines found the colors of these cherts attractive

288

and sought them simply for that reason. On a more general level of interpretation, the presence of exotic lithic materials is an indicator of the scale of social relationships external to the immediate area of the site. Such an expanded social network could have been based upon either inter or intralineage mechanisms of exchange, or both. Thus the presence of exotic raw materials may reflect the ultimate ecological imperative in the Western Desert, which is to find ways of overcoming uncertainties of food and water resources in this arid, nonseasonal habitat.

Finally, not all of the patterns observed in the Puntutjarpa data on adzes can be explained yet. For example, we know that opaline was used in spite of its poor mechanical efficiency, but we do not know why. No evidence exists that local opaline in the Warburton area was sought due to sacred associations. Opaline there is easy to find, especially in creek beds, but there is no assurance that any or all of the opaline found at Puntutjarpa originated in the local area. Perhaps opaline was simply being tried out for various uses by the Aborigines. Given the possibility of sacred associations as a factor in Aboriginal selection of lithic raw materials, it could also be that the opaline occuring at Puntutjarpa was obtained from distantly located sacred sites. One such sacred site was observed on a trip with some Aborigines a few miles south of the Blackstone Range in 1967. This site, roughly 125 miles east of the Warburton Mission, contains opaline that my guides said was collected for toolmaking. In fact, several of these men took pieces away with them, although I never saw what kinds of tools were eventually produced from these stones. Perhaps laboratory procedures like neutron activation analysis and trace element studies can test this material one day to help determine its sources of origin.

Ethnographic flakescraper data suggest that the more casual the approach to making and using a paroicular class of tool, the more likely one is to find that class of tool being made from generally available raw materials rather than from quarried stones. At Puntutjarpa, unpatterned variability of form within this tool type correlates with an unusually even distribution of preferences in raw material, as if no particular preference occurred. But this interpretation still does not explain the low but persistent use of exotic cherts for making flakescrapers, and no ethnographic observations were made that would bear directly upon this point. Perhaps the exotic chert flakes used for making flakescrapers were only leftovers from adze manufacture, along the lines shown for white chert, but that idea is mainly conjectural.

Backed blades have no ethnographic analogue in the Western Desert, but it is still possible to suggest that the unusually heavy use of exotic cherts for making these tools reflects an exotic origin for this artifact type. Backed-blade technology certainly did not originate at Puntutjarpa, and earlier dates for backed blades in Australia are known, most notably at the Graman Rockshelter site in New South Wales (McBryde 1974:321-23) at around 3500 B.C. In the absence of experimental and direct ethnographic observations, the preferences for certain stones in making backed blades remain difficult to interpret. It seems possible that trade connections and social contacts expanded somewhat in the Western Desert during the period when backed blades came into use at Puntutjarpa, since the percentages of exotic chert increased there during this period.

The overwhelming predominance of quartz as a lithic raw material throughout the Puntutjarpa sequence is most economically explained by its ready availability in amounts on the surface nearby. Ease of accessibility in this case seems to have overridden this material's rather poor edge-holding qualities (at least for woodworking) and difficulties in manufacture. Ethnographic observations emphasize the casual nature of Western Desert Aborigine stone toolmaking, with the prediction, here fulfilled, that even coarse stone materials will be preferred for most immediate tasks that do not require well-shaped tools if these materials can be obtained close at hand without the need for special arrangements like a trip to a quarry or trading partners. The relatively high percentage of quartz used for backed-blade manufacture clearly violates this interpretation and stands in contrast to the ethnographic pattern.

Thus backed backed blades stand out from the rest of the Puntutjarpa assemblage, not only in terms of form, but also in terms of their raw material associations. There are no analogies to guide us in interpreting the role of this class of stone artifacts. Instead, it is the contrasts that are most useful in this case. Backed blades are clearly anomalous in terms of the total lithic assemblage of Puntutjarpa, whether looked at from a typological or a technological point of view. Uncontrolled analogies of a general nature are always possible, like the idea that these stone artifacts may have been used as inset blades on knives (suggested by Natufian sickle-blades or the ethnographic *taap*

290

knife of southwestern Australia) or as inset barbs for a spear tip (as suggested by archaeological evidence from the Upper Kenya Capsian or by ethnographic "death spears" from certain areas of Australia). These generalized analogies get some support from the fact that ethnographic Western Desert Aborigines possess an effective technology for hafting small stone tools like adzes, suggesting that their ancestors could have hafted backed blades as well. However, such uncontrolled analogies do not take us far, since, short of finding ancient backed blades still set into their hafts, we cannot effectively test these propositions.

None of the predictions that are possible on the basis of ethnographic observations in the Western Desert will directly explain the archaeological pattern for backed blades. But contrasts with these predictions offer a basis for proposing alternative explanations for these patterns. The unusually high percentage of exotic raw materials used to produce these artifacts suggests that some kind of symbolic associations existed for them. The fact that the overall percentage of exotic lithic materials in the total Puntutjarpa assemblage effectively doubled after backed blades were introduced there suggests the appearance of a trade relationship different in kind from what had prevailed. If my previous arguments are accepted, we can propose that the presence of exotic raw materials at Puntutjarpa for most tool types is most easily explained in terms of an ethnographic model of intra lineage exchange based on shared sentiments among members of the same patrilineage that place a high value on the sacred associations of the material with the place it was quarried. But backed blades depart from this pattern enough for me to suggest that these tools may have been imbued with sacred associations of a higher order than other artifact types in the assemblage. Perhaps some of these tools or the raw materials from which they were made arrived at Puntutjarpa along a network of interlineage trade. This general argument is supported, too, by the relatively high percentage of quartz used in backed blade manufacture (including at least one piece made of clear quartz). Quartz crystals and artifacts made from them are regarded by the ethnographic Western Desert Aborigines as *mapanpa*, a class of substances left behind by totemic ancestors, though not necessarily at or near sacred sites. Included in this category are other items like pearl shell, tektites, and, nowadays, even old eyeglass lenses, pieces of Bakelite plastic, and other oddments of European origin. If any of the backed blades found at Puntutjarpa were made from quartz crystals (as opposed to the more common rough pieces of quartz found scattered on the surface), they might have been imbued with this same sort of sacred—though not necessarily secret—significance. The contrast, then, between the prevailing ethnographic pattern and the situation surrounding backed blades can be used as a basis for suggesting interlineage trade as a possible explanation for the selective preferences for exotic and otherwise "sacred" raw materials in producing this class of artifacts. In considering backed blades, the ethnographic pattern of intralineage exchange and transport of lithic raw materials provides a baseline for comparison that allows us to infer how differently backed blades may have been integrated into the total lithic assemblage at Puntutjarpa from other classes of tools.

This small-scale demonstration is intended to show the value of interpreting archaeological correlations in a behavioral context. While there is clearly a need for ethnoarchaeologists to discern the nature of general relationships between various aspects of material culture and behavior (the lawlike propositions discussed earlier), there is an equally pressing need to find ways to relate observed relationships to specific patterns encountered in sites during archaeological excavation and survey. One could propose a law to describe the relationships between different lithic raw materials and tool types based upon experimental and ethnographic observations of Western Desert Aborigine material culture, but such a law would necessarily have to combine considerations of mechanical efficiency, procurement efficiency, and sacred attitudes. Could one law effectively describe all of the variables observed? If it could, how valid would it be in describing the processes of lithic selection in another culture? The case of the ethnographic Western Desert Aborigines demonstrates the extent to which specific beliefs and traditionally held values impinge upon the process of lithic selection and resource procurement, and it suggests something of the complexity of the relationships between the variables that determine which lithic raw materials will be used for making a particular type of tool. Rather than attempting to qualify or multiply invariable laws to suit such specific cases, perhaps we will be better off to use such cases as baselines for comparison with prehistoric situations as discovered through archaeology. Then each comparison becomes, in itself, a test of the relationships between various kinds of material remains and human behavior without presupposing any kind of uniformitarian bias. In ethnoarchaeology, what you see is not what you get, since there is much more to what you get than what you see in archaeological correlations alone. Ethnoarchaeology, as the systematic exploration of alternative human behaviors, provides a basis for inferences that transform these correlations into ideas about past human behavior.

References

ABERLE, DAVID F.
1970   "Comments," in *Reconstructing Prehistoric Pueblo Societies*, ed. William A.
        Longacre (Albuquerque: University of New Mexico Press, School of American
        Research Advanced Seminar Series).

ADAMS, ROBERT McC.
1974a   "Anthropological Perspectives on Ancient Trade," *Current Anthropology*
        15:239-58.
1974b   "The Mesopotamian Social Landscape: A View from the Frontier," in
        Reconstructing Complex Societies, ed. C.B. Moore, supplement to the *Bulletin
        of the American Schools of Oriental Research*, no. 20. (Cambridge, Mass.:
        M.I.T. Press).

ADAMS, WILLIAM H.
1973   "An Ethnoarchaeological Study of a Rural American Community: Silcott,
        Washington, 1900-1930," *Ethnohistory* 20:335-46.

ADELSON, J. F., E. ASP, AND I. NOBLE
1961   "Household Records of Foods Used and Discarded," *Journal of the American
        Dietetic Association* 39:578-84.

ADELSON, J. F., I. DELANEY, C. MILLER, AND I. NOBLE
1963   "Discard of Edible Food in Households," *Journal of Home Economics*
        55:633-38.

ALLAND, ALEXANDER, JR., AND BONNIE McCAY
1973   "The Concept of Adaptation in Biological and Cultural Evolution," in
        Handbook of Social and Cultural Adaptation, ed. J. Honigmann (Chicago:
        Rand McNally and Co.).

ALLEN, HARRY
1972   "Land Where the Crow Flies Backwards" (Ph.D. diss., Australian National
        University).

ALLEN, J. R. L.
1963   "The Classification of Cross-Stratified Units, With Some Notes on Their
        Origin," *Sedimentology* 2:93-114.

ALMAGOR, URI
1971   "Social Organization of the Dassanetch of the Lower Omo" (Ph.D. diss.,
        University of Manchester, England).

AMANOLAHI-BAHARVAND, SEKANDAR
1975   "The Baharvand, Former Pastoralists of Iran" (Ph.D. diss., Rice University).

ANDERSON, KEITH M.
1969   "Ethnographic Analogy and Archeological Interpretation," *Science*
        1963:133-38.

ANDERSON, W.
1776-77 "Anderson's Journal on Cook's Third Voyage" (photostat in Mitchell Library,
        Sydney).

APODACA, ANACLETO
1952   "Corn and Custom," in *Human Problems in Technological Change*, ed. Edward
        H. Spicer (New York: Russell Sage Foundation).

295

ARNOLD, DEAN E.
1971   "Ethnomineralogy of Ticul, Yucatan Potters: Etics and Emics," *American Antiquity* 36:20-40.
ASCHER, ROBERT
1961a   "Analogy in Archaeological Interpretation," *Southwestern Journal of Anthropology* 17:317-25.
1961b   "Experimental Archeology," *American Anthropologist* 63:793-816.
1962   "Ethnography for Archaeology: A Case from the Seri Indians," *Ethnology* 1:360-69.
1968   "Time's Arrow and the Archaeology of a Contemporary Community," in *Settlement Archaeology*, ed. K. C. Chang (Palo Alto, Calif.: National Press Books).
1974   "Tin-Can Archaeology," *Historical Archaeology* 8:7-16.
BACKHOUSE, J.
1843   *A Narrative of a Visit to the Australian Colonies* (London).
BAL, D. C., J. H. O'HORA, AND B. W. PORTER
1973a   *Pima County E.C.H.O. [Evidence for Community Health Organization] Report, October 1972-June 1973* (Tucson, Ariz.: Pima County Health Department).
1973b   *Arizona E.C.H.O.: Reference and Procedures Manual* (Phoenix: Arizona State Department of Health).
BARRAU, JACQUES
1963   "L'agriculture des îles Wallis et Futuna," *Journal de la Société des Océanistes* (Paris) 19:157-71.
1965a   "L'humide et le sec: An Essay on Ethnobiological Adaptation to Contrastive Environments in the Indo-Pacific Area," *Journal of the Polynesian Society* 74:329-46.
1965b   "Witnesses of the Past: Notes on Some Food Plants of Oceania," *Ethnology* 4:282-94.
1965c   "Histoire et préhistoire horticoles de l'Océanie tropicale," *Journal de la Société des Océanistes* (Paris) 21:55-78.
BARTH, FREDRIK
1956   "Ecologic Relationships of Ethnic Groups in Swat, North Pakistan," *American Anthropologist* 58:1079-89.
1964   *Nomads of South Persia* (London: George Allen and Unwin).
BEAGLEHOLE, J. C. (ed.)
1967   *The Voyage of the Resolution and Discovery, 1776–1780*, 2 pts. (Cambridge: Cambridge University Press for the Hakluyt Society).
BEALE, THOMAS W., AND PAUL F. HEALY
1975   "Archaeological Films: The Past as Present," *American Anthropologist* 77:889-97.
BEHRENSMEYER, ANNA K.
1975   *The Taphonomy and Paleoecology of Plio-Pleistocene Vertebrate Assemblages East of Lake Rudolf, Kenya*, Bulletin of the Museum of Comparative Zoology, vol. 146, no. 1.
BENNETT, JOHN W.
1969   *Northern Plainsmen* (Chicago: Aldine Publishing Co.).
BEVERIDGE, W. I. B.
1961   *The Art of Scientific Investigation* (London: Mercury).
BIGARELLA, JOAO J.
1972   "Eolian Environments: Their Characteristics, Recognition, and Importance," in *Recognition of Ancient Sedimentary Environments*, ed. J. K. Rigby and W. K.

References

Hamblin (Tulsa, Okla.: Society of Economic Paleontologists and Mineralogists).

BINFORD, LEWIS R.

1965   "Archaeological Systematics and the Study of Culture Process," *American Antiquity* 31:203-10.

1967   "Smudge Pits and Hide Smoking: The Use of Analogy in Archaeological Reasoning," *American Antiquity* 32:1-12.

1968   "Methodological Considerations of the Archeological Use of Ethnographic Data," in *Man the Hunter*, ed. Richard B. Lee and Irven DeVore (Chicago: Aldine Publishing Co.).

1972   *An Archaeological Perspective* (New York: Academic Press).

1973   "Interassemblage Variability—The Mousterian and the 'Functional' Argument," in *The Explanation of Culture Change: Models in Prehistory*, ed. Colin Renfrew (London: G. Duckworth & Co.).

1975   "Historical Archeology: Is It Historical or Archeological?" *Popular Archeology* 4:11-30.

in press   "A Case Study in the Character of Some Archaeological Formation Processes."

BINFORD, LEWIS R., AND SALLY R. BINFORD

1966   "A Preliminary Analysis of Functional Variability in the Mousterian of Lavallois Facies," *American Anthropologist* 68:238-95.

BIRKET-SMITH, KAJ

1959   *The Eskimos* (London: Methuen & Co.).

BLACK, JACOB

1972   "Tyranny as a Strategy for Survival in an 'Egalitarian' Society: Luri Facts versus an Anthropological Mystique," *Man* 7:614-34.

BLAKE, IAN

1969   "Climate, Survival and the Second-Class Societies in Palestine Before 3000 B.C.," *Advancement of Science* 25:409-21.

BONNICHSEN, ROBSON

1973   "Millie's Camp: An Experiment in Archaeology," *World Archaeology* 4:277-91.

BONNICHSEN, ROBSON, AND R. MORLAN

1974   "Experiments in Lithic Technology: A Cognitive Approach to Bifaces," paper presented at the Symposium on Prehistoric Art and Technology, Calgary.

BORDAZ, JACQUES

1970   "The Suberde Excavations, Southwestern Turkey, An Interim Report," *Türk Arkeoloji Dergisi Sayi* 17:43-71.

BORDES, FRANCOIS

1971   "Essai de préhistoire experimentale—Fabrication d'un epieu de bais," in *Mélanges de préhistoire, d'archéocivilisation et d'ethnologie* (Paris: Sevpen).

1973   "On the Chronology and Contemporaneity of Different Paleolithic Cultures in France," in *The Explanation of Culture Change: Models in Prehistory*, ed. Colin Renfrew (London: G. Duckworth & Co.).

BOSERUP, ESTER

1965   *The Conditions of Agricultural Growth* (London: George Allen and Unwin).

BOSHIER, ADRIAN K.

1965   "Effects of Pounding by Africans of North-west Transvaal on Hard and Soft Stones," *South African Archaeological Bulletin* 20:131-36.

BOWDLER, SANDRA

1970   "Bass Point: The Excavation of a Southeast Shell Midden Showing Cultural and Economic Change" (B.A. thesis, University of Sydney).

1974a   *An Account of an Archaeological Reconnaissance of Hunters' Isles, North West Tasmania, 1973/74*, Records of the Queen Victoria Museum, Launceston, Tasmania, no. 54.

1974b   "Pleistocene Date for Man in Tasmania," *Nature* 252:697-98.

1975   "Further Radiocarbon Dates from Cave Bay Cave, Hunter Island, North West Tasmania," *Australian Archaeology: Newsletter of the Australian Archaeological Association* 3:24-26.

BOWEN, THOMAS, AND EDWARD MOSER

1968   "Seri Pottery," *The Kiva* 33:89-132.

BOWLER, J. M., RHYS JONES, H. R. ALLEN, AND A. G. THORNE

1970   "Pleistocene Human Remains from Australia: A Living Site and Human Cremation from Lake Mungo," *World Archaeology* 12:39-60.

BOYD, DAWKINS, W.

1874   *Cave Hunting: Researches on the Evidence of Caves Respecting the Early Inhabitants of Europe* (London).

BRONSTEIN, NANCY

1977   "Report on a Replicative Experiment in the Manufacture and Use of Western Desert Micro-Adzes," in "Puntutjarpa Rockshelter and the Australian Desert Culture," by Richard A. Gould, in *Anthropological Papers of the American Museum of Natural History* 54, part 1 (New York).

BROOKFIELD, HAROLD C.

1972   "Intensification And Disintensification in Pacific Agriculture: A Theoretical Approach," *Pacific Viewpoint* 13:30-48.

BROTHWELL, D., AND E. HIGGS

1969   *Science in Archaeology* (London: Thames and Hudson).

BROWN, MARLEY, III

1973   "The Use of Oral and Documentary Sources in Historical Archaeology: Ethnohistory at the Mott Farm," *Ethnohistory* 20:347-60.

BUNZEL, RUTH

1929   *The Pueblo Potter: A Study of Creative Imagination in Primitive Art* (New York: Columbia University Press).

BURGH, ROBERT F.

1959   "Ceramic Profiles in the Western Mound at Awatovi, Northeastern Arizona," *American Antiquity* 36:20-40.

BURROWS, EDWIN G.

1936   *Ethnology of Futuna*, Bernice P. Bishop Museum Bulletin 138 (Honolulu).

1937   *Ethnology of Uvea*, Bernice P. Bishop Museum Bulletin 145 (Honolulu).

BUTZER, KARL W.

1971   *Recent History of an Ethiopian Delta*, Department of Geography Research Paper 136 (Chicago: University of Chicago).

CALLAHAN, ERRETT (ed.)

1972   *Experimental Archaeology Newsletter* #1: *A Sampling* (Richmond: Virginia Commonwealth University).

CARNEIRO, ROBERT L.

1970a   "A Quantitative Law in Anthropology," *American Antiquity* 35:492-94.

1970b   "A Theory of the Origin of the State," *Science* 169:733-38.

CARR, CLAUDIA J.

1977   *A System of Societal/Environmental Interaction: The Dassanetch of Southwest Ethiopia*, Department of Geography Research Paper (Chicago: University of Chicago).

CAUVIN, JACQUES

1974   "Troisième campagne de fouilles à Tell Mureibet," *Annales Archéologiques Arabes Syriennes* 24:47-58.

CHAMBERLIN, T. C.

1965   "The Method of Multiple Working Hypotheses," *Science* 148:754-59.

References

CHAPMAN, KENNETH M.
1970   *The Pottery of San Ildefonso Pueblo*, School of American Research Monograph 28, ed. F. H. Harlow, Jr. (Albuquerque: University of New Mexico Press).
CHARLTON, THOMAS H.
1972   "Population Trends in the Teotihuacan Valley, A.D. 1400-1969," *World Archaeology* 4:106-23.
CHILDE, V. GORDON
1956   *Piecing Together the Past* (London: Routledge and Kegan Paul).
CHURCHMAN, C. W.
1948   *Theory of Experimental Inference* (New York: Macmillan Co.).
CLAASSEN, CHERYL
1975   "Antiques—Objects of Lateral Cycling?" *Proceedings of the Arkansas Academy of Science* 29:36.
CLARK, A. McFADYEN, AND DONALD W. CLARK
1974   "Koyukon Athapaskan Houses as Seen Through Oral Tradition and Through Archaeology," *Arctic Anthropology* 11(supplement):29-38.
CLARKE, DAVID L.
1968   *Analytical Archaeology* (London: Methuen & Co.).
1972   "A Provisional Model of Iron Age Society and Its Settlement System," in *Models in Archaeology*, ed. David L. Clarke (London: Methuen & Co.).
1973   "Archaeology: The Loss of Innocence," *Antiquity* 47:6-18.
CLARKE, J. D. GRAHAME
1952   *Prehistoric Europe: The Economic Basis* (London: Methuen & Co.).
1957   *Archaeology and Society* (London: Methuen & Co.).
1970   *Aspects of Prehistory* (Berkeley and Los Angeles: University of California Press).
COE, MICHAEL D., AND KENT V. FLANNERY
1964   "Microenvironments and Mesoamerican Prehistory," *Science* 143:650-54.
COHEN, YEHUDI A.
1968   "Culture as Adaptation," in *Man in Adaptation*, ed. Yehudi A. Cohen (Chicago: Aldine Publishing Co.).
COLEMAN, EMILY
1966   "An Analysis of Small Samples from West Point Shell Midden" (B.A. thesis, University of Sydney).
COLES, JOHN
1973   *Archaeology by Experiment* (New York: Charles Scribner's Sons).
COLLINGWOOD, R. G.
1940   *Metaphysics* (London: Oxford University Press).
1946   *The Idea of History* (London: Oxford University Press).
COLLINS, D.
1789-1802 *An Account of the English Colony in New South Wales*, 2 vols. (London).
COLLINS, DESMOND
1973   "Epistemology and Culture Tradition Theory," in *The Explanation of Culture Change: Models in Prehistory*, ed. Colin Renfrew (London: G. Duckworth & Co.).
COLTON, HAROLD S.
1939   "Primitive Pottery Firing Methods," *Museum of Northern Arizona, Museum Notes* 11:63-66.
1951   "Hopi Firing Temperatures," *Plateau* 24:73-76.
COMPTON, ROBERT R.
1962   *Manual of Field Geology*. (New York: John Wiley & Sons).
CONKLIN, HAROLD C.
1954   "An Ethnoecological Approach to Shifting Cultivation," *Transactions of the New York Academy of Science* 17:133-42.

1963   *The Study of Shifting Cultivation*, Pan American Union Studies and Monographs, no. 6 (Washington, D.C.).

COOK, JAMES
1776-79 "Journal, Third Voyage" (photostat in Mitchell Library, Sydney).

COON, CARLETON S.
1958   *A Reader in General Anthropology* (New York: Holt and Rinehart).

CORNELL, CHRISTINE (trans.)
1974   *The Journal of Post Captain Nicolas Baudin . . . Assigned by Order of the Government to a Voyage of Discovery* (Adelaide: Libraries Board of South Australia).

COUTTS, P. J. F.
1967   "Pottery of Eastern New Guinea and Papua," *Mankind* 6:482-88.

COWGILL, GEORGE L.
1970   "Some Sampling and Reliability Problems in Archaeology," in *Archéologie et calculateurs* (Paris: Editions du Centre National de la Recherche Scientifique).

CRABTREE, DON E.
1966   "A Stoneworker's Approach to Analyzing and Replicating the Lindenmeier Folsom," *Tebiwa* 9:3-39.
1973   "Experiments in Replicating Hokoham Points," *Tebiwa* 16:10-45.

CRAWFORD, I. M., AND R. TONKINSON
1969   "Report on Sites Lying within the Area Leased by International Nickel in the Vicinity of Wingellina, Which Are Thought to be Sacred to Aborigines," paper presented to the Advisory Panel to the Minister for Native Welfare, Perth, Western Australia.

CROZET, J. M.
1783   *Nouveau voya;e à la mer du sud, commencé sous les ordres de M. Marion* (Paris).

CUSHING, FRANK HAMILTON
1886   "A Study of Pueblo Pottery as Illustrative of Zuni Culture-Growth," in *Fourth Annual Report of the Bureau of Ethnology, 1882-83*.
1920   *Zuni Breadstuff*, Indian Notes and Monographs, no. 8 (New York: Heye Foundation).

DAVID, NICHOLAS
1971   "The Fulani Compound and the Archaeologist," *World Archaeology* 3:111-31.
1972   "On the Life Span of Pottery, Type Frequencies, and Archaeological Inference," *American Antiquity* 37:141-42.

DAVID, NICHOLAS AND HILKE HENNIG
1972   *The Ethnography of Pottery: A Fulani Case Seen in Archaeological Perspective*, Addison-Wesley Modular Publications in Anthropology, no. 21 (Reading, Mass.).

DeBOER, WARREN R.
1974   "Ceramic Longevity and Archaeological Interpretation: An Example from the Upper Ucayali, Peru," *American Antiquity* 39:335-42.

DEETZ, JAMES F.
1965   *The Dynamics of Stylistic Change in Arikara Ceramics*, Illinois Studies in Anthropology, no. 4 (Urbana: University of Illinois).
1968a   "Cultural Patterning of Behavior as Reflected by Archaeological Materials," in *Settlement Archaeology*, ed. K. C. Chang (Palo Alto, Calif.: National Press Books).
1968b   "Hunters in Archaeological Perspective," in *Man the Hunter*, ed. Richard B. Lee and Irven DeVore (Chicago: Aldine Publishing Co.).

References

1970 "Archeology as a Social Science," in *Current Directions in Anthropology*, ed. Ann Fischer, American Anthropological Association Bulletin 3(3), pt. 2.

1971 "Must Archaeologists Dig?" in *Man's Imprint from the Past*, ed. James Deetz (Boston: Little, Brown & Co.).

1973 "Ceramics from Plymouth, 1635-1835: The Archaeological Evidence," in *Ceramics in America*, ed. I. M. G. Quimby (Charlottesville: University of Virginia Press).

DEPNER, DEBBIE
1972 "To Store or Discard" (manuscript, Arizona State Museum Library, University of Arizona, Tucson).

DE QUATREFAGES, A.
1884 *Hommes fossiles et hommes sauvages: Etudes d'antropologie* (Paris).

DIAMOND, JARED
1977 "Distributional Strategies," in *Sunda and Sahul: Prehistoric Studies in South East Asia, Melanesia and Australia*, ed. J. Allen, J. Golson, and R. Jones (London: Academic Press).

DiPESO, CHARLES
1950 "A Guaraheo Potter," *The Kiva* 16:1-5.

DOBZHANSKY, THEODOSIUS
1962 *Mankind Evolving* (New Haven, Conn.: Yale University Press).

DONNAN, CHRISTOPHER B.
1971 "Ancient Peruvian Potters' Marks and Their Interpretation Through Ethnographic Analogy," *American Antiquity* 36:460-66.

DONNAN, CHRISTOPHER B., AND C. WILLIAM CLEWLOW, JR. (eds.)
1974 *Ethnoarchaeology*, University of California, Los Angeles, Institute of Archaeology, Monograph 4.

DOSTAL, W.
1967 *Die Beduinen in SüdArabien*, Wiener Beiträge zur Kulturegeschichte und Linguistik, Band 16 (Horn, Austria: Ferdinand Berger & Sons).

DOZIER, EDWARD P.
1951 "Resistance to Acculturation and Assimilation in an Indian Pueblo," *American Anthropologist* 53:56-66.

1954 "The Hopi-Tewa of Arizona," *University of California Publications in American Archaeology and Ethnology* 44:259-376.

DROWER, M. S.
1969 "The Domestication of the Horse," in *The Domestication and Exploitation of Plants and Animals*, ed. Peter J. Ucko and G. W. Dimbleby (London: G. Duckworth & Co.).

EDELBERG, LENNART
1966-67 "Seasonal Dwellings of Farmers in North-Western Luristan," *Folk* 8-9:377-401.

EIGHMY, J. L.
n.d. "The Use of Material Culture in Anthropological Research" (manuscript, Arizona State Museum Library, University of Arizona, Tucson).

ELLEN, ROY F., AND I. C. GLOVER
1974 "Pottery Manufacture and Trade in the Central Moluccas, Indonesia: The Modern Situation and the Historical Implications," *Man* 9:353-79.

ELLIS, FLORENCE HAWLEY
1961 "The Hopi, Their History and Use of Lands," Defendant's Exhibit No. E500, Docket No. 229, Indian Claims Commission (Washington, D.C.).

ELSTER, E.
1976 "The Chipped Stone Industry," in *Neolithic Macedonia as Reflected*

by Excavations at Anza, Southeast Yugoslavia, ed. M. Gimbutas (Los Angeles: University of California, Los Angeles, Institute of Archaeology).

EPA (ENVIRONMENTAL PROTECTION AGENCY)
1974   *Solid Waste Management: Recycling and the Consumer (SW-117)* (Washington, D.C.).

EVANS, JOHN
1872   *The Ancient Stone Implements, Weapons and Ornaments of Great Britain* (London: Longmans).

EWERS, JOHN C.
1955   *The Horse in Blackfoot Indian Culture*, Bureau of American Ethnology Bulletin 159 (Washington, D.C.).

FAGAN, B.
1975   *In the Beginning*, 2d ed. (Boston: Little, Brown & Co.).

FARRAND, W. R.
1972   "Late Quaternary Paleoclimates of the Eastern Mediterranean Area," in *The late Cenozoic Glacial Ages*, ed. K. K. Turekian (New Haven, Conn.: Yale University Press).

FAULKNER, A.
1972   "Mechanical Principles of Flintworking" (Ph.D. diss., University of Washington).

FENTON, WILLIAM N.
1974   "The Advancement of Material Culture Studies in Modern Anthropological Research," in *The Human Mirror*, ed. Miles Richardson (Baton Rouge: Louisiana State University Press).

FIRTH, RAYMOND
1975   "An Appraisal of Modern Social Anthropology," in *Annual Review of Anthropology 4*, ed. B. J. Siegel (Palo Alto, Calif.: Annual Reviews).

FLANNERY, KENT V.
1965   "The Ecology of Early Food Production in Mesopotamia," *Science* 147:1247-56.
1968   "Archeological Systems Theory and Early Mesoamerica," in *Anthropological Archeology in the Americas,*ned. Betty J. Meggers (Washington, D.C.: Anthropological Society of Washington).

FONTANA, BERNARD L.
1968   "Bottles and History: The Case of Magdalena de Kino, Sonora, Mexico," *Historical Archaeology*: 45-55 (Society for Historical Archaeology).

FONTANA, B. L., W. J. ROBINSON, C. W. CARMACK,
AND E. E. LEAVITT, JR.
1962   *Papago Indian Pottery* (Seattle: University of Washington Press).

FORD, JAMES A.
1954   "The Type Concept Revisited," *American Anthropologist* 56:42-53.

FORD, JANET L., AND MARTHA A. ROLINGSON
1972   "Site Destruction Due to Agricultural Practices in Southeast Arkansas," *Arkansas Archeological Survey, Research Series* 3:1-40.

FORD, RICHARD I.
1972   "Barter, Gift, or Violence: An Analysis of Tewa Intertribal Exchange," in *Social Exchange and Interaction*, Anthropological Papers of the University of Michigan Museum of Anthropology, no. 46 (Ann Arbor).

FOSBERG, F. R., B. J. GARNIER, AND W. A. KUCHLER
1961   "Delimitation of the Humid Tropics," *Geographical Review* 51:333-47.

302

References

FOSTER, GEORGE M.
1960   "Life-Expectancy of Utilitarian Pottery in Tzintzuntzan, Michoacan, Mexico," *American Antiquity* 25:606-9.
1973   *Traditional Societies and Technological Change*, 2d ed. (New York: Harper and Row).

FRANKE, PAUL R., AND DON WATSON
1936   "An Experimental Corn Field in Mesa Verde National Park," in *Symposium on Prehistoric Agriculture*, ed. Donald D. Brand, University of New Mexico Bulletin 296 (Albuquerque: University of New Mexico Press).

FREEMAN, L. G., JR.
1968   "A Theoretical Framework for Interpreting Archeological Materials," in *Man the Hunter*, ed. Richard B. Lee and Irven DeVore (Chicago: Aldine Publishing Co.).

FRERE, JOHN
1800   "Account of Flint Weapons Discovered in Suffolk," *Archaeologia* 13:204-5.

FRIEDRICH, MARGARET HARDIN
1970   "Design Structure and Social Interaction: Archaeological Implications of an Ethnographic Analysis," *American Antiquity* 35:332-43.

FRITZ, J. M., AND F. T. PLOG
1970   "The Nature of Archaeological Explanation," *American Antiquity* 35:405-12.

GILL, E. D., AND M. R. BANKS
1956   *Cainozoic History of Mowbray Swamp and Other Areas of Northwestern Tasmania*, Records of the Queen Victoria Museum, Launceston, Tasmania, n.s. 6.

GODELIER, M., AND J. GARANGER
1973   "Outils de pierre, outils d'acier chez les Baraya de Nouvelle-Guinie," *L'Homme* 13:187-220.

GOLSON, JACK
1974   "Archaeology and Agricultural History in the New Guinea Highlands" (manuscript, Anthropology Department, Bernice P. Bishop Museum, Honolulu).

GORMAN, CHESTER F.
1969   "Hoabinhian: A Pebble-Tool Complex with Early Plant Associations in Southeast Asia," *Science* 163:671-73.

GOULD, RICHARD A.
1968   "Living Archaeology: The Ngatatjara of Western Australia," *Southwestern Journal of Anthropology* 24:101-22.
1971   "The Archaeologist as Ethnographer: A Case from the Western Desert of Australia," *World Archaeology* 3:143-77.
1973   *Australian Archaeology in ecological and Ethnographic Perspective*, Warner Modular Publications, no. 7.
1974   "Some Current Problems in Ethnoarchaeology," in *Ethnoarchaeology*, ed. Christopher B. Donnan and C. William Clewlow, Jr., University of California, Los Angeles, Institute of Archaeology, Monograph 4.
1977   "Ethnoarchaeology; Or, Where Do Models Come From?" in *Proceedings of the 1974 Biennial Conference of the Australian Institute of Aboriginal Studies*, ed. R. V. S. Wright (Canberra).

GOULD, RICHARD A., DOROTHY A. KOSTER, AND ANN H. L. SONTZ
1971   "The Lithic Assemblage of the Western Desert Aborigines of Australia," *American Antiquity* 36:149-69.

GRAHAM, J., R. HEIZER, AND T. HESTER
1972   A *Bibliography of Replicative Experiments in Archaeology* (Berkeley, Calif.:
        Archaeological Research Facility).
GREEN, R. C.
1972   "Aspects of the Neolithic in Oceania: Polynesia," in *Early Chinese Art and Its
        Possible Influence in the Pacific Basin*, ed. N. Barnard (New York: Intercultural
        Arts Press).
GRIFFIN, JAMES B.
1956   "The Study of Early Cultures," in *Man, Culture, and Society*, ed. Harry L.
        Shapiro (London: Oxford University Press).
GROUBE, L. M.
1971   "Tonga, Lapita Pottery, and Polynesian Origins," *Journal of the Polynesian
        Society* 80:278-316.
GUNTHER, R. T.
1945   *Life and Letters of Edward Lhuyd* (Oxford: Oxford University Press).
GUTHE, CARL E.
1925   *Pueblo Pottery Making: A Study at the Village of San Ildefonso* (Andover,
        Mass.: Phillips Academy).
HALL, EDWARD T.
1966   *The Hidden Dimension* (Garden City, N.Y.: Doubleday & Co.).
HALL, ELIZABETH
1975   "The Sufi Tradition: A Conversation with Indries Shah," *Psychology Today*,
        July, pp. 53-61.
HARLAN, JACK
1971   "Agricultural Origins: Centers and Noncenters," *Science* 174:468-74.
HARRIS, DAVID R.
1972   "The Origins of Agriculture in the Tropics," *American Scientist* 60:180-93.
HARRIS, MARVIN
1964   *The Nature of Cultural Things* (New York: Random House).
1968a   "Comments," in *New Perspectives in Archaeology*, ed. Sally R. Binford and
        Lewis R. Binford (Chicago: Aldine Publishing Co.).
1968b   *The Rise of Anthropological Theory* (New York: Thomas Y. Crowell Co.).
HARRISON, G. G.
n.d.   "Socio-Cultural Correlates of Food Utilization and Waste in a Sample of Urban
        Households" (Ph.D. diss., University of Arizona).
HARRISON, G. G., W. L. RATHJE, AND W. W. HUGHES
1974   "Socioeconomic Correlates of Food Consumption and Waste Behavior: The
        Garbage Project," paper presented at the annual meeting of the American
        Public Health Association, New Orleans.
1975   "Food Waste Behavior in an Urban Population," *Journal of Nutrition
        Education* 7:13-16.
HART, C. M. W.
1943   "A Reconsideration of Natchez Social Structure," *American Anthropologist*
        45:374-86.
HARVEY, BYRON, III
1964   "Is Pottery Making a Dying Art?" *Masterkey* 38:55-65.
HAYDEN, BRIAN, AND JOHAN KAMMINGA
1973   "Gould, Koster, and Sontz on 'Microwear': A Critical Review," *Newsletter of
        Lithic Technology* 2:3-13.
HAYDEN, JULIAN
1959   "Notes on Pima Pottery Making," *The Kiva* 24:10-16.

References

HEIDER, KARL G.
1967   "Archaeological Assumptions and Ethnographical Facts: A Cautionary Tale from New Guinea," *Southwestern Journal of Anthropology* 23:52-64.

HEMPEL, CARL G.
1965   *Aspects of Scientific Explanation* (New York: Free Press).

HENRY, DON, AND FRANK SERVELLO
1974   "Compendium of C-14 Determinations Derived From Near Eastern Prehistoric Sites," *Paléorient* 2:19-44.

HIATT, BETTY
1967-68 "The Food Quest and the Economy of the Tasmanian Aborigines," *Oceania* 38:99-133, 190-219.

HIATT, L. R.
1965   *Kinship and Conflict* (Canberra: Australian National University Press).

HIGGS, E. S., AND M. R. JARMAN
1972   "The Origins of Animal and Plant Husbandry," in *Papers in Economic Prehistory*, ed. E. S. Higgs (Cambridge: Cambridge University Press).

HILL, ANDREW P.
1975   "Taphonomy of Contemporary and Late Cenozoic East African Vertebrates" (Ph.D. diss., University of London).

HILL, JAMES N.
1968   "Broken K Pueblo: Patterns of Form and Function," in *New Perspectives in Archeology*, ed. Sally R. Binford and Lewis R. Binford (Chicago: Aldine Press).
1970a   *Broken K Pueblo*, Anthropological Papers of the University of Arizona, no. 18.
1970b   "Prehistoric Social Organization in the American Southwest: Theory and Method," in *Reconstructing Prehistoric Pueblo Societies*, ed. William A. Longacre (Albuquerque: University of New Mexico Press, School of American Research Advanced Seminar Series).

HOLE, FRANK
1975   "The Sondage of Tappeh Tula'i," in *Proceedings of the Third Annual Symposium on Archaeological Research in Iran* (Tehran: Museh-e Iran-e Bastan).

HOLE, FRANK, AND R. F. HEIZER
1973   *An Introduction to Prehistoric Archeology*, 3d ed. (New York: Holt, Rinehart and Winston).

HOWELLS, WILLIAM
1973   *The Pacific Islanders* (New York: Charles Scribner's Sons).

HOWITT, A. W.
1904   *The Native Tribes of South East Australia* (London).

ISAAC, GLYNN L.
1967   "Towards the Interpretation of Occupation Debris: Some Experiments and Observations," *Kroeber Anthropological Society Papers* 37:31-57.
1971   "Whither Archaeology?" *Antiquity* 45:123-29.

ISAAC, GLYNN L., AND E. McCOWN
1976   *Human Origins* (Menlo Park, Calif.: W.A. Benjamin).

IVERSEN, J.
1956   "Forest Clearance in the Stone Age," *Scientific American* 194:36-41.

JANZEN, DANIEL H.
1973   "Tropical Agroecosystems," *Science* 182:1212-19.

JARMAN, M. R.
1972   "European Deer Economies and the Advent of the Neolithic," in *Papers in Economic Prehistory*, ed. E. S. Higgs (Cambridge: Cambridge University Press).

JEWELL, P. A., AND G. W. DIMBLEBY
1966   "The Experimental Earthwork on Overton Down, Wiltshire, England: The First Four Years," *Proceedings of the Prehistoric Society* 32:313-42.

JOHNSON, SAMUEL
1775   *A Journey to the Western Islands of Scotland* (London). (Reprinted 1970, ed. R. W. Chapman. Oxford: Oxford University Press).

JONES, RHYS
1965   "Archaeological Reconnaissance in Tasmania, Summer 1963/1964," *Oceania* 35:191–201.
1966   *A Speculative Archaeological Sequence for North West Tasmania*, Records of the Queen Victoria Museum, Launceston, Tasmania, n.s. 25.
1968   "The Geographical Background to the Arrival of Man in Australia and Tasmania," *Archaeology and Physical Anthropology in Oceania* 3:186–215.
1970   "Tasmanian Aborigines and Dogs," *Mankind* 7:256–71.
1971   "Rocky Cape and the Problem of the Tasmanians" (Ph.D. diss., University of Sydney).
1973   "Emerging Picture of Pleistocene Australians," *Nature* 246:278–81.
1974   "Tasmanian Tribes," appendix to *Aboriginal Tribes of Australia*, by Norman B. Tindale (Berkeley and Los Angeles: University of California Press; Canberra: Australian National University Press).
1975   "The Neolithic Palaeolithic and the Hunting Gardeners: Man and Land in the Antipodes," in *Quaternary Studies: Selected Papers from IX INQUA Congress, Christchurch, New Zealand, 2-10 December 1973*, ed. R. P. Suggate and M. M. Cresswell (Wellington: Royal Society of New Zealand, Bulletin 13).
1976   "Tasmania: Aquatic Machines and Offshore Islands," in *Problems in Economic and Social Archaeology*, ed. G. de G. Sieveking, I. H. Longworth, and K. E. Wilson (London: Duckworth).
1977   "Man as an Element of a Continental Fauna: The Case of the Sundering of the Bassian Bridge," in *Sunda and and Sahul: Prehistoric Studies in South East Asia, Melanesia and Australia*, ed. J. Allen, J. Golson, and R. Jones (London: Academic Press).
in press "The Tasmanian Paradox," in *Stone Tools as Cultural Markers: Change, Evolution, and Complexity*, ed. R. V. S. Wright (Canberra: Australian Institute of Aboriginal Studies).

JUNGHANS, S., E. SANGMEISTER, AND M. SCHROEDER
1960   *Metallanalysen kupferzeithlicher unde fruhbronzezeitlicher Bodenfunde aus Europa*, Studien zu den Anfängen der Metallurgie, no 1 (W. Berlin: Gebrüder Mann).

KEESING, ROGER M.
1974   "Theories of Culture," in *Annual Review of Anthropology* 3, ed. B. J. Siegel. (Palo Alto, Calif.: Annual Reviews).

KEHOE, ALICE B., AND T. F. KEHOE
1973   "Cognitive Models for Archaeological Interpretation," *American Antiquity* 38:150-54.

KELLY, RAYMOND C.
1968   "Demographic Pressure and Descent Group Structure in the New Guinea Highlands," *Oceania* 39:36-63.

KEMP, T. B.
1963   "The Prehistory of the Tasmanian Aborigines," *Australian Natural History* 14:242-47.

References

KIRCH, PATRICK V.
1975   "Cultural Adaptation and Ecology in Western Polynesia: An Ethnoarchaeological Study" (Ph.d. diss., Yale University).
1976   "Ethnoarchaeological Investigations in Futuna and Uvea (Western Polynesia): A Preliminary Report," *Journal of the Polynesian Society* 85:27-69.
in press "Rapport préliminaire sur l'investigation archéologique des iles Wallis et Futuna (Polynésie Occidentale)," *Journal de la Société des Océanistes* (Paris).

KIRKBRIDE, DIANA
1972   "Umm Dabaghiyah 1971: A Preliminary Report," *Iraq* 34:3-15.
1973a   "Umm Dabaghiyah 1972: A Second Preliminary Report," *Iraq* 35:1-7.
1973b   "Umm Dabaghiyah 1973: A Third Preliminary Report," *Iraq* 35:205-9.
1974   "Umm Dabaghiyah 1974: A Fourth Preliminary Report," *Iraq* 36:3-10.

KLEINDIENST, MAXINE R., AND PATTY JO WATSON
1956   "Action Archeology: The Archeological Inventory of a Living Community," *Anthropology Tomorrow* 5:75-78.

KNIFFEN, FRED B.
1974   "Material Culture in the Geographic Interpretation of the Landscape," in *The Human Mirror*, ed. Miles Richardson (Baton Rouge: Louisiana State University Press).

KRAMER, S. N.
1961   *History Begins at Sumer* (London: Thames and Hudson).

LABILLARDIERE, J. J. H. DE
1800   *Rélation du voyage à la recherche de La Pérouse* . . . (Paris). Pagination references are to the English translation by J. Stockdale (London, 1800).

LANGE, FREDERICK W., AND CHARLES R. RYDBERG
1972   "Abandonment and Post-Abandonment Behavior at a Rural Central American Housesite," *American Antiquity* 37:419-32.

LARSON, ETHEL
1972   "Correlation Between Replacement Cost and Use-Life of Elements" (manuscript, Arizona State Museum Library, University of Arizona, Tucson).

LAUER, PETER K.
1970   "Amphlett Islands' Pottery Trade and the Kula," *Mankind* 7:165-76.
1971   "Preliminary Report on Ethnoarchaeological Research in the Northwestern Massim, TPNG," *Asian Perspectives* 14:69-75.

LAUGHLIN, WILLIAM S.
1969   "Foreword," in *Hunters of the Northern Ice* by Richard K. Nelson (Chicago: University of Chicago Press).

LEE, IDA
1920   *Captain Bligh's Second Voyage to the South Sea* (London: Longmans, Green and Co.)

LEE, RICHARD B.
1966   "Kalahari-1: A Site Report," in *The Study of Man*, Anthropology Curriculum Study Project.

LeFREE, BETTY
1975   *Santa Clara Pottery Today*, School of American Research Monograph 29 (Albuquerque: University of New Mexico Press).

LEGGE, A. J.
1972   "Prehistoric Exploitation of the Gazelle in Palestine," in *Papers in Economic Prehistory*, ed. E. S. Higgs (Cambridge: Cambridge University Press).

LEONE, MARK P.
1972   "Issues in Anthropological Archaeology," in *Contemporary Archaeology*, ed.
        Mark P. Leone (Carbondale: Southern Illinois University Press).
1973   "Archeology as the Science of Technology: Mormon Town Plans and Fences,"
        in *Research and Theory in Current Archeology*, ed. Charles L. Redman (New
        York: Wiley-Interscience).

LEROI-GOURHAN, ANDRE, AND MICHEL BREZILLON
1966   "L'habitation magdalenienne No. 1 de Pincevent près Montereau
        (Seine-et-Marne)," *Gallia Préhistoire* 9:263-385.

LEVINS, RICHARD
1968   *Evolution in Changing Environments*, Monographs in Population Biology,
        no. 2 (Princeton, N.J.).

LEWIS, O.
1969   "The Possessions of the Poor," *Scientific American* 221:114-25.

LINTON, RALPH
1936   *The Study of Man* (New York: Appleton-Century-Crofts).

LISTER, FLORENCE C., AND ROBERT H. LISTER
1972   "Making Majolica Pottery in Modern Mexico," *El Palacio* 78:21-32.

LLOYD, G. T.
1862   *Thirty-three Years in Tasmania and Victoria* (London).

LONGACRE, WILLIAM A.
1964a   "Archeology as Anthropology: A Case of Study," *Science* 144:1454-55.
1964b   "Sociological Implications of the Ceramic Analysis," *Fieldiana Anthropology*
        55:155-70.
1968   "Some Aspects of Prehistoric Society in East-Central Arizona," in *New
        Perspectives in Archeology*, ed. Sally R. Binford and Lewis R. Binford (Chicago:
        Aldine Publishing Co.).
1970   *Reconstructing Prehistoric Pueblo Societies* (Albuquerque: University of New
(ed.)   Mexico Press, School of American Research Advanced Seminar Series).
1974   "Kalinga Pottery-Making: The Evolution of a Research Design," in *Frontiers in
        Anthropology*, ed. Murray Leaf (New York: Van Nostrand).
1975   "Ethnoarchaeology of the Kalinga, Kalinga-Apayao Province, Northern
        Luzon, the Philippines" (research proposal submitted to the National Science
        Foundation).

LONGACRE, WILLIAM A., AND JAMES A. AYRES
1968   "Archeological Lessons from an Apache Wickiup," in *New Perspectives in
        Archeology*, edited by Sally R. Binford and Lewis R. Binford (Chicago: Aldine
        Publishing Co.).

LONGRIGG, S. H.
1953   *Iraq, 1900 to 1950: A Political, Social, and Economic History* (London: Oxford
        University Press).

LOURANDOS, HARRY
1970   "Coast and Hinterland: The Archaeological Sites of Eastern Tasmania" (M.A.
        thesis, Australian National University).

LUBBOCK, JOHN
1869   *Prehistoric Times as Illustrated by Ancient Remains and the Manners and
        Customs of Modern Savages* (London and Edinburgh).

LUEBBERS, ROGER
1975   "Ancient Boomerangs Discovered in South Australia," *Nature* 253:39.

308

References

LYON, PATRICIA J.
1970   "Differential Bone Destruction: An Ethnographic Example," *American Antiquity* 35:213-15.

McBRYDE, ISABEL
1974   *Aboriginal Prehistory in New England* (Sydney: Sydney University Press).

McCARTHY, F. D.
1939   "'Trade' in Aboriginal Australia, and 'Trade' Relationships with Torres Strait, New Guinea and Malaya," *Oceania* 9:405-38.

MacDANIELS, L. H.
1947   *A Study of the Fe'i Banana and Its Distribution with Reference to Polynesian Migrations*, Bernice P. Bishop Museum Bulletin 190 (Honolulu).

McKELLAR, JUDITH
1973   "Correlations and the Explanation of Distributions" (manuscript, Arizona State Museum Library, University of Arizona, Tucson).

McKERN, W. C.
1929   *The Archaeology of Tonga*, Bernice P. Bishop Museum Bulletin 60 (Honolulu).

MALINOWSKI, BRONISLAW
1922   *Argonauts of the Western Pacific* (London: Routledge).

MARRIOTT, ALICE
1968   *Maria, Potter of San Ildefonso* (Norman: University of Oklahoma Press).

MAXWELL MUSEUM OF ANTHROPOLOGY
1974   *Seven Families in Pueblo Pottery* (Albuquerque: University of New Mexico Press).

MAYER-OAKES, WILLIAM J.
1974   "Review of *Contemporary Archaeology: A Guide to Theory and Contributions*, ed. Mark P. Leone," *American Anthropologist* 76:651-56.

MEAD, MARGARET
1976   "Towards a Human Science," *Science* 191:903-9.

MEDAWAR, PETER BRIAN
1969   *Induction and Intuition in Scientific Thought* (Philadelphia: American Philosophical Society).

MEDFORD, LARRY D.
1972   "Agricultural Destruction of Archeological Sites in Northeast Arkansas," *Arkansas Archeological Survey, Research Series* 3:41-82.

MEEHAN, BETTY
in press "Hunters by the Seashore," *Journal of Human Evolution*.

MELLARS, P.
1973   "The Character of the Middle-Upper Palaeolithic Transition in South Western France," in *The Explanation of Culture Change: Models in Prehistory*, ed. Colin Renfrew (London: G. Duckworth & Co.).

MESTON, A. L.
1956   "Miscellaneous Notes on the Culture of the Tasmanian Aboriginal," *Memoirs of the National Museum of Victoria* 20:191-99.

MILLIGAN, J.
1863   "Shell Mounds," *Transactions of the Ethnological Society of London* 2:128-29.

MINDELEFF, COSMOS
1900   "Localization of Tusayan Clans," *Bureau of American Ethnology Annual Report* 19:639-53.

MINER, HORACE
1956   "Body Ritual Among the Nacirema," *American Anthropologist* 58:503-7.

MOORE, A. M. T.
1975   "The Excavation of Tell Abu Hureyra: A Preliminary Report," *Proceedings of the Prehistoric Society* 41:50-77.
MOORE, F. G. T.
1969   *The Observation of Savage Peoples by J. M. Degérando* (London: Routledge and Kegan Paul).
MORTENSEN, PEDER
1972   "Seasonal Camps and Early Villages in the Zagros," in *Man, Settlement and Urbanism*, ed. Peter J. Ucko and G. W. Dimbleby (London: G. Duckworth & Co).
MOTZ, A.
n.d.   "Individual Bathroom Decoration Coordinated with Educational Level and Drug Use," paper prepared for Anthropology 136 (manuscript, Arizona State Museum Library, University of Arizona, Tucson).
MULVANEY, D. J.
1975   *The Prehistory of Australia*, 2d ed. (London and Melbourne: Penguin Books).
MUNSEN, P.
1969   "Comments on Binford's 'Smudge-Pits and Hide Smoking': The Use of Analogy in Archaeological Reasoning," *American Antiquity* 34:83-85.
NELSON, RICHARD K.
1969   *Hunters of the Northern Ice* (Chicago: University of Chicago Press).
NETTLES, ISOLDE
1972   "The Effect of Mass on Distance to Repair Using Time Mechanisms as an Example" (manuscript, Arizona State Museum Library, University of Arizona, Tucson).
NEWTON, DOLORES
1974   "The Timbira Hammock as a Cultural Indicator of Social Boundaries," in *The Human Mirror*, ed. Miles Richardson (Baton Rouge: Louisiana State University Press).
NILSSON, S.
1868   *The Primitive Inhabitants of Scandinavia* (London: Longmans, Green and Co.).
NISSEN, K., AND M. DITTEMORE
1974   "Ethnographic Data and Wear Pattern Analysis: A Study of Socketed Eskimo Scrapers," *Tebiwa* 17:67-88.
O'CONNELL, JAMES F.
1974   "Spoons, Knives and Scrapers: The Function of Yilugwa in Central Australia," *Mankind* 9:189-94.
ODELL, GEORGE
1974   "L'analyse fonctionnelle microscopique des pierres taillées. Un nouveau système," paper presented at the Congrès Préhistorique de France, 20th session, Martigues.
in press "Préliminaires d'une analyse fonctionelle des microlithiques pointus de Bergumemeer," *Bulletin de la Société Préhistorique Française*.
O'KELLY, M. J.
1954   "Excavation and Experiments in Ancient Irish Cooking-Places," *Journal of the Royal Society of Antiquity, Ireland* 84:105-55.
OLIVER, DOUGLAS L.
1949   *Economic and Social Uses of Domestic Pigs in Siuai, Southern Bougainville, Solomon Islands*, Papers of the Peabody Museum of Archaeology and Ethnology, vol. 24, no. 3 (Cambridge, Mass.: Harvard University).

References

OLSON, E. C.
1962   "Late Permian Terrestrial Vertebrates, U.S.A. and U.S.S.R.," *Transactions of the American Philosophical Society* 52(2).

ORME, BRYONY
1974   "Twentieth-Century Prehistorians and the Idea of Ethnographic Parallels," *Man* 9:199-212.

OSWALT, WENDELL H.
1974   "Ethnoarchaeology," in *Ethnoarchaeology*, ed. Christopher B. Donnan and C. William Clewlow, Jr., University of California, Los Angeles, Institute of Archaeology, Monograph 4.

PANOFF, MICHEL
1970   *La terre et l'organisation sociale en polynésie* (Paris: Editions Payot).

PARSONS, ELSIE CLEWS
1940   "Relations between Ethnology and Archaeology in the Southwest," *American Antiquity* o.s. 3:214-20.

PARSONS, JEFFREY R.
1972   "Archaeological Settlement Patterns," in *Annual Review of Anthropology 1*, ed. B. J. Siegel (Palo Alto, Calif.: Annual Reviews).

PASTRON, ALLEN G.
1974   "Preliminary Ethnoarchaeological Investigations among the Tarahumara," in *Ethnoarchaeology*, ed. Christopher B. Donnan and C. William Clewlow, Jr., University of California, Los Angeles, Institute of Archaeology, Monograph 4.

PAWLEY, ANDREW, AND ROGER GREEN
1973   "Dating the Dispersal of the Oceanic Languages," *Oceanic Linguistics* 12:1-67.

PEPPER, GEORGE H.
1920   *Pueblo Bonito*, American Museum of Natural History Anthropological Papers, no. 27 (New York).

PERIN, CONSTANCE
1970   *With Man in Mind: An Interdisciplinary Prospectus for Environmental Design* (Cambridge, Mass.: M.I.T. Press).

PERKINS, D., AND P. DALY
1968   "A Hunter's Village in Neolithic Turkey," *Scientific American* 219:96-106.

PERON, F.
1807-16 *Voyage de découvertes aux Terres Australes*, 2 vols. (Paris). Pagination references are to the English translation by Richard Phillips (London, 1810).

PERROT, JEAN
1966   *Préhistoire du Proche Orient*, Supplément au Dictionnaire de la Bible (Paris: Editions Letouzey et Ané).

PETERSON, NICOLAS
1968   "The Pestle and Mortar: An Ethnographic Analogy for Archaeology in Arnhem Land," *Mankind* 6:567-70.
1971   "Open Sites and the Ethnographic Approach to the Archaeology of Hunter-Gatherers," in *Aboriginal Man and Environment in Australia*, ed. D. J. Mulvaney and J. Golson (Canberra: Australian National University Press).
1973   "Camp Site Location Amongst Australian Hunter-Gatherers: Archaeological and Ethnographic Evidence for a Key Determinant," *Archaeology and Physical Anthropology in Oceania* 8:173-93.

PIGGOTT, STUART
1976   *Ruins in a Landscape: Essays in Antiquarianism* (Edinburgh: Edinburgh University Press).

PLATT, JOHN R.
1964   "Strong Inference," *Science* 146:347-53.

PLOMLEY, N. J. B
1966   *Friendly Mission: The Tasmanian Journals and Papers of George Augustus Robinson, 1829-1834* (Hobart: Tasmanian Historical Research Association).
1969   *An Annotated Bibliography of the Tasmanian Aborigines*, Royal Anthropological Institute Occasional Paper no. 28 (London).

POLLARD, JACK, ed.
1969   *Australian and New Zealand Fishing* (Deewhy West, N.S.W.).

POPPER, K.
1963   *Conjectures and Refutations* (London: Routledge and Kegan Paul).

PRICE, JAMES E., CYNTHIA PRICE, JOHN COTTIER, SUZANNE HARRIS, AND JOHN H. HOUSE
1975   *An Assessment of the Cultural Resources of the Little Black Watershed* (Columbia: University of Missouri).

PULESTON, DENNIS E.
1971   "An Experimental Approach to the Function of Classic Maya Chultuns," *American Antiquity* 36:322-34.

PULLEINE, R. H.
1929   "The Tasmanians and Their Stone-Culture," *Reports of the Australian Association of Advancement of Science* 19:294-314.

QUA'TÖQTI
1974   "First Mesa Potters Relate History of Nampeyo's Pottery," *Qua'töqti: The Eagle's Cry* (Oraibi, Ariz.), September 5, p. 3.

QUATREFAGES, A. DE
1884   *Hommes fossiles et hommes sauvages: Etudes d'antropologie* (Paris).

RAPOPORT, AMOS
1969   *House Form and Culture* (Englewood Cliffs, N.J.: Prentice-Hall).

RAPPAPORT, ROY A.
1967   *Pigs for the Ancestors* (New Haven, Conn.: Yale University Press).
1971   "Nature, Culture, and Ecological Anthropology," in *Man, Culture, and Society*, ed. Harry L. Shapiro (London: Oxford University Press).

RATHJE, WILLIAM L.
1974   "The Garbage Project: A New Way of Looking at the Problems of Archaeology," *Archaeology* 27:236-41.
1975   "In Praise of Archaeology: Le Projet du Garbage," paper presented at the annual meeting of the Society for Historical Archaeology, Charleston, S.C.

RATHJE, W. L., AND F. J. GORMAN
n.d.   "The Garbage Project: Report No. 1" (manuscript, Arizona State Museum Library, University of Arizona, Tucson).

RATHJE, WILLIAM L., AND WILSON W. HUGHES
1975   "The Garbage Project as a Nonreactive Approach: Garbage in . . . Garbage out?" in *Perspectives on Attitude Assessment: Surveys and Their Alternatives*, ed. H. Wallace Sinaiko and Laurie A. Broedling, Manpower Research and Advisory Services Technical Report 2 (Washington, D.C.: Office of Naval Research, Navy Manpower R & D Program, and Smithsonian Institution).

READ, CATHERINE E.
1971   "Animal Bones and Human Behavior: Approaches to Faunal Analysis in Archeology" (Ph.D. diss., University of California, Los Angeles).

References

REDMAN, CHARLES L.
1973   "Multistage Fieldwork and Analytical Techniques," *American Antiquity* 38:61-79.
1974   *Archeological Sampling Strategies*, Addison-Wesley Modular Publications (Reading, Mass.).
REID, J. JEFFERSON, MICHAEL B. SCHIFFER, AND JEFFREY M. NEFF
1975   "Archaeological Considerations of Intrasite Sampling," in *Sampling in Archaeology*, ed. James W. Mueller (Tucson: University of Arizona Press).
REID, J. JEFFERSON, MICHAEL B. SCHIFFER, AND WILLIAM L. RATHJE
1975   "Behavioral Archaeology: Four Strategies," *American Anthropologist* 77:864-69.
REYNOLDS, P. J.
1967   "Experiment in Iron Age Agriculture I," *Transactions of the Bristol and Gloucester Archaeological Society* 86:60-73.
RICHARDS, P. W.
1952   *The Tropical Rain Forest* (London: Cambridge University Press).
RICHARDSON, MILES, ed.
1974   *The Human Mirror* (Baton Rouge: Louisiana State University Press).
ROBBINS, L. H.
1973   "Turkana Material Culture Viewed from an Archaeological Perspective," *World Archaeology* 5:209-14.
ROBBINS, MICHAEL C., AND RICHARD B. POLLNAC
1974   "A Multivariate Analysis of the Relationships of Artifactual to Cultural Modernity in Rural Buganda," in *The Human Mirror*, ed. Miles Richardson (Baton Rouge: Louisiana State University Press).
ROBINSON, GEORGE AUGUSTUS
1829-34 Tasmanian Journals and Papers (see Plomley 1966). Original MSS in the Mitchell Library, Sydney.
ROSSEL, E. P. E. DE
1808   *Voyage de Dentrecasteaux, envoyé à la recherche de La Pérouse* (Paris).
ROTH, H. LING
1899   *The Aborigines of Tasmania*, 2d ed. (Halifax).
ROUGHLEY, T. C.
1953   *Fish and Fisheries of Australia*, rev. ed. (Sydney: Angus and Robertson).
ROUSE, IRVING
1973   "Analytic, Synthetic, and Comparative Archeology," in *Research and Theory in Current Archeology*, ed. Charles L. Redman (New York: Wiley-Interscience).
ROWE, JOHN H.
1959   "Archaeological Dating and Cultural Process," *Southwestern Journal of Anthropology* 15:317-24.
ROWLANDS, M. J.
1971   "The Archaeological Interpretation of Prehistoric Metalworking," *World Archaeology* 3:210-24.
ROWTON, M. B.
1973   "Urban Autonomy in a Nomadic Environment," *Journal of Near Eastern Studies* 32:201-15.
1974   "Enclosed Nomadism," *Journal of the Economic and Social History of the Orient* 17:1-30.
RUST, ALFRED
1943   *Stellmoor* (Neümünster, Germany: Karl Wachholtz).

RYDER, M.
1969   "Remains of Fishes and Other Aquatic Animals," in *Science in Archaeology*, ed.
        D. Brothwell and E. Higgs, 2d ed. (London: Thames and Hudson).
SABLOFF, J., T. BEALE, AND A. KURLAND
1973   "Recent Developments in Archaeology," *Annals of the American Academy of
        Political and Social Science* 408:103-18.
SAHLINS, MARSHALL
1972   *Stone Age Economics* (Chicago: Aldine Publishing Co.).
SAILE, DAVID, JAMES ANDERSON, RONJI BOROOAH, ALICE RAY,
KENNETH ROHLFING, CHERYL SIMPSON, ALAN SUTTON, AND MALDWYN
WILLIAMS
1972   *Families in Public Housing: An Evaluation of Three Residential Environments
        in Rockford, Illinois*, University of Illinois at Urbana Committee on Housing
        Research and Development, Research Report.
SALMON, MERRILEE H.
1975   "Confirmation and Explanation in Archaeology," *American Antiquity*
        40:459-64.
1976   " 'Deductive' vs. 'Inductive' Archaeology," *American Antiquity* 41:376-81.
SALWEN, BERT
1973   "Archaeology in Megalopolis," in *Research and Theory in Current Archeology*,
        ed. Charles L. Redman (New York: Wiley-Interscience).
SAMWELL, DAVID
1776-78 "Some Account of a Voyage to South Seas in 1776-1777-1778" (MS in British
        Museum, London: Egerton MS 2591).
SARAYDER, D., AND I. SHIMADA
1971   "A Quantitative Comparison of Efficiency Between a Stone Ax and a Steel Ax,"
        American Antiquity 36:216-17.
1973   "Experimental Archaeology: A New Outlook," *American Antiquity* 38:344-50.
SAXON, E. C.
1974   "The Mobile Herding Economy of Kebarah Cave, Mt. Carmel: An Economic
        Analysis of the Faunal Remains," *Journal of Archaeological Science* 1:27-45.
SCHIFFER, MICHAEL B.
1971   "The Economy of Social Interaction: A Proxemic View," *Anthropology UCLA*
        3:74-83.
1972a   "Archaeological Context and Systemic Context," *American Antiquity*
        37:156-65.
1972b   "Cultural Laws and the Reconstruction of Past Lifeways," *The Kiva* 37:148-57.
1973a   "Cultural Formation Processes of the Archaeological Record: Applications at
        the Joint Site, East-Central Arizona" (Ph.D. diss., University of Arizona).
1973b   "The Relationship Between Access Volume and Content Diversity of Storage
        Facilities," *American Antiquity* 38:114-16.
1974   "On Whallon's Use of Dimensional Analysis of Variance at Guila Naquitz,"
        American Antiquity 39:490-92.
1975a   "An Alternative to Morse's Dalton Settlement Pattern Hypothesis," *Plains
        Anthropologist* 20:253-66.
1975b   "Archaeology as Behavioral Science," *American Anthropologist* 77:836-48.
1975c   "Behavioral Chain Analysis: Activities, Organization, and the Use of Space,"
        Fieldiana: Anthropology 65:103-19.
1975d   "Cultural Formation Processes of the Archaeological Record: A General
        Formulation," paper presented at the Eighth Annual Meeting of the Society for
        Historical Archaeology, Charleston, S.C.

314

References

1975e   "The Effects of Occupation Span on Site Content," in *The Cache River Archeological Project: An Experiment in Contract Archeology*, assembled by Michael B. Schiffer and John H. House, Arkansas Archeological Survey, Research Series 8.

1976   *Behavioral Archeology* (New York: Academic Press).

n.d.   "Prospects for the Archeological Study of Reuse Processes in Modern America" (manuscript, Arizona State Museum Library, University of Arizona, Tucson).

SCHIFFER, MICHAEL B., AND JOHN H. HOUSE

1975   "Indirect Impacts of the Channelization Project on the Archeological Resources," in *The Cache River Archeological Project: An Experiment in Contract Archeology*, assembled by Michael B. Schiffer and John H. House, Arkansas Archeological Survey, Research Series 8.

SCHIFFER, MICHAEL B., AND WILLIAM L. RATHJE

1973   "Efficient Exploitation of the Archaeological Record: Penetrating Problems," in *Research and Theory in Current Archaeology*, ed. Charles Redman (New York: Wiley-Interscience).

SELLEY, F.

1970   *Ancient Sedimentary Environments* (Ithaca, N.Y.: Cornell University Press).

SEMENOV, S. A.

1964   *Prehistoric Technology*, trans. M. W. Thompson (London: Cory, Adams and Mackay).

SHARP, LAURISTON

1952   "Steel Axes for Stone Age Australians," in *Human Problems in Technological Change*, ed. Edward H. Spicer (New York: Russell Sage Foundation).

SHEETS, PAYSON

1975   "Behavioral Analysis and the Structure of a Prehistoric Industry," *Current Anthropology* 16:369-91.

SHIMADA, IZUMI

n.d.   "Threefold Analysis of Human Behavior: A Case Study in Experimental Archaeology" (manuscript submitted for publication).

SHUTLER, RICHARD, JR., AND MARY E. SHUTLER

1975   *Oceanic Prehistory* (Menlo Park, Calif: Cummings Publishing Co.).

SIPE, BARRY

1973   "Original Research in Behavioral Archaeology: Patterns of Primary Refuse at Recreation Areas" (manuscript, Arizona State Museum Library, University of Arizona, Tucson).

SMITH, WATSON

1952   *Kiva Mural Decorations at Awatovi and Kawaika-a with a Survey of Other Wall Paintings in the Pueblo Southwest*, Papers of the Peabody Museum of Archaeology and Ethnology, 37 (Cambridge, Mass.: Harvard University).

1971   *Painted Ceramics of the Western Mound at Awatovi*, Papers of the Peabody Museum of Archaeology and Ethnology, 38 (Cambridge, Mass.: Harvard University).

1972   *Prehistoric Kivas of Antelope Mesa*, Papers of the Peabody Museum of Archaeology and Ethnology, vol. 39, no. 1 (Cambridge, Mass.: Harvard University).

SOLECKI, RALPH

1963   "Prehistory in Shanidar Valley, Northern Iraq," *Science* 139:179-93.

SOLECKI, ROSE L.

1964   "Zawi Chemi Shanidar, A Post-Pleistocene Village Site in Northern Iraq," in *Sixth International Congress on Quaternary, Warsaw 1961*, 4:405-12.

SOLLAS, W. J.
1911   *Ancient Hunters and Their Modern Representatives* (London: Macmillan and Co.).

SPAULDING, ALBERT C.
1973   "Archaeology in the Active Voice: The New Anthropology," in *Research and Theory in Current Archeology*, ed. Charles L. Redman (New York: Wiley-Interscience).

SPENCER, J. E.
1966   *Shifting Cultivation in Southeastern Asia*, University of California Publications in Geography, no. 19 (Berkeley).

SPETH, J.
1974   "Experimental Investigation of Hard-Hammer Percussion Flaking," *Tebiwa* 17:7-36.
in press "The Role of Platform Angle and Core Size in Hard-Hammer Percussion Flaking," in *Lithic Analysis in Archaeology* ed. R. Tringham (New York: Academic Press).

SPETH, J., AND G. JOHNSON
1976   "Problems in the Use of Correlation for the Investigation of Tool Kits and Activity Areas," in *Cultural Change and Continuity*, ed. C. E. Cleland (New York: Academic Press).

SPICER, EDWARD H.
1952   *Human Problems in Technological Change* (New York: Russell Sage Foundation).
1962   *Cycles of Conquest: The Impact of Spain, Mexico and the United States on the Indians of the Southwest, 1533-1960* (Tucson: University of Arizona Press).

SPOONER, BRIAN (ed.)
1972   *Population Growth: Anthropological Implications* (Cambridge, Mass.: M.I.T. Press).

STANISLAWSKI, MICHAEL B.
1969a   "The Ethno-archaeology of Hopi Pottery Making," *Plateau* 42:27-33.
1969b   "What Good Is a Broken Pot? An Experiment in Hopi-Tewa Ethno-archaeology," *Southwestern Lore* 35:11-18.
1973   "Ethnoarchaeology and Settlement Archaeology," *Ethnohistory* 20:375-92.
1974   "The Relationships of Ethnoarchaeology, Traditional, and Systems Archaeology," in *Ethnoarchaeology*, ed. Christopher B. Donnan and C. William Clewlow, Jr., University of California, Los Angeles, Institute of Archaeology, Monograph 4.
in press "Hopi and Hopi-Tewa Pottery Making Styles of Learning," in *Experimental Archeology*, ed. John E. Yellen (New York: Columbia University Press).

STANISLAWSKI, MICHAEL B., AND BARBARA B. STANISLAWSKI
1974   "Hopi and Hopi-Tewa Ceramic Tradition Networks," paper presented at the Seventy-third Annual Meeting of the American Anthropological Association, Mexico City.

STEENSBERG, A.
1955   "Mit Braggender Flamme," *Kuml* 63-130.

STEWARD, JULIAN H.
1937   "Ecological Aspects of Southwestern Society," *Anthropos* 32:87-104.
1955   *Theory of Culture Change* (Urbana: University of Illinois Press).

References

STREUVER, STUART
1968   "Problems, Methods and Organization: A Disparity in the Growth of Archeology," in *Anthropological Archeology in the Americas*, ed. Betty J. Meggers (Washington: Anthropological Society of Washington).

STURTEVANT, W. C.
1964   "Studies in Ethnoscience," *American Anthropologist* 66:99-131.

SWAN, LAWRENCE
1972   "Testing for Status Symbol Changes in Modern Material Culture" (manuscript, Arizona State Museum Library, University of Arizona, Tucson).

TANSLEY, ARTHUR G.
1935   "The Use and Abuse of Certain Vegetational Concepts and Terms," *Ecology* 16:299.

THOMAS, DAVID H.
1973   "An Empirical Test for Steward's Model of Great Basin Settlement Patterns," *American Antiquity* 38:155-76.
1974   *Predicting the Past* (New York: Holt, Rinehart and Winston).

THOMPSON, RAYMOND H.
1958   *Modern Yucatecan Maya Pottery Making*, Memoirs of the Society for American Archaeology 15 (Washington, D. C.).

THOMSON, DONALD F.
1964   "Some Wood and Stone Implements of the Bindibu Tribe of Central Western Australia," *Proceedings of the Prehistoric Society* 30:400-422.

TINDALE, NORMAN B.
1941   "The Hand Axe Used in the Western Desert of Australia," *Mankind* 3:37-41.
1965   "Stone Implement Making among the Nakako, Ngadadjara and Pitjandjara of the Great Western Desert," *Records of the South Australian Museum* 15:131-64.

TRETYAKOV, P. N.
1935   "Kistorii boklassovogo obshchestva verkhnevo pobolzhya," *Izvestiya Gos. Akad, Istorii Mat. Kult.* 106:97-180.

TRIGGER, BRUCE G.
1970   "Aims in Prehistoric Archaeology," *Antiquity* 44:26-37.
1973   "The Future of Archeology Is the Past," in *Research and Theory in Current Archeology*, ed. Charles L. Redman (New York: Wiley-Interscience).

TRINGHAM, RUTH
1973   "The Function, Technology and Typology of the Chipped Stone Industry at Bylany," in *Die Aktuelle Fragen der Bandkeramik*, ed. J. Fitz (Szekesfehervar: A Fejér Megyei Múzemok Igazgatósága).
in press "Analysis of the chipped stone industry of Divostin, Yugoslavia," in *Divostin*,
a   ed. A. McPherron and D. Srejovic (Belgrade).
in press "Analysis of the flaked stone industry of Sitagroi," in *Sitagroi*, ed. A. C.
b   Renfrew.
in press "Application of Functional Information in Lithic Analysis, in *Lithic Analysis in*
c   *Archaeology*, ed. R. Tringham (New York: Academic Press).

TRINGHAM, RUTH, GLENN COOPER, GEORGE ODELL, BARBARA VOYTEK, AND ANNE WHITMAN
1974   "Experimentation in the Formation of Edge Damage: A New Approach to Lithic Analysis," *Journal of Field Archaeology* 1:186-96.

TSCHOPIK, H., JR.
1950   "An Andean Ceramic Tradition in Historical Perspective," *American Antiquity* 15:196-218.

TSIRK, A.
1974   "Continuum Mechanics and Flaking: Some Comments and Questions," paper presented at the Symposium on Primitive Technology and Art, Calgary.

TUGGLE, H. DAVID, ALEX H. TOWNSHEND, AND THOMAS J. RILEY
1972   "Laws, Systems, and Research Designs: A Discussion of Explanation in Archaeology," *American Antiquity* 37:3-12.

TUMIN, M. M.
1952   *Caste in a Peasant Society: A Case Study in the Dynamics of Caste (Princeton, N.J.: Princeton University Press)*.

TYLOR, EDWARD B.
1865   *Researches into the Early History of Mankind and the Development of Civilisation* (London: John Murray).

UCKO, PETER J.
1969a   "Ethnography and Archaeological Interpretation of Funerary Remains," *World Archaeology* 1:262-80.
1969b   "Penis Sheaths: A Comparative Study," *Proceedings of the Royal Anthropological Society* 27-67.

UCKO, PETER J., AND ANDREE ROSENFELD
1968   *Palaeolothic Cave Art* (London: World University Press).

USDA (UNITED STATES DEPARTMENT OF AGRICULTURE)
1969   *Dietary Levels of Households in the United States, Spring 1965: Household Food Consumption Survey 1965-66*, Report no. 6 (Washington, D.C.: USDA-ARS).

VAN DER MERWE, NIKOLAAS F., AND ROBERT T. K. SCULLY
1971   "The Phalaborwa Story: Archaeological and Ethnographic Investigation of a South African Iron Age Group," *World Archaeology* 3:178-96.

VAN ZEIST, W.
1969   "Reflections on Prehistoric Environments in the Near East," in *The Domestication and Exploitation of Plants and Animals*, ed. Peter J. Ucko and G. W. Dimbleby (London: G. Duckworth & Co.).

VARNER, DUDLEY M.
1974   "Two Ethnographic Functions of Bird-Form Pottery from Oaxaca, Mexico," *American Antiquity* 39:616-17.

VAYDA, ANDREW P.
1961   "Expansion and Warfare Among Swidden Agriculturalists," *American Anthropologist* 63:346-58.

VAYDA, ANDREW P., AND ROY A. RAPPAPORT
1968   "Ecology, Cultural and Non-Cultural," in *Introduction to Cultural Anthropology*, ed. J. A. Clifton (Boston: Houghton Mifflin Co.).

VISHER, GLENN S.
1972   "Physical Characteristics of Fluvial Deposits," in *Recognition of Ancient Sedimentary Environments*, ed. J. K. Rigby and W. K. Hamblin (Tulsa, Okla.: Society of Economic Paleontologists and Mineralogists).

VOLTAIRE, F. M. A. DE
1764   *Philosophical Dictionary*. Ed. and trans. T. Besterman, 1971 (Harmondsworth, Eng.: Penguin Books).

VOORHIES, MICHAEL R.
1969a   *Taphonomy and Population Dynamics of an Early Pliocene Vertebrate Fauna, Knox County, Nebraska*, Contributions to Geology, Special Paper No. 1 (Laramie: University of Wyoming).

References

1969b   "Sampling Difficulties in Reconstructing Late Tertiary Mammalian Communities," *Proceedings of the North American Paleontological Convention, September, 1969*, Part E:454-68.

VOYTEK, BARBARA

1974   "An Example of Microwear Analysis: Its Contribution to Stone Tool Typologies" (B.A. thesis, Harvard University).

in press "A Microwear Study of the Flints from Fengate, Y-4, England," in *The Second Fengate Report*, ed. F. Pryor, Royal Ontario Museum Archaeological Monograph Series (Toronto).

WALL, KATHY

1973   "Primary and Secondary Refuse at the KOA Campground," (manuscript, Arizona State Museum Library, University of Arizona, Tucson).

WALLACE, A. F. C.

1962   "Culture and Cognition," *Science* 135:351-57.

WARNER, W. L., M. MEEKER, AND K. EELLS

1960   *Social Class in America: A Manual of Procedure for the Measurement of Social Status* (New York: Harper and Row).

WATERBOLK, H. T., AND J. J. BUTLER

1965   "Comments on the Use of Metallurgical Analysis in Prehistoric Studies," *Helinium* 5:227-51.

WATSON, PATTY JO

1975   "Archaeological Ethnography in Western Iran," paper presented at the Seventy-Fourth Annual Meeting of the American Anthropological Association, San Francisco.

WAUCHOPE, ROBERT

1966   *Archaeological Survey of Northern Georgia with a Test of Some Cultural Hypotheses*, Memoirs of the Society for American Archaeology, no. 21 (Washington, D.C.).

WEBB, EUGENE J., DONALD T. CAMPBELL, RICHARD D. SCHWARTZ, AND LEE SECHREST

1966   *Unobtrusive Measures: Nonreactive Research in the Social Sciences* (Chicago: Rand McNally).

WEBB, MALCOLM C.

1974   "Exchange Networks: Prehistory," in *Annual Review of Anthropology 3*, ed. B. J. Siegel (Palo Alto, Calif.: Annual Reviews).

WEIGAND, P. C.

1969   *Modern Huichol Ceramics*, University Museum Mesoamerican Studies (Carbondale: Southern Illinois University).

WENDORF, FRED

1968   "Late Paleolithic Sites in Egyptian Nubia," in *The Late Prehistory of Nubia*, vol. 2, ed. F. Wendorf (Dallas, Tex.: Southern Methodist University Press).

WFA (WAR FOOD ADMINISTRATION)

1943   "Facts on Food Waste," War Food Administration Working Paper (Washington, D.C.: Food Distribution Administration, Nutrition and Food Conservation Branch).

WHALLON, ROBERT

1974   "Spatial Analysis of Occupation Floors II: The Application of Nearest Neighbor Analysis," *American Antiquity* 39:16-34.

WHEAT, JOE BEN

1972   *The Olsen-Chubbuck Site: A Paleo-Indian Bison Kill*, Memoirs of the Society for American Archaeology, no 26 (Washington, D.C.).

WHITE, CARMEL
1971 "Man and Environment in North West Arnhem Land," in *Aboriginal Man and Environment in Australia*, ed. D. J. Mulvaney and J. Golson (Canberra: Australian National University Press).
WHITE, DOUGLAS R., GEORGE P. MURDOCK, AND RICHARD SCAGLION
1971 "Natchez Class and Rank Reconsidered," *Ethnology* 10:369-88.
WHITE, J. PETER
1967 "Ethno-archaeology in New Guinea: Two Examples," *Mankind* 6:409-14.
1968a "Fabricators, Outils Écailles or Scalar Cores," *Mankind* 6:658-66.
1968b "Ston Naip Bilong Tumbina: The Living Stone Age in New Guinea," in *La Préhistoire: problemmes et tendances*, ed. Denise de Sonneville-Bordes (Paris: Editions du Centre National de la Recherche Scientifique).
WHITE, J. P., AND C. N. MODJESKA
1974 "Mental Templates: An Ethnographic Experiment," paper presented at Biennial Conference of the Australian Institute of Aboriginal Studies, Canberra.
WHITE, J. P., AND DAVID H. THOMAS
1972 "What Mean These Stones? Ethno-taxonomic Models and Archaeological Interpretations in the New Guinea Highlands," in *Models in Archaeology*, ed. David L. Clarke (London: Methuen & Co.).
WHITE, LESLIE A.
1949 *The Science of Culture* (New York: Grove Press).
1959 *The Evolution of Culture: The Development of Civilization to the Fall of Rome* (New York: McGraw-Hill).
WHITMAN, ANNE, AND BARBARA VOYTEK
in press "Etude des traces d'utilisation sur les lamelles à bord abattu de Pierre Chatel," *Etudes Quarternaires: Géologie, Paléontologie, Préhistoire*.
WILMSEN, EDWIN N.
1970 *Lithic Analysis and Cultural Inference: A Paleo-Indian Case*, Anthropological Papers of the University of Arizona, no. 16. (Tucson).
WILSON, E. B.
1952 *An Introduction to Scientific Research* (New York: McGraw-Hill).
WINSHIP, GEORGE PARKER
1896 *The Coronado Expedition, 1540-1542*, Fourteenth Annual Report of the Bureau of American Ethnology (Washington, D.C.).
WISDOM, J. O.
1952 *Foundation of Inference in the Natural Sciences* (London: Methuen & Co.).
WITTFOGEL, KARL A.
1957 *Oriental Despotism* (New Haven, Conn.: Yale University Press).
WOOLSEY, JANET (ed.)
1973 *Newsletter of Experimental Archeology no. 2* (Richmond: Virginia Commonwealth University).
WRIGHT, GARY
1971 "Origins of Food Production in Southwestern Asia: A Survey of Ideas," *Current Anthropology* 12:447-77.
WRIGHT, H. E.
1968 "Natural Environment of Early Food Production," *Science* 161:334-39.
YELLEN, JOHN E.
1974 "The !Kung Settlement Pattern: An Archaeological Perspective" (Ph. D. diss., Harvard University).

References

in press "Cultural Patterning in Faunal Remains: Evidence from the !Kung Bushmen,"
    in *Experimental Archaeology*, ed. J. E. Yellen (New York: Columbia University
    Press).

YELLEN, JOHN, AND HENRY HARPENDING
1972 "Hunter-gatherer Populations and Archaeological Inference," *World
    Archaeology* 4:244-53.

YEN, D. E.
1971 "The Development of Agriculture in Oceania," in *Studies in Oceanic Culture
    History*, vol. 2, ed. R. C. Green and M. Kelly, Pacific Anthropological Records
    12 (Honolulu).
1973 "The Origins of Oceanic Agriculture," *Archaeology and Physical Anthropology
    in Oceania* 8:68-85.
1974 *The Sweet Potato and Oceania*, Bernice P. Bishop Museum Bulletin 236
    (Honolulu).
1976 "Indigenous Food Processing in Oceania," in *Gastronomy: The Anthropology of
    Food and Food Habits*, ed. Margaret L. Arnott (Chicago: Aldine Publishing
    Co.).

YEN, D. E., P. V. KIRCH, P. ROSENDAHL, AND T. RILEY
1972 "Prehistoric Agriculture in the Upper Valley of Makaha, Oahu," in *Makaha
    Valley Historical Project Interim Report No. 3*, ed. Ladd and Yen, Pacific
    Anthropological Records, no. 18.

ZIPF, GEORGE K.
1949 *Human Behavior and the Principle of Least Effort* (Cambridge, Mass:
    Addison-Wesley).

ZUBROW, EZRA B. W.
1972 "Environment, Subsistence, and Society: The Changing Archaeological
    Perspective," in *Annual Review of Anthropology 1*, ed. B. J. Siegel (Palo Alto,
    Calif.: Annual Reviews).

Index

Index

Index

Meehan, Betty, 33, 36–41
Meeker, M., 53
Melanesia, 111
Mellars, P., 191
Mesoamerica, seed crops in, 105
Mesopotamia, pastoral nomadism in, 127–67
Meston, A. L., 22
Mexico, 73, 210
Milligan, J., 14
Mindeleff, Cosmos, 221, 223
Miner, Horace, 230
Mississippi Valley, smudge pits in, 187–90
Modjeska, C. N., 4, 184, 194
Moore, A. M. T., 135
Moore, F. C. T., 12
Morlan, R., 171
Mormon architecture, 209
Mortensen, Peder, 137
Moser, Edward, 216, 242
Motz, A., 54
Mt. Weld Station, Australia, 284
Mulvaney, D. J., 24, 270
Munsen, P., 187–89
Murdock, George P., 238
Mureybet, Iran, 135, 137
Museum of Northern Arizona, 211

Nacirema, 82, 230, 243–47
Nairobi, Kenya, 90
Nampeyo, Hopi potter, 214, 216, 219–20, 224
Natchez Paradox, 238
National Science Foundation, 125
Natufian sickle-blades, 290
Navajo tribe, 222
Near East, seed crops in, 105
Neely, James, 154
Neff, Jeffrey M., 233
Nelson, Richard K., 207
Nettles, Isolde, 245
New Guinea, 5, 121, 183–84, 186, 195–96, 263; Kula ring, 208, 222
New South Wales, Australia, 20, 42, 290
Newton, Dolores, 202, 217
Newton, Isaac, 12
Nilsson, S., 191
Nissen, K., 184, 195
Niuatoputapu Island, Polynesia, 125
Noble, I., 69
nomadic society: and natural processes affecting cultural materials, 77–101; pastoralism in, 4–5, 127–67; social factors in, 155–59; in Western Iran, 127–67
Nullarbor Plain, Tasmania, 12
Nunamiut Eskimo, 206, 239

O'Connell, James F., 196, 231, 234–36, 254
Odell, George, 194
O'Hora, J. H., 60
O'Kelly, M. J., 171
Oliver, Douglas L., 122
Omo River Delta, Ethiopia, 84, 87
Orme, Bryony, 185, 233
Oswalt, Wendell H., 230

Panoff, Michel, 121–22
Papago pottery, 214–15
Parsons, Elsie Clews, 226
Parsons, Jeffrey R., 211
pastoral nomadism, 4–5; in Western Iran, 127–67
Pastron, Allen G., 224, 236–37
Pawley, Andrew, 116
Pepper, George H., 232
Perin, Constance, 236
Perkins, D., 137
Péron, François, 12, 15
Perrot, Jean, 136
Peru, 210, 215
Peterson, Nicolas, 229, 232, 241–42
Picuris pottery, 215
Piggott, Stuart, 13
Pima County (Ariz.) Health Department, 60
Pima-Papago area, 225
Platt, John R., 208
Plymouth Plantation, 74
Plog, F. T., 170, 250
Plomley, N. J. B., 11, 13, 15, 18–19, 22, 35–36, 44–45
Polacca, Arizona, 211–12
Pollard, Jack, 39
Pollnac, Richard B., 202, 204
Polynesia, 5, 263; Western, and agriculture, 103–25
Popper, K., 179
Porter, B. W., 60
pots and pottery, 201–27; Hopi, 6, 207, 209–27, 231
prayer sticks, 232
Price, James E., 242
Pueblo Bonito, 232
Pueblo Indians, 232; kachina dance, 209
Puleston, Dennis E., 185
Pulleine, R. H., 21
Puntutjarpa Rockshelter, Australia, 5, 9, 254–93

Qadan sites, 136

Rapoport, Amos, 236
Rappaport, Roy A., 50, 107

327

Index

Throssel, Lake, Australia, 278
Ticul pottery, 214
Timbira tribes, 217
Tindale, Norman B., 263, 270
Tongan Archipelago, 125
Tonkinson, R., 287
tool making and use, 3; stone tools, 191–98
totemism, 6
Townshend, Alex H., 250–51
Tretyakov, P. N., 174
Trigger, Bruce G., 210
Tringham, Ruth, 8–10, 171, 173, 177, 178, 180, 191, 193, 194, 195, 208
Trobrianders, 222
tropical agriculture, 4, 103–25
Tschopik, H., Jr., 210, 226
Tsirk, A., 182, 192
Tucson. See Garbage Project
Tucson Sanitation Division, 49–75
Tuggle, H. David, 250–51
Tumin, M. M., 50
Turkana, Lake, 78–101
Twain, Mark, 249–50
Tylor, Edward B., 14

Ucko, Peter J., 185, 189, 209
Umm Dabaghiyah, 141–42
U. S. Department of Agriculture, 68–69
University of Arizona, 235; Medical School, 58
University of California, Berkeley, Department of Hydraulic Engineering, 97
Upper Kenya Capsian, 291
Ussher, James, 12
Uvea (Wallis Islands), 4, 111–25

Van der Merwe, Nikolaas F., 204, 241
Van Diemaners, 15
Van Zeist, W., 135
Varner, Dudley M., 241
Vayda, Andrew P., 107
Visher, Glenn S., 83
Volga Basin, 174
Voorhies, Michael R., 83–84
Voytek, Barbara, 194

Wadi Tharthar, 142

Wainwright Eskimo, 207
Wali of Pusht-i-Kuh, 158
Wall, Kathy, 244
Wallace, A. F. C., 209
Walpi, Arizona, 211–12
Warburton Range area, 259–60, 262–85
War Food Administration, 74
Warner, W. L., 53
waste behavior, 2–10
Waterbolk, H. T., 176
Watson, Don, 171, 183
Watson, Patty Jo, 208, 247
Wauchope, Robert, 241
Webb, Eugene J., 51–52, 59, 236
Webb, Malcolm C., 208
Weigand, P. C., 214, 222–23
Wendorf, Fred, 136
Western Mining Corporation, Ltd., 260
Western Polynesia, agriculture in, 111–25
Whallon, Robert, 173
Wheat, Joe Ben, 78
White, Douglas R., 238
White, J. P., 4, 184, 194, 229, 241
White, Leslie A., 210, 251
Whitman, Anne, 194
Wilmsen, Edwin N., 250
Wilson, E. B., 177–78, 182–83
Wingellina Hills, Australia, 262, 278, 285, 287
Winship, George Parker, 253
Wisdom, J. O., 172, 177, 179
Wittfogel, Karl A., 210
Woolsey, Janet, 230
Wright, Gary, 135
Wright, H. E., 135

Yellen, John E., 2, 78–79, 81–82, 171, 184, 210, 232, 244
Yen, D. E., 110–11, 117, 121, 123
Yir Yoront people, 222
Yucatan Maya pottery, 239
Yugoslavia, 194

Zagros Mountains, pastoral nomadism in, 132, 134–37, 150, 159
Zarzian sites, 136
Zawi Chemi, Iran, 135, 137
Zuni pottery, 215–16, 219, 221–22, 224–25
Zipf, George K., 242–43, 245
Zubrow, Ezra B. W., 120

329